Rethinking Strategy

edited by

Henk W. Volberda and Tom Elfring

SAGE Publications
London • Thousand Oaks • New Delhi

SAGE Publications Ltd
6 Bonhill Street
London EC2A 4PU

SAGE Publications Inc
2455 Teller Road
Thousand Oaks, California 91320

SAGE Publications India Pvt Ltd
32, M-Block Market
Greater Kailash - I
New Delhi 110 048

British Library Cataloguing in Publication data

A catalogue record for this book
is available from the British Library

ISBN 0 7619 5644 1
ISBN 0 7619 5645 X (pbk)

Library of Congress catalog card number available

Typeset by Siva Math Setters, Chennai, India
Printed in Great Britain by Biddles Ltd, Guildford, Survey

To our wives and children

Anna, Lisa and Celine – HV

Judith, Jasper, Roel and Paulien – TE

Contents

Notes on Contributors

Henk W. Volberda is Professor of Strategic Management and Business Policy at the Rotterdam School of Management, Erasmus University. He has worked as a consultant for many large European corporations and has published in many refereed books and journals. He is Director of the Erasmus Strategic Renewal Centre, programme director of the Erasmus Institute of Management, Board member of the Rotterdam School of Management, and Secretary of the Dutch-Flemish Academy of Management. He is also Editor-in-Chief of *M&O* and *Management Select*, Senior Editor of *Long Range Planning*, and member of the editorial boards of *Organization Science* and *Tijdschrift voor Bedrijfsadministratie* (*TBA*). He has received many awards for his research on organizational flexibility and strategic change. His book, *Building the Flexible Firm; How to Remain Competitive*, received wide acclaim.

Tom Elfring has a chair in Innovative Entrepreneurship at Wageningen University and is Associate Professor of Strategic Management at the Rotterdam School of Management, Erasmus University. He did his PhD research in Economics at the European University Institute in Florence, Italy, and his studies have been published in refereed books and journals. He has been the Director of the PhD programme at the Rotterdam School of Management and Vice-president of EDAMBA.

Bruce Ahlstrand author of *The Quest for Productivity* (Cambridge University Press, 1990) and co-author of *Human Resource Management in the Multi-Divisional Company* (Oxford University Press, 1994), is a Professor of Management at Trent University, Ontario.

Charles Baden-Fuller has established a reputation on rejuvenating mature firms through his work with CEOs, his academic articles and his book *Rejuvenating the Mature Business* (Harvard Business Press). He currently works on issues of knowledge management and entrepreneurship in high technology firms, including the practical use of real options and alliance structures. Professor Baden-Fuller holds degrees in Mathematics and Economics from Oxford, Cornell and London Business School of Economics. He is also the current Editor of *Long Range Planning*, a leading international strategy journal.

Andy Bailey is a Senior Fellow in the Management Development Division of Lancaster University Management School. His research interests focus on the nature of strategy development, organizational change and processes of increasing individual effectiveness in strategy formulation. He has written a number of papers in the area of strategy process and has worked as a consultant on strategy development and management development with a number of public and private sector organizations.

Patrice Cooper lectures in Management and Business Strategy at University College, Cork. She is currently pursuing a PhD, concerning leadership and knowledge management. Other research interests include: perspectives on strategy formation, strategic change/corporate transformation and structural change across various industries.

Thomas Ericson has a PhD in Business Administration from Linköping University. He joined Jönköping International Business School in 1998 as a Research Fellow/Assistant Professor. His research is concentrated on organizational change and leadership with a special focus on social/psychological aspects such as the role of sensemaking in change processes. He is a teacher in organization theory and behaviour.

Nicolai J. Foss is Professor of Economic Organization, Copenhagen Business School, and Director of the Learning, Incentives and Knowledge Project. His research centres on the understanding of the efficient organization of knowledge and learning processes. His work has appeared in journals such as *Organization Science* and *Industrial and Corporate Change*.

Gerry Johnson is Professor of Strategic Management at the University of Strathclyde Graduate Business School. He is the author of *Strategic Change in the Management Process* (Blackwells) and co-author of *Exploring Corporate Strategy* (Prentice Hall) with Kevan Scholes. His main research interests are in the fields of strategy development and strategic change in which he has published numerous papers.

Paula Kirjavainen is a Post-doctoral Researcher at the Institute for Executive Education, TSEBA, where she is leading a multi-client research and development project on strategic competence management.

Christian Koenig Associate Professor at ESSEC, received a Masters degree from Harvard University and his PhD from the University of Paris-Dauphine. He has been working on alliance strategies in an international context and on organizational issues related to globalization. As the current Director of the ESSEC MBA programme, he is also involved in innovations in management education. He is the co-author of *Perspectives en Management Stratégique, vol. 4.*

Joseph Lampel is a Reader in Management at the University of St Andrews, Scotland. He is a founding member of the Institute for Research on Emergent Policy Processes, and a senior fellow of the International Project in the Management of Engineering and Construction.

Michael Lawless is at Duke University where he researches and teaches strategic management and management of innovation. His research has been published in *AMJ, SMJ, Management Science* and *Organization Science* among other journals. He was Chair of the TIM Division of the Academy of Management, co-founded the *Journal of High Tech Management Research*, and has held editorial positions at *AMJ* and *Organization Science*.

Joseph T. Mahoney is Associate Professor of Business Administration at the University of Illinois at Urbana-Champaign. He received his PhD in Business Economics from the Wharton School of Business, University of Pennsylvania. His current research interests include vertical co-ordination, transaction costs theory, resource-based theory and dynamic capabilities.

Anders Melander is a Research Fellow/Assistant Professor at Jönköping International Business School. He has a PhD in Business Administration. His research focuses on the role of industrial wisdom in strategic change and the strategic network as a vehicle to achieve strategic marketing development.

Leif Melin is Professor of Management at Jönköping International Business School. He is also Head of the Department of Entrepreneurship, Marketing and Management and responsible for the PhD programme. He has a Master of Political Science from Lund University and a PhD in Industrial Marketing from Linköping Institute of Technology, Linköping University. He has published his research results in several books and journals and in the periodical book series 'Advances in International Marketing'.

Henry Mintzberg is Cleghorn Professor of Management Studies at McGill University, Montreal, and Visiting Scholar at INSEAD in Fontainebleau, France. He is the author of many books and articles, including *Strategy Safari* (with Bruce Ahlstrand and Joseph Lampel). He is currently writing a book entitled *Developing Managers, not MBAs*.

Johannes M. Pennings is Professor of Organization Behaviour at the Wharton School, University of Pennsylvania. He received his PhD from the University of Michigan. Prior to his current status, he was affiliated with Carnegie Mellon University and Columbia University. His recent research has involved the role of human and social capital for innovation and performance.

Patrick Regnér is Assistant Professor of Business Policy and Strategy at the Institute of International Business at the Stockholm School of Economics. He received his PhD in 1999, based on his dissertation 'Strategy creation and change in complexity: adaptive and creative learning dynamics in the firm'.

Ron Sanchez teaches, publishes and consults in the areas of competence-based strategic management and technology strategy. He has degrees in psychology, comparative literature, architecture, engineering, and management, and received his PhD in Technology Strategy from MIT. He has published several books on the competence-based perspective in strategic management, as well as numerous papers in leading strategic management, marketing, and technology management journals.

Paul J.H. Schoemaker is Research Director of the Emerging Technology Program at Wharton School, University of Pennsylvania, where he also serves as Adjunct Professor of Marketing. Dr Schoemaker is the founder and Chairman of Decision Strategies International, Inc. His numerous articles and books have been published in over ten languages.

J.-C. Spender is Dean of the Business and Technology Division at SUNY-FIT, New York. Initially trained as a nuclear engineer and computer salesman, he received his PhD in Corporate Strategy from Manchester Business School in 1980. He also served on the faculties of City University (London), UCLA, Glasgow and Rutgers. He has taught in Japan, New Zealand, Finland, Norway and Sweden.

Janine Stiles is Head of Strategic Management at Henley Management College. Her research interests over the past seven years have been in strategic alliances and value-added partnerships, developing more recently into issues associated with public/private sector partnerships. Her publications include a number of articles and book reviews in business journals, co-authorship of a book on finance for the general manager and contributions to a number of edited business texts.

Howard Thomas is Dean of the Warwick Business School at the University of Warwick in England; formerly he was Dean (1991–2000) and the James F. Towey Distinguished Professor of Strategic Management at the College of Commerce and Business Administration at the University of Illinois at Urbana-Champaign.

Frans A.J. van den Bosch Professor of Management, received his Masters in Economics from the Erasmus University Rotterdam and a PhD from Leyden University. He is a Fellow of the Erasmus Research Institute of Management (ERIM). He has written and contributed to several books and over 80 articles in scientific journals. Among others, his scientific papers have appeared in *Corporate Governance, European Management Journal* and *Organization Science*.

Gilles van Wijk is Professor of Business Policy at ESSEC. Since 1995, he has been Dean of the faculty. He holds a PhD in Management of Organizations from Columbia University, and a diploma in Physics from the Swiss Federal Institute of Technology in Zurich. His research interests include trust, strategic alliances and entrepreneurial strategy.

Preface

As we have entered the 2000s, strategy as a field of study has fallen on hard times. Thoughtful members of the academic community are increasingly arguing that the concepts and tools of analysis that formed the backbone of the strategy literature during its major growth, need a basic re-evaluation in order to pave the way for new ideas. At the same time, changing competitive environments are forcing companies in almost every sector to re-examine their strategy. There seems to be a growing consensus among managers that the path to future success leads away from traditional prescriptions advocating top-down control, formal planning and industry analysis. Managers and practitioners are heralding strategy revolution as the new hallmark of organizational excellence. Moreover, the popular business literature on strategic management is replete with prescriptions and directives with regard to successful strategic recipes: downsizing, re-engineering, strategic alliances, strategy innovation, revitalization strategies, etc.

Despite all these signposts for rethinking strategy, there has been relatively little accumulation of theory. Instead of progress in terms of shared concepts and paradigms, there seems to be academic disillusionment with the value of strategy literature and schools of thought. Managers in today's competitive environment are engaged in strategic experiments without the guidance of appropriate theories of strategic management. We believe that the need for strategic theorizing during the 21st century is greater than ever. Of course, numerous management gurus have convincingly promoted the 'one and only' strategic recipe based on experience with one or a few successful firms. However, is it true that the object of strategic management is so variable and is changing so rapidly that new concepts and research findings are obsolete before they can be applied? In our opinion, closer scrutiny will reveal much less variety and much more continuity in strategic management. Numerous so-called 'new' concepts are old wine in new bottles. We do need new directions in theory and managerial practice, but not new words for the same phenomena.

In this book, we derive new directions in strategy; not on the basis of a random selection of successful firms but on the basis of a systematic treatment of paradigm or schools of thought in strategy. Our aim is not to increase fragmentation in the field further, but to contribute to strategy synthesis. This collective endeavour started in 1995 with the international workshop, 'Schools of Thought in Strategic Management: Beyond Fragmentation', organized by the Rotterdam School of Management in collaboration with the European Institute of Advanced Studies of Management. Well-known scholars in the field, experienced academics as well as fresh PhDs starting in the subject presented and discussed papers on the following topics:

- conceptual studies on defining and categorizing schools of thought in strategic management
- quantitative and qualitative empirical studies on how firms, CEOs, business unit managers or venture managers form strategies; these empirical studies were based on surveys, theoretical case studies and longitudinal case studies
- conceptual studies on fragmentation in the field of strategic management
- studies on various methodological perspectives in strategic management
- integration efforts in strategic management
- conceptual and empirical studies on emerging schools in strategic management.

Besides presentations and lively debates about state-of-the-art strategic management, some scholars were asked to give a personal view and reflections on new directions in the strategy field: Henry Mintzberg on schools of thought, Gery Johnson and Michael Lubatkin on strategy classifications, Charles Baden-Fuller on shifting firm boundaries, Howard Thomas and Ron Sanchez on developing dynamic capabilities and Hans Pennings and Michael Lawless on the role of configurations in strategic management. Besides disagreement on methodological approaches and selection of dominant concepts, there was some consensus on agendas for future research directions in strategic management.

- In a pre-paradigmatic field such as strategy we should appreciate pluralism, as theories and concepts from various related and non-related disciplines have really expanded and enriched the knowledge base of strategic management.
- The field of strategic management is well beyond the classification stage and some focusing is now due in the field's steady evolution. From an academic standpoint, the integration of various complementary strategy perspectives along certain lines (the role of the strategist, type of rationalities, considering time) should be stimulated.
- To overcome the fragmentation–integration dilemma, real progress in the strategy field may be achieved by synthesis in certain problem areas: redrawing firm boundaries (boundary school), developing dynamic capabilities (dynamic capability school) and finding new viable configurations (configurational school).

After this inspiring conference, we thought that we should really do something with these ideas. We also invited some scholars who had not been able to attend the workshop for their suggestions. J.-C. Spender provided us with ideas on strategy as a professional field, Paul Schoemaker was willing to reflect on integration efforts and Nicolai Foss laid down the foundations of the boundary school in strategic management. With the assistance of Thijs Spigt, we developed a road map for a volume on fragmentation, integration and synthesis in strategy. The outcome is, we think, not an ordinary edited volume but a structured effort to show new directions in strategy. As a result, this book is not only interesting for strategy scholars and PhDs new to the subject, but also extremely helpful for students of strategic management. Moreover, reflective practitioners and managers can use the theories and tools provided as a basis for new sources of competitive advantage.

Starting with the pluralism in strategic management (Part I), we continue with a consideration of various efforts of integration (Part II). Subsequently, we show various attempts of strategy synthesis: the boundary school (Part III), the dynamic capability school (Part IV) and the configurational school (Part V). Finally, we reflect on these multiple directions of strategy synthesis (Part VI).

A volume such as this comes about only through the combined efforts of many people, not least of whom are the authors. We thank them for their willingness to write and rewrite chapters in this book, and to reflect on and review other chapters in the book. In particular, we want to thank those who wrote the commentaries: Henry Mintzberg, Paul Schoemaker, Nicolai Foss, Charles Baden-Fuller, Ron Sanchez, Howard Thomas and Johannes M. Pennings.

We are also indebted to Thijs Spigt, who was the 'speed boss' of this project. Thijs had to send out many letters and make an uncountable number of phone calls. It is true to say that he was the driver that kept us on the road to completion of the project.

Of course, our colleagues in the Department of Strategic Management and Business Environment of the Rotterdam School of Management also deserve recognition for their valuable suggestions. We especially want to thank Frans van den Bosch, chair of our department, for his support of this project.

This book was also enriched by the many pleasant and stimulating discussions we had with students in the Strategic Management Major of the Rotterdam School of Management. The class discussions on schools of thought in strategic management as well as the presentations of group projects helped us to fine tune our line of reasoning and forced us to simplify and clarify the arguments made. Moreover, our colleagues Wynand Bodewes and Stelios Zyglydopolous, with whom we taught the introductionary Strategic Management course, provided us with helpful comments. In addition, the many interactions with managers participating in MBA executive and in-company programmes on strategy proved to be extremely useful in developing this volume. Also, the academic debates we had with peers in the field, as well as comments from reviewers, served as the impetus for progress.

We would also like to acknowledge the efforts of Wil Geurtsen for her endless help in composing the final manuscript. Without her editing skills, this would have been an impossible mission. Also, Martijn Bax, Marijn Hoff, Imke Lampe and Marten Stienstra were of great help in finalizing the reference list. Furthermore, we want to express our gratitude to Claire Roth, Kiren Shoman and Louise Wise of Sage, who showed great patience and gave us much autonomy as well as helpful directions during production of this book.

Finally, we are grateful to our closest partners in this endeavour: our wives and children. This work would not have been accomplished without their unconditional support. We dedicate this joint work to them.

Henk W. Volberda and Tom Elfring

PART I

THEORY, SCHOOLS AND PRACTICE

1

Schools of Thought in Strategic Management: Fragmentation, Integration or Synthesis

Tom Elfring and Henk W. Volberda

Over the last thirty years, strategic management has become established as a legitimate field of research and managerial practice (Shrivastava, 1986: 363). In the evolution of strategy research, a diversity of partly competitive and partly supplementary paradigms have emerged. To provide an unequivocal definition would mean ignoring the versatility of strategic management. The choice of a definition and the application of specific strategic management techniques is greatly dependent on which paradigmatic schools of thought in strategic management one prefers. In this book, we will therefore review the various schools of thought and their contribution to the theory and practice of strategy.

A school of thought is understood to be the range of thought of a specific group of researchers, which has crystallized within the field of strategic management (Brown, 1993). In other words, a school of thought can be seen as an institutionalized paradigm. Besides reflecting on the variety of schools in strategy, we will also sketch out new promising directions in strategy research and practice. Although some strategy scholars have argued that the achieved multiformity in schools of thought signifies an enrichment of the research within the field of study (cf. Mahoney, 1993), other scholars from related disciplines complain about the lack of consistency and coherence (Camerer, 1985). In particular, they argue that the field of strategic management is extremely fragmented and that there is no agreement concerning the underlying theoretical dimensions nor the methodological approach to be employed. In response, many strategists have advocated increased integration of theories within the strategy field.

What is needed is a greater emphasis on integration rather than differentiation of views. Research needs to be more concerned with reducing conceptual or theoretical barriers between disciplines and literatures and the consequent emphasis on eclectic approaches to explain organizational behaviour. (Hrebiniak and Joyce, 1985: 348)

Additional synthesis and pluralism is needed to advance integrated theory development – as opposed to fractionalism or applied functionalism – in the field of strategy. (Schoemaker, 1993: 108)

What are the new directions in strategy? Should we just accept the fragmentation in the field, strive towards an integration or even try to achieve a strategy synthesis? This opening chapter has a dual purpose. First we want to review the literature and discuss the issues of fragmentation and integration. What do we mean by fragmentation and what is the evidence that the strategy field is fragmented? There is also the question of why the field has become fragmented. Although not all strategy scholars see fragmentation as an inhibiting factor for progress, there is a general feeling that it is worth pursuing the challenge of integration at this stage in the field's development (see Schoemaker, 1993 and his commentary in Chapter 8 of this book).

A variety of such attempts at integration within the field will be mapped out in this chapter. While the field could make progress via the integration of theories and the development of meta-theories, we suggest another scenario – that of synthesis of theory and practice, along some well-delineated research directions. In particular, we suggest further attention to three synthesizing schools, namely the 'boundary' school, the 'dynamic capability' school and the 'configurational' school. In contrast to the traditional schools, synthesizing schools are based on a number of disciplines and strongly connected to the practical problem areas within the field of study.

The second purpose of this chapter is to provide a roadmap for this book. We want to position the 19 contributors in our discussion of the field, centred around the debates on fragmentation, integration and three synthesizing schools.

The strategy literature provides us with diverse lists of different schools of thought (cf. Chaffee, 1985; Mintzberg, 1990b; Whittington, 1993). In this chapter, we shall shortly review different schools of thought based on a classification developed by Mintzberg (1990b) and Mintzberg et al. (1998). This particular way to distinguish nine different schools illustrates the fragmentation of the field. The over-accentuation of the base disciplines has led to theoretical frameworks that have little to say about the practical problems in strategic management. In contrast with an over-emphasis on base disciplines in the strategy field, Spender argues in Chapter 2, 'Business Policy and Strategy as a Professional Field', that strategy is a professional field with complex links to executive practice rather than an academic science or a coherent body of integrated theory. He debates that a proper balance between theory building and attention to the notion of executive praxis is crucial. Over-emphasis on theory construction may result in a splintering of the field into unconnected academic specialities. Spender does not judge the degree of fragmentation to be alarming. On the contrary, he believes 'that there are several lines of theorizing converging on a new and powerful paradigm of strategic analysis' (see Chapter 2, this volume).

Classifying Schools of Thought

The number of publications in the field of strategic management has greatly increased in size over the last 30 years. In the mid-1960s Andrews (1965) and Ansoff (1965) were the first to give the discipline of strategic management a separate profile. However, they can hardly be considered as the founders of strategic management. Many of the current lines of reasoning or schools of thought within strategic management have not built on their range of ideas or are actually inconsistent with the 'design' and 'planning' schools of thought associated with Andrews and Ansoff, respectively. In a number of classifications their contribution was labelled as the classical perspective (Rouleau and Séquin, 1995; Whittington, 1993). In contrast to many previous classification attempts, the taxonomies devised by Rouleau and Séquin and Whittington try to relate the classification criteria to the underlying principles of the various contributions in strategic management. Whittington's four perspectives differ fundamentally along two dimensions: the outcome of strategy and the process by which it is made. Similarly, Rouleau and Séquin identify four 'forms' of strategic discourse, each of which suggests a particular arrangement of representations concerning the individual, the organization and its environment. These classifications are an improvement on some previous attempts. Distinctions of 'content' versus 'process' and strategy formulation versus strategy implementation are of limited value for a deeper understanding of the principles of these classifications, largely because they relate to practical categories (Rouleau and Séquin, 1995). Mintzberg has also developed a taxonomy that goes beyond the simple dichotomous classifications. In his view the differences between the schools are very much governed by the underlying base discipline. However, the unit of analysis (similar to Rouleau and Séquin, 1995) and the process of strategy (similar to Whittington, 1993) also have an impact on the dividing lines between the distinguished schools in his classification. Among the many typologies (cf. Chaffee, 1985; Whittington, 1993), we have chosen to use Mintzberg's classification of nine schools of thought as a starting point for our discussion, because this classification clarifies on the most detailed level each school's specific contribution to the strategy field. The characteristic contribution of each school is often the result of a clear choice with respect to approach and assumptions about the content, the process and the context of strategy formation. The distinctive contribution of each school can also be related to its roots in a specific base discipline.

The first distinction to be made between the nine schools of thought is between a prescriptive and a descriptive approach. The 'design' and 'planning' schools are both prescriptive in character, as is the 'positioning' school of thought. The other six schools belong to the descriptive category. First, the three more normative or prescriptive schools of thought will be briefly discussed. For each of the three prescriptive schools of thought a clear indication will be given of their own contribution to the field.

The 'design' school is responsible for the development of the Strength Weaknesses Opportunities Threats (SWOT) model. In this model the strengths and weaknesses of a company are mapped, together with the opportunities and threats in the market place. The data can be used to analyse various strategic options, which both exploit the internal opportunities and anticipate the market situation. Reaching a good fit between the internal opportunities (strengths and weaknesses) and the external circumstances (opportunities and threats) can be considered to be the central guideline of this school of thought. A key role in the strategy formation is played by the board of directors, and in particular by the chairperson. This approach can be further formalized into a more systematic approach. In this perspective, strategy formation consists of developing, formalizing and implementing an explicit plan. This school is known as the 'planning' school; strategy formation is developed not so much by the chair of the board but rather by the planners in a staff division.

The central focus of the 'positioning' school is the industrial–economic angle, with the work of Porter (1980, 1985) being particularly important. Competition and a competitive position are analysed mostly on the basis of economic concepts, and in this approach companies in a certain industry must choose one out of three generic strategies: cost-leadership, differentiation or focus. This school of thought is strongly influenced by economics while the 'planning' school has its theoretical roots in system theory and cybernetics. For the 'design' school it is very difficult to point to a specific root discipline. The approach used there has emerged from an attempt to develop an integrative perspective based on practice.

In the three schools of thought discussed above, the environment is seen as relatively constant. The challenge for strategy formation is to influence the environment, either responding to it or adjusting the organization to it. The underlying assumption here is that the environment can be analysed and that a company's opportunities and threats can be distilled from it. Another assumption is that the company has the time, using a planned or unplanned approach, to realize the potential of a certain strategy. The 'design' school still works on the assumption that the CEO can design an explicit 'grand strategy' for the entire enterprise. Research by Mintzberg and Waters (1985) shows, however, that strategies are not always explicitly formulated, but can come about spontaneously without a priori intentions. It is also shown in empirical research carried out by Burgelman (1983) and the strategic decision-making models of Bourgeois and Brodwin (1984) that strategies often take place bottom-up and that the top management approves of these afterwards ('retrospective sense making'). Likewise the 'planning' school assumes that a correct strategy can only come about by means of frequent and systematic forecasting, planning and control. Empirical research by Fredrickson (1983), Fredrickson and Mitchell (1984) and Mintzberg (1973a) shows that in turbulent environments planning is, however, often insufficient and leads to rigidity. The annual planning rituals within an organization restrict its innovative potential; options are fixed and new options are not noticed.

As a consequence of the untenability of the normative assumptions of the above-mentioned prescriptive schools, the more descriptive schools are increasingly gaining influence in the discipline (see Table 1.1). The latter schools, like the 'entrepreneurial', the 'cognitive' and the 'learning' schools are not prescriptive but they try instead to describe the actual strategy formation in enterprises on the basis of empirical research.

TABLE 1.1   *Normative assumptions of prescriptive schools reconsidered*

Prescription	Description
• Top-down	• Bottom-up
• Planning	• Spontaneous
• Analytical	• Visionary
• Perfect rationality	• Bounded rationality

In the 'entrepreneurial' school, the environment is not a stable factor; it can be influenced and manipulated. Entrepreneurs are capable of bringing new innovative products and services onto the market, developed on the basis of idiosyncratic dynamics, quite detached from the existing 'laws' of the market. Baden-Fuller and Stopford (1994) show that the choice of the branch of industry only determines the profit expectations for a very small part, and that the 'firm' and not the branch of industry is a decisive measure of success. At the same time, these authors argue that successful enterprises like McDonalds, Benneton and Toyota do not opt for a 'generic strategy', but instead opt for a combination of 'low cost' and 'differentiation.' This does not lead to the 'stuck in the middle' effect feared by Porter, because the 'positioning' school does not take into consideration internal organizational factors such as culture and ideology. It is the entrepreneurs with a vision of the future who determine the environment and not vice versa. Strategic management viewed from this perspective cannot be traced back directly to a specific discipline, although the economist Schumpeter (1934) can be seen as its intellectual progenitor.

The next two schools of thought, the 'cognitive' and the 'learning' schools, have psychology as their root discipline. They consider the environment to be very demanding and/or difficult to comprehend. In the cognitive school the individual is the unit of analysis and strategy formation is based on 'mental maps.' March and Simon (1958) and Simon (1976) have made an important contribution to the cognitive school. In particular, the concept of 'bounded rationality' has been important. In these schools strategy will be not so much planned, but rather incremental and 'emerging'. According to the supporters of the 'learning' school, whose pioneers were Lindblom, Quinn and Weick, a strategy unfolds. It was Lindblom (1959) who concluded that strategic management was not a linear process, but an incremental process of 'muddling through'. This incremental vision was confirmed by Cyert and March (1963) and the article by Wrapp (1967) entitled 'Good managers don't make policy decisions'. Etzioni (1968: 282–309) took on an intermediate position, namely 'mixed scanning', whereby strategists must develop a long-term vision while approaching the short-term step by step. On the basis of nine longitudinal case studies in large enterprises confronted with changes, Quinn (1980a) concluded that incrementalism is logical because of the iterative character of strategic management processes and the need to adjust strategies continuously. According to this founder of the 'learning' school, strategic management is necessarily a fragmented process, whereby initiatives arise from different subsystems and top management defines strategies as broadly as possible and leaves options open as long as possible. On the other hand, Johnson (1988) and others propose, on the grounds of a longitudinal case study, that incrementalism is not logical but a result of cognitive schemes (Weick, 1979), cultural idea systems (Smircich and Stubbart, 1985) or political processes (Pettigrew, 1977). This 'non-logical' incrementalism forms the basis for the 'cultural' and the 'political' schools.

The contribution of the political school of thought to the strategic management field consists of concepts such as power and coalitions. Important studies that brought the factor power into strategic management literature were those of Allison (1971) and Perrow (1970). Strategic in this school means choosing your position and thinking in terms of move and counter-move. Making a distinction between power formation within an organization and between organizations is significant. The latter level of analysis is the meso level in which the environment is clearly malleable. Securing a position in order to be able to determine the rules of the game can be a great influence in the competitive position of an organization. As far as the micro level is concerned, it is often assumed that organizations have a single face, thus ignoring the large differences of opinion and the existence of a variety of power blocks within organizations. The importance of recognizing the different sorts of strategy formation and implementation and the development of these concepts in order to analyse them can be attributed to the political school of thought. It has been clearly demonstrated that this school of thought is strongly influenced by political science.

In contrast to the schools already discussed, influencing the environment has very little to do with the following schools of thought. In the cultural school of thought, developing a common perspective for the organization is the central issue. The contribution of this school lies particularly in the insights offered into the importance of a common company culture for the formulation, and particularly the implementation, of a strategy. A strategy can only be successful if it is deeply rooted in the company culture and, accordingly, the development of common values and insights is a central issue. Strategy formation here is not bottom-up or top-down but must be approached from a collective perspective. The conceptual breeding ground for this school of thought is anthropology, and Normann (1977) has made an important contribution to the development of the theory.

The last school of thought is the environmental school. This school has been strongly influenced by the work of 'population-ecologists', like Hannan and Freeman (1977). By analogy to biology they look at organizations with the aid of the variation–selection–retention model. Strategies are positions in the market and if the favourable conditions that gave rise to the growth of the firm change, the organization is doomed. This approach is exceedingly deterministic and the room available for management to formulate strategies is non-existent.

Each of the nine schools represents a specific angle or approach to strategy formulation (see Table 1.2). The separation of the discipline into clearly defined schools of thought furnishes us with insights into the backgrounds and the often implicit assumptions of a great number of trends in the field. Mintzberg, however, shows that each school of thought is concerned with a certain aspect of the

TABLE 1.2 *Nine schools of thought in strategic management*

Dimensions	Prescriptive			Descriptive					
	Design	**Planning**	**Positioning**	**Entrepreneurial**	**Cognitive**	**Learning**	**Political**	**Cultural**	**Environmental**
Key author(s)	Andrews, 1965	Ansoff, 1965	Porter, 1980	Schumpeter, 1934	Simon, 1976	Lindblom, 1959; Quinn, 1980a	Allison, 1971; Perrow, 1970	Normann, 1977	Hannan and Freeman, 1977
Base discipline	None	Systems theory, cybernetics	Economics	None	Psychology	Psychology	Political science	Anthropology	Biology
Vocabulary	SWOT model, fit	Formalizing, programming, budgeting	Analysing, generic strategy	Vision, leadership, innovation	Bounded rationality, map, mental model reframe	Incremental, 'emerging'	Power, coalition dominant	Ideology, values	Reaction, selection, retention
Central actor	President/ director	Planners	Analysts	Leader	Brain	Everybody who learns	Everybody with power	Collectivity	Stakeholders
Environment	Opportunities and threats	Stable and controlled	Analysable in economic variables	Manoeuverable	Overwhelming for cognition	Demanding	Intractable, malleable	Incidental	Dominant, deterministic
Strategy	Explicit perspective	Explicit plan	Explicit generic positions	Implicit perspective	Mental perspective	Implicit patterns	Positions, plays	Collective perspective	Specific position

Source: Mintzberg, 1990b

total picture, ignoring the other aspects along the way. If the contributions, shortcomings, assumptions and context of the diverse schools of thought are made more explicit, the fragmentation within strategic management is made painfully obvious.

Fragmentation: Evidence and Explanation

Looking at the issue of fragmentation solely from the point of view of the number of distinct schools of thought is too narrow. What are the other indicators of fragmentation? In this section the existence of fragmentation in the field is illustrated based on the differences concerning the underlying theoretical dimensions and the variety of methodological perspectives.

Theoretical Dimensions

From the perspective of the nine distinct schools of thought, strategic management would appear to be a fragmented discipline. A variety of entirely idiosyncratic approaches sheds light on the specific aspects of the strategic management process. This can be illustrated by showing the position of each of the schools of thought on some underlying theoretical dimensions (see Figure 1.1). We have distinguished five dimensions, i.e. prescriptive versus descriptive schools, voluntaristic versus deterministic schools, the unit of analysis of the schools, the research area of each of the schools and the extent to which each of these schools applies a static or a dynamic perspective. Concerning the first dimension, it has been argued that the first three schools (design, planning and positioning) can be characterized as prescriptive, while the other six are more descriptive in nature.

In addition to the prescriptive–descriptive dimension, one can also look at the degree to which each school has room for strategic choice (voluntarism) or whether successful strategies are selected by the environment (determinism). An extreme example of the latter is the environmental school (cf. Hannan and Freeman, 1984). This is quite opposite to the cognitive school, in which there is room for slack (Cyert and March, 1963), to the learning school, in which there is leeway for 'strategic choice' (Child, 1972) and to the political school, in which there is room for decisions from the dominant coalition (Thompson, 1967). Although the latter mentioned schools employ a more voluntary perspective, it must be stated that an increasing number of theoretical contributions within these schools assume that the room for choice is limited by internal organizational factors such as the routines that have built up over the years and the cognitive limitations of policy makers (cf. Nelson and Winter, 1982).

The unit of analysis varies greatly too. The entrepreneurial and cognitive schools address themselves in particular to the individual, namely the entrepreneur and the manager. The learning school, however, focuses far more on the group level, while the unit of analysis in the design, planning and positioning schools is the organization. Finally, in the environmental school the branch, the industry or the environment is the chosen aggregation level.

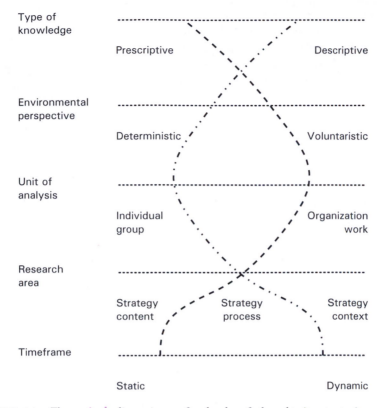

FIGURE 1.1   *Theoretical dimensions of schools of thought in strategic management; – – –, positioning school; – · · – learning school*

In addition to the level of analysis, there are great differences between the schools of thought with respect to their focus on a specific area of interest in strategic management. According to Pettigrew (1990) the research area can be divided into interest in the strategy content, the strategy process and the context in which the process takes place. The positioning school is particularly interested in the strategy content in terms of generic strategies: what is the best generic strategy for management to choose? On the other hand, the planning and design schools are more concerned with the process of strategic management from a prescriptive perspective and the cognitive, learning and political schools from a more descriptive perspective. The environmental and, to a lesser extent, the cultural schools are particularly interested in the strategic context, being concerned with the environmental factors and national or professional cultures, respectively.

Finally, most of the prescriptive schools give a static description of strategy formation, while, for example, the learning school employs a more dynamic perspective and distinguishes different strategic learning routes. On the basis of these underlying theoretical dimensions, each school can be positioned in the profile above. As an example, the positioning school and the learning school have been filled in as two antipoles (see Figure 1.1). The differences between the schools concerning the underlying theoretical dimensions can be seen as an illustration of the fragmentation in the field.

Methodological Perspectives

Another way to examine the degree of fragmentation in the discipline is to look for common elements in the methodological perspective. Methodology is the way in which knowledge is acquired for strategic management questions. According to Camerer (1985), in his much discussed article 'Redirecting research in business policy and strategy', it is the lack of a disciplined methodology that is the cause of the fragmentation in strategic management.

> For all the energetic research on strategy and policy, the state of the art is disappointing. Theories are ambiguous, untested and tend to replace other theories with little apparent progress. (Camerer, 1985: 5)

The author argues that many concepts are ambiguous and that there is no clarity on definitions. The distinction between 'strategy' and 'policy' is, for example, extremely vague. He also mentions that theories and checklists are seldom tested or compared with competing theories. Most research in strategic management is inductive and based on a limited number of case studies. The result of this weak methodological basis is that there is no accumulation of knowledge, only a substitution of theories and schools of thought. Camerer therefore proposes a strictly hypothetical–deductive approach to research in strategic management, which according to him flourishes best in 'harder' theories such as 'agency-theory', 'game theory', 'industrial organization' and 'decision theory'.

In contrast to the Popperian Camerer, Teece (1990) argued, in the same way as Lakatos (1970), that within strategic management progress could only be made by developing dominant research programmes such as the traditional 'competitive forces' perspective or the 'resourced-based' perspective.

> Until there is a framework and some accepted core of theoretical ideas, the field cannot build cumulatively. One cannot have meaningful exchanges in any field until there is some agreement on terminology, assumptions, causal structure and recognition of where different approaches may be applicable. (Teece et al., 1990: 3)

While Camerer opts for a disciplined methodological approach and Teece for dominant research programmes, Mahoney (1993) chooses the opposite, the more pragmatic approach of methodological pluralism under the pretext of 'good science is good conversation'. According to Mahoney, or equally Daft and Buenger (1990) and Hambrick (1990), these authors employ a strongly instrumental approach, which excludes new insights that do not fit within a hard theory or dominant research programme. Furthermore, these so-called harder sciences face the same problems in that their concepts are also often ambiguous and not clearly defined. Instead of looking for universal methodological criteria, Mahoney argues that the continual attunement of rivalling schools of thought in strategic management should be promoted (see also Cooper, Chapter 7, this volume).

To summarize, Camerer is very unhappy with the present state of fragmentation, Teece wants to reduce this fragmentation to some extent by developing dominant research programmes and Mahoney, on the contrary, appreciates the versatility of the field. On the basis of this heated debate concerning the 'best' methodology, it is clear that the differences not only refer to content but also to the methodological approach.

Causes of Fragmentation

In the previous sections we provided some evidence of the fragmented character of the strategic management field. A large number of distinct schools, diversity in underlying theoretical dimensions and different views on methodology give an indication of what can be seen as important characteristics of fragmentation. This provides an answer to the question of what we mean by fragmentation, but it leaves open the question of why. What are the causes of the observed fragmentation? The analysis by Whitley (1984) provides valuable insights into examination of the why issue.

A fragmented discipline can be characterized according to Whitley by a high degree of task uncertainty and a low degree of co-ordination of research procedures and strategies between researchers. The existence of a great degree of uncertainty can be explained by the fact that three target groups can be isolated, each with its own criteria for research and research procedures, namely the strategy field, the base disciplines and management as the end-users. In addition to the criteria within the first target group, which strategic management researchers have more or less accepted, one can also look at the criteria that are valid for the different base disciplines. The base disciplines upon which strategic management builds can be seen as the second target group. The demands that can be made, for example, of economic research, are different from those for research into strategy. In many cases this is due to the distinction between monodisciplinarity and interdisciplinarity. The third distinct target group can be seen as the management. Ultimately, users employ their own criteria for the assessment of research. The existence of these three groups alongside one another leads to task uncertainty, resulting in fragmentation of the strategy field if no conscious attempts are made towards integration and synthesis. Researchers and research institutes are not dependent on any of these three groups for their assessment or for obtaining, for example, financial support. If one group rejects research proposals then the researcher can turn to one of the other groups. Quality control is not in the hands of an elite, which is often the case in the more theoretically oriented monodisciplines.

The relative independence of research efforts means that alignment and co-ordination are not seen as being an absolute necessity. This conclusion on the fragmentation within strategic management is in line with the observation that many potential scientific conflicts are conceivable within the field but that the factual conflicts and/or heated debates are limited. The escape routes for assessment and financing are numerous compared to most of the social sciences.

For further development of strategic management a certain degree of integration and synthesis is necessary, but the required degree of integration varies. In this book we can distinguish different categories of reaction to this assertion in order to reach a satisfactory degree of integration. The first reaction is very much in line with Mahoney (1993), who favours pluriformity and only a limited degree of integration. It is considered acceptable that only certain fundamentals are established and agreed upon. This position is argued and defended by Patrice Cooper in her chapter entitled 'Fragmentation in Strategic Management', in which the fragmented nature of the research efforts on acquisitions is reviewed (Chapter 7, this book). In her chapter three distinct schools of acquisitive research are identified: the Capital Market School, the Strategic School and the Organizational Behaviour School. Each addresses different questions/issues at different levels of analysis and with different methodologies. It is argued that the evolution of these diverse perspectives had facilitated rather than slowed the advancement of knowledge within this area. And for future research Cooper consequently recommends greater attention to understanding the similarities and differences among existing schools, as opposed to the development of integrative approaches or metatheories.

The second reaction to fragmentation is integration of these diverse strands of research. Three chapters in this book, by Patrick Regnér on multiple rationalities (Chapter 4), by Thomas Ericson, Anders Melander and Leif Melin on the role of the strategist (Chapter 5) and by Frans van den Bosch on time (Chapter 6) are examples of integration approaches. The authors explore the possibilities of integrating complementary perspectives of the different strategy schools. Their approaches are in line with the suggestions of Schoemaker (1993). In the next section we will shortly discuss these three different approaches to accomplishing integration.

The third reaction to fragmentation is synthesis in a very pragmatic way. This synthesis, in our view, should be concentrated on bringing together the three distinct groups. Varying clusters of problem areas must be connected to a combination of perspectives and schools of thought. This results in three synthesizing schools. The third part of this book is devoted to examining the synthetic approach in more detail.

Perspectives on Integration

A variety of authors are convinced (Bowman and Hurry, 1993; Chakravarthy and Doz, 1992; Schoemaker, 1993) that further theory formation within strategic management can be achieved now by integration. Segmentation and fragmentation will hamper the development of the discipline. A number of integration approaches will be discussed, in particular Schoemaker's proposals. He has distinguished three more or less related approaches. These integration approaches are based on the complimentary rather than conflicting aspects of the different schools.

In the first approach, the underlying assumptions must be as close to reality as possible. In Schoemaker's terminology, they must show 'assumptional fit'. In a number of cases the strategic problem of the firm will be relatively clear cut, because assumptions about high efficiency levels, rationality and common goals are more or less compatible with the situation concerned. The rational schools of thought such as the planning and positioning schools can be used for the analysis. These schools would be unsuitable if there were a dominance of opposing interests and conflicting ideas about the aims to be pursued. Problem fields that are characterized as such might be studied on the basis of the political school. The fit of the assumptions to reality emphasizes the complementarity of the various schools and thereby brings about a certain integration.

Chapter 4 by Patrick Regnér, 'Complexity and Multiple Rationalities in Strategy Processes', deals with different assumptions about rationality. Strategy processes are handled by firms and managers through bounded and variable multiple rationalities. Depending on the complexity of the situation, rationality varies. According to Regnér the applied nature of strategic management acquires a multi-dimensional view, incorporating diverse complexities, rationalities and strategies. The contribution by Regnér can be positioned on the intersection between economics-oriented dynamics, resource-based models and the behavioural-based organizational learning models. The former emphasize mechanisms for capability creation and the latter focus on the firm as a cognitive entity. The purpose of his chapter is to integrate these different strategy approaches by looking for a fit between different complexities and multiple rationalities.

A second approach tries to realize complimentarity by employing the 'unit of analysis' as an important criterion for the choice of a specific school of thought. Chakravarthy and Doz (1992) use that criterion to illustrate the complimentarity between strategy process and strategy content research. Schoemaker argues that the design and positioning schools are applicable to problems in which the external development and their impact on the strategy of a firm are the key issues. On the other side of the continuum, the emphasis appears to lie on the detailed developments within a firm, whereby individuals, teams and their mutual relations are central to research. With this kind of focus, the learning, cognitive and cultural schools will be able to provide more insights.

It is exactly that combination of schools that is centre stage in Chapter 5 by Thomas Ericson, Anders Melander and Leif Melin. In 'The Role of the Strategist', they discuss the contribution of the strategist in strategy formation. The strategist is used as an 'umbrella concept' to focus on the human actor who may play a crucial role in strategy processes. They adopt a multilevel approach, examining simultaneously the firm level, the industry levels and the individual actor. Concerning the role of the strategist, they make a distinction between the formal role of top management and the role of the strategist. A review of the literature is presented on the role of the strategist, which results in a typology. This typology helps us to understand why the strategist is either over-emphasized or under-emphasized and seldom put into a process context. According to the authors, the process context of the strategic arena is defined through the dialogue around issues that are strategic to the local organization. The analysis and decision making concerning these issues provide a platform 'to integrate and use a wide set of schools to create a more holistic understanding of the interplay between different forces influencing strategic change processes', (Ericson, Melander and Melin, Chapter 5).

The third approach, working on the basis of the different models being complementary, makes use of the dichotomy presented by the presence or absence of equilibrium. This concerns the degree to which a firm is able to adjust to a constantly changing environment. Schoemaker argues that in the last decade there have been different periods in which firms were fairly well equipped to react to new market situations. In such a situation of relative stability, schools based on the rational actor model, such as the positioning school, are appropriate. A more turbulent environment with a great level of uncertainty, for example with the introduction of new technology or a change in the rules of competition, can lead to disequilibrium. In this situation, firms need structural alterations or organizational innovations (Chandler, 1977) to adapt to the continually changing situation. Other schools are more appropriate in these circumstances, for example, schools in which the emphasis lies on core competences, capabilities and invisible assets (cf. Amit and Schoemaker, 1993; Itami, 1987; Prahalad and Hamal, 1990) or the entrepreneurial school in which the creation of new combinations is relevant.

This type of complementarity is used by Frans van den Bosch in Chapter 6 'What Makes Time Strategic?'. He examines, for example, the punctuated equilibrium model to elaborate on the concept of the nature of strategic change over time. This model allows us to investigate simultaneously the incremental and revolutionary change of organizations and how these different types of change are connected. The punctuated equilibrium model is one of the three dynamic theories of strategy analysed in van den Bosch's chapter, the other two being the commitment approach of Ghemawat (1991) and the chain of causality approach of Porter (1991). One of the main questions is how these theories deal with the concept of time. In order to answer that question van den Bosch distinguishes three key strategic characteristics of time. These are irreversibility, nature of strategic change and interconnectedness. The core of the analysis is to see whether and how these three strategic characteristics of time are reflected in the three dynamic theories of strategy. Following that analysis, van den Bosch discusses how the strategic time construct can contribute to integration efforts in the strategy field.

In his commentary 'The Elusive Search for Integration', Paul Schoemaker examines two key questions. Why is integration so challenging in the domain of strategy and is it worth pursuing vigorously at this stage in the field's development? The difficulties for integration are largely the result of the diversity of the field concerning the domain, approach and purpose of the inquiry. The difficulty, according to Schoemaker, is to achieve integration on all those attributes. However, most integration efforts in the field and also in the chapters in this book focus on one or two of those attributes. Schoemaker offers two approaches to the challenge of fully fledged rather than partial integration.

The various attempts at integration or the positioning of the different schools of thought in an integrative framework are of importance for further theory building. This means that the similarities and differences between various concepts are clarified and the boundaries of the different schools are put into perspective. However, it is questionable whether developing a grand design or meta-theory is realistic if the current state of affairs is taken into account. The theoretical problems within the different integrative approaches have not yet been solved; it is not clear on what grounds certain situations or problems should be classified into an integrative framework. The theoretical basis and consistency of concepts poses serious problems. We suggest a modest and practical attempt at synthesis. In our approach, the development of a meta-theory is not the central focus, but the search for a restricted number of schools, making the link between theories and some clusters of practical problems of the greatest importance. It is a practical approach (see also the contribution of Foss in Chapter 9) and it is in line with Spender's arguments (Chapter 2) about strategy as a professional field.

One of the key issues in the fragmentation versus the integration debate is the integration of valuable insights from the base disciplines into an integrating framework of strategic management. Apart from the difficulties already mentioned in realizing such a meta-theory, it also remains to be seen if such an approach really will reduce fragmentation. According to Whitley's analysis (1984) such an approach does not tackle the causes of fragmentation. The integration effort is limited to a linkage between the field of strategic management and the contributing base disciplines. The third group involved in Whitley's analysis, the practical field, is left aside. As a result, an important source of knowledge is not used in theory building. Knowledge stemming from practice and the field experience of prescriptive do-statements and theory driven consultancy is of importance for the development of the discipline, whether dealing with either practical or theoretical problems. Bearing in mind the causes of fragmentation, strategic management should provide a synthesis between theory building and the use of various base disciplines on the one hand and the knowledge developed in the practical arena of the business community on the other.

A Synthetic Approach: Three Emerging Strategy Schools

The attempts at integration discussed so far do not actually contribute to a reduction of fragmentation in the field of strategic management. The over-accentuation of base disciplines and the 'artificial' searching processes for common dimensions has led to theoretical frameworks that have little, if anything, to say about the practical problems in strategic management. Neither do they offer new perspectives for scholars in the strategy field.

Bowman (1990: 17) quite rightly remarks that no central paradigm can be developed in strategic management. The most important cause in Bowman's view is the great dilemma between theory-oriented schools and more practically oriented design schools. To give a polarized view, one could maintain that within the field of strategic management there is an extreme separation between analytical approaches (Volberda, 1992), which are strongly anchored in a specific base discipline, and clinical approaches, which are strongly concerned with the development of concepts and techniques for strategic management (see Figure 1.2). Following Whitley's terminology (1984), we could argue that within the analytical approach the strategy researcher chooses a base discipline as the target group,

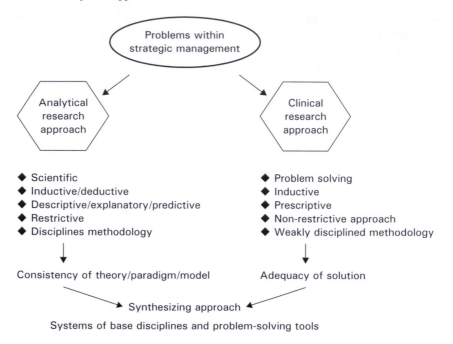

FIGURE 1.2 *The synthesizing research approach in strategic management (Volberda, 1992)*

while in the clinical approach the researcher focuses primarily on management as the target group.

The analytical approach is a theory-oriented and scientific approach based on systematic observation and measurement, employing an absolute separation between the researcher and research object. The formal inductive and deductive logic applies results in descriptive, explanatory and, at most, predictive knowledge. In this restrictive or monodisciplinary approach, the central focus is on the consistency of the underlying theory of the school of thought. All the researchers in such an analytical school in strategic management act according to the same strict methodological principles. In this respect one could label the positioning, cognitive and environmental schools as analytical schools.

On the other hand, the clinical approach is far more problem oriented. This inductive approach is based on the experience of the researcher, subjective assessment, trial and error and mainly qualitative data. The result is prescriptive knowledge in the form of concepts, 'tools' and 'do's and don'ts' for the strategist. In this clinical approach to strategic management, the researchers are not building on one specific theory. Furthermore, they do not apply generally accepted methodological rules. It is more of a multidisciplinary approach whereby the most important assessment criterion is the adequacy of the solution. The design and planning schools in particular are based on this clinical approach. Researchers with a great deal of practical experience in the field of strategic management (in particular Ansoff, 1965 and Selznick, 1957) and strategy consultants have contributed to these prescriptive schools and the development of concepts and methods.

The disadvantage of the analytical schools of thought is that they address themselves to the relatively unimportant problems that fit into their analytical framework (Schön, 1984). Often the researcher who is not involved in the strategic problem area, uses indirect measuring techniques such as large-scale surveys and focuses on quantifiable data. The knowledge provided, in the form of general hypotheses, is often very trivial for practitioners and is not directly applicable for the strategists (cf. Lindblom, 1987: 512; Thomas and Tymon, 1982; Weick, 1989: 516). On the other hand, the clinical schools have not developed any explicit criteria by which knowledge may be evaluated. In many situations, practical relevance and feasibility dominates, and this often leads to opportunistic research behaviour without ex-ante methodological considerations. Many concepts in strategic management, such as the SWOT analysis, the Boston consultancy matrix, the GE business screen and the 7 S's model are often applied but seldom tested. It is therefore not surprising that many of the excellent enterprises raised by Peters and Waterman (1982), which were consistent according to the 7 S's model, were not successful the following year.

In summary, the discipline suffers from a discord that is leading to great fragmentation. We therefore advocate a more synthesizing approach, which is both theory oriented and problem oriented (Volberda, 1993). The fragmentation in our discipline will not be solved by choosing one school at the expense of another, but by synthesis. Schendel puts it this way:

> This tension between base disciplines versus more practically oriented scholars in strategy (and perhaps the entire business school) is best seen and solved not as a choice of one field and perspective over the other, but in relative, balanced terms. A good metaphor is that of the engineer, who has one foot firmly planted in physical sciences and theory, with the other just as firmly planted in practice and problem-solving. (Schendel, 1991: 2)

An important guideline in our attempt at synthesis has been the result of Whitley's analysis of the causes of fragmentation in a field like strategic management. Synthesis serves to integrate the three different target groups of research, namely the base disciplines, the body of knowledge of strategic management and, finally, management as the user. In this context, synthesizing schools differ from the prevailing analytical and clinical schools in strategic management in the sense that they:

- are based on theories from various base disciplines (T) with an explicit reference to these disciplines
- are related to a cluster of problem areas (P) in strategic management
- develop clear problem-solving tools (T') from a chosen range of theories (see Figure 1.3).

In other words, a synthesizing school of thought in strategic management consists of more than one base discipline and one set of problem-solving techniques to deal with a specific range of strategic problems. The application of specific tools

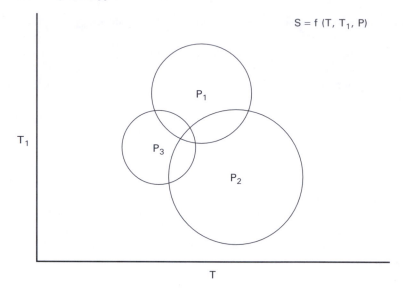

$$S = f (T, T_1, P)$$

FIGURE 1.3   *Synthesizing schools in strategic management; P, cluster of problems areas; T, base disciplines; T₁, problem-solving tools; S, synthesizing schools of thought*

for strategic problem areas may even lead to an adjustment of the basic theories. In this book, we shall attempt to describe synthesizing schools of thought (see Parts III, IV, and V). Of course, such a description can never be complete. On the basis of a literature study, we have distinguished three emerging schools of thought with synthesizing characteristics: the boundary school, the dynamic capability school and the configurational school. Each of these schools will be examined in more detail in Parts III, IV and V. In the following paragraphs we briefly discuss the main research questions and summarize the aim and contributions of the chapters are summarized.

The Boundary School

In the 1980s, the vertically integrated firm as guiding principle became increasingly controversial. The advantages of scale and control appeared to be losing ground to the disadvantages of bureaucracy and inflexibility. Partly due to the influence of increased international competition, the blurring of the boundaries of industry and uncertainty, companies increasingly turned to their core activities. They tried to enhance their flexibility and innovation. Thus, the strategic response to these new developments was that firms should not make everything themselves, but concentrate on their core competences while contracting out the other parts of the production process to other specialists (Mahoney, 1992). This question of make or buy does not only apply to existing production processes, but also to the development of new products and services. Besides the make or buy options, we can distinguish a third hybrid option of co-operation, for example minority and majority participation, joint ventures and network structures (cf. Jarillo, 1988; Powell 1987). As a result of these make, buy and co-operate decisions the boundaries of the organization are becoming increasingly vague. Research into the boundaries of the organization is therefore the central focus of the boundary school. Important research questions for this school are as follows.

- What are the advantages and disadvantages of doing it yourself and contracting out, respectively?
- When is co-operation preferable to doing it yourself or contracting out and how must co-operation be organized?
- What are the strategic implications of make, buy or cooperate?
- How can make, buy or cooperate decisions be implemented and how should these dynamic relationships be managed?

In the boundary school strategy is a boundary decision and it basically concerns two issues: where to draw the boundary and how to manage the fuzzy dividing line between the firm and its environment. The issue of where to draw the boundary of the firm has a bearing on questions concerning outsourcing, partnering, alliances, virtual organizations and also diversification. The way a firm responds to these challenges has a direct impact on its competitive position and, therefore, these boundary questions are directly related to the core of strategy formation. The boundary questions are, however, addressed and answered in different ways by different perspectives in the social sciences. In fact, research dealing with boundary questions is rooted in various base disciplines, varying from economics to sociology and from psychology to history.

In Chapter 9 Nicolai Foss discusses a number of theories that may be seen as constituting the boundary school. He reviews the contributions to the boundary school of transaction cost economics, the resource-dependency approach by Pfeffer and Salancik (1978), the networks perspectives and lastly the capabilities approach to firms. He explores how some of these theories are related and can be harmonized. For example, there are some parallels between the (sociological) resource-dependency approach and transaction cost economics, and many network arguments can be given a straightforward transaction cost interpretation. However, besides this similarity Foss also examines the extent to which these theories are fundamentally different or are even in conflict. Foss maps out the common and complementary aspects of the diverse constituent theories of the boundary school. He addresses in particular the issue of where to draw the boundary of the firm. His emphasis is therefore on the content rather than the process of strategic management. The process part is closely connected to the second main issue in the boundary school, i.e. how to manage across the divide.

In Chapter 10 'Managing Beyond Boundaries: the Dynamics of Trust in Alliances' Koenig and van Wijk focus on the processes underlying co-operative relationships. One of the unanswered questions in the alliances literature is how trust, power and information processes affect the outcomes of co-operation. It is exactly this problem that Koening and van Wijk address. Their purpose is to present a new perspective on the dynamics of co-operation. The building blocks of that perspective are the concepts of trust, contracts and interaction.

They examine these concepts in detail and trace the variety of their academic roots. They view trust as a learning process, which grows out of interaction and is not solely derived from shared norms and values. The analysis of the key concepts is followed by an examination of the relationships between them. For example, trust is not excluded by contracts; they are complementary or even mutually reinforcing. Trust is what allows contracts to emerge and is also secured by these same contracts.

The last chapter contributing to the boundary school blends the content and process perspectives. Chapter 11 on strategic alliances by Stiles investigates what influences a firm to act in a co-operative or a competitive way within the alliances, and how this has an impact on the organizational arrangement. Stiles evaluates six major theoretical streams in terms of their potential contribution in order to enhance our understanding of the development of alliances. These are strategic choice or positioning theory, international business theory, negotiations theory, transaction cost theory and resource-dependency theory. These theories are used in an eclectic way to identify the factors that are likely to influence the extent to which firms adopt a co-operative and/or a competitive stance. These stances should not be viewed as opposing and mutually excluding factors, but as a combination of characteristics. Stiles develops a framework based on the potential ability of the partners involved to realize the competitive and/or co-operative stance. This framework may help us understand the dynamics in alliances and it may be used as an instrument for managers evaluating and shaping alliances.

Charles Baden-Fuller discusses the chapters in Part III in his commentary. He examines the added insights of the chapters concerning two main questions of the boundary school: where should an organization draw its boundaries, and how should it manage across the divide?

The Dynamic Capability School

The dynamic capability school considers strategic management as a collective learning process aimed at developing distinctive capabilities that are difficult to imitate. The theoretical basis of the dynamic capability school is largely based on the work of Amit and Schoemaker (1993), Barney (1991) and Prahalad and Hamel (1990), Teece et al. (1990). This synthesizing school is not focused on developing an optimal strategy through industry and segment selection and the manipulation of market structure to create market power (Porter, 1980). Instead of using such an outside-in approach where the importance lies with the environment, the dynamic capability school employs an inside-out approach. If markets are in a state of flux, then the internal resources and capabilities of a firm would appear to be a more suitable basis for strategy formulation than the external customer focus that has traditionally been associated with the marketing orientation to strategy (Grant, 1996). On the basis of a reservoir of developed capabilities and acquired resources, the firm must exploit a distinctive competence in different end-markets. The most important research questions for this school are these:

- How do organizations develop firm-specific capabilities?
- How can organizations develop new capabilities that are complementary or that substitute existing capabilities?
- What are the determinants of successful development routes?
- How can one determine or measure the collective capabilities of a firm?

In Chapter 13 Ron Sanchez gives an overview of the dynamic capability school. He has expanded the name of the school to 'resources, dynamic capability and competence' to emphasize the progression of concepts, each of which significantly extends the ability to achieve integration of diverse approaches to strategy theory. Sanchez first reviews the concept of resources for the integration of ideas about the firm and its competitive environment. The notion of dynamic capability is portrayed as an extension of the concept of resources. His perspective on dynamic capability is the firm's relative ability to use current resources, to create new resources and to develop new ways of using current or new resources. The concept of competence is examined as it builds on and extends the concepts of resources and dynamic capabilities into a theory of competence-based competition. Finally, Sanchez discusses how these conceptual building blocks may provide a foundation for integrating a number of approaches to strategy theory. He argues that the emerging theory of competence-based competition appears to facilitate integration of separate approaches, such as process and content, competition and co-operation views of strategy and internal and external approaches to understanding competitive dynamics.

The conceptual review is followed by Chapter 14 on modularity and dynamic capabilities by Ron Sanchez and Joseph T. Mahoney. Here the authors argue that modularity in an organization's product and process architecture can improve strategic flexibility and organizational learning. Achieving strategic flexibility by modularity can be understood as the ability to substitute component variations, thereby increasing the variety of products a firm can develop in a relatively short period with relatively small costs. Cutting down the design process into modular components facilitates the concurrent development of components by loosely coupled development organizations, which is important for producing products in turbulent markets. Concerning learning capability, Sanchez and Mahoney suggest that modular product architectures may provide a framework for improving organizational learning processes.

In Chapter 15 Paula Kirjavainen aims to increase our understanding of how learning affects the processes of strategy formation and strategic change in knowledge-intensive firms. This chapter is based on case-based research at the leading Finnish knowledge-intensive firms. It is argued that the strategy of a knowledge-intensive firm may be seen as the development of capabilities to transform the firm's diverse individual and organizational knowledge resources into core competences that consistently provide superior value to clients or customers. The concept of strategic learning is introduced and depicted as a cyclical process that occurs at two levels – learning and meta-learning – and involves intertwined changes of the knowledge of individual managers and the development of a collective paradigm of the group of significant actors. Thus strategic learning is characterized as a learning process through which a firm develops its portfolio of competences. In the conceptualization of strategic learning, Kirjavainen suggests the need for and the possibility of integrating three levels of analysis – individual, organizational and paradigmatic – of learning processes.

The commentary in Part IV on the dynamic capabilities school is written by Howard Thomas. He not only reflects on the three chapters but also gives his view on the development of the dynamic capabilities perspective within the field of strategic management research. Furthermore, he addresses a set of issues that may guide future competitive strategy research.

The Configurational School

This school considers strategic management as an episodic process in which certain strategy configurations dominate, depending on the organizational environment. The configurational school was posited by Mintzberg (1990b) as a collective school for all nine distinct schools in his classification. In each episode, a certain strategy school can dominate depending on the context. This school mainly focuses on the following research questions.

- In what environment are specific strategy configurations effective?
- What are the relevant dimensions that explain the variety of strategy configurations?
- How can an organization pass through a transition from one configuration to the other?

The configurational school is mainly oriented towards explaining the variety of strategic configurations and has resulted in numerous ex-ante taxonomies and ex-post typologies in the form of strategy modes, archetypes, configurations, periods, stages and life cycles. This school came to development through the work of Khandwalla (1977), who has given a systematic categorization of relevant dimensions, Miller and Friesen (1980), who have developed a typology of strategic archetypes and, of course, the work of Mintzberg himself (1973a, 1978) concerning strategy modes and organizational configurations.

In contrast to an integrative research approach, this school does not only show interest when certain configurations are plausible but also tries to explain dynamic trajectories of change. In doing so, its work is based on socially oriented organizational sciences, which, with the aid of ideal examples, try to explain the variety in strategy and structure configurations (cf. Lammers, 1987; Perrow, 1986; Weber, 1946). At the same time, this school has strong roots in business history, seeing certain business 'recipes' as dominant in certain periods (cf. Chandler, 1962).

In Chapter 17, Mintzberg, Ahlstrand and Lampel reviews the historical antecedents and some of the key contributions of this school. Furthermore, they discuss some of the criticism raised in the literature concerning the foundations of the configuration school. The basic idea of the configuration approach dates back to the findings of Khandwalla (1970). The effectiveness of organizations could be related to a set of complementary characteristics. Later work at McGill University, Canada and elsewhere added the factor 'time' in the analysis, and transitions of one configuration to another became the central focus of the configuration perspective. These research efforts and their results are examined in Chapter 17, which provides the conceptual ground for the next two chapters on configurations.

The main concern in the second chapter on configurations, 'A Framework for a Managerial Understanding of Strategy Development' by Andy Bailey and Gerry Johnson, is to understand how managers perceive the strategy process. This process cannot be captured through one-dimensional analysis and therefore the authors propose and test a multidimensional framework for analysing managers' perceptions. On the basis of the literature they draw six perspectives – planning, incrementalism, cultural, political, command and enforced choice. Survey data are used to test the extent to which these perspectives adequately describe the strategy development process as understood by those managers. The results are used to advance a number of propositions that explore specific configurations in the strategy development process.

In his chapter 'Strategy Configurations in the Evolution of Markets' Michael Lawless explains configurations in terms of the co-evolution of firms and markets. He defines a configuration as a set of capabilities and strategies common to a particular group of firms in a market over time. The empirical basis of the configuration school has been much more developed than the theoretical underpinning. Lawless' aim is to come up with an explanatory mechanism to enable us to understand why configurations emerge and persist. He wants to complement the empirical basis of the configuration approach with a theoretical grounding. Evolutionary economics and resource-oriented strategy literature provide the theoretical concepts to give insight into the underlying mechanisms of the dynamics of configurations.

The chapters in Part V are discussed in the commentary on configurations by Johannes Pennings. The focus of the discussion is on the added value of the chapters to theory building in management science and in particular to the configurational school. Pennings also addresses the issue of the boundaries of the configurational school. Furthermore, he makes a distinction between studies coming up with typologies of an 'armchair variety' and investigations in which the typology is based on statistical data reduction techniques, each of which has a particular role in theory building.

Conclusions

In this introductory chapter we have systematically discussed a variety of schools of thought in strategic management. The fragmentation in the field was illustrated by considering the underlying theoretical dimensions of the schools and the various methodological perspectives applied by strategy researchers. The questions this throws up are: what are common theoretical dimensions, and are methodological differences reconcilable? By considering various theoretical dimensions, we concluded that it is not possible to reach a definite clustering of schools of thought. Reduction of fragmentation in this way is difficult to realize. A similar conclusion was drawn with respect to the search for a common methodological perspective. In view of the clear differences, it is not likely that fragmentation can be reduced by means of a disciplined methodological approach.

Should we then accept fragmentation in the strategy field? According to Howard Thomas' commentary (Chapter 16) the use of multiple lenses for viewing phenomena, increased precision in the definition of various strategy constructs and the measures used to test them, and a focus on multiple units of analysis will all contribute to a further understanding of the ways companies co-operate or compete for sustained advantage. By contrast, accumulation of knowledge and further development of the central concepts in strategic management can, in many researchers' view, only come about through integration of the various schools in the strategy field. This dilemma of differentiation versus integration raises the question of whether we should pursue integration more vigorously or keep expanding our knowledge base in a pluralistic fashion. What is the best balance? According to Schoemaker (Chapter 8), the field of strategy is well beyond the classification stage, as evidenced by the explosion of research in the past few decades and the rich plurality of concepts, theories and approaches. He concludes that considering the current stage of development of the strategy field, more differentiation is probably counterproductive to the field's cohesion and progress. On the other hand, we have to admit that various attempts at integration have led to theoretical frameworks that are relatively separate from actual problems in strategic management.

In escaping this differentiation–integration dilemma, we suggest an increased effort toward synthesis. Synthesis is less far-reaching than integration. It does not attempt to develop a single paradigm consisting of universal concepts and laws covering the entire strategic management field. Instead it is anchored in a few clusters of strategic management problem areas, which we have called synthesizing schools. In this book an attempt is made to distinguish the main dimensions of the synthesizing schools. Synthesis serves to develop a coherent body of knowledge for each of the identified problem areas by combining the insights from the three different target groups of research, namely the base disciplines, the body of knowledge of strategic management and management as the user. To start such a synthesis, we provide three emerging schools of thought in strategic management, namely the boundary school, the dynamic capabilities school and the configurational school. Each of these synthesizing schools of thought consists of more than one base discipline and one set of problem-solving techniques for tackling a specific range of strategic problems. As far as methodology is concerned, the synthetic schools try to span the divide between the analytical and clinical approaches. These three synthesizing schools of thought are designed to neutralize the causes of fragmentation at the source. In this sense, our proposal for three schools of thought is new. It is not a repeated attempt to arrive at a meta-theory for strategic management and neither is it a classification of schools of thought that harbour inherent fragmenting powers. Further development of the three distinct synthesizing schools of thought will meet the widely experienced need to accumulate insights and knowledge in the field of strategic management.

In this book we will further elaborate these synthesizing schools, discuss their central research questions, the base disciplines upon which they build and the problem-solving tools they offer. They provide a useful guide for the discovery of the new directions in strategic management. Moreover, from a practitioner's perspective, the application of these synthesizing schools may open up new sources of competitive advantage.

2

Business Policy and Strategy as a Professional Field

J.-C. Spender

This chapter has three sections. In the first we trace some features of BPS's recent development. In the second, beginning with a reconsideration of how Chandler reconstructed the field, we examine deeper reasons for the present variety of views. In the final section we evaluate some of the recent progress towards the three-dimensional framework of a dynamic theory of organizational strategy.

We have seen some change in what strategy theory is about. In the 1960s we said it was the planning necessary to reach the firm's goals or, in contemporary parlance, it was the task of re-engineering the firm around its current objectives. Now we realize it is not so simple. Strategy, like much of the world, seems more complex. Strategy's essence may now lie among the processes of gaining competitive advantage by developing strong cultures, acquiring difficult to imitate skills, pinpointing and exploiting others' weaknesses, innovating and appropriating economic rents, evolving and diffusing 'best practice' and organizational routines, establishing strategic alliances, creating business information and organizational learning systems that lead to knowledge asymmetries, or by effective teaming of empowered employees. Such diversity is clearly confusing and threatening.

Appropriating theory from other disciplines, our field has been pushed beyond yesterday's quasi-mechanical strategy/structure models into the disturbingly understructured area of idiosyncratic knowledge and skills. These developments are forcing us to reconsider the two presuppositions, which up to now gave strategy its meaning: (a) economic rationality and (b) the notion of the firm. The stability of these concepts provided a foundation for the term strategy. But these concepts' abstractness also separated them from the firm's executive and organizational practices, with their tacit components and creative and ethical features. Now we see that strategy is not merely about goal setting and mechanical planning, it is also about creating and re-creating organizations and their culture, morality, practices and rationalities; but we pay a stiff price for this advance. Aside from the increased complexity, we risk becoming so wedded to the new theoretical tools that we forget the real objective, which is to help analyse and evaluate the executive's part in the creation and direction of the firm, and of the wider socio-economy of which it is a part. As soon as we forget this strategic task and become absorbed in subsidiary theoretical arguments, our field splinters into unconnected academic specializations. (See also the discussion in Chapter 1 by Tom Elfring and Henk W. Volberda.)

But in this chapter we argue, on the contrary, that there are several lines of theorizing converging on a new and powerful emerging paradigm of strategic analysis that draws us back towards Barnard, Penrose and Schumpeter, and to their efforts to place leadership, entrepreneurship and economic growth in a truly dynamic framework. These new models find the organization's identity and competitive advantage in the dynamic of its idiosyncratic knowledge, skills and practices and its learning processes.

Recent conferences have been marked by vigorous discussions about whether our area is distinctive and, if so, in what way. In these sessions we display a certain disingenuity as we confess our inability to define our field. Despite strategy specialists being among the most populous in management education, it appears that we are still searching for a professional identity. This display is clearly unsettling to executives, as well as to our doctoral students, newly minted PhDs and junior faculty. Such uncertainty is not new (Bower, 1982; Bracker, 1980; Schendel and Hofer, 1979), indeed it is not long since doctoral students were being actively dissuaded from researching business policy and strategy (Taylor and Macmillan, 1973). Nor are these doubts diminishing (Ghemawat, 1991; Summer et al., 1990). Schendel (1991), in particular, has called for a new set of questions to help define our field.

Some disputes about our field are extremely public (Ansoff, 1991; Mintzberg, 1991). Others are played out in the varied syllabuses of individual schools. Incredibly, many business policy and strategy (BPS) professors still focus on strategy as the process of developing a fit between the organization and its environment. Others have moved on and focus on industry analysis, negotiation and game theory, protecting economic rents or the management of cultural change. Reflecting this diversity, our field's important papers appear in at least six different journals (MacMillan, 1989). At the same time the marketing and financial strategists ignore our journals and professional meetings, and the legal and political theorists of organization periodically claim our territory. Occasionally papers appear protesting this confusion and proposing theoretical closure (for example, Camerer, 1985; Shrivastava, 1987).

Practitioners also seem increasingly dissatisfied and some charge our business schools with failing the nation. Our journals clearly serve our institutional promotion and tenure process well, but do so at the expense of alienating this clientele (Behrman and Levin, 1984; Porter and McKibbin, 1988). Much of this criticism is directed at our inability to deal with the practical aspects of BPS: executive leadership, business ethics, global competitiveness, the commercialization of research and development, the social and environmental responsibilities of corporations and so forth. There have been piecemeal responses from individual business schools, but there is little consensus on the nature or place of BPS in management education, although, prior to the International Association for

Management Education's recent reforms, it had its special place as the capstone course. General criticisms are matched by more specific complaints. Many practitioners expect our field to be normative, to help them develop winning ways and methods, yet research in BPS seldom carries forceful prescriptive recommendations (Bettis, 1991). Some would say our field is about helping managers identify and think through their difficulties, but it is clear that our colleagues in economics, health care, education, psychology and politics have an impact on executives that we do not. While we have provided useful terms, such as 'competitive advantage' and 'core competencies', we have provided little substantive theory that strategists can use to design their organizations or forecast business outcomes. So we might be excused for some despair, thinking the field of such little use that, along with astrology, it should be pushed beyond the professional pale.

The Development of Our Field

We sometimes try to explain this sorry state of affairs by saying that our field is 'young' (for example, Huff, 1989; Lamb, 1984). This is historically incorrect. Business policy has been a required course in American business schools for well over half a century (Schendel and Hofer, 1979) and executive level business education goes much further back than the founding of the Harvard Business School in 1909 (Redlich, 1957). The real historical dynamic, as Schendel and Hofer remind us, is the interplay of academic rigour and managerial relevance (1979). Prior to the 1950s there was no recognizable academic field, though there was widespread university teaching. The strategy faculty came from other disciplines. There were no strategy journals, no theoretical literature, no professional society and no BPS doctoral students. A distinctive field emerged only as analysis replaced anecdote (Gilmore, 1970). The initial framework was that of Learned et al. (1965). Their concept of business strategy resolved a four-way tension between what the management wanted to do, thought it might do, considered it was able to do and thought it ought to do (Porter, 1981). This framing was sufficiently subtle to encompass the ethical and political dimensions of business leadership, as well as the more tangible matters of production, profit and competitive position. Given such subtlety, the case method remained our field's principal pedagogical technique (Christensen and Hansen, 1987).

The Analytic Tradition and its Failure

In the late 1950s the quantitative analytic methods developed during World War II swept through business management (Gilmore, 1970). New computational methods and equipment became available, Ansoff and Steiner provided the essential seminal texts and articles, and new journals such as *Management Science* and *Long Range Planning* were started. A new professional identity, that of the quantitative forecaster and strategic planner, began to take shape. But research was difficult, requiring access to confidential decision processes in boardrooms and planning departments. To the few who gained access it was immediately obvious that the planning literature was much too prescriptive and bore scant relation to practice. The espoused theories of rational decision-making had little to do with the way strategizing was actually done. While some strategists sampled populations of decisions and sought generalizations that would vault over the detail of specific strategy decisions, the Harvard Business School (HBS) stuck doggedly to the case method and 'situational analysis' (Christensen and Hansen, 1987: 30). They felt the relevance-seeking practitioner needed protection against academics' abstract theories and rigorous statistics.

Strategy, Structure and the Discovery of New Categories

Chandler (1962) changed the relationship between theoretical rigour and practical relevance, and thereby transformed our field. Using historical methods, he sampled 70 leading American companies and exposed general relationships that had both explanatory power and practical policy implications. He provided a way of defining, measuring and relating the organization and its environment that was well suited to the needs of professors and researchers, as well as to practitioners. BPS research flowered, especially when, following the microeconomists but rejecting the older traditions of both the HBS case writers and Chandler's own painstaking historical methodology, secondary data about diversification and financial performance became acceptable for doctoral work. In the 1970s, Scott, Wrigley, Rumelt, Thanheiser, and Channon effectively built a new version of BPS by exploring the concepts of strategy, structure, fit and performance.

This new choice of phenomena and method immediately brought the academic work on strategy closer to industrial organization (IO) economics. But the same manoeuver pushed corporate ethics, social responsibility and executive judgment even further out of the analysis. Another potentially devastating result was the training of a new generation of academics who had neither the historian's passion for detail nor the intuition and insight into executive practice that normally resulted from prolonged field research (Mintzberg, 1973b). This further widened the gap between academic strategists and corporate executives, though the gap must also be understood in the context of the 1959 Ford and Carnegie reports and business schools' struggles for academic legitimacy among their academic peers. For many the strategy–structure–fit paradigm still remains the main definition of our field (Summer et al., 1990: 364). Yet, as today's attention to networking and organizational learning reminds us, strategy and structure have become inadequate concepts, and the pivotal notion of fit seems an incomprehensible hang-over from microeconomic equilibrium theory (Drazin and van de Ven, 1985; Rumelt, 1987: 141; Rumelt et al., 1991: 10; Venkatraman and Prescott, 1990).

New Categories for Strategy Research

Chandler's work profoundly influenced the basic definition of our field in ways quite separable from the particulars of the strategy/structure research paradigm. He showed, reinforced later by the work of Bower, Mintzberg, Child and

Isenberg, that executives do not think in the ways presumed by the older planning and decision-making models. Assailed by so many details, senior executives struggle to focus on a few broad topics. By identifying these, Chandler gave the field the specific new categories that opened up a new theoretical territory based wholly on strategic practice. Whereas the planning paradigm treated strategy as part of the rational decision process of an economic machine, Chandler relocated strategy in the broader framework of the economic history of a society and its organizational institutions. Even though much of the work derived from Chandler's retreating back into purely economic models, neglecting this broader institutionally determined framework, our field was pushed forward by these new categories and intellectual frameworks. Its readiness to absorb them was a sure sign of its intellectual vigour. But the discovery of new categories is an overlooked part of the research process (see also Part V on the configurational school). It stands dialectically opposed to the more familiar process of hypothesizing, sampling and statistical analysis. For too many students and researchers, methodology starts and stops with hypothesis testing, though we see that far greater progress comes with establishing new categories (Daft et al., 1987). Category generation research, such as Chandler performed when he argued for the distinctions between multidivisional, centralized and regional firms, remains high risk, while hypothesis testing, using secondary data, is a safer method that appeals to our field's prevailing tenure and promotion pathologies.

The next crucial step forward was the move to investigate the strategist's idiosyncratic categories and rationality (cf. Chapter 5, this volume). As soon as researchers accepted Simon's (1976) argument that economic rationality was problematic, no longer pre-supposed, they were forced to develop alternatives, if only because the strategist's rationality also becomes the basis for an explanation of his/her action (cf. Chapter 4, this volume). In the social sciences new frameworks generally come from the actors involved in the phenomena of interest, i.e. managers, workers, deal-makers, entrepreneurs, inventors, etc., or are borrowed from the other social sciences. Some BPS researchers, such as Mintzberg, remain committed to these actors' views and intuitions, pointing out the irrelevance of decision-making theory (Mintzberg, 1994). In this sense Mintzberg's entire *oeuvre* is a prolonged attack on our field's typically uncritical pre-supposition of economic rationality. In his best-known paper (Mintzberg, 1976), Mintzberg adopts the split brain metaphor to argue that business strategy is more art than science. This critique goes to the heart of strategic theory, suggesting that business strategy can be distinguished from all else, such as decision making, tactics, pricing or market positioning, by being inexplicable within the framework of a priori rationalism. For Mintzberg, strategy is the creative outcome of managerial experience, judgment and introspection, only researchable because it guides practice and thereby reveals the shape and working of the managerial or organizational unconscious. An easier option is to borrow from the other social sciences and assume the actor's rationality is relatively pre-defined, a reflection of his/her cultural or mental map, whether that is located in an organization, work group, profession, industry or nation. Starting from Simon's notion of 'bounded rationality', strategy is redefined as the process of sense-making, of creating the local rationality or framework of analysis. The strategic process becomes the construction and dissemination of a particular rationality. Strategic change is not simply the redirection of the enterprise towards different product markets or levels of performance, it may also be the displacement of one rationality or culture (Miles and Snow, 1978) or one industry recipe (Spender, 1989) by another.

Note that this attack on economic rationality also suggests a framework in which multiple actors and multiple rationalities might be active at one time. (See also Chapters 4 and 8, this volume.) Game theory begins with a two person zero-sum game in which both actors adopt the same rationality. Negotiation begins as actors with divergent rationalities seek outcomes that benefit both. In the same way we can expect different rationalities to result from the division of interest between a principal and his/her agent. Unless the latter is adequately bonded or policed, he/she will make decisions that run against the owner's interest. Child, Pfeffer, Pettigrew and others mount a similar attack on rationality from political theory. Political theory argues that competition between actors with different rationalities may not be reconcilable unless those with power suppress the differences, superimposing their rationality on others. Under conditions of multiple rationality the organization loses its identity and it becomes impossible to distinguish the interests of the organization from those of the dominant coalition. Similar problems arise with the socio-psychological research of Hambrick, Finkelstein, Castanias and Helfat, and others investigating top management teams, looking at, for instance, the relationship between its members' backgrounds and their strategic choices. Before the attack on economic rationality many of these difficulties used to be sidelined by separating strategy formulation from its implementation (Schendel and Hofer, 1979: 14). The field has benefited hugely from Simon's insights into the limitations of economic rationality by showing that cognitive theory denies the distinction between formulation and implementation.

Any attack on economic rationality is damaging. With one sweep it wipes away the familiar structure of goal-oriented strategic analysis while also cutting the ground for analyses that treat the organization as the principal unit of analysis. Both the individual's bounded decision making and the group's political processes become crucial, and much greater attention needs to be paid to teamwork (Alchian and Demsetz, 1972). The damage is so severe that many writers still refuse to recognize these implications of Simon's critique. But to ignore Simon's work is to miss the way our field has been successfully pushed through these 'paradigm barriers'. No longer presuming economic rationality, we ask completely new questions about the nature of organizations and their management. The field's new answers revolve around knowledge and skills, what managers and employees actually know and bring to the workplace. We puzzle over the subtle combination of objective and tacit knowledge (Polanyi, 1962), and the heuristics and intuitions that were being denied by our previous presumption of economic rationality. Bounded rationality drives a wedge between rational decision making and managerial practice, and so creates the appropriate theoretical space for tacit knowledge as a new mode of explanation. It makes it important to understand how managers and work groups fashion intendedly rational decisions from their tacit knowledge, and this brings their morality, ethics and leadership back into the analysis.

To a Different Level of Analysis

The attack on economic rationality also threatens our concept of the firm. It is not that the firm is a-rational, without a rationality. It is that its rationality, boundaries and integrity must now be explained if we are to identify the firm, for we can no longer presume its nature. Political theorists do this by equating the organization with its dominant coalition. Cognitive theorists equate the organization with its cognitive frame or organizational culture. These are alternative sources of the actor's rationality and the theorist's explanation. But the search for an alternative organizational rationality can still be side-stepped by retaining the presumption of economic rationality at some other level above or below that of the firm, i.e. at the industry or strategic group level, or at the sub-unit, transaction or divisional level. Reactionary theorists, such as the transaction cost economists, who wish to remain true to the neo-economic tradition, retreat from the level being attacked. They find it is no longer necessary to have a clear notion of the organization 'as a whole', as the object of their analytic attention.

Industrial organization economics shifts the analytic level upwards. The industry or strategic group becomes the principal unit of analysis; the firm is simply a member of that group. There is a complementary shift in the economic approach. Given interfirm competition, the group's stability needs to be explained. This might arise because an industry or strategic group recipe is the primary source of its member firms' rationality (Spender, 1989). It might also arise in ways described by Chamberlin's (1933) theory of monopolistic competition, in which the industry emerges as a set of institutionalized behaviours that create both stable interfirm differentiation and collective market power. The initial interest in IO was to generate methods of measuring the industry's market power, so that government could act to eliminate the collusive restraints on competition, which Bain (1968) dubbed 'barriers to entry' (Conner, 1991). Porter (1980) turned Bain's framework upside down, suggesting that individual firms could equally well discover these barriers for themselves and either manipulate them or reposition the firm to take advantage of them. The firm is defined as a group member and its strategic decision is limited to deciding which industry or strategic group to join and which barriers to erect.

While IO shifts the level of analysis upwards, transaction cost analysis (TCA) shifts it downwards, below the level of the firm or even the operating unit, to that of the individual economic transaction. The firm's strategic decision is now to choose each transaction's mode of governance or, in everyday language, to choose whether to make or buy. When the firm can do things more cheaply than they can be done elsewhere, it has a competitive advantage conceptually identical to that of being 'behind' an entry barrier. But uncertainty and opportunism also lead to costs. So Williamson (1975) argues that transactions are better performed within the firm when they are too 'impacted' by these cost-increasing factors to organize across the market place. Strategy is then about minimizing the costs at the transaction level wherever these can be determined. Where they cannot, it is about minimizing the firm's exposure to opportunism and its costs. While not a comprehensive theory of the firm, TCA is a suggestive heuristic so long as the firm is treated as a loosely constrained 'bundle' of transactions or a 'nexus' of the contracts governing those transactions.

Progress, Rich Confusion or Fragmentation?

In the sections above we touched on several theories drawn from disciplines previously peripheral to strategic theory. We argued that they enabled our field to push through two major theoretical barriers, and thereby take us beyond the 'fit and performance' model. The first breakthrough was the rejection of universal economic rationality, the second the rejection of the organization as an unproblematic unit of analysis. The first forces us to focus on the diverse knowledge, skills and heuristics that organizational actors adopt under conditions of uncertainty. The second forces us to question our analytical level or, more importantly, our analytical strategy. Must we consider each transaction or actor separately or should we generalize at the level of the work group, the professional's background, the organization, the strategic group, the industry or the national culture?

With hindsight we see strategy was previously limited to the questions surrounding the direction of an existing enterprise, and was never about its creation or the reasons for its integrity or persistence under conditions of uncertainty. Given BPS's recent progress, we can no longer take the organization, its boundaries, integrity or rationality for granted. By drawing in theories from other disciplines the strategic agenda has been enriched and extended – and pushed much closer to the strategic concerns of practising managers. In today's turbulent times, with mergers and acquisitions booming, in addition to global hypercompetition, managers are no longer able to kick back and presume the existence and persistence of their firm. They appreciate that it must be continually restructured and re-engineered around the new circumstances it confronts. The simplicity has gone. The comfortable and easily taught strategy–structure–fit–performance and strategy–industry conduct–performance paradigms have been pushed aside.

At the same time we see that BPS is in danger of being reduced to a series of specialized sub-fields that find it increasingly difficult to communicate with each other. Language and methodologies diverge as some analysts pursue cases, or use ethnographic, semiotic or deconstructionist methods, while others pursue increasingly sophisticated quantitative analyses or game theory. The levels of analysis vary widely, too. Some work with individual decisions, some with autonomous work groups, others with industries and nations. To cover contemporary BPS research we would have to touch on all of the following, providing each with an assessment of its research methodologies and findings, and its relationship to organizational performance:

- planning, implementation, accounting and information systems
- strategy/structure, fit
- growth stages and life cycles
- horizontal and vertical integration and outsourcing

- joint ventures, mergers, acquisitions and portfolio management
- top, middle management and workplace teamwork
- game theory, bargaining and co-operation
- industrial organization, strategic groups and oligopoly
- institutional and transaction cost economics
- agency theory, property rights and corporate control
- technology strategy, developing and protecting intangible assets
- skills, tacit knowledge and organizational learning
- organizational culture, symbolism, communication and change management
- interorganizational networking and strategic alliances
- globalization, localization and international competitiveness.

Though this list is not exhaustive, it seems a forbidding menu of ways for thinking about why one firm performs better than another or about why firms differ (Schendel, 1991). At its worst it is little more than a laundry list of fashionable 'strategic lenses', but even then its scope implies how rich is the strategy theory we now seek, how great is the progress made since the 1960s.

Toward a Dynamic Theory of Organizational Strategy

In this final section we argue that our field's fragmentation is more apparent than real. Far from dividing into discipline-oriented sub-fields, BPS is actually coherent and in an energetic phase of progressive critical science. The preceding sections show that the field has advanced to the point where strategy is still about organizations, but its scope has been significantly increased. We have made problematic what was previously taken for granted about the creation, persistence and performance of organizations under conditions of bounded rationality, internal heterogeneity and internal and external uncertainty. The persistence of the field, given the onslaught from these other disciplines, is also an expression of our faith in its ability to capture management's strategic contributions. Strategy remains distinct from economics, psychology, political theory, operational research, mathematics and the other fields from which it borrows, only so long as it captures and reflects management's agency, intuitions, tacit knowledge and creativity, and thereby appropriates these other disciplines' categories to its own purposes.

The familiar parts of BPS, planning, implementation, control, market analysis, environmental assessment, fit, competitive activity and the application of new technology, are riddled with genuine theoretical problems. Yet we cannot let managerial practice be subordinated to purely 'academic' concerns. If we have trouble with the TCA, biased decision, and game theory approaches, and think they are going to split our field, it is only because we have too little intuition about how these can be used to illuminate managerial practice. Ghemawat's (1991) descriptions of the use of game theory in oil lease bids, Burgelman's (1991) analysis of technology choice at Intel, or Dutton and Dukerich's (1991) analysis of image management at the NY Port Authority, are reminders of the absolute necessity to stick close to the actors who develop these intuitions. Insisting on this attachment is Mintzberg's enduring contribution to our field.So long as we retain good intuition about the organization and its strategic problems we will be able to make use of many new category systems. We suffer fragmentation only when we get taken up with these other disciplines' theoretical disputes. Interfunctional capstone courses no longer carry the clout they once did, even at HBS, and no-one gets tenure now for teaching or writing cases. But if our field abandons its commitment to managerial practice and no longer troubles to discover the strategic practitioner's core intuitions and heuristics, it will become a dry husk, ready to be ripped apart and subordinated to these other disciplines. One look at our history shows this tension is not new; it came with the territory (Redlich, 1957) and is an unavoidable consequence of applying the abstractions of science to the rich complexity of human affairs. The tension is always potentially damaging, but it is also the principal source of our discipline's dynamism.

In the preceding sections we have argued that the field has been extended in two directions: (a) to a richer understanding of the multiple rationalities behind strategic activity and (b) to multiple levels, so embracing the systemic structures and processes above and below the firm. These alternative analyses are well understood by practitioners. Their intuitions about managing the limits of rationality have been obvious in their attachment to political theories of the firm and, more recently, their ready adoption of organizational culture and its analysis. Their familiarity with multiple levels has been evident in their use of both cost accounting and total quality management (TQM) at the transaction level and of the industry analysis in Porter's model. In short, we could argue that managers are used to working with a two-dimensional analytical matrix. One dimension deals with rationalities, from the universal profit maximizing of economics to the arbitrary and idiosyncratic (such as the founding entrepreneur's). The other dimension deals with alternative levels of analysis, from the elemental activity of work study through the transaction and organizational levels, up to the industry, national and global levels. Practitioners are able to meld these dimensions so long as they maintain a strong sense of the relationship between their praxis and the organization's purposes. As they ask 'what does it mean for us?' they seek to transform the abstractions of the analysis with their intuitive sense of the organization's ontology, i.e. what really matters to the firm. Academics often lack this sense of the organization's identity and so conclude our field is fragmenting. In the next section we suggest that the organization's identity emerges from its practices. This opens up a third dimension of analysis, one that enables us to move towards a truly dynamic framework that narrows the gap between theory and practice even further. (See also the discussion on synthesizing schools Chapter 1.) It will, of course, cause many in academia to see further fragmentation.

The Dynamics of Organization: Knowledge, Routines, Learning and Heuristics

The discussions of tacit knowledge, intangible firm-specific assets, learning by doing and creative destruction suggest a new phase of strategic theorizing as we move towards the knowledge-based theory of the firm. The focus on organizational knowledge and learning shows a new convergence between institutional economics, political theory, game theory and cognitive theory, especially in the technology strategy area (Grant, 1995, 1996; Itami, 1987; Kogut and Zander, 1992; Leonard-Barton, 1995; Nelson and Winter, 1982; Nonaka, 1990b; Nonaka and Takeuchi, 1995; Spender, 1996; Teece, 1987; Weick, 1995; Winter, 1987). Despite the many levels at which these concepts are applied, there is growing agreement that, in a reasonably efficient and competitive market economy, knowledge and skills are the principal sources of sustained competitive advantage. Yet, as Conner points out, this kind of analysis is perilously close to being tautologous (1991: 145). Some new categorizing scheme is required if this line of theorizing is to progress. At one level it will be necessary to distinguish whether a firm is simply reducible to its definable resources, as the resource-based view implies, or whether it also comprises 'non-resources' such as culture, trust, commitment or *esprit de corps*.

The key question becomes, 'How do we acquire, protect, apply and sustain these intangible resources?' and it moves us away from the static categories and frameworks that are bounded by the laws of physics, the conservation of matter and the second law of thermodynamics. We escape the zero-sum and open the way to a dynamic Schumpeterian or Penrosian theory of business strategy, of the growth of the firm, its resources and the economy. But our field still struggles to fit such dynamic notions into its familiar static structures (see Frans van den Bosch on dynamic theories, Chapter 6). If the firm's knowledge is idiosyncratic, scarce and the source of sustainable competitive advantage, it is being considered a tangible but essentially static asset. Theories grounded in the immobility or 'unimitability' of core skills are attempts to quash the dynamic and save the static concepts of traditional economic thought (Lippman and Rumelt, 1982). They delay the time at which the field commits to a more dynamic theory and methodology. But strategic practitioners are telling us that that time has arrived.

Theories of organization learning abound (Cohen and Sproull, 1996; Healy and Bourne, 1995; Moingeon and Edmondson, 1996; von Krogh and Roos, 1996). Despite their seeming diversity, these theories actually converge on the criteria that BPS researchers need in order to capture the recent contributions from other fields. For instance, transaction cost economics tells us to look at the effect of conflicting individual rationalities and opportunism under impacted information. The strategist's response is neither the economist's nor the political theorist's. While economists look to agency theory and performance bonds and political theorists look to power, strategists look to the kind of organizational learning that restrains moral hazard and generates trust (Fukuyama, 1995). Political theory tells us that individuals struggle to protect their own interests, but society exists and functions because these individuals also learn that it is in their own interests to accept political and social institutions. Likewise, industrial organization economics tells us to look at mobility barriers, but switching costs, product differentiation and customer loyalty are individual learning institutionalized into economic behaviours. Game theory now informs us about the possibility of individual learning, which, institutionalized, becomes group co-operation (Axelrod, 1984; Shapiro, 1989; Taylor, 1987). Such learning leads us to look at the institutional structures that bind diverse and competing economic actors together into economic systems and, in so doing, provide their rationality. Increasingly, as learning seems the key to the emerging strategic paradigm, these institutional structures become the real focus of strategic analysis in our expanded theoretical agenda. The effect is to shift the emphasis onto how the firm's executives influence these structures and thereby manage the processes of individual and organizational learning, and how these processes interrelate as individuals coalesce into an institutionalized community-of-practice (Brown and Duguid, 1991). The knowledge generated is both diffused around the organization, the essence of Nonaka and Takeuchi's (1995) analysis, and institutionalized in the organization's routines (Nelson and Winter, 1982).

Dealing with Practice

To break through into a truly dynamic knowledge-based paradigm we need to address the concepts of organizational and individual practice. Practice lies at the core of the discussion of tacit knowledge and skills, and it opens up a third 'action' dimension of the emerging framework of strategic theorizing. To the two previous dimensions of strategic analysis, the need to deal with multiple rationalities and levels of analysis, we add the distinction between reasoned analysis and human action. We argue that human action cannot be fully analysed as the unproblematic consequence of reasoned decision making. Some action may be treated this way, but much cannot, especially that which is strategic and performed under conditions of uncertainty (Spender, 1989: 42). By introducing this third dimension we suggest that much of the executive creativity that results in strategic advantage emerges only through action, and as we delve into the notion of practice we shall see that our field's notions of rationality and levels of analysis also change.

Polanyi's (1962) discussion of tacit knowledge is often summarized in the maxim 'we know more than we can tell', the point being that much of human knowledge is embedded in practice and cannot be readily articulated using the abstractions of language. Strategists have recently taken up the tacit/explicit distinction, recognizing that the firm's tacit knowledge, embedded in organizational routines, is likely to be inimitable and so the source of persistent economic rents. But the distinction may be more profound than this. For us, tacit knowledge is not simply an under-articulated form of explicit organizational or individual knowledge. It also suggests that the ability to engage skilfully (and heedfully) in organizational practice is a form of knowing that differs from the explicit form of knowing associated with managerial decision making. The point is not language's inability to grasp what some people reveal in their practice, rather that the knowledge captured by language is itself not in the 'world' of organizational activity. This is most obviously true when we build theoretical models that are deliberately abstracted and generalized away from the world we experience. Practice, by definition, is immediate, in the world and contextualized, and not possible to be wholly captured in linguistic generalities.

The implication is that to grasp organizational practice fully we may have to move away from the idea of generality. Action is always in context, and strategic advantage is always in the world. Thus theorists are forced to make strategic judgments about the 'local-ness' or contextuality of their general analyses, trading off the particular against the applicable elsewhere. Every context has its own rationality so theorists must pay close attention to the boundaries around the activities being analysed. Far from moving into the era of 'boundary-less' organizations heralded by some academic theorists, practising business strategists are already showing us, through their attention to empowerment, teamwork, strategic alliances and networking, that they are continually redefining the boundaries around the organizational practices they manage. In general, managers have been far quicker to reconceptualize the new objects of attention than have the academics. As a result, managers are becoming less concerned with the firm's tangible assets and their ownership, the basis of a microeconomic theory, than with the pattern of economic activities that they can influence to produce appropriable consequences.

This shift of attention presents us with severe methodological challenges because (a) our established tradition of focusing on abstract models may no longer be appropriate to this new action-oriented research objective and (b) the abstractions of language may not be able to capture the immediacy of the skilful practices on which this new approach to strategy is focused. Strategy researchers must, therefore, work out new questions – and new strategies for generating answers. One strategy, analogous to the research into managerial cognition which avoided pre-supposing the actor's rationality and, following Simon (1976), looked for its sources, is to look indirectly at the sources of skilful practice. Here, institutional theory might be of considerable help. Those who have analysed the professions, such as Abbott (1988), show how newcomers are socialized into the institutional frameworks that define skilled practice. As Cassell (1991) illustrates, the expert's theoretical learning often shapes professional practice less than the institutional structures of the world into which those practices must be fitted. We also know that professional institutions are extraordinarily sensitive about the boundaries around the activities they wish to influence, and this provides us with a metaphor for strategic management of the organization as a system of professional practice. Identifying the boundaries around the system give us a way of speaking about practice, which avoids sacrificing its immediacy and contextuality. Brown and Duguid (1991) lull us into accepting the boundary around Orr's community of photocopier technicians as a way of identifying both the explicit and the implicit elements of the body of knowledge articulated in their practice. This achieves the complex double objective of giving us a sense of (a) the knowledge shared among the photocopier technicians and (b) the story telling that results in an institutional fabric that holds together the heterogeneity of individual experience, skill and interest evident in the technicians' group. The latter, of course, is the result of the technicians' commitment to their ongoing system of practice.

Since these systems or communities of professional practice are 'in the world', they can never be designed in the abstract in the way that organization theory pre-supposes organizations can be designed. Organizations are, instead, partially emergent and quasi-autonomous systems of organic order, in many respects more like the informal system that we know infuses every attempt to design an organization. The strategic manager's role is redefined as helping to shape these systems in the light of the historical, socio-economic, technological and institutional contexts in which they are embedded. To grasp organizations as quasi-autonomous systems of professional practice, strategy theory must, therefore, abandon the mechanistic notion of organization designer and pay greater attention to the 'affordances' (Norman, 1989: 9) or the means and 'levers' through which managers might influence such systems. The idea that strategists are attempting to influence systems of practice containing diverse rationalities and multiple levels of action, as individuals, groups, organizations, institutions and interests interact, is richly illustrated in Latour's (1996) extended analysis of the history of the Aramis personal rapid transit project. In so far as this gives us a sense of what the new knowledge-based paradigm of strategic theorizing might be like, we might see several characteristic features emerging. We are no longer abstract theorists trying to give managers the universal laws of an economic process 'out there' that they then use to design their firms. Instead we have to become professional practitioners, depending on our intuitions, as well as on the data, as we offer practical advice about how managers might more effectively influence the specific systems of which they are part. We offer heuristics such as (a) look for the system's affordances or levers, (b) get a sense of the heterogeneity of the actors' rationalities or the system's 'interpretive flexibility' (Bijker, Hughes and Pinch, 1987: 4), (c) probe the dynamics of institutional structures and learning processes that hold the diversity together and result in the sense of identity emerging among the actors and (d) think through how the emerging boundaries can be managed, extended with alliances to draw in more activity or reduced by 'outsourcing' and 'downsizing'. These may seem small steps, but they constitute a significant movement towards a completely new paradigm of strategic analysis that treats the firm as a real system of dynamic knowledge processes, contextualized and 'in the world'.

Conclusion

In this chapter we explored recent changes in the field of business policy and strategy. Over the last decade there has been a vast increase in the variety of methods and concepts being applied. It is especially obvious that the field's traditional tendency to borrow from other disciplines has accelerated. Industrial anthropology and cognitive theory opened up the analysis of organizational culture and employee rationality. Economics, both the industrial organization (IO) and the transaction cost analysis (TCA) varieties, made major new impacts. Game theory helped us develop complex rigorous models of interfirm competition. International business theorists pursue ever more eclectic models. As a result many writers consider BPS to be fragmented, bordering on the chaotic. We argue that this is typical of a field developing rapidly through a period of critical science. Within BPS the questions now being considered are richer and more fundamental than ever before. With the benefit of hindsight, we can see that strategic analysis used to be only about the direction of an extant enterprise towards objectives given by the owners or their agents. We understood little about the competitive, cognitive and market constraints over these goals. These became clearer after (a) Chandler (1962) reshaped the field around the internal structuring and market engagements of firms and (b) Simon (1976) drew our attention to bounded rationality. Now, after Porter (1980), Williamson (1975) and Nelson and Winter (1982) we see that strategic analysis is also about the creation of the enterprise, the resolution of divergent interests and rationalities, the choice of governance mode and of conduct towards competitors, and the management of the firm's body of intangible and hard-to-imitate knowledge. We now introduce the notion of practice, in particular the idea of communities and systems of practice, as a third dimension of the emerging strategic analysis. This allows us to draw attention to the institutional structures and practices that hold diverse rationalities and interests together long enough for a sense of organizational identity to emerge. We concluded with suggestions about how managers might influence these systems of practice, offering four types of heuristic for looking at the system's (a) affordances, (b) interpretive flexibility, (c) institutional identity and (d) boundary management.

3

Thoughts on Schools

Henry Mintzberg

I am a great believer in the flat Earth theory. We thought we discovered the truth several hundred years ago: the Earth is not flat, it is round. Out with the old, in with the new.

Well, I flew into Schiphol Airport in Amsterdam recently, and looking out of the window, I thought: can anyone really believe they corrected for the curvature of the Earth in building that runway? In other words, for certain very practical purposes, the flat Earth theory remains perfectly acceptable. Of course, I hope the pilot didn't use it on his flight from Gothenburg. For flying aeroplanes, the round Earth theory isn't bad. But it is no more true than the flat Earth theory, or else aeroplanes coming into Geneva from Italy would smash into the Alps, i.e. the Earth is not perfectly round either; it is bumpy. In fact, it is not really round at all, since it bulges at the poles.

The point is that it is arrogant to consider any theory true, whether new or old. (Physical scientists, it has been said, stand on the shoulders of their predecessors, while we social scientists stand on their faces!) All theories are false – they are just words and/or figures on pieces of paper. Theories are more or less useful, that is all, depending on the circumstances, which means old theories can sometimes be as useful as new ones. (I'll bet we still rely on Newton's physics more than Einstein's physics.)

The ten schools were meant to capture old and new theories. I have my preferences, but that merely reflects what I find more useful, maybe just to promote my own publications! Of course, while each school may represent a theory (or set of theories), there is also the need for more integrative theory across the ten. Typologies are a weak form of theorizing, but they, too, may be useful, if only to delineate the territory.

Darwin once distinguished 'splitters' and 'lumpers'. Lumpers love categories, nice boxes in which to put things. Splitters complain that the world is not like that. Everything is nuanced. Well, lumping helps – there are often central tendencies – even if splitters do have a point. We need to identify categories and at the same time we need to recognize their limitations.

In that regard, it is the integrative schools that interest me most. Not that we shall ever have a theory of strategy – I certainly hope not, anyway! I proposed the configurational school as integrative – to set the other schools in context by considering sequences of phases in the strategy making process. That is, of course, one integrative approach among many.

Tom Elfring and Henk W. Volberda propose two others, a boundary school and a dynamic capabilities school. But since ten is a nice round number, I must consider these very carefully. I see the boundary school in the passive spirit of the environmental school, and the dynamic capabilities school as a kind of hybrid of the design and learning schools. Of course, hybrids are integrative in a way, and we could be looking for all kinds of hybrids among these and other schools.

Leif Melin also suggested to me a 'network' school. But I would be tempted to put it into the political school or, more exactly, to use it to rethink the political school, since it suggests strategy as a negotiated process among different organizational entities. Maybe the power or political school would be better labelled the 'negotiation' school, to designate strategy as a negotiated process internally (organizational politics) and externally (the organization negotiating in its environment, or else developing its strategy collectively in a network).

The point is that the schools were presented as a history of sorts, a kind of snapshot of where the strategy field was when I wrote it and where it had been. If that can help to take us further – if, in other words, the framework can be treated as flexible and dynamic – then so much the better. Our world of strategy is also flat and round, bumpy and bulging.

PART II

INTEGRATION EFFORTS IN THE FIELD

4

Complexity and Multiple Rationalities in Strategy Processes

Patrick Regnér

This chapter attempts to integrate various strategy perspectives. It is argued that strategy resides in complexity and is best studied in terms of a multiple rationality set tied to the firm's capability to learn. Strategy is interpreted in terms of adaptive and alterable learning mechanisms that could potentially allow superior knowledge to be used in strategic capabilities and be a source of competitive advantage. These strategic learning mechanisms, based on both calculated and systemic rationalities, emerge through knowledge assimilation and integration by means of human assets where the firm's resources and market forces meet. Four strategic learning modes are presented as an illustration of interacting learning practices in strategy processes and as an outline for empirical research and implications for management.

Strategic Complexity: Challenging Strategy Theories

Strategy research has from its early days been concerned with both external positions and opportunities and internal resources and capabilities (Andrews, 1971; Ansoff, 1965). Some theories have emphasized one or the other to a higher degree, prescribing market (Porter, 1980) or resource stances (Wernerfelt, 1984). These external and internal positions are both achieved through complex strategy processes influenced by organizational decisions and characteristics as well as processual and contextual properties. It is from this complexity of attaining and maintaining secure market positions that the practice of business strategy originates. In contrast, strategy theory terminates in confrontation with this complexity, as it seems to be unable to capture complexity.

It is not particularly controversial to assert that the traditional view of strategy as a controlled and conscious plan made in advance, including a clear separation of formulation and implementation (Andrews, 1971; Ansoff, 1965) has been demonstrated to be incorrect (Hayes, 1985; Mintzberg, 1978, 1990a, 1994; Mintzberg and Waters, 1985; Quinn, 1980a). Strategy is, rather, an adaptive process where piecemeal strategic decisions are taken based on continuous feedback between formulation and implementation in an emergent pattern over time. Unfortunately, interpretations of this latter view have not moved beyond the portrayal of strategy as an ambiguous and uncontrollable process in history. This process is described as guided either by power and politics or by random combinations of events or environmental selections or isomorphic forces, all involving few possibilities for manoeuver for managers (Cohen et al., 1972; Di Maggio and Powell, 1983; Hannan and Freeman, 1977; Pettigrew, 1973, 1985). If managers are perfectly rational in traditional (and some political) views, they are imperfectly rational in these perspectives. Apparently, there is a need for a more holistic view. This view must recognize that managers and firms face considerable constraints due to environmental complexities, but at the same time have an important potential to adapt to, manage, modify and create complexity. What we need is a view incorporating the applied nature of strategy, without surrendering it to random and uncontrollable processes.

Perspectives emphasizing strategy development as an incremental, complex, but purposeful process (Mintzberg and Waters, 1985; Quinn, 1980a) move in the right direction. However, besides pure descriptions of strategy processes, these views do not seem to explore the kind of considerations strategy involves or what the implications are for managers; the actual substance of strategy is more or less left out. The related integration of various strategy perspectives in configurational approaches are also promising (Miller and Friesen, 1980; Mintzberg and McHugh, 1985; Mintzberg et al., 1976), but it is doubtful whether strategy develops sequentially in independent and categorical segments (cf. Part V on the configurational school, this volume). It seems more likely to be an interweaved process involving diverse rationalities and strategies simultaneously rather than individual rationalities and strategies as distinct lumps in a process of episodic stages.

Within economics-oriented strategy research it is primarily resource-based dynamic capabilities perspectives (for example, Teece et al., 1990) that offer encouraging ideas for the future. However, when we leave the simple and static supply and demand of resources and capabilities and move into more dynamic properties, involving the development of strategic capabilities, economics alone is insufficient. Here, organizational beliefs, values and knowledge become fundamental, and behavioural theories step in and have more to say. Organizational learning seems particularly applicable.[1] Economics does not seem to be able to examine satisfactorily several manifestations of strategy, i.e. processes, uncertainty, power and coalitions. The organization is simply considered as a bundle of assets and change is often represented by deterministic environmental selection (Bettis, 1991; Hirsch et al., 1990). The economics tradition of strategy research has contributed significantly to the development of the strategy field during the last decade, but it is now time for behaviourally oriented research to follow on.

The applied nature of strategic management requires a multidimensional view, incorporating diverse complexities, rationalities and strategies, where managers and firms face constraints, but also have manoeuvering possibilities and act as active knowledge assimilators and arbitrators. We believe research on strategy processes can make progress in the intersection between the economics-oriented dynamic resource-based models, emphasizing the mechanisms of capability creation, and the behavioural-based organizational learning models, focusing on the firm as a cognitive entity. Certainly there is a danger of becoming too eclectic in an integrative effort, but the whole strategy field is multiparadigmatic by nature, which is definitely no coincidence. Also, despite the inherent risk of fragmentation it seems as though behavioural as well as economics-oriented researchers within strategy are now promoting a pluralistic development regarding both theory and methodologies (Bettis, 1991; Bowman, 1990; Daft and Buenger, 1990; Rumelt et al., 1991). The purpose of this chapter is to provide a multidimensional strategy perspective and integrate different strategy approaches based on a view of strategic complexity and multiple rationality, focusing on strategic learning and knowledge management as decisive mechanisms in the management of strategy.

Coping with Strategic Complexity via Multiple Rationalities

Rent opportunities flourish in the strategic complexity of problems that prevail between order and disorder. In an environment characterized by total unconnectedness there is no room for strategy as situations can be optimized easily and instantly, so strategy becomes tactics (Emery and Trist, 1965). In a very turbulent environment, total interconnectedness prevails and the situation is non-manageable, so no strategy is feasible (McCann and Selsky, 1984). Potentials for economic rent abound between these two states of non-complexity, in interconnectedness, where organizations face turbulence, but are still able to manage and form strategy. (See Schoemaker, 1990 for a similar point of view.) Hence, under conditions of order and simplicity, where optimization is rudimentary, potentials for economic rents diminish. Similarly, where complete chaos abides, optimization has no meaning and economic rent possibilities dwindle (Figure 4.1). It follows from this reasoning that strategy is meaningful and valuable only under conditions of complexity, between the states of order and disorder. (According to this definition total chaos and total stability are not complex (cf. Simon, 1962).) There is a whole array of various strategy process interactions between internal firm resources and external market forces contributing to strategic complexity and, in turn, to opportunities for rents. This strategic complexity can be illustrated by various concepts discussed in the strategy literature, for example, entry barriers, market impediments and friction forces including diverse market imperfections such as various economies, imperfect information, transaction costs and product differentiation (Porter, 1980; Schoemaker, 1990; Yao, 1988).

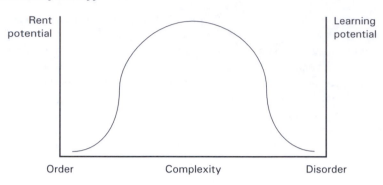

FIGURE 4.1   *Rent and learning potentials in complexity and non-complexity (partially adapted from Schoemaker, 1990)*

The weakness in much of strategy research is that complexity, where strategy is possible and rent opportunities high, has been neglected in the sense that either the models (a) presume more or less perfect rationality, which can only be achieved in order or non-complexity or (b) stress imperfect rationality to the extent that it concerns complete disorder or non-complexity. This is also illustrated by the fact that two of the main disciplines upon which strategy research has relied are basically suspicious about business strategy. In economics, any supranormal profits due to successful strategy will dissipate into the market as competition force rents to zero (perfect rationality) or the firm is considered to be a function of environmental selection in history rather than a result of deliberate strategies (imperfect rationality). In many organization theory perspectives the dominant role of inevitable external forces requires the firm to adapt passively, leaving no room for strategy (imperfect rationality). When we move into specific strategic planning theories, managers are assumed to have more or less perfect information (perfect rationality).

An alternative to the afore-mentioned polarized perfect/imperfect rationality approaches might be a multiple rationality perspective. If we examine the two views of rationality discussed above we note that they correspond to different views of making strategy. In the first case (perfect rationality), strategy is a controlled and conscious plan made in advance with complete knowledge; a strategy formulation perspective (for example, Andrews, 1971; Ansoff, 1965). In the second case (imperfect rationality), strategy is an emergent, uncontrolled and ambiguous process with basically deceptive knowledge; a strategy formation perspective (for example, Cohen et al., 1972; Hannan and Freeman, 1977; Lindblom, 1959). Hence, it can be suggested that there is a correlation between various rationality and strategy perspectives. Essentially, strategy could be conceived as rationality, which relaxes the traditional view of rationality as strictly relating to individuals and strategy mainly relating to organizations (Singer, 1994).

It is a widely accepted notion in contemporary strategic management research that rationality is not perfect, but bounded (Simon, 1955). It must be acknowledged that bounded or limited rationality neither implies that strategy is completely left to deterministic external forces, nor that it is identical for all firms. Managers still have considerable room for manoeuver in order to adapt actively, manage, modify and create complexities. The skill of doing so will differ from one actor to another, which implies that rationality is not only bounded, but variable (Schoemaker, 1990). We suggest that bounded or limited rationality might be conceived as including a whole set of rationalities coping with different complexities, from strong rationality, where management has more direct influence over strategy, to adaptive rationality, where management has less direct say. Hence, depending on the complexity of the problem, strategy will be based on a set of multiple rationalities and the capability of handling these will differ from firm to firm, as rationalities are both bounded and variable (see also Chapter 2, this volume).

An analysis of strategy processes benefits from a multiple rationality perspective. As rationality will vary depending on each strategic problem within the process, different rationalities in a strategy process can exist simultaneously, but for diverse complexities. For example, where the strategy process is characterized by low complexity it might include strong rationality, in higher complexity it might involve contextual and process rationality, taking contextual and processual influences into consideration (Cohen et al., 1972; Lindblom, 1959) or adaptive rationality, emphasizing experiential learning by individuals and organizations (Cyert and March, 1963; March, 1978). Finally, in a strategy process characterized by very high complexity the only possibility might be posterior rationality, where objectives are revealed in the interpretation of action (March, 1978; Weick, 1979) or selected rationality – a selection procedure based on the survival or growth of strategies, where managers have very little or no say (Hannan and Freeman, 1977).[2] For these multiple rationalities there are variations among actors and managers and firms will cope with the various complexities in different ways. This variation is the very foundation for firms exhibiting different strategies and, thus, different profitabilities.

The proposal that strategy processes ought to be examined in terms of various rationalities corresponding to variations in complexity within the process, rather than analysing the whole process in terms of one rationality perspective, can be described as a configurational perspective (cf. Mintzberg, 1979, 1989, 1990b), but not on the level of the organization or strategy process. It is, rather, a configurational view on the level of individual complexities within the strategy process where each corresponds to a particular rationality configuration. Hence, a strategy process could involve all sorts of complexities and, thus, rationalities and therefore it does not make sense to analyse it according to a single rationality view. Strategy strives in the set of bounded and variable rationalities both from firm to firm and within firms, which provides a suitable foundation for integrating different perspectives.

Calculated and Systemic Rationality in Strategic Learning

Given our reasoning above, strategy processes can be analysed in terms of the various ways in which knowledge is generated and informs strategy. In lower complexity, strategy can be based on calculated rationality (i.e. strong, contextual, process), where actions are connected consciously and intentionally to knowledge. For problems of higher complexity we have to shift to systemic rationality (i.e. adaptive, posterior, selective), which is based on the fact that knowledge evolves 'over time within a system and accumulates across time, people, and organizations without complete current consciousness of its history' (March, 1978: 592). Correspondingly, strategy is informed by means of deducing optimal alternatives based on formal strategic methods, such as strategic models, algorithms and tools, in low complexity. As we move into areas of higher complexity, where rent opportunities are higher, this becomes less feasible. Instead, strategy must be generated by various types of approximations, based on what others do, previous experiences, hypotheses, experiments, heuristics, etc. Hence, strategy in higher complexity must rely more on inductive reasoning than on the deduction of optimal strategies. Doing a jigzaw puzzle is a good illustration, where the beginning and end are more based on deduction and possible optimization, and in those phases the strategic problem essentially becomes tactics. In between them the only possibility seems to be a strategy based on inductive reasoning through gathering of information, guesses, comparisons, assumptions, trial and error, etc.[3] Therefore, strategy in complexity is not primarily about deliberately locating either resource or market stances through deduction, but rather a question of managing the process of inductions where these develop. The strategy process seems to be analogous to an adaptive and changeable learning process where various learning mechanisms such as information gathering, experiences, experiments and so on guide strategy.

Consequently, in order to analyse strategy processes in terms of strategic complexities and multiple and varying rationalities, a learning perspective seems appropriate. Ideal learning conditions appear to prevail in complexity, between complete order and chaos (Figure 4.1). Simple, stable and benevolent environments on the one hand and highly chaotic, rapidly changing and threatening environments on the other, both offer poor opportunities for learning (Hedberg, 1981).[4] It has been verified by several studies that organizational learning is a powerful device in the development of organizational intelligence, although not simple (Levitt and March, 1988). In our framework, firms cope with different complexity settings through various interweaved strategic learning mechanisms based on systemic as well as calculated rationality. Strategic learning involves various adaptive and alterable learning practices, such as scanning, intelligence gathering, experiments, etc. Accordingly, strategic learning is perceived as inferences from observations and operations transferring into learning and guiding strategy development. These various forms of observations (for example, intelligence, scanning) and operations (for example, previous experiences, experiments), depending on learning skills, might generate superior knowledge that can be used in strategic capabilities. Strategic learning emerges within and among human assets in the intersection between a firm's other resources, such as physical assets, and market forces, i.e. competitive forces, and has the potential to generate strategic capabilities (for example, product or market innovations, manufacturing flexibility) that, in turn, may provide above average returns (cf. Amit and Schoemaker, 1993).

In the same way as we argue that organizations exhibit rationality through strategy we argue that they exhibit learning through adaptation or alteration processes. The more we emphasize social interaction and transmission between individuals and between different hierarchical levels as being important for individual learning in the organization, the closer we seem to come to definitions that accept explicitly that organizational level learning exists (cf. Hedlund and Nonaka, 1993; Levitt and March, 1988). In line with our prior discussion on multiple rationalities we argue that organizations, like individuals, are likely to be able to perform miscellaneous forms of learning. We believe that organizational learning is something more than the sum of individuals' learning.[5] When individuals learn so does the organization, and, moreover, initiating or altering interactions between individuals generates organizational knowledge.

So which possible sources of learning skills are there? It has been suggested that 'organizational climate' (Hansen and Wernerfelt, 1989) or 'organizational culture' (Barney, 1986b) may be determinants of sustained competitive advantage. Accordingly, one important source of unique learning advantages could be the cognitive structure of the firm. This has been described in various forms as an interpretative system or scheme (Daft and Weick, 1984), paradigm (Johnson, 1988), industry recipe (Grinyer and Spender, 1979a; Spender, 1989) and knowledge structure (Lyles and Schwenk, 1992). As our discussion is based on a learning and knowledge metaphor we will use the latter term. The knowledge structure is a group of shared premises, beliefs, assumptions, etc. that shape the organization's comprehension of itself, its environment and the relationship between the two. It provides the organization's worldview and can be seen as part of the organizational culture. The knowledge structure can be viewed as a forceful learning foundation in the sense that it controls the conditions suited for various learning mechanisms and also contains heuristics and routines that guide strategy. It provides a basis for mutual understanding within the organization and provides accessible knowledge accumulated over years, which can be used in given situations.

However, learning, like rationality, is not perfect, but bounded. It is vulnerable to a whole range of cognitive, contextual and political learning barriers (Huber, 1991; Levinthal and March, 1993; Levitt and March, 1988; Schwenk, 1984). Firms will display various skills in handling these barriers, thus, they will vary not only among, but also within firms. The variable learning skills from player to player determine variations in profitability; if learning skills were generalized to firms, there would obviously be no room either for strategy or above average returns.

Strategy as a Set of Strategic Learning Practices

Strategy in complexity can be illustrated as a continuous knowledge assimilation process involving various strategic learning modes based on learning through observations and operations, including intelligence, informal scanning, experience and experiment. Different modes deal with various levels of strategic complexity. These learning practices determine the ability to adapt to, manage, modify and create strategic complexities and to devise a set of managerial and organizational means of strategic action. Intelligence and scanning are based on more passive learning by observing with a particular focus on market forces. Experience and experiment build on learning by doing, are more active and are based on internal resources and capabilities. It is out of the interaction process between these modes that knowledge emerges and strategy develops. The combined outcome of the modes might produce valuable strategic knowledge.

Intelligence is the formal search in the environment for information and intelligence likely to invoke strategy changes (Ghoshal and Kim, 1986; Ghoshal and Westney, 1991; Lenz and Engledow, 1986; Prescott and Smith, 1989). It relies more on formal and hard data and might involve more or less formalized business intelligence units, directing, collecting, analysing and disseminating intelligence.

Informal scanning is an informal search for changes and opportunities in the environment (Aguilar, 1967; Daft et al., 1988; Fahey and King, 1977; Hambrick, 1982; Jain, 1984; Keegan, 1974). It is based on more soft and subjective processes, such as casual personal contacts, maybe in terms of hearsay, gossip and speculation, rather than written intelligence reports, and these processes bring about hunches or intuitions rather than objective statements (cf. Mintzberg, 1973b, 1975, 1976).

In experience we turn to more active processes involving first hand knowledge. In these processes the foundation for strategy is knowledge acquired through direct experience (Argyris and Schön, 1978; Cyert and March, 1963; Levitt and March, 1988) either formally through systematic efforts or through more informal accidental and haphazard processes (Huber, 1991). Hence, experiential learning is based on inferences from strategy implementation.

Experiment includes formal organizational experiments (Lawler, 1977) aimed at adaptation, for example, market tests. It also involves experimenting organizations, emphasizing regular changes in goals, organization structures, processes, markets, etc. (Hedberg et al., 1976) and the active generation of knowledge through creation of ambiguity and chaos (Nonaka, 1988, 1990a, 1994) directed towards enhancement of adaptability.[6]

It might be argued that our inclusion of diverse knowledge assimilation processes in a single context is illogical, as they involve distinct processes and are, at least partly, based on theories that can be distinguished from each other (Levitt and March, 1988; Scott, 1992). At the same time, a distinction between them will be rather subjective and indefinite as they are considerably interwoven in practice and can to some degree be substituted for each other. Therefore, for our purpose, which is integrating schools of strategy, a unification of these different mechanisms through which knowledge is assimilated is perfectly logical.

It is important to note that the modes are interwoven with each other and belong on a continuum or in a 'forcefield' rather than in distinct and separate sections (Figure 4.2). Portions of intelligence might involve more informal and subjective processes and, thus, be similar to scanning. Similarly, experiences based on organizational searches for suitable strategies might certainly involve scanning characteristics and, clearly, experience and experiment blend with each other.

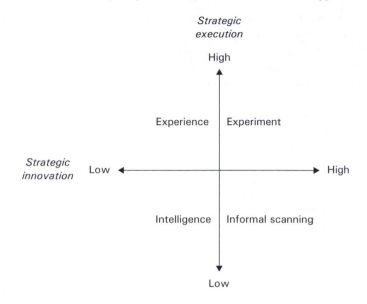

FIGURE 4.2   *Strategic learning modes*

We noted above that the various modes differ when it comes to strategic execution (learning by observing versus learning by doing) and concerning their relative focus on external market forces and internal resources. Another important difference is in terms of innovation emphasis (exploitation versus exploration) (see Figure 4.2). In addition, the strategic learning modes correspond to various complexities, face various learning barriers, differ in terms of uniqueness and imitability and have various management implications. Each aspect is discussed below.

Regarding complexity the intelligence and experience modes inform strategy in lower interconnectedness where specific articulated bits and pieces of information can be gathered and certain strategies can be sought. In higher complexity, where only subtle cues can be perceived and trial and error is used, the informal scanning and experiment modes guide strategy.

The strategic learning modes are vulnerable to various learning barriers that make companies differ in their learning skills and, in turn, differ in strategic capabilities and profitability. Numerous cognitive simplification processes pertaining to strategy and decision making (Hogarth and Makridakis, 1981; March and Sevón, 1988; Schwenk, 1984) and a range of organizational learning and adaptation impediments (Holland, 1975; Huber, 1991; Levinthal and March, 1993; Levitt and March, 1988) have been examined in the literature. Cognitive simplification processes are most prominent when there is consensus among decision makers (Janis, 1972; Schwenk, 1984) and, although it might seem contradictory, one of the most important learning barriers is the prevailing knowledge structure of the organization. This defines the learning framework at the outset of each mode and contains heuristics and routines guiding strategy. Hence, while the knowledge structure can be a primary asset in terms of learning, it might also be an impediment in the learning process. Formal intelligence relies on the existing knowledge structure and bias confirming evidence, as it is frequently initiated in order to support prevailing strategies, while informal scanning might be more secluded. Experience will be backed by the knowledge structure as action is heavily based on the employment of existing resources and capabilities, building on the established knowledge structure. In experimental learning there is potential that the knowledge structure will be more profoundly deviated from and possibly questioned, as it is a mode specifically directed at creating new ideas and beliefs.

The various strategic learning practices differ when it comes to uniqueness and imitability, too. Formal intelligence will not be a major source for sustainable above average returns as it guides strategy via public available knowledge, similar to that acquired by others. Still, firms with unique methods for acquisition and analysis and better skills in applying them might have the possibility to gain above average returns. However, the predicament is that methods for acquisition of information and the analysis of it and even the skill with which these are employed may be in the public domain as well (Barney, 1986a), yet we have reason to expect some inertia in their dissipation, allowing for temporary competitive advantages. Potentials for above average returns are more likely when valuable firm-specific interactions between firm resources and market forces are involved in the learning process. Interactions will be firm-specific if the resources and strategic capabilities involved and/or the relationships (i.e. human assets) in the interaction are laborious and costly for competitors to imitate. Thus, as we move into valuable, more unique and non-imitable firm resource/market force interaction processes, the potential for above average returns is better. Valuable first-hand informal scanning is more based on unique connections and trust, which is hard to imitate compared to second hand formal intelligence and may, therefore, be more likely to provide superior knowledge and above average returns. Similarly, strategy can be informed via firm-specific interaction processes in the experience and experiment mode. Interactions are likely to be more unique and non-imitable in experiments compared to experience, but the probability that they will be valuable is obviously lower.

The fact that adaptive and alterable processes in organizations require a balance between exploration and exploitation is reflected in many theories of organizations and firms in the past (Holland, 1975; Penrose, 1959) and central to many modern thoughts of organization as well (Hedlund and Rolander, 1990; March, 1991a, 1991b; Senge, 1990; Wernerfelt, 1984). It is apparent that the learning modes will vary concerning the exploration/exploitation balance. Intelligence will primarily support exploitation, in particular regarding focused searches, which tend to be close to action and more short sighted, capitalizing on existing market forces. Informal scanning, being further from action and entailing a more holistic use of knowledge, entails more exploration properties, investigating new opportunities among market forces. Experience through the use of firm resources leans more toward exploitation and constrains exploration as experiential learning is particularly sensitive to 'successes in the temporal and spatial neighbourhood of action' (March, 1991b: 17). Experiments through firm resources obviously encompass exploration; it is specifically focused on the generation of novelty in the long run, even if the current exploitation and exploration mix happens to be optimal.

Managing Strategy through Strategic Learning Modes

Implicit in our discussion lies the assumption that learning may improve strategic intelligence and we have suggested that some firms may possess learning advantages over others. Hence, some firms would be better at managing the learning modes than others. Below we propose some general suggestions on how the strategic learning modes can be managed in order to enhance knowledge assimilation. However, as indicated earlier in our discussion on learning barriers, the learning modes face major obstacles, many of which are very difficult to overcome and, clearly, learning via the modes does not invariably lead to intelligent strategies. It is important to observe that knowledge management (cf. Hedlund, 1994) in high complexity is not primarily about directly trying to eliminate or circumvent learning barriers, but rather a matter of improving the ability to assimilate and integrate knowledge via various forms of inductions in order to inform strategy. It is specifically the interaction among diverse strategic learning modes that is essential.

Formal intelligence can be improved through management of the organization and procedures of intelligence. Numerous 'business intelligence system' designs have been suggested in the management literature, based on various tools and techniques for searching the environment (for example, Fuld, 1984; Gilad, 1989, 1994; Meyer, 1987; Sammon et al., 1984; Tyson, 1986). However, as discussed, it seems that the most valuable knowledge is not provided through formal business intelligence units (or other formal strategic methods), but through more informal and 'soft' processes. Accordingly, informal intelligence procedures become meaningful. For informal scanning it seems that building networks of contacts and establishing trust within them is of the most importance, emphasizing firm-specific interaction processes between firm resources and market forces. Interactions are also the foundation for experience as a source of knowledge. Procedures for analysing and observing experiences can be improved and management can promote new ventures and ideas as a way to increase the opportunities for learning and, furthermore, promote sharing of experience through diffusion (Levitt and March, 1988). However, there is a risk that experience relies on an outdated and rigid knowledge structure, as discussed above. In that case, experimentation is especially appropriate, as the lack of alternative assumptions and solutions has to be clarified with more innovative and unorthodox approaches, including the destruction of old structures and the encouragement of conflicts, letting alternatives prosper. The experimentation mode can be actively initiated through the purposeful introduction of peculiar ideas, conflicts, errors, etc. (Nonaka, 1988; von Krogh and Vicari, 1993) or it can be more passively promoted through conditions nurturing experiments via organizational slack (March, 1981) and allowance for conflict with established structures.

Summary and Conclusion

This chapter has attempted to integrate various strategy perspectives and strived to provide a multidimensional view of strategy in terms of various learning mechanisms. The aim has been to emphasize the applied nature of strategic management. We have suggested that strategy processes can be studied in terms of different complexities and a multiple rationality set tied to the firm's capability to learn. Strategy derives its meaning and usefulness in complexity. We concluded that complex interactions between firm resources and market forces contribute to strategic complexities. Complexity in strategy processes is handled by firms and managers through bounded and variable multiple rationalities, both from firm to firm and within firms. Depending on the complexity of the situation, rationality ranges from perfect in complete order to strong in low complexity, adaptive in high complexity and selective in disorder.

Strategy in complexity was portrayed as an adaptive and alterable learning process of exploration and exploitation based on observations and operations. The various strategic learning mechanisms, based on calculated as well as systemic rationality, emerge through knowledge assimilation and integration via human assets where firm resources and market forces meet. Depending on learning skills the outcome of this process may be superior knowledge that can be used in strategic capabilities and may provide above average returns. According to this view, learning may be a source of competitive advantage, and learning skill may be derived from the knowledge structure of the firm. Learning practices were specified in terms of strategic learning modes – intelligence, informal scanning, experience and experiment – that inform strategy in complementary ways. They differ in terms of execution (learning by observing versus learning by doing), innovation (exploration versus exploitation) and complexity focus, and in terms of learning barriers, uniqueness and managerial implications. In our approach, the firm is a vehicle for knowledge assimilation and integration through human assets, emerging in the intersection between firm-specific resources and market forces. The firm is especially required to handle strategic complexity while in more ordered circumstances the market would do this. Herein, then, lies a proposition that the firm is anticipated to co-ordinate complexity whereas more simple structures would be arranged through the market.

In our framework, management's role becomes one of managing strategy in contrast to directing or dominating strategy, as in strategic management and strategic planning perspectives, respectively. Managing strategy concerns knowledge management in terms of actively cultivating and enriching conditions for knowledge assimilation in high complexity, but also, more traditionally, in lower complexity it concerns improving procedures and organization of knowledge assimilation. We especially emphasize the role of experimentation and the active invitation to ambiguity and contradictions in strategy processes. Bounded and variable creativity may even be regarded as a conclusive source of competitive advantage.

If strategy formulation schools give managers an exaggerated role, strategy formation schools give them an understated one. The perspective presented here could be portrayed as a strategy 'fomentation' perspective, emphasizing managers' roles in stimulating and provoking knowledge assimilation. Naturally, there is a grain of truth in each of the perspectives; managers do formulate some strategies that have to be formed through fomentation during the process. The view offered here is an effort to replace one-dimensional views of strategy processes involving exaggerated or understated capacities of managers with a more multidimensional one.

Implicit in our discussion lies the supposition that adaptive and alterable learning can improve the intelligence and performance of the firm. Learning mechanisms are powerful instruments in strategy processes and if we extend our strategic learning modes with more sophisticated learning mechanisms we might be able to sketch some properties of the intelligent firm. However, as discussed, we confront formidable obstacles in using learning for intelligence in organizations. Hence, it is important to observe that we do not conceive of learning as a new miraculous strategy tool for managers. This would simply take us back into strategy formulation schools, proposing another remarkable management method for strategy making. On the contrary, this perspective recognizes the limitations of managers in terms of learning and suggests that, on the whole, restrictions in learning skill are the very foundation for strategy and above average returns.

A fair criticism of the approach in this chapter would be that it is eclectic and fragmentary in its nature, without any solid theoretical foundation. On the other hand, the whole strategic management field is multiparadigmatic and, especially as we approach the application of strategic management within behavioural-based research, a more pluralistic view is necessary. Maybe in the future, when adequately developed, a strategic and organizational learning research field, involving multiple learning dimensions, may provide a sound theoretical base for the multidimensional nature of strategic management. This chapter has strived to integrate various aspects of strategic management in an effort to reflect the applied and multifaceted character of strategic management. Hopefully, this integrative and multidimensional approach has provided some inspiration to others to continue this work.

Notes

1 The comments of Rumelt et al. (1991: 22, 27) on the influence of the economics discipline on strategy are a good example. 'But the applied nature of strategic management and its extensive scope will require intersection with theory from other social science disciplines as well ... Where the co-ordination and accumulation of knowledge is key, and where patterns of belief and attitude are important, other disciplines will have more to say.'

2 Naturally, this process is even more complicated as rationality will vary depending on the level in the organization (for example, individual, group, organization) and depending on the time perspective. Rationality from the viewpoint of one level is not necessarily the same from another; in fact we have to deal with a whole set of interacting rationalities. However, this chapter will not go into depth with analysing ecologies of rationalities.

3 In doing a puzzle the arrangement of the first pieces, sides and corners, sorting pieces into heaps depending on colours and structures, etc. are rudimentary as is fitting the last pieces, but in between we have to rely on more approximate procedures like comparing

pieces, trying them, adapting ideas about the motive, trying what worked before, copying, drawing analogies with other parts, etc.

4 Note that we have made a distinction between complexity and chaos. In Hedberg's (1981) presentation the ability to learn diminishes once complexity has reached a certain level.

5 A factor complicating the analysis of learning, as with rationality, is that learning will differ and interact between levels and there will also be interactions with other organizations' learning (March, 1991b). For example, what is learned in one part interacts with what is learned in other parts and the returns and learning from a strategy in one organization are dependent on those of others (network externalities). While illustrating that learning is a relevant analogy, this ecological character of learning can also result in serious learning barriers (discussed in the next section).

6 See Huber (1991) for the distinction between organizational experiments aimed at adaptation and experimenting organizations directed towards adaptability.

5

The Role of the Strategist

Thomas Ericson, Anders Melander and Leif Melin

The Nature of the Strategy Process – some Basic Assumptions

This chapter is based on the assumption that strategy processes are complex, embedded in different contexts, dynamic in nature and driven by both structures and social actors. Therefore, strategy processes must be analysed and understood with the help of multiple theories, both contrasted and integrated into synthesized knowledge. But this assumption seems not to be shared by most students of strategy making, which means that it needs to be further developed in arguments based on rigorous research. The majority of all research efforts in this field is still done in research projects where single, one-dimensional problems unrelated to internal and external contexts are analysed based on static data, and where almost no regard is taken of the social construction dimension of the strategic reality studied.

This paper has its roots in 15 years of strategy research, where the ambition has been to take the complexity, the holism, the dynamics and the social actor seriously into account (see, for example, Hellgren and Melin, 1992, 1993; Melin, 1985, 1987, 1989). The field-of-force metaphor (Melin, 1985, 1989) was an attempt to express the need for three simultaneous perspectives in order to comprehend the different driving and counteracting forces that shape the strategy formation and strategic development of all organizations. External forces express the degree of determinism and contextual embeddedness that the external environment may always represent. Strategic (or interactive) forces describe the competitive and collaborative means that all players in an industrial field are using, reactively or proactively, to defend or change its position. Internal (intraorganizational) forces represent the cultural, cognitive, political, competence-based and structural dimensions that shape the internal conditions for strategic action in the focal organization.

The field-of-force metaphor has been further developed in the industrial field approach (Hellgren et al., 1993) by emphasizing the need for combining several theoretical perspectives and for simultaneously considering three different units of analysis in strategy studies.

Such a multilevel approach implies that we stress not only the firm (as in most business strategy research) and the industry (as in the industrial organization research), but also the individual actor(s) as a crucial level for analysis. Through combining these three units of analysis we may be able to understand both the dynamics within each level as well as the dynamic interplay between them. All three levels should be seen in their specific social context, and in the context of time, longitudinally (cf. the contextualist approach, Pettigrew, 1985; Pettigrew and Whipp, 1991). Furthermore, we emphasize three theoretical dimensions within the industrial field approach: the factual dimension, the relational dimension and the ideational dimension of strategic change. (These three dimensions show some similarity with the typology of structure presented by Fombrun, 1986.) We will elaborate further and argue for such an integrative approach in the discussion section at the end of the chapter, but first we will focus mainly on the level of individual actors, by emphasizing one important agent in the strategy process: the strategist of the focal organization.

The Strategist in Focus

On the one hand there is a wide literature on leadership, on the other hand the knowledge about strategic change is growing. However, we still have a rather weakly developed knowledge about the role of the strategist in the strategy formation process. In this chapter we review different theoretical schools and perspectives in order to see what contributions they give to an understanding of the role of the strategist. We also discuss possible reasons as to why the strategist is weakly represented in strategy process research. However, our conclusion is not that the strategist is missing but rather that the social actor perspective in general is poorly developed in schools of thought on strategy.

The strategist is used as an umbrella concept to focus the human actor(s) who could be expected to play a rather crucial role in strategy processes (if any single human actor really does), such as the CEO, the president, the owner-manager, the managerial elite, the upper echelon top manager(s), the top management team, etc. In practice, the role of the strategist as the premier strategy-maker is rather institutionalized in most countries, both in commercial laws about limited companies, and more informally in social belief systems.

The strategist is, of course, related to the existence of strategies to formulate, strategic issues or problems to tackle, and strategic decisions to make. However, what is strategic is not entirely clear. Hickson et al. (1986) define strategic decisions as decisions made at the top about big matters. However, they partly modify this view by saying that strategic decisions '... are towards one end of a continuum, at the other end of which are the trivial everyday questions ... (and) those who are involved believe (these decisions) will play a bigger rather than smaller part in shaping what happens for a long while afterwards' (Hickson et al., 1986: 27). Furthermore, they are 'comparatively organization-wide in (their) consequences' (Hickson et al., 1986: 28).

Whittington (1993: 5) identifies four perspectives on strategy where each perspective has its own view on strategy making, and Mintzberg (1990b) distinguishes ten schools of thought in strategy (as discussed in Chapter 1). It is obvious that such a variation of perspectives on the formation of strategy implies a wide variation on the meaning and role of the strategist, which will be further evident from the following literature review.

In Search of the Strategist in Strategy Research

In this section we present the appearance of the strategist in theoretical schools within, or closely related to, the strategy field, i.e. schools of thought of relevance for understanding strategy making in general and, more specifically, the strategist as a possible role/agent in strategy processes. The review starts with contributions from the contingency school(s). Gradually, the focus shifts to literature giving greater emphasis to the role of processes rather than structures in strategy formation. Finally, we examine research that gives the strategist as an individual actor a more obvious role within the process of strategy formation.

The Sometimes Absent or Mainly Passive Strategist

The contingency literature argues that a number of situational factors, such as organizational size, technology and environment, determine a certain type of organizational design. With this argument follows the statement that there is no best way of designing organizations. An increasing interest in the organization–environment relationship was a driving force in the development of this stream of research. Regarding organizations as 'closed and rational systems' may be seen increasingly as naive (Scott, 1992). Several well-known contributions emphasizing different contingency factors emanated from this perspective (Burns and Stalker, 1961; Lawrence and Lorsch, 1967; Perrow, 1967; Woodward, 1965). The Aston group (Hickson et al., 1971; Hinings et al., 1974; Pugh et al., 1968) represent another contingency school where structural conditions determine the outcome of processes.

Thompson (1967) questioned the deterministic role of the environment by showing the possibilities for the organization to influence environmental forces through negotiation with other organizations within its domain. The strategies in use were co-operation, coalition and co-optation. However, Thompson also held the organization as the negotiation unit, keeping the strategist rather impersonal. Child (1972) criticized the deterministic orientation of most contingency schools and called attention to the fact that organizations have opportunities for making their own more voluntary strategic choices. This view introduced the role of the actor more directly, i.e. the individual or group was seen to be making a choice. Child argued that managers most often have a range of alternative possible actions, despite the pressure on them from situational factors.

With Chandler (1962), strategy was introduced as a determining factor on the design of the organization, such that change in organizational structure followed the implementation of a new strategy. In the empirical evidence (historical cases) that Chandler presented, the strategist was visible. However, in the conceptual framework, the strategist was put into the less important background.

Some important works following on from Chandler (Miles and Snow, 1978; Miller, 1987; Porter, 1980) share the assumption that different environmental conditions shape unique strategies, which are related to specific organizational forms. In the framework of generic strategies (Porter, 1980) strategic managers seem to be rather passive or machine-like in an organization seen as a black box. When top management is considered at all, it is merely as a function of the specific structure that is described, as the task of the headquarters in different structures (Chandler, 1962). When noted, the managerial role is mainly to 'keep a look out' (Burns and Stalker, 1961) and to interpret the environment (Miles and Snow, 1978).

Moving from the contingency view to a configurational view, several determining factors may affect an organization simultaneously and in different ways. Mintzberg (1979) presented a typology of five (later seven) organizational configurations deriving from forces represented by several contingency factors and built up by several design parameters. All configurations consist of five basic parts. Mintzberg labelled one part the strategic apex, which is formed by 'those at the very top of the hierarchy ... those people charged with overall responsibility for the organization – the chief executive officer (whether called president, superintendent, Pope or whatever), and any other top-level managers whose concerns are global' (Mintzberg, 1979: 24–25). Mintzberg identifies three sets of duties for the strategic apex, of which one is issues related to the development of the organization's strategy. Generally, strategy formulation 'involves the interpretation of the environment and the development of consistent patterns in streams of organizational decisions' (Mintzberg, 1979: 25). Mintzberg and Waters (1985) argue that the role of the strategist tends to take different expressions depending on what kind of configuration is in focus. Different organizational configurations influence and set preconditions for management and the overall strategy formation process. Three different organizational configurations (the simple structure, the machine bureaucracy and the adhocracy) are compared regarding the mode of strategy formation and the role of leadership in this process.

In the simple structure, top management, i.e. the strategist, is a significant factor in the strategy formation process. The simple structure is characterized by a relatively low degree of hierarchy and minimal formalization of behaviour, and the strategist in this type of configuration has a great deal of influence. The role of the strategist is to search for opportunities and to develop a 'one-brain' visionary strategy. The strategist creates a concept of the business. '[L]eadership in the simple structure – what we here call the entrepreneurial mode – is very much tied up with the creation of vision, essentially with concept attainment' (Mintzberg and Waters, 1985: 69). In this configuration, leadership is actually taking the lead.

In the second configuration, the machine bureaucracy demands a different type of leadership because of the size of the organization and the need for increased co-ordination. In this configuration, top management is becoming more focused on planning and formalization. The planning may result in a strategic plan that is implemented in a formal way, which means that there is a rationalistic perception of the strategy formation process. Moreover, the strategist in the machine bureaucracy often tends to be a 'caretaker' of an already existing strategy (Mintzberg, 1990a). The organization becomes more and more bureaucratic and the role of the strategist defuses. Compared to the simple structure, with the strategist as a concept attainer, the strategist of '… the machine bureaucracy is a planner, or perhaps a pigeonholder who slots generic strategies into well-defined conditions and then hangs onto them for dear life' (Mintzberg and Waters, 1985: 75). Here, the organization is taking the lead in the machine bureaucracy.

In the third configuration, the adhocracy, it is important to be adaptive to environmental changes. If we could identify a rationalistic view of the strategy process in the machine bureaucracy, the opposite would be found in an adhocracy. This configuration avoids standardization and formalization, and power is divided among members in a complex coalition. As the environment tends to take the lead in the adhocracy, the strategist's role is to handle uncertainty and new situations, i.e. 'a pattern recognizer, seeking to detect emerging patterns' (Mintzberg and Waters, 1985: 81). The strategist has to be successful in negotiating with stakeholders both outside and inside the organization.

An underlying premise in both the contingency and the configurational literature is that it is not until after having taken the situation into consideration that the management system can be properly worked out. As we have seen, the literature within this stream of research does not totally disparage or minimize the possible value of the strategist. Top managers may play an important role, but are seldom considered as an important determinant to organizational change and design. For instance, Miles and Snow (1978) claim that management must be adjusted to fit the specific organizational configuration. Different configurations demand different kinds of management, '… for it is our belief that no form of organization can be operated effectively unless it has an appropriate accompanying managerial theory' (Miles and Snow, 1978: 129). But the environment is not given objectively and the strategist has the role of defining trustworthy images of the environment and manipulating the social setting in which the organization is embedded (Pfeffer and Salancik, 1978).

The Formation Process in Focus with a More or Less Evident Strategist

Contingency theorists tend to neglect the role of the strategist in strategy formation partly because they avoid focusing the formation process through which strategies emerge. In this section we will concentrate on the literature that employs a more processual view of strategy formation.

Two quite recent British studies attempt to focus the processual character of strategic change (Pettigrew and Hendry, 1992; Pettigrew and Whipp, 1991). They argue that in order to understand strategic change on the organizational level the whole competitive environment must be considered, including both the sector and the economy. Their results indicate that managing change involves the strategist focusing on environmental assessment, linking strategic and operational change, creating a human resources management philosophy, and 'building a receptive climate for change'. However, the strategist must also have an ability to set new visions and values, guiding the organization into the future. Pettigrew and Whipp (1991) conclude that all these abilities must be seen as different pieces in a 'juggling game'. The overall strategic role is to achieve a kind of organizational *gestalt*, which in turn means placing an emphasis on the continuous evolutionary process of change.

> The essence of coherence appears to be not the simple fit between an organization and its competitive environment. On the contrary, the skill relates much more to the ability to hold the business together as a totality while simultaneously changing it, often over lengthy periods of time. (Pettigrew and Whipp, 1991: 283)

The authors stress that shaping strategic change takes considerable time and that the necessary energy for renewal does not need to come from outside. They found several cases where the existing managements were able to infuse the organizations with renewed energy.

Another less optimistic view of the possibilities for evolutionary change is presented by Johnson (1987). His standpoint is that organizations inevitably reach a point where the organizational paradigm has to change. The paradigmatic change is defined as 'a change in those taken-for-granted assumptions about how things are done and why the organization is successful' (Johnson, 1987: 291). Johnson concludes that this is the reason why there is often a change of top managers when organizations go through paradigmatic changes. The change 'is not necessarily because the new chief executive has the "answers" to the problems facing the business, but because he or she will be prepared to support and foster the mechanisms for change' (Johnson, 1987: 293).

A strong belief in the necessity of new managerial blood is found in some of the 'turnaround' literature. Turnaround is broadly defined as 'the process that takes the firm from a position of weak performance to a position of sustained good performance' (Brege and Brandes, 1993). The process of turnaround seems to require new top management in the organization. Nyström and Starbuck (1984) declare that the only way to achieve a turnaround is to replace the strategists. The reason given is that the old strategists, even if they are competent, are no longer trustworthy. The symbolic signal in changing the strategist is considered very important. The role of the new management is to create a new perception of reality and new ideas. Strategists have to be risk takers, acting fast and motivating all members of the organization.

There is a debate about whether it is possible to make a turnaround in an organization without a severe crisis (Barker and Mone, 1994; Pearce and Robbins, 1994; Robbins and Pearce, 1992). The debate concerns the necessity and causal effect of retrenchment and successful turnaround. Grinyer et al. (1988) have studied successful turnarounds, known as 'sharpbenders', and they argue that as performance of organizations is measured by expectations, the match between expectations and performance determines the need for a turnaround. Companies doing quite well can go through a turnaround, if expectations change. Grinyer and McKiernan (1992) discuss typologies of recovery strategies and find three recovery patterns:

1 anticipatory organizations that are implementing strategic changes when performance is still on acceptable levels
2 organizations facing extinction that are forced to make immediate revolutionary changes (such change most often involves a change of management)

3   organizations in an intermediate position that are recovering, only to fall back
    into low performance because the actions taken only addressed the symptoms.

The management role in the studied recovering organizations was devoted to
action, communication, values, customer opinions, people and delegation of
tasks.

Grinyer and McKiernan (1992) vitalize the often rather analytical view of turnarounds by stressing that the need for change is not always objectively given by
a situation. Expectations are socially constructed and follow on from historic performance, and demands are made by stakeholders both outside and within the
company. This notion makes us reconsider the importance of the strategist in
the strategy formation process.

A line of literature following this argument and giving the strategist an obvious role in the formation process is the popular management literature (Fombrun,
1992; Kotter, 1996; Moss Kanter, 1983; Peters, 1987; Peters and Waterman,
1982). A basic idea in this literature is that companies forget the individual, and
his/her way of functioning. The recipe is that the strategist's role is to create
organizational situations that promote creativity and change. Control devices in
such organizations are the creation and maintenance of basic values. The authors
argue that decision making and daily operations can then be highly decentralized.
Peters and Waterman (1982) focused on incremental changes and often identified
some former strategist (or in a few cases a present strategist) that had the ability
to implement strong normative values in the organization. To keep this kind of
'inspirational' management is seen as the key to successfully creating a climate
with an entrepreneurial spirit. Focusing the need for more revolutionary changes,
Kotter (1996) represents the view that the strategist must actively create a sense
of urgency or crisis.

As stated above, the focus on processes of change is one way to avoid the often
static relationship between the environment, organizational structures and organizational strategy. The processual literature is, however, divided between those
authors who focus mainly on the organizational processes (Pettigrew and Hendry,
1992; Pettigrew and Whipp, 1991) and those who give the individuals a larger
role to play within the strategy formation process (Kotter, 1996; Peters and
Waterman, 1982).

The Leadership of Strategy Formation

As discussed, the literature focusing on processual aspects of strategy formation
also shows clear differences on the view of the strategist. The key theme in the
literature emphasizing the incremental ability to change is that this is done by an
inspirational management, through a combination of motivation, inspiration and
strong guiding values. This motivational and cultural role of management is seen
as more important than organizational structure, size, technology and other contingency components. The belief is that commitment to organizational goals is
the single most important parameter in the strategy formation process.

Another view in this stream of literature is that a cultural web 'filters' all
information from the environment, creating an organizational reality separated

from the outside reality. The strive for coherence in values and norms in order to achieve action is viewed as leading to group thinking (Janis, 1972) and, eventually, inertia (Morgan, 1986). The strength of inertia is the core of the debate. When the need for rethinking occurs, will the dominating organizational values represented by the strategist lead to an organizational blindness? Is the strategist in a position to rethink the values and norms that may be built and implemented by himself? Is the leader able intentionally to manage a process in which a sense of meaning for the organizational members is changing repeatedly? Or, is the strategist caught in the same organizational reality as the rest of the organization's members? If so, then the manager only takes (or is given) a managerial role. After a while he *is* a managerial role and, consequently, the manager has to leave in order to precipitate changes of organizational reality (Nyström and Starbuck, 1984).

These questions about the role of top managers in the strategy formation process lead us to consider literature focusing on organizational leadership and the socio-cognitive dimension of strategy formation (cf. Gioia and Sims, 1986; Hosking and Morley, 1991; Katz and Kahn, 1978; Smircich, 1983; Weick, 1979). The socio-cognitive perspective can be illustrated with two core concepts: sense making and enactment (Weick 1995). Sense making is the process of interpretation and active construction of a social world, a process that takes place in the mind of individuals often within an organizational context. Enactment focuses on the behavioural aspect, holding that individuals often produce parts of the environments they face (Smircich and Stubbart, 1985).

On the individual level this perspective is based on cognitive psychology. A cognitive scheme is, for instance, a mental map or structure of thought that guides the individual in a particular situation. The scheme creates meaning and coherence for individuals. It facilitates interpretation in different situations and guides individuals' action (Gioia and Manz, 1985; Lord and Foti, 1986). The cognitive scheme represents rules that direct information processing (Lord and Foti, 1986), guide our attention, guide our memory to a 'scheme consistent' behaviour, and fill in 'white spots' where information is missing (Gioia and Poole, 1984). Cognitive schemes are constructed through our previous experiences. Through these processes an 'interpretation reservoir' is developed (Melin, 1991), which is unique to each individual actor. Consequently, the 'way-of-thinking' (Hellgren and Melin, 1993) of a strategist consists of a number of relatively stable thematic sets of values, assumptions and thoughts about management and strategic development, in addition to reflecting the life experience and personality of the strategist him/herself.

The socio-cognitive perspective focuses on the political, cognitive and social aspects of the strategy formation processes. Hosking and Morley (1991) focus on three social processes in which the strategists are involved: networking, negotiation and enabling. Networking refers to the active participation in the creation of a dialogue with the organizational members and stakeholders outside the organization. Networking can also help the strategist to make sense of the ongoing flow of events in ways that will enhance the strategy formation process. Negotiation focuses on the content of the networking, i.e. the ongoing conversation. In negotiations the products of the sense-making process are communicated and organizational members are asked to 'buy in' and act on the views presented by the strategist (cf. Andersen, 1987). Finally, the process of enabling helps others to help themselves enact ways for future development both mentally and socially; this is often called empowerment.

This view focuses on the possible options for the strategist in strategy formation processes. Hellgren and Melin (1993) illustrate both options and dangers in a study of the strategy process during two decades in a large Swedish manufacturing firm. They found that strategic change in this organization was closely related to the strategist's 'way-of-thinking', due to the institutionalized power distribution. As an example of this, the 'way-of-thinking' of a new CEO became very influential for the strategic changes that occurred in the organization. This new strategist was expected (by the members of the board) to fulfill the successful strategic plans of his predecessor. Instead, he implemented his own 'way-of-thinking', developed during his managerial career of 15 years. When introduced into this new organizational context his stable 'way-of-thinking' meant frame-breaking and radical strategic initiatives.

The socio-cognitive perspective emphasizes the role of the strategist in the strategy formation process; a role that was either under-emphasized or stereotyped in the earlier part of the review. However, the observation of the role of the institutionalized power distribution within the organization in the Hellgren and Melin (1993) study brings the context back to the fore and illustrates the importance of combining the understanding of the individual, the organizational and the environmental processes and structures in order to understand strategy formation processes.

The Strategist in the Strategy Formation Process: some Findings

The purpose of this chapter is to discuss and develop knowledge about the role of the strategist in the strategy formation process. In the review of the literature we have focused on research that makes explicit contributions to our knowledge of this particular subject. It is important to make clear that the purpose of the literature review was simply to illustrate our point, and it is not a full review of the literature.

Analysing the literature, five broad themes emerge. These themes illustrate the general tendencies in the literature and are rather disparate, which stresses the fact that the role of the strategist in the strategy formation process is a complex phenomenon.

1 The first theme we found is that contingency factors often influence the strategist's possibilities of acting, i.e. the strategist's space of action is only free within the limits of certain restrictions. By this we mean that the strategist has quite a different role in the 'machine bureaucracy' from that in a 'simple structure'.

2 The second theme is that the strategist is treated as synonymous with the top management of an organization. In most cases there is no doubt that

the strategist *is* the top manager or part of a top management team. The exceptions to this assumption are rare. Terms such as CEO, president, manager and top leader are often used to mean 'strategist'.

3   The third most important role of the strategist is symbolic and inspirational. The strategist is seen, especially in recent literature, as a motivator or organizational energizer, infusing the organization with high spirits, and eventually controlling the enactment of organizational reality.

4   The fourth theme, most literature seems to conclude, whether implicitly or explicitly, is that the strategist's 'way-of-thinking' is stable over long periods of time. For instance, Mintzberg (1978) indicates this in his study of Volkswagen. In order to change the overall strategy when the company was facing serious problems, the old top management had to leave and a new leader was introduced to the company. This is even clearer in all 'turnaround' literature and in research within the socio-cognitive perspective, where some authors explicitly state that radical change must be preceded by a change in top management, i.e. a change of the dominant strategic mindset within the organization.

5   The fifth theme generally sees the strategist as rational within some boundaries. The strategist's cognitive structures are stable, and he/she is intentionally logical within these structures. This theme is strongly interconnected to the fourth theme.

Using our integrative framework presented in the introduction and the insight gained from the analysis of the literature review we now suggest a typology of strategist roles; roles that are more or less prominent in research about the strategist in strategy formation processes. This typology aims to galvanize further research on the role of the strategist and we will therefore finally suggest some ways to proceed in operational research at the end of the chapter.

The Missing Strategist

Here the strategist is downplayed. Following our integrative framework we may argue that the factual dimension, which refers to the objective reality view of industries (as expressed in traditional analytical perspectives, such as the industrial organization (for example, Bain, 1968; Scherer, 1980) and business policy (for example, Ansoff, 1965; Porter, 1980; Rumelt, 1974)) dominates this type. In this view the strategist is rather paradoxical. In spite of his/her rational and analytical abilities his/her contributions to the strategy formation are few. Instead, the structures take the lead. When the strategist is emphasized he is often seen as playing more of an symbolic role.

The Great Strategist

Here the strategist's importance is highly recognized. He/she is regarded as of great importance for the future development of the organization. The role is often inspirational, motivational and rather visionary. By enacting visions of the future the strategist can mobilize energy in the organizations such that they are able to resist and overcome obstacles in the world around them. However, in this type the great strategist must also be able to fail. A great success can, therefore, also be a great failure. To achieve radical changes the view is that the strategist often has to be replaced, because he/she is so dependent on his/her personal commitment to the future of the organization, i.e. his/her vision of the future.

The Coalition View of the Strategist

Here the strategist is seen as a *gestalt*, rather than as a single human being. The strategist here is the top management group or other coalitions of stakeholders playing an important role in the organizational strategy process. In this typology, networking and politicking are important means to achieve ends in the strategy formation process. The networking and politicking does, however, presume both internal and external perspectives on the formation process. The strategist consisting of coalitional groups may extend beyond formal organizational boundaries.

The Invisible Strategist

In the introduction, the dominating view of the strategist in the literature was described as connecting the role of the strategist with one or a small group of top managers in an organization. This view also dominated in most of the literature (see theme 2). This view is also taken in the three first typologies, but in this fourth typology we leave this assumption and reformulate the implicit definition of the strategist. Here the strategist is seen as a force with a dominating influence on the strategy formation process. In this case, for example, the organizational values and beliefs (organizational culture) and the industrial recipe (Spender, 1989) describing dominating values at the sector or industry level, in addition to national cultures may have a dominating influence on the strategy formation process.

Operational Research on the Strategist

Following Bourdieu (1993), we argue that research about the strategist role in the strategy formation process must start with the construction of the strategist. It is our belief that the separation of the formal role of the manager (CEO, president and so on) and the role of the strategist is vital for understanding the strategy formation process. According to Goffman (1959) the manager is a role played on the 'front region'. Using Goffman's language, the individual plays the role of manager according to social expectations, i.e. giving the 'right' answers when a single interview is conducted or a questionnaire is filled in.

However, in order to identify the strategist we have to enter the 'back region' (Goffman, 1959) in the organization. The strategist must be seen as socially constructed (if existing?) in a certain context. Goffman states, however, that the back region is hard for the student to enter. In the back region the roles played upfront are redefined. The formal position of 'manager' acknowledged by organizational members in the 'front region' may be of low value when the internal processes not visible to outside observers are considered. The only way to approach the 'back region' and to reveal the strategist is by studying the organization and its members over a substantial period – the study of several organizational layers and repeated interviews with a large number of individuals. As a test, we are using this methodology in an ongoing study of the strategy formation process in a large hospital. The following data illustrate the size of the study. Three doctoral and one senior researcher are involved, more than 150 interviews are being conducted, and participative observations are frequently conducted both in administrative and operational parts of the organization. The study has been going on for more than five years and obviously a multitude of hierarchical levels are being examined.

In order to avoid the classic problem of mixing the role of manager and strategist our suggestion is to take the process itself as the starting point. In our hospital study we operationalize the process with the help of an 'issue perspective' on strategy formation processes. Research has shown the advantages of studying change processes through the concept of strategic issues (for example, Dutton, 1988; Dutton et al., 1990). As the issue concept is combined with the concept of the strategic arena a fruitful analytical framework emerges. The strategic arena is defined through the dialogues around issues that are strategic to the individual organization. Following this line of thought it is important to note that the arena includes all possible situations that offer an opportunity for communication of strategic issues and thereby reproduce or change the organizational reality. This framework allows for a separation of the formal top management and the role of the strategist.

The focus on issues in the strategic arena is a way to avoid the focus on one single (or a few) force(s) affecting strategic change processes. As the hospital study proceeds we reveal the changing nature of the formation process and the interaction between the organizational context and the formation process. We are also able to construct the role of the strategist within this context. The issue perspective makes it possible to integrate and use a wide set of theoretical schools to create a more holistic understanding of the interplay between different forces influencing strategic change processes.

Conclusions

The aim of this chapter was to review theoretical schools and perspectives, in order to see what contributions they give to our understanding of the role of the strategist in strategy formation processes. The literature review was summarized in five themes. The literature revealed that basic assumptions differed in the theoretical schools and so, therefore, did the view of the role of the strategist. The literature review and the five broad themes that emerged led us to develop a typology of the strategist role in strategy formation. It is our belief that this typology can be used as a theoretical tool in further research into strategy formation in organizations. In the last part of the chapter we took the opportunity to include some ideas of how research can advance in a more operational way.

6

What Makes Time Strategic?

Frans A.J. van den Bosch

The body of knowledge in the strategy field shows a growing number of distinctive schools. Each of these schools stresses the supremacy of its chosen perspective. This development could lead to fragmentation of the field. As a reaction to this development, researchers pointed out the necessity of going beyond fragmentation and of efforts aiming at putting pieces together, for example, by the development of synthesizing schools of thought (Elfring and Volberda, Chapter 1, this volume; Mintzberg, 1990b; Schoemaker, 1993). Going beyond fragmentation, however, will not be easy. It will be a real scientific challenge! To contribute to this challenge, we suggest that these integration efforts can benefit from taking time seriously in strategy research.

To this end we will investigate the following research question: 'What makes time strategic?' Furthermore, we will discuss why the preliminary answers to this question are helpful for the ongoing integration efforts in the strategy field. Based on a brief review of the literature, two propositions are suggested that deal with key strategic dimensions and key strategic characteristics of time, respectively. Subsequently, three recent dynamic theories of strategy are confronted with these propositions. For that purpose the punctuated equilibrium model (Romanelli and Tushman, 1994; Tushman and Romanelli, 1990), the commitment approach of Ghemawat (1991) and Porter's (1991) chain of causality approach will be used. In the concluding section we point out that integration efforts in the strategy field can indeed benefit from taking time seriously.

Theories of Strategy: Comparative Statics versus Dynamic Approaches

Theories of strategy are usually of a static nature or, at best, of a comparatively static nature. This fact is widely recognized. In a special issue of the *Strategic Management Journal* dedicated to the inherently dynamic phenomenon of the strategy process, this is pointed out as follows: 'Much of strategic management writing, like a good deal of the social sciences, is an exercise in comparative statics' (Pettigrew, 1992a: 5). Because of the strong ties between the strategy field and disciplines such as economics and sociology, in which comparative statics approaches are still dominant, the focus on comparative statics in strategy as well is not at all surprising.

The need for dynamic theories, however, is increasingly noticeable, not only in the base disciplines, but also in the strategy field. The growing attention given to the process dimension of strategy, to the accumulation over time of firm-specific resources and to the rejuvenating processes of firms (Baden-Fuller and Stopford, 1994) has contributed to this need. The resource-based theory of the firm has been influential, as this theory focuses on the internal make-up over time of firm-specific resources, capabilities and competences. Dierickx and Cool (1989: 1506) point out that 'strategic asset stocks are accumulated by choosing appropriate time paths of flows over a period of time'. The dynamic capabilities approach takes the argument even further. It links environmental dynamics with internal and interorganizational processes. According to Teece et al.,

> The term 'dynamic' refers to the shifting character of the environment ... The term 'capabilities' emphasizes the key role of strategic management in appropriately adapting, integrating, and re-configuring internal and external organizational skills, resources, and functional competences toward changing environments. [...] only recently have researchers begun to focus on the specific aspects of how some organizations first develop firm-specific capabilities and how they renew competencies to respond to shifts in the business environment. (1994: 12)

Other recent examples of contributions to dynamic approaches in the strategy field are Ghemawat (1991) and Porter (1991).

The role of time in theories of strategy can be assessed in a number of ways. One of these is to analyse various schools of thought in strategy research. Mintzberg (1990b) offers an interesting starting point. He discerns nine distinct schools with respect to strategy formation and adds another one, the so-called 'configurational school'. Mintzberg compares the schools by use of five different dimensions, of which the process dimension and the contextual dimension seem to be the most appropriate for our purposes. The process dimension focuses on how strategy gets formed and in particular on change (incremental versus revolutionary), while the contextual dimension focuses on conditions surrounding the strategy formation, in particular, situation, structure and stage. For our purposes, the nature of change in Mintzberg's process dimension is of particular importance. Mintzberg's contextual dimension of schools of thought tries to specify the stages during which the different approaches of the schools would be likely to be present. For example, the design school would be present during periods of reconception and the entrepreneurial school during start-ups and turnarounds. Taking time seriously in theories of strategy presupposes specifying the periods or stages most appropriate for the theories involved.

In his description of the configurational school, Mintzberg (1990b) raises the interesting question of which schools of thought would be likely to be present during the specified stages. This chapter, however will not deal with this aspect of dynamic theories in strategy.

The important role of time in the so-called contextualist approach, proposed by Pettigrew, is also of interest when finding clues for contributions to our research question.

> A contextualist analysis of a process such as change draws on phenomena at vertical and horizontal levels of analysis and the interconnections between these levels through time. [...] The horizontal level refers to the sequential interconnectedness among phenomena in historical, present, and future time. An approach that offers both multilevel or vertical analysis and processual, or horizontal, analysis is said to be contextualist in character. (Pettigrew, 1990: 270)

The contextualist approach emphasizes the importance of embeddedness, both with regard to interconnected levels of analysis and the temporal interconnectedness. Because of the central role of time in a contextualist approach, this research method offers valuable insights, too, especially regarding the implications of time for temporal interconnectedness and for strategic change, as argued by Hellgren et al. (1993).

Both Mintzberg's schools of thought in strategy and the contextualist approach seem to offer interesting clues for developing dynamic theories of strategy. This assumes, however, that strategy itself is a dynamic concept and is defined accordingly. Although many definitions of strategy have been proposed in the literature, identification of the necessary and sufficient conditions of key features of the strategy concept have received remarkably little attention. Tang and Thomas (1994) explicitly pay attention to this important issue. They propose a so-called dominance-based definition of strategy, by defining strategy as the highest-level decision in the hierarchy, exhibiting three features of dominance: vertical, horizontal and dynamic. Tang and Thomas (1994: 209) point out that:

> A vertically dominant strategy is one that determines, directly or indirectly, other decisions of a firm. A horizontally dominant strategy seeks to optimize the value of the firm according to some criteria. Dynamic dominance implies that strategy should affect the subsequent decisions of a firm over a relevant period of time.

They consider a decision to be strategic if it satisfies these three features of strategy. For the purposes of this chapter, the third dimension is very important. Although dynamic theories of strategy presume a dynamic concept of strategy, in this chapter it is explicitly assumed that the strategy concept is a dynamic concept in search of dynamic theories.

What Makes Time Strategic?

Key concepts in strategy are time based, such as long-term objectives, planning cycles and sustainable competitive advantage. This temporal dimension is highlighted even more by the emerging interest in time-related strategies, such as time based competition (Stalk and Hout, 1990). The growing interest in strategic renewal stresses the importance of exploring the evolution of strategy over time as well (Huff et al., 1992). In all these contributions to incorporating time into strategy concepts and theories, however, the concept of clock-time or calendar-time dominates. The observation that strategy deals with clock- or calendar-time is a partial answer to the fundamental question: 'What makes time strategic?' We would like to contribute to this question by distinguishing at least two types of attributes of time in strategy:

1 key strategic dimensions of time, i.e. different conceptual lenses to look at time
2 key strategic characteristics of time, giving rise to different strategic implications for management.

Strategic Dimensions of Time

A few conceptual lenses to look at time, or dimensions of time as we prefer to call them, are distinguished in the literature. According to Das (1991: 50), 'the most widely prevalent view of time is that of clock-time or calendar-time. This conception of time, which is also called physical time, is evident in all discussions of time management.' We prefer to label this conceptual lens the objective dimension of time. Das (1991) also draws attention to the psychological dimension of time in the sense of pre-existing individual differences in the psychological conceptions of the future. This is called here the subjective dimension of time, and is also proposed by Vinton (1992: 15) who stresses the need for 'an understanding of the complexity of temporally related beliefs, values, and behaviors that influence behavior at individual, work group, and organizational levels'. The difference between these basic dimensions is that in the first dimension time is considered to be a universal and quantifiable phenomenon, while in the second dimension the human perception of time is central. Regarding the subjective time dimension, different units of analysis may be discerned. Time has meaning not only to individuals, but also to groups or organizations and national cultures. One of the ways a national culture distinguishes itself from others is by differences regarding attitudes to time (Trompenaars, 1993). The way in which societies look at time gives rise to the concept of cultural time. Cultural time is an important example of the subjective dimension of time.

The perspectives or metaphors chosen in the analysis of organizations are connected to different dimensions of time, albeit in an implicit way. For example, Morgan (1986: 12) points out, 'our theories and explanations of organizational life are based on metaphors that lead us to see and understand organizations in distinctive yet partial ways'. Using the metaphor of organizations as machines, the mechanical way of thinking and, therefore, the objective dimension of time, will be more ingrained in comparison to Morgan's metaphor of organizations as flux and transformation. The latter metaphor stresses the necessity of understanding the logic of change shaping social life. In this metaphor a mechanical way of thinking about time associated with the objective dimension of time will no longer be sufficient. Using the subjective dimension of time will contribute to a more thorough understanding.

Different types of knowledge produced in management studies are also connected with different dimensions of time. This is illustrated by comparison of Mintzberg's configurational school with the contextualist approach to strategy.

Mintzberg's configuration school is an example of the use of the objective dimension of time in strategy formation. Here, 'strategies themselves were identified as episodes – patterns in action that sustained themselves for identifiable periods of time. These strategies were then lined up against one another to identify distinct periods in the history of the organization.' (Mintzberg, 1990b: 183).

The contextualism research method does not, however, emphasize the objective dimension of time, i.e. clock-time, but the historic event in its context. This research method claims an event is never what is immediately available: it includes its contiguous past and present as well (Tsoukas, 1994). The notion of time as the temporal ordering of distinct events is rejected. According to Tsoukas (1994: 767): 'contextualism is *synthetic*: it takes a pattern, a gestalt, as the object of study, rather than a set of discrete facts. Its root metaphor is the historic event, continuously changing over time.' This research method, however, does not offer the opportunity to make generalized statements about empirical regularities over time. Therefore Tsoukas (1994: 767) concludes:

> … contextualism is dispersive: the multitudes of facts it seeks to register are assumed to be loosely structured, not systematically connected by virtue of a lawful relationship. There is no search for underlying structures, and the distinction between appearances and an underlying reality is not accepted.

Tsoukas compares contextualism to organicism as rivalling structural approaches to the creation of a body of knowledge in management studies. Tsoukas argues on the basis of the work of Pepper (1942) that organicism offers opportunities for determining generalized statements about empirical regularities in time.

> Organicism deals with historic processes which are regarded as essentially organic processes: the unfolding of a logic that is immanent into the object of study. […] The process unfolds in the direction of greater inclusiveness, determinateness and organicity. (Tsoukas, 1994: 769)

Tsoukas compares examples of theories based on an organic approach with Mintzberg's (1979) organizational configurations and the quantum models of change such as Tushman and Romanelli's (1990). These types of models are discussed further in the next section.

Strategic Characteristics of Time

First some observations will be made regarding key strategic characteristics of time as the second attribute of time in strategy. Obviously, these observations depend on choices made with regard to the relevant dimensions of time and, related to that, the chosen level(s) of analysis, as well as the types of management knowledge in which one is interested. The focus will not be on the behaviour of individuals within organizations, but on the structural and ecological levels of analysis (Scott, 1987) and the influence of organizational and national culture on time will be disregarded. It seems appropriate, therefore, to focus primarily on the objective dimension of time. The second choice, related to the first, is made in favour of a type of management knowledge producing, in principle, generalized statements about empirical regularities over time. Based on these choices, three key strategic characteristics of time are distinguished as follows:

1   strategic time is irreversible
2   strategic time is related to the nature of strategic change
3   strategic time interconnects the context, content and process of strategy at various levels of analysis.

Each of these characteristics will be elaborated on briefly. The idea that important strategic decisions of firms are simply reversible is becoming increasingly open to criticism. Although Stinchcombe (1965) pointed out some 30 years ago that many organizations retain their structural characteristics long after their founding, and Hannan and Freeman (1977) have stressed the importance of organizational inertia, the growing support for the idea that 'history matters' is quite recent. Bartlett and Ghoshal (1989) describe companies as captives of their own past, coining the notion of administrative heritage as both an organizational asset and constraint.

> A company's ability to respond to the strategic task demand of today's international operating environment is constrained by its internal capabilities, which are shaped by the company's administrative heritage. Internal capability is developed over a long period of time and cannot be changed overnight or by management decree. (Bartlett and Ghoshal, 1989: 35)

The dynamic capabilities perspective established the idea of path dependencies. Teece et al. (1994: 24) state, 'The notion of path dependencies recognizes that 'history matters'. Bygones are rarely bygones, despite the predictions of rational actor theory. Thus a firm's previous investments and its repertoire of routines (its 'history') constrain its future behavior.' This notion of path dependency is elaborated by Ghemawat (1991), who criticizes the tendency of managers to think of strategy as a search for timeless bases of success. He stresses the necessity of bringing time back into strategy by recognizing that previous strategic choices constrain later ones, and he defines the concept of commitment as the tendency of strategy to persist over time. Ghemawat links commitment with irreversibility as being implicit in his concept of commitment: 'Commitment is a superior way of thinking about strategy not just because it is a dynamic theory, but because it is *the* dynamic theory implied by irreversibility' (Ghemawat, 1991: 31, italics in original). Related to this, it is interesting to note that Teece et al. (1994: 31) point out that: '… firms, at various points in time, make longterm, quasi-irreversible commitments to certain domains of competence … In this regard, the work of Ghemawat (1991) is highly germane to the dynamic capabilities approach to strategy.' The concepts of administrative heritage, organizational inertia, path dependencies and commitment and their theoretical underpinning suggest that a first key strategic characteristic of time should be its irreversibility.

Strategic time is related to strategic change. One cannot imagine strategic change or strategic renewal without the passing of time. Moreover, strategic time and strategic change seem to be irreversible for the same reasons. An important aspect of strategic change is whether it is incremental or radical. The punctuated equilibrium paradigm (Gersick, 1991) examines both. This paradigm claims that firms evolve through the alternation of periods of equilibrium, in which persistent underlying structures permit only incremental change, and periods of radical change. During periods of radical or revolutionary change, these underlying structures are altered in a fundamental way. From a strategy perspective both the duration of time and the impact of time in periods of equilibrium and in revolutionary periods are quite different. This suggests a second key strategic characteristic of time: the nature of strategic change (incremental or radical).

In discussing a multilevel exploration of the punctuated equilibrium approach, in which at different levels of analysis revolutionary change takes place in relatively brief periods, Gersick (1991) draws attention to the need and possibilities for multilevel research. Time in strategy not only connects vertical levels of analysis, i.e. higher or lower levels of analysis with respect to developments of phenomena or variables to be explained, but also at the horizontal level of the sequential interconnectedness among phenomena or variables over time. Time in strategy connects the context, content and process at multiple levels of analysis. This interconnectedness characteristic will be labelled the third key strategic characteristic of time. This characteristic concerns both vertical interconnectedness and horizontal connectedness and is inspired by the research method of contextualist analysis.

Our argument here can be summarized by two basic propositions about the strategic time construct as shown in Table 6.1. In the next section three existing dynamic theories of strategy will be confronted with these propositions.

TABLE 6.1 *What makes time strategic: two propositions on the strategic time construct*

Proposition 1
Developing dynamic theories of strategy can benefit by taking into account different key strategic dimensions of time.
Proposition 1a
Key strategic dimensions of time are:
1 the objective dimension of clock time
2 the subjective dimension of time.
Proposition 2
Dynamic theories of strategy can benefit by taking into account different key strategic characteristics of time.
Proposition 2a
Key strategic characteristics of time are:
1 strategic time is irreversible (irreversibility characteristics)
2 strategic time is related to the nature of strategic change
3 strategic time connects the context, content and process of strategy at the various levels of analysis (interconnectedness characteristic).

Do Dynamic Theories of Strategy Reflect Different Dimensions and Strategic Characteristics of Time?

The purpose of confronting existing dynamic theories of strategy with the two propositions presented in Table 6.1 is not to discriminate between 'good' (i.e. dynamic) and 'bad' (i.e. static) theories of strategy. Our purpose is to illustrate the usefulness of distinguishing both strategic dimensions and strategic characteristics of time for improving existing theories and building new dynamic theories of strategy. Moreover, the purpose is to provoke ideas about how the strategic time construct can contribute to integration efforts in the strategy field. In selecting the three existing dynamic theories of strategy, two criteria were used. First, relatively recent contributions to the literature were analysed. Second, only those contributions that the authors themselves judged to use dynamic theories or approaches were selected. Based on these two criteria, the following three theories may be distinguished: first, the punctuated equilibrium model, second, the commitment approach and third, the chain of causality approach. Table 6.2 depicts the results of the confrontation of these theories with the two propositions. In order to explain Table 6.2, these theories will be discussed very briefly. The emphasis is on assessing whether strategic dimensions and strategic characteristics of time are discerned in these theories or whether they play an explicit or implicit role.

TABLE 6.2   *Do dynamic theories of strategy reflect different key strategic dimensions of time and key strategic characteristics of time?*

	Three existing dynamic theories of strategy		
	Punctuated equilibrium approach	Commitment approach	Chain of causality approach
Key strategic dimensions Are different dimensions recognized?			
1 Objective	Yes	Yes	Yes
2 Subjective	No	No	No
Key strategic characteristics Are different characteristics recognized?			
1 Irreversibility characteristics	Yes	**Yes**	Yes
2 Nature of strategic change:			
incremental	**Yes**	Yes	Yes
revolutionary	**Yes**	No	No
3 Interconnectedness characteristics	Yes	No	**Yes**

Bold indicates the best illustration of these strategic characteristics of time

The punctuated equilibrium model of organizational transformation has emerged as an interesting approach for simultaneously investigating both incremental and revolutionary strategic change of organizations (Gersick, 1991; Miller and Friesen, 1984; Romanelli and Tushman, 1994; Tushman and Romanelli, 1990). For our purpose it is important to note that the model integrates three distinct dynamic perspectives on organizational evolution: ecological models, adaptation models and transformational models. The punctuated equilibrium model states that organizations progress through convergent periods punctuated by re-orientations.

> Convergent periods refer to relatively long time spans of incremental change and adaptation which elaborate structures, systems, controls and resources towards increased co-alignment ... Re-orientations are relatively short periods of discontinuous

change where strategies, power, structure and systems are fundamentally transformed towards a new basis of alignment. (Tushman and Romanelli, 1990: 141)

The model assumes that an organization's prior pattern of convergence and re-orientation set the stage and create the context for current behaviour. According to Romanelli and Tushman (1994) few aspects of the model have been tested up until now. Their empirical test of the model is based on objective life histories of companies using archival data and trying to eliminate '... biases in information, particularly from firm-generated documents' (Romanelli and Tushman, 1994: 1148). This emphasis on creating objective life histories could indicate that in the punctuated equilibrium model no other time dimensions are discerned than the objective dimension. With respect to the assessment of the key strategic characteristics of time in this model, filling in Table 6.2 is not very difficult. A key element of this model is the elaborated concept of the nature of strategic change discerning both incremental and revolutionary changes and stressing important aspects of the vertical interconnectedness. To a large extent the model also illustrates the irreversibility characteristic, at least with respect to revolutionary change and the interconnectedness characteristic. With respect to the latter characteristic, Gersick (1991: 33) also stresses the possibilities for multilevel research with this model.

The commitment approach, i.e. the tendency of strategies to persist over time (Ghemawat, 1991), is the second example of a dynamic theory of strategy. This approach is related to the punctuated equilibrium model in the sense that Ghemawat (1991: 16–17) claims: 'Commitment seems to be the only logical explanation for punctuated equilibria ... There is no easy explanation for punctuated equilibria unless history matters in the way implied by commitment.' Commitment is caused by so-called lock-in and lock-out processes due to difficulties of disposing of, and then regaining, 'sticky' factors, i.e. durable, specialized and untradeable factors. Furthermore, commitment is caused by lags in adjusting the stocks of 'sticky' factors to the desired levels. Ghemawat considers these three causes to be related to the economics of factor adjustment. The only non-economic cause, organizational inertia, as the fourth cause of commitment, is not elaborated explicit in his model.

The key role of the irreversibility characteristic of time in a dynamic theory of strategy is stated most clearly by Ghemawat (1991: 31).

> Irreversibility is simply a recognition of the fact that the arrow of time points away from the past and towards the future. The unidirectionality of time seems fundamental enough to serve as the foundation of strategy, one that may finally allow the field to progress like a normal (i.e. cumulative) science.

Based on this key quotation, it is not difficult to conclude that the commitment approach takes the irreversibility characteristic seriously, as shown in Table 6.2. However, to make a clear assessment of the nature of strategic change and the interconnectedness characteristic in the commitment approach, fewer clues are present. The same is true of the dimension of time used. Given the fact that the majority of the causes of commitment are economic in nature, it is presumed here that the objective dimension of time is dominant in this dynamic theory.

Porter's (1991) chain of causality approach was chosen as a third example of a contribution towards a dynamic theory of strategy. His contribution discusses in particular the necessity of a truly dynamic theory of strategy, in which the importance of distinguishing between a cross-section approach and a longitudinal approach in explaining a firm's success and its origins of competitive advantage is stressed. Porter points at three promising theories that address the longitudinal problem in strategy: game theoretical models, the commitment and uncertainty approach and the resource-based view of the firm. After reviewing these theories Porter (1991: 109) concludes that 'We are still short of a dynamic theory of strategy, although we are beginning to learn about the subprocesses involved.' Although Porter refers to Ghemawat's (1991) commitment approach, he criticizes it for assuming the environment to be relatively stable.

To understand the dynamics of strategy, Porter proposes a chain of causality framework, incorporating both the cross-sectional and the longitudinal approach and taking seriously the mutual influence over time between the firm and its business environment. In the chain of causality, four successive links structure the cross-sectional approach, from the broadest industry level to the underlying sources of competitive advantage, i.e. the so-called drivers of the firm. Each successive link contributes to the understanding of a firm's success. Next to these four links, two additional links further back in the chain of causality are proposed. These two links together constitute the longitudinal approach with regard to a firm's initial conditions and its managerial choices and the (national and local) environment structured by Porter's (1990) diamond framework.

Confronting the chain of causality framework with the two attributes of strategic time it seems remarkable that Porter (1991) does not raise these issues at all. The only dimension discussed is the objective dimension of clock-time as the following quotation reveals. 'Should we be building theories for explaining success over two or three years, over decades, or over centuries?' (Porter, 1991: 99). Although Porter does not use the concept of irreversibility of strategy, his proposed chain of causality framework clearly stresses this key strategic characteristic of time. His framework makes no explicit statements about the nature of strategic change. It seems safe to assume, however, that his framework is more in line with incremental change. Of the three theories compared in Table 6.2, Porter's chain of causality framework is, in my opinion, the best illustration of the interconnectedness characteristic of time (van den Bosch, 1997; van den Bosch and de Man, 1997), especially with respect to connecting the different levels of analysis over time with the strategy context and content. The strategy process and the nature of strategic change, however, are not very well elaborated in his framework.

Summarizing this section, we will reflect on the preliminary findings shown in Table 6.2. As the first two rows of the table show, the objective time dimension is the only discernable dimension in the three theories discussed. The other three rows in Table 6.2 relate to the three key strategic characteristics of time, displaying a somewhat fragmented picture. In none of the theories discussed are all three strategic characteristics of time present. On the contrary, it appears that each theory offers to some extent the best elaboration for only one of the key strategic characteristics. The irreversibility characteristic of time is a key feature of the commitment approach. The punctuated equilibrium model highlights both the incremental and the revolutionary nature of the strategic change of firms over time. As stated above, the chain of causality approach provides an interesting example of the necessity of introducing the interconnectedness characteristic for dynamic theories of strategy.

Reflecting on these findings, it is interesting to note that we need different theories, each with a different perspective on time and focusing on different levels of analysis, to illustrate the three key strategic characteristics of time. Juxtaposing dynamic theories of strategy in this way shows how each theory offers insights to the others and thereby also offers clues for integration efforts in strategy.

Integration Efforts in the Strategy Field can Benefit from Taking Time Seriously

In reflecting on the preliminary findings, the question of how integration efforts in the strategy field can benefit from taking time seriously will now be discussed further. Special attention will be given to levels of analysis issues both in time and over time and to the integrative role of the strategic time construct.

As concluded in the previous section, it is quite remarkable that in the three selected dynamic theories of strategy, contrary to the first proposition, strategic time is regarded as one dimensional. As discussed at the start of the chapter, the same is true with respect to the dimension of time in the premises of Mintzberg's configurational school. The premises of this school are those of the other nine schools of thought, such as the design school and the learning school, brought together. Mintzberg's (1990b) overview of schools of thought clearly indicates that these schools have a bias towards the objective time dimension. Paying more attention to the social-psychological level of analysis in which individual behaviour within an organization is central as well as to issues of managerial cognition and perceptions in theories of strategy, would certainly challenge this bias. Since the focus here is primarily on the objective time dimension this challenge will not be addressed.

With respect to the second proposition, we shall comment on each of the three key strategic characteristics of time. The irreversibility characteristic seems to be crucial with respect to improving causality in theories of strategy; it permits us to distinguish between past and future, in which cause and effect are distinct. This characteristic enables, among other things, the formulation of propositions in strategy that can be tested in longitudinal case studies. Chandler's (1962) work provides good examples of this. The second key strategic characteristic deals with the nature of strategic change over time.

Focusing on the combined effects of the first and second characteristics, one could wonder what the implications are of accepting the first key strategic characteristic of time for the second characteristic, i.e. the nature of strategic change. As it seems obvious that revolutionary strategic change almost by definition is irreversible, proponents of non-revolutionary or incremental strategic change have to investigate the irreversibility of accumulated incremental change over time as well. Incidentally, this suggestion is absent from the recommendations of a recent empirical test of the punctuated equilibrium model (Romanelli and Tushman, 1994: 1163). As the third key strategic characteristic of time proposes interconnectedness, both vertical and horizontal, this characteristic is clearly of great importance for theories of strategy aiming at explaining cross-functional and cross-level strategic phenomena.

This brings us to the possible contribution of the strategic time construct to integration efforts in the strategy field. We will limit ourselves here by pointing briefly at the potential contribution of the objective dimension and of the inter-connectedness characteristic of time. Integration efforts in the strategy field aim at going beyond the theoretical fragmentation of the field. A minimum pre-requisite for these efforts seems to be to see the world of affairs in terms of inte-grated categories and problems, in the way that 'lumpers' do, in contrast to 'splitters' in strategy (Mintzberg, 1990b). In such a more integrated approach one of the challenges is to look for constructs that in principle can connect existing theories of strategy that address different levels of analysis. For that purpose, multilevel models are necessary, i.e. models that are used simultaneously to examine phenomena at two or more levels of analysis. Examples of multilevel models are Klein et al.'s (1994) cross-level and multilevel models. Cross-level models describe the relationship between the independent and dependent variables at different levels of analysis. Multilevel models specify patterns of relationships replicated across the levels of analysis involved.

Whether strategic time can indeed be used as a construct connecting existing theories of strategy addressing different levels of analysis is an interesting ques-tion. Two possible integrative functions of the strategic time construct will be suggested with regard to this question. Seen from the perspective of the objective dimension of time, the strategic time construct connects the different levels of analysis, including the relevant strategy concepts and theories, both at the same moment and over time. Research guided by this first integrative function can lead to new cross-level and even 'compound' models. Besides this first integrative function of the strategic time construct a second integrative function (directly related to the first) can be discerned, namely strategic time as a multilevel construct, which is, in principle, applicable at all the relevant levels of analysis. Needless to say, strategic time as a multilevel construct can stimulate the devel-opment of multiple level theories of strategy, such as the industrial field approach proposed by Hellgren et al. (1993).

These two inter-related integrative functions of the strategic time construct stem from a common theoretical source: the interconnectedness characteristic of strategic time. That is why the use of the strategic time construct and in particu-lar this characteristic is here considered as being of great importance for new directions in strategy that go beyond fragmentation of the field.

Summary and Conclusion

This chapter addresses the research question, 'What makes time strategic?' Although this question seems rather simple, the answer has been shown to be complex. This stems from the fact that dynamic theories of strategy are still in their infancy. By distinguishing key strategic dimensions and characteristics of time two propositions regarding the strategic time construct were suggested. Subsequently, three recent dynamic theories of strategy were confronted with these propositions. In discussing the preliminary findings, two mutually related integrative functions of the strategic time construct were discerned. First, the objective dimension of strategic time connects the different levels of analysis, including those of the relevant strategy concepts, both at the same time and over time. Second, strategic time is a multilevel construct. As strategy research stresses the dynamic and multilevel contexts in which managerial phenomena are embedded, both integrative functions are important. Taking time seriously in strategy research clearly contributes to integration efforts in the strategy field.

Acknowledgements

I would like to thank Charles Baden-Fuller, Raymond van Wijk and the editors of this volume for helpful comments on an earlier version of this paper.

7

Fragmentation in Strategic Management

Patrice Cooper

Confusion regarding the meaning of particular concepts is no stranger to the strategic management literature. Camerer (1985) and Leontiades (1982) spoke of the approaches, checklists or typologies, developed by strategy researchers, which tend to be loosely constructed, ambiguous, fundamentally debatable and difficult to teach. Years later, this discussion continues with entire texts devoted to the issue of defining what strategy is (Whittington, 1993). Indeed, the strategic management literature abounds with differing perspectives on the concept of strategy formation, for example, Fredrickson (1992), Mintzberg (1973a, 1978, 1987a, 1987b, 1990b), Mintzberg et al. (1976), and Mintzberg and Waters (1985). The existence of such varying schools gives rise to the notion that the strategic management field could be described as fragmented (see Elfring and Volberda, Chapter 1). Disciplinary fragmentation typically suggests a multiplicity of competing schools with little consensus or sharing of beliefs about theory, methodology, techniques or problems (Connolly, 1984; Lodahl and Gordon, 1972; Zammuto and Connolly, 1984). Consequently, for some time now a number of authors have argued in favour of increased integration (Biggadike, 1981; Chaffee, 1985; Jemison, 1981b; Porter, 1981; Schoemaker, 1993; Teece, 1990). In the words of Jemison, 'Strategic management has reached the point where more integrative research approaches are necessary for the continued progress of the field' (Jemison, 1981b: 601).

This chapter explores this argument. It is organized into three parts. Part one examines the notion of fragmentation in a single area of strategic enquiry – the research on acquisitive growth.[1] The reasons for and the implications of such fragmentation are explored. This part concludes with the issue of integration itself. Can consensus among these various perspectives be achieved, or is agreement likely to remain elusive? If the latter is the case, is this acceptable? Part two explores the need for integration through examining the real costs of continued fragmentation. On the basis of the arguments developed in the context of the acquisition literature, the concluding section, part three, considers some general lessons for the future development of the strategy field.

Part One – Empirical Research on Acquisitive Growth

As the frequency, number and size of acquisitions have increased, acquisitions have inevitably drawn the attention of many groups of scholars and practitioners. Space limitations preclude an in-depth coverage of the broad scope of acquisitive research here. The most comprehensive review of the extant literature (Haspeslagh and Jemison, 1991), identifies three broadly defined schools of thought: the capital markets school, the strategic school and the organizational behaviour school. Recently scholars have combined strategic and organizational considerations, adopting a process perspective. In some instances the extensive and eclectic streams of research within each perspective have resulted in the appearance of subschools or subgroups. Figure 7.1 provides an overview of these schools, including an indicative bibliography for each and their interconnections.

At first glance the diverse nature of Figure 7.1, in terms of the number of schools/subschools, is suggestive of an area of enquiry that is seriously fragmented. What is the cause of such fragmentation; why have so many schools emerged from a single subject area? In an attempt to provide an answer to this question, the following section explores the theoretical and methodological foci of each school.

Acquisitive Research: an Overview of the Core Research Streams

Although all these schools pursue questions related to acquisitions, each line of research is anchored in a different central question, and each approaches its question from a particular perspective with different sets of assumptions, and with a different set of methodologies. For example, the central question asked by financial economists, on whose research the capital markets school is based is, 'Do acquisitions create value, and if so for whom?' The performance impact of acquisitions is studied through adopting an event study approach, i.e. through measuring the changes in the share price that occur during the short period surrounding the acquisition announcement.[2] When the net change (beyond that attributed to the movement of the market in general) is positive, financial economists conclude that wealth has been created. Empirical findings emanating from capital markets studies are largely consistent, with shareholders of target firms making significant gains, while acquiring firms neither gain nor lose. Thus, financial economists conclude, acquisitions benefit society by creating wealth. Two major limitations have been identified, however, in applying a capital markets perspective. First, it assumes shareholders can understand the way in which a firm's strategy is likely to evolve. The works of Lindblom (1959), Mintzberg (1973b), Quinn (1980a) and Wrapp (1967) suggest strategy is not a predictable, deterministic process, but rather concerns a set of evolving decisions. Second, the inherent assumption that firms always act to maximize shareholder value is contradicted by streams of research identifying other motives (Cyert and March, 1963; Donaldson and Lorsch, 1983; Simon, 1976).

In contrast to the financial economists' perspective, which is primarily interested in the effect of acquisitions on the economy, the strategic school is

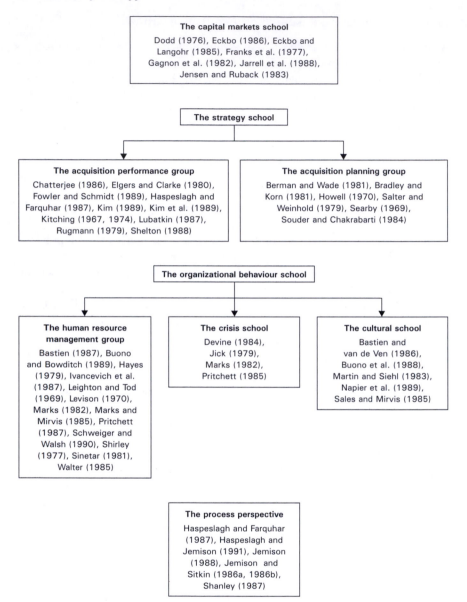

FIGURE 7.1   *Research schools on acquisitions*

interested in their impact on individual firms. Figure 7.1 identifies two sub-groups. The acquisition performance researchers are interested in identifying the types of acquisitions that are more likely to be successful for an acquiring firm. The methods used in uncovering variables that might discriminate between different types of acquisitions and consequent performance levels vary from event studies to managerial opinion. The variables deemed to be associated positively with performance include relative size, market share, pre-acquisition profitability, pre-acquisition growth and pre-acquisition experience (Fowler and Schmidt, 1989; Kitching, 1967, 1974). While the issue of relatedness has received the greatest attention (Chatterjee, 1986; Elgers and Clarke, 1980; Kitching, 1974; Lubatkin, 1987; Shelton, 1988; Singh and Montgomery, 1987), support for relatedness as a determinant of acquisition performance is inconclusive at best. In short, while relatedness provides an ex-ante indication of potential sources of value creation it does not guarantee such value (Haspeslagh, 1986; Haspeslagh and Jemison, 1987). This tendency to take relatedness and value creating synergies for granted is symptomatic of a fundamental weakness of the strategy school – there is a disproportionate emphasis on the strategic task, leaving aside practical considerations, such as interpersonal, interorganizational and intercultural friction (Haspeslagh and Farquhar, 1987).

Other strategy researchers, the acquisition planning group, have addressed the difficulty of implementation through a concern for better pre-acquisition analysis and planning (Berman and Wade, 1981; Bradley and Korn, 1981; Howell, 1970; Salter and Weinhold, 1979; Searby, 1969) or post-acquisition planning (Howell, 1970). Central to these prescriptions is the logical decomposition of the acquisition process into a number of steps, including the definition of acquisition objectives, acquisition search and screening, strategic evaluation, financial valuation and negotiation (Salter and Weinhold, 1979). While such prescriptions are logical and useful, in reality acquisitions do not conform to the planning/implementation mode (Souder and Charkrabarti, 1984).

Organizational behaviour scholars are concerned with the broad question of what effect acquisitions have on individuals. The human resource management tradition has focused on the human resource impact of acquisitions and how this impact can be managed (Bastien, 1987; Buono and Bowditch, 1989; Hayes, 1979; Ivancevich et al., 1987; Leighton and Tod, 1969; Levison, 1970; Marks, 1982; Marks and Mirvis, 1985; Pritchett, 1987; Schweiger and Walsh, 1990; Shirley, 1977; Sinetar, 1981; Walter, 1985). While these studies examine the pre- and post-acquisition impact, there is a tendency to over-concentrate on the negative aspects of the acquisition. Many studies focus on feelings of conflict, alienation, tension, career uncertainty, etc. (Buono et al., 1988; Marks and Mirvis, 1985; Sales and Mirvis, 1985; Sutton, 1983). Other studies (Pritchett, 1985; Schweiger and Walsh, 1990; Walsh, 1988) focus on the relationship between acquisitions and employee turnover. The issue of acceptance with regard to the new owners/managers has also been examined (Graves, 1981; Shirley, 1977). The underlying assumption of all of these studies is that the identification of the major human resource related problems in an acquisition facilitates a fairer and less conflict-ridden implementation.

The crisis literature views the negative consequences of acquisitions to some extent as rites of passage, a necessary organizational crisis requiring individuals to progress through several stages akin to the grieving process: shock, defensive retreat, acknowledgement and finally adaptation (Devine, 1984; Jick, 1979; Marks, 1982). The organization of appropriate mourning periods has been prescribed by some consultants (Pritchett, 1985).

The cultural compatibility school sees acquisition integration primarily as a culturally driven phenomenon. Drawing on research that examines interorganizational and intraorganizational cultural differences (Martin and Siehl, 1983), these researchers argue that in a decision regarding an acquisition much emphasis should be placed on the idea of cultural compatibility between the organizations (Sales and Mirvis, 1985).

Historically, acquisition outcomes have been seen as a result of achieving both strategic and organizational fit between the two firms. However, with numerous acquisitions not yielding the expected results, these two perspectives have recently been called into question. In response, a series of studies emerged that sought to understand better the factors associated with successful or unsuccessful acquisitive strategies. One of these studies (Jemison and Sitkin, 1986a), was the first to recognize that the acquisition process itself (the interactions between members of both organizations and the problems and facilitating factors arising in the process) is a potentially important determinant of acquisition outcome. In response, the process perspective has arisen. This school retains the role of strategic and organizational fit but adds consideration of how aspects of the decision and integration process can affect the final acquisition outcomes (Jemison and Sitkin, 1986a). A number of academic studies have since espoused a process view (Haspeslagh and Farquhar, 1987; Haspeslagh and Jemison, 1991; Shanley, 1987) or addressed process-related issues (Jemison, 1988; Jemison and Sitkin, 1986b).

Fragmentation in Acquisitive Research: The Causes and Consequences

The above overview illustrates that the vast and growing literature on acquisitions has developed unevenly along various lines. Thus, at its most basic, the prime reason for fragmentation in this area arises from the tendency of different researchers to focus non-cumulatively on varying dimensions of the same research issue. This heterogeneity is compounded by the diversity of research lenses employed.[3] Such variations arise from the different paradigmatic perspectives of the nature of the subject matter being studied (Burrell and Morgan, 1979), which gives rise to different assumptions, different research questions (Ritzer, 1975), and may produce seemingly incompatible views of the same phenomenon (Astley and van de Ven, 1983).

Similarly, the more obvious consequences relate to the contradictory and inconclusive nature of the advice emanating from each school on what are considered to be the important aspects of an acquisition strategy. For example, consideration of questions such as: 'What are the criteria by which an acquisition should be judged?' elicit varying responses. The capital markets perspective asserts that the merits of an acquisition should be assessed on the immediate value created for shareholders. Some strategy researchers suggest the focus should be on the extent of relatedness to the firm's existing business. Still other researchers argue that in a decision regarding an acquisition great weight should be given to the idea of cultural compatibility between organizations. 'How can a management team improve its success with acquisitions?' Again the existence of different schools suggests a variety of routes to success. The human resource management group suggests identification of the major human resource-related problems in an acquisition facilitates a fairer and less conflict-ridden implementation. Meanwhile, the process perspective emphasizes pre-acquisition decision making and post-acquisition integration as important determinants of a successful acquisition outcome.

Is Consensus Possible? Is Integration Desirable?

So far a number of very distinct schools of acquisitive research have been identified, each of which addresses different questions and issues at different levels of analysis and with different methodologies. The focus individual schools place on such diverse aspects of acquisitions suggests scholars of each school will continue to examine their partial, albeit important, questions. In other words, such inevitable or irreducible differences are inherent in the very nature of the phenomena under study and, consequently, consensus among the different areas of research is unlikely. If we assume this to be the case, how should we cope with such fragmentation? Typically, when faced with a multitude of definitions, reviewers of the strategy literature 'try to put out the fire with gasoline' (Camerer, 1985), combining these diverse working definitions into a new improved super definition. Should we adopt this approach? Should we seek to develop some form of meta-theory or super-school to pull the various theoretical orientations together? In short, is integration the answer? Recent evidence suggests that it is. Ramanujam and Varadarajan (1989) make the following point with regard to research on corporate diversification.

> ... An impressive volume of work has grown around the topic, yet the findings of this vast body of research continue to be fragmentary ... Suggestions for future research on this topic include the need for integration. (Ramanujam and Varadarajan, 1989: 544)

This desire for some form of common language or unified theory is shared by the business community.

> As managers there are no integrated criteria to help us to assess or evaluate potential acquisitions – nor how to deal with post-acquisition blues. (Irish Managing Director)

Quotations such as these and arguments from the literature already referenced (Biggadike, 1981; Jemison, 1981b; Porter, 1981; Teece, 1990) strongly advocate increased integration. The next section explores the attractiveness of this option through examining the real costs of continued fragmentation.

Part Two – The Costs of Disciplinary Fragmentation

The notion of consensus has been linked repeatedly to the level of paradigm development within a given field (Lodahl and Gordon, 1972; Pfeffer, 1993; Zammuto and Connolly, 1984), whereby a field considered paradigmatically developed is characterized by more efficient communication and an accepted and shared vocabulary for discussing the field's content (Lodahl and Gordon, 1972). Subsequently, there is a reduction in time spent defining terms or explaining concepts. In a similar vein, the import of ideas by fields with less developed paradigms from fields with highly developed paradigms, for example, the import of economic concepts into strategic management (Porter, 1981; Rumelt et al., 1991), means the boundaries and domains of the less paradigmatically developed fields are most often in contest and under negotiation (Pfeffer, 1993). Thus fragmentation[4] represents a cost in terms of time spent on definitional and boundary maintenance activity.

On a less conceptual level, in the absence of a well-developed paradigm, a field incurs costs in numerous areas, such as teaching, where there is less agreement on course content and more time devoted to graduate doctoral students, administration, where there is an absence of criteria for judging individual projects or programmes (Zammuto and Connolly, 1984), research, where there is less collaborative research and less agreement on what are considered to be the more significant research issues for the future (Webster and Starbuck, 1988), and longer lead times for publication due to a greater numbers of re-writes and higher rejection rates (Zuckerman and Merton, 1971).

Pfeffer (1993) developed these arguments. Drawing on various studies within the organizational sciences, he compiled a list of outcomes effected by the level of paradigm development. It is argued, because of the greater visibility and predictability of their actions, that paradigmatically developed fields fare better in a number of areas, including internal resource allocation, external funding and autonomy from central university administration.

Knowledge Advancement:
The Real Cost of Continued Fragmentation

The preceding discussion suggests fragmentation within a given field can hamper its development in what are considered to be a number of important aspects. However, a more fundamental point, and one which has formed the core of the organizational sciences debate, suggests that fragmentation presents a serious obstacle to scientific growth of a field (Connolly, 1984). Pfeffer (1993) supports this view.

> Consensus, however achieved, is a vital component for the advancement of knowledge in a field: without some minimal level of consensus about research questions and methods, fields can scarcely expect to produce knowledge in a cumulative, developmental process. (Pfeffer, 1993: 611)

This argument is not new. Cole (1983), Kuhn (1970), Lakatos (1970), Polanyi (1958) and Ziman (1968) have argued convincingly that some degree of consensus is a necessary (though not sufficient) condition for the accumulation of knowledge in science or in any other type of intellectual activity. Whether consensus implies knowledge development is itself open to dispute. Indeed a person's position regarding a paradigm becomes clearer when one uses terms such as knowledge development or advancement, because whether knowledge develops or not depends on one's paradigm (Cannella and Paetzold, 1994). Thus, while Pfeffer (1993) viewed knowledge advancement as 'a cumulative developmental process', Cannella and Paetzold (1994) believe the enforced consensus and dominant paradigms being called for by Pfeffer, would lead to stagnation in knowledge evolution. It is suggested that knowledge advancement is best achieved when

> ... there are critics among us who constantly push us to reassess our assumptions and refine our theories. One's understanding can be justified ... only by comparisons to other understandings and perspectives. (Cannella and Paetzold, 1994: 337)

Many authors have argued against the introduction of theoretical and methodological certainty (Bourgeois, 1984; Dewey, 1929) and in favour of more theoretical and methodological pluralism (Boland, 1982; Bowman, 1990; Burrell and Morgan, 1979; Denzin, 1989; Marsden, 1993; Reed, 1985). In the words of Feyeraband:

> The search for the absolute paradigm is the search for absolute conformism. Any method that encourages uniformity is a method of deception. It enforces an unenlightened conformism, it results in the deterioration of intellectual capabilities. (Feyeraband, 1975: 45)

Knowledge Advancement:
Where Does the Study of Acquisitions Stand?

The preceding discussions suggest the subject domain of acquisitive research is in a pre-paradigmatic stage of development. Existing research streams have tended to remain fragmented in their orientation (although some effort has been made by the process perspective to combine strategic and organizational considerations). The question thus arises as to how this fragmentation has impacted on the development of knowledge concerning acquisitions. This chapter argues that the evolution of diverse perspectives has facilitated rather than slowed the advancement of knowledge in this area. The most basic definition of knowledge advancement – increased understanding about one's subject area – is assumed. The argument is a very simple one. It is not that the existing literature lacks coherence, but the prevailing view that makes it seem that way. Viewed in isolation, each acquisitive school remains inchoate, as if they were unconnected, rather than varying aspects of a common phenomena. Viewed together, not only does each school cast new light on some aspect of acquisitions, but in some instances it does so through advancing the work of previous schools. For example, the strategy performance researchers claimed that the average performance findings of the financial economists would be of little relevance to individual firms, so they set out to examine a whole range of variables that might distinguish potential successes. While on balance the strategy school considered the problems of implementation, the organizational behaviour school addressed another important implementation issue – the people aspect. Finally, the process school advanced one stage further – while it retained the important role of issues of strategic and organizational fit, it added consideration of how aspects of the acquisition decision-making and integration processes can affect the final outcome.

The advancing nature of each of these schools, in terms of their success in addressing previously unanswered questions or issues and their more refined foci (the impact of acquisitions on the economy, the firm and the individual), supports the idea that the existence of diverse acquisitive schools has facilitated rather than inhibited knowledge advancement. The difficulty is this: while each school builds on the limitations or absences of others, there is a tendency for schools to over-state their own views. For example, while the organizational behaviour school provides an antidote to the financial or strategic perspective on acquisitions, these studies tend to go too far the other way, that is, they let organizational issues out-weigh an acquisition's strategic potential and consider integration issues primar-ily from the standpoint of whether individuals accept the new situation. In the end, by purely concentrating on one set of factors other issues that need to be addressed may be ignored or become clouded in the researcher's mind.

The Acknowledgement of Conflicting Views:
'Vive La Difference'

What does this discussion contribute to the integration versus fragmentation debate? As we have shown, the fragmented nature of the literature on acquisitive growth has not hindered the development of knowledge but encouraged it. Therefore, in this way at least, fragmentation, diversity and knowledge advance-ment can co-exist. Problems arise when each school or perspective becomes totally blinded by its own view, because while each school advances research through addressing previously unanswered questions it does so at the expense of other viewpoints. Mintzberg (1989b) quotes Rumelt (1979), 'What is strategic depends on where you sit' – the biases inherent in each school and the fact that each school is unduly skewed towards its own separate agenda, are purely down to a matter of sitting position. So what do we need to do? What is needed is to move our chairs a little so that we can both see and hear the views of other schools. In doing so we could establish a new form of consensus. This consensus should entail an agreement to acknowledge the differences and similarities across the different research streams. The differences and similarities will con-cern fundamental issues such as research questions, units of analysis, timeframes, methodological perspectives and the underlying assumptions and influencing base disciplines. This may provide the much sought after 'connective tissue', facilitating a step towards addressing previously untouched issues. In essence, what will most benefit the area of acquisitive research at this time is not an 'inte-grating school' but a shared understanding of the fundamental research issues underlying the entire subject area. Refocusing future research to confront these issues and projecting the likely issues for the future should be the chief concern.

Part Three – Conclusions

The field of strategic management is an interdisciplinary domain in a nascent pre-paradigmatic stage of development (Rumelt et al., 1994). It is hardly surprising, therefore, that subareas such as acquisitions exhibit disagreement about assump-tions, methods and research issues. What is interesting is the way we endeavour to deal with this – the development of encompassing frameworks that integrate different schools – in some ways the development of schools about schools about schools. There is nothing unusual about this – in the main when faced with complexity people prefer to think in terms of categories or envelopes of attributes (Miller and Mintzberg, 1983). However, as this chapter has argued, such 'lumping' (Mintzberg, 1989; Chapter 3, this volume) is unnecessary. As shown here, diverse perspectives concerning acquisitive growth have facilitated rather than hindered knowledge advancement within this area. Thus fragmentation, diversity and knowledge advancement can co-exist. What is needed, therefore, is not further integrative schools but an acceptable level of correspondence and agreement among different schools.

To conclude, this chapter argues for the extension of this argument to the strategic management field in its entirety. Thus, agreeing with Mahoney (1993) we should continue the conversation within the field, rather than insisting on universal criteria within that conversation. This should be of significant benefit in bringing strategic management into the future. As Schendel (1994) suggested

> What will most benefit strategic management is not a unifying paradigm, but the articulation of the fundamental issues underlying the field and a refocusing of research to confront them. (Schendel, 1994: 2)

Notes

1 The strategic management field has numerous topic domains that probably vary in the extent to which they exhibit consensus. Therefore, this chapter concentrates on examining consensus in a single area of research enquiry. Reviewing field consensus at a subject domain level has been previously employed and found useful (Webster and Starbuck, 1988).

2 Financial economists base their work on several fundamental concepts: the efficient market hypothesis, agency theory (Eisenhardt, 1989b), free cashflow (Jensen, 1987), the market for corporate control (Manne, 1965) and the capital asset pricing model (Brealy and Myers, 1988; Weston and Copeland, 1986).

3 Parkhe (1993) makes a similar point about international joint ventures.

4 This chapter agrees with Lodahl and Gordon's view (1972), that fragmentation denotes an absence of consensus.

8

The Elusive Search for Integration

Paul J.H. Schoemaker

I was invited to comment on four chapters, each of which offers a distinct perspective on the challenges and promises of integration. Regnér (Chapter 4) emphasizes the role of multiple rationalities and complexity as possible ways to synthesize strands of research and theory in strategy, to which I am very sympathetic (see Schoemaker, 1990, 1993). Van den Bosch (Chapter 6) proposes time as a promising variable, while Ericson et al. (Chapter 5) focus on the role of the individual actor in the drama called strategy. Lastly, Cooper (Chapter 7) explores the challenges of integration in the context of corporate acquisitions. The pluralism of these four approaches highlights the challenge before us: various meta-theories of strategy integration are themselves in need of integration.

This leads me to examine two key questions in this commentary: first, why is integration so challenging in the domain of strategy and, second, is it worth pursuing vigorously at this stage in the field's development? Both questions are complex, and my comments are offered in the spirit of a perspective to encourage dialogue rather than as answers. Nonetheless, it is important to develop a viewpoint on both, to guide our research and allocate our limited resources in the most promising directions. Should we pursue integration more vigorously or keep expanding our knowledge base in a pluralistic fashion? What is the best balance?

Why is Integration so Challenging?

As the authors of Part II justly emphasize, the field of strategy is highly diverse and fragmented in three core dimensions:

1   the domain of inquiry, ranging from the strategy of nations to individuals competing just against nature (for example, a mountain climber or explorer)
2   the approach of inquiry, ranging from clinical anecdotes to abstract theory
3   the purpose of the inquiry, ranging from descriptive to predictive to normative (see Schoemaker, 1982, 1991).

Further compounding our problem is the fact that the prescriptive side of strategy is about how best to exploit the uniqueness of the circumstances in which a strategizing agent (a nation, firm, individual or perhaps an animal) finds itself. But if too much uniqueness is perceived, the opportunity to draw similarities from other cases is reduced. Herein lies the essence of the prescriptive challenge: balancing the tradeoff between exploiting uniqueness and importing the lessons from analogous but not quite identical cases. Historically, the field of strategy has been rooted in case studies and only later were significant strides made in theoretical integration, at first using economic theory and later organization sciences (see Mintzberg et al., 1998; Rumelt et al., 1994).

The more we understand the uniqueness of any one case, the less we appreciate the similarities to other cases unless we know how to abstract from the specifics and think more in terms of canonical forms. The ideal strategy advisor is one who keenly understands the subtleties of the problem at hand and yet can invoke broad, synthetic knowledge, gleaned from other cases, and apply it to the present situation. Psychologists refer to this process of problem solving as pattern matching. The more patterns a person's repertoire contains, the greater the chance that a similar case is encountered. Appropriate search algorithms must exist to allow for an efficient and effective similarity comparison to occur. Hence, some form of abstraction is needed from the specific case in the person's database of prior cases. This feature-matching process constitutes a form of integration.

Approaches to Integration

A case in point is Cooper's review of research on corporate acquisitions. Three major academic strands are identified, each of which has several substrands. In judging the desirability of a new proposed acquisition, the strategist can explore similarities between past cases (either in raw or codified form) and then make adjustments from these anchors to reflect the uniqueness of the case at hand. If the question is whether the proposed acquisition will create stockholder wealth, numerous financial models can be applied. In assessing the organizational problem likely in the post-acquisition phase, a broad spectrum of views and hypotheses can be drawn upon, and so on. Integration is at its essence the recognition of similarities and differences among numerous cases, at a higher level of abstraction than that at which the cases themselves were documented.

Without sound theories, concepts, primitives and exemplars, the integration process will remain an art rather than a science. The field of strategy needs to deepen as well as expand the codification and synthesizing frameworks to achieve the level of integration needed for grounded, as opposed to ad hoc, solutions. Thus far, the field of strategy has liberally borrowed from economics, management science, organization and sociology, biology and military science, among others. Each offers useful constructs and empirical insights, but their union presents a patchwork of disciplinary confusion and prejudice that is counterproductive to the field's cohesion and progress. Ideally, we would have a hierarchy of attributes of increasing abstraction, which connect the numerous modules of strategic insight into a coherent framework. A starting point, top-down, would be the three attributes I referred to earlier, concerning the domain, approach and purpose of the inquiry.

These three attributes are just a start and others are needed, too. Erickson et al. (Chapter 5) seek an integration by acknowledging the role of the individual strategist who operates within an organizational context and industry setting. The type of context, from simple to bureaucratically complex, will exert a great influence on the degrees of freedom the strategic actor possesses. This form of integration addresses both the domain question (from individual to societal) and the role of context. What is lacking are clear pointers that tell us when and how to focus on the role of the actor. My ideal form of integration is literally a data-base with search engines and valuation functions that tell the user, for any given strategy problem that has been coded in the language of the program, where to search for analogous cases, theoretical principles, empirical findings, relevant concepts and even ideological preferences.

Van den Bosch (Chapter 6) seeks an integration along process lines, specifi-cally regarding the role of time, which he parses into subjective versus objective time, as well as other dimensions. Using only the time dimension allows him to distinguish various strategy theories (from punctuated equilibria to dynamic capabilities and commitment), although additional dimensions will be needed to differentiate the theories more fully. No doubt, the dimension of time is impor-tant, but we need more guidance, for instance on when the role of time versus the role of the individual actor merits more attention. Each of these two approaches highlights important attributes, namely unit of analysis, context and time, via which the pattern matching process referred to above may be performed. But additional attributes will be needed, too – notably those of intent (descriptive versus prescriptive) and worldview (rational versus behavioural) in order to allow a search algorithm to guide us toward solutions for specific cases.

Is Further Integration Worth Pursuing at this Time?

Without integrating theories, each case will be solved anew and in isolation. We re-invent the wheel and make slow incremental progress. Both practitioners and scholars of strategy must in some way or other reduce a given strategy problem, with all its attendant complexity, to a canonical structure that reveals both the similarities and differences vis-à-vis other exemplars for which outright solutions or useful insights exist. Then, upon transferring the solutions from these related domains, in reduced and abstract form, to the present situation, significant tailor-ing and adaptation may be needed, which often requires a high level of clinical expertise.

I see the challenge of integration we face in strategy as similar to the ones encountered in the field of decision sciences. Each decision, whether strategic or tactical, is unique in its fine detail and yet amenable to theoretical analysis in reduced or canonical form. The primitives of this canonical form are acts, probabilities, outcomes, preferences, etc. The tools and frameworks that render these primitives relevant and operational include expected utility theory, Bayesian analysis, and others (Schoemaker, 1982). The decision sciences approach to problem solving utilizes pattern matching (for example, the problem about a choice under certainty, risk, uncertainty or conflict) as well as design principles, such as constructing decision trees or utility functions. My remarks above have especially highlighted the pattern-matching approach to integration. The other one that merits attention is 'design from first principles', in which creativity and deduction play different roles.

Design from first principles requires a generic conceptual framework, and a set of parameters within that framework that can be tailored to the case at hand. This approach, by definition, is more abstract and relies on fewer archetypes. Instead of a similarity comparison, its essence consists of building up, block by block, a representation that is a special case within the general framework. This requires creativity and design excellence, especially in the formulation of the options set. The field of medicine offers a good example. Treatment regimes can be based on pattern matching (which requires only superficial expertise but a large database) or on tailored therapies designed from a basic understanding of the underlying medical science (which requires deep medical expertise plus the clinical skill of application and translation). The training of physicians consequently requires a deep immersion in theory as well as a vast exposure to clinical cases. The training of strategists may have to pursue a similar path.

As emphasized in a recent synthesis of the diverse fields of decision sciences, good prescription emanates from sound description, aided by the existence of normative theories that give guidance (Kleindorfer et al., 1993). It was also argued that a process perspective can tie together the disparate strands of theory and empiricism that currently define the field of decision sciences. A process perspective encourages sensitivity to temporal order and context, assuring that the ensuing analysis remains connected to the realities of the problem being faced. In addition, the unit of analysis problem was emphasized, covering the full range of social aggregation (from individual to societal decision making). Lastly, the descriptive, normative and prescriptive approaches were contrasted. All too often, the prescriptive sciences abstract and distort the reality at hand to make their tools more applicable, which is, of course, an insidious inversion of priorities.

Consider again the case of corporate acquisition. The financial approach to valuation entails a net present value analysis and embedded options valuations. Various assumptions will have to be made to operationalize these models, such as what cashflows to project or what discount rate to use. The fundamental trade-off in developing these models is between internal and external validity. A financial model that is internally consistent, i.e. entails proper calculation and deduction but is based on shaky assumptions adds little value, no matter how elegant. Strategy advisors should be especially mindful that internal validity means little without external validity, at least to the practitioner. Conversely, high external validity without internal validity may result in biased or ad hoc advice. The challenge is one of striking a judicious balance, which in turn requires proper models for judging both types of validity. This recognition offers yet another form of integration: that between reality and our representation of it.

A key lesson for the field of strategy is that integration without appropriate primitives and associated theory is bound to fail. We must continue to enlarge the set of exemplars from which theory can derive and to which it can be applied. At an early stage of development in any science, fragmentation is welcome since researchers need to reflect the fine detail of the cases encountered. Biologists first started with observation and classification into taxonomies based on readily observable features, for example, collecting and sorting butterflies. It would be premature to forge integration when the set of exemplars, or the development of primitives and associated theory are in an embryonic stage. However, once the classification phase matures, the time is ripe for re-conceptualization, which Darwin did in the grandest of manners in biology and Newton or Einstein in physics.

My personal view is that the field of strategy is well beyond the classification stage. Just consider the extensive business case library developed at Harvard and elsewhere, the explosion of grounded research over the past few decades, and the rich plurality of concepts, theories and approaches referenced in this book and beyond. On the other hand, the field of strategy has not yet seen the integrative equivalent of a Newton or a Darwin, let alone an Einstein. In this sense, the field is still in a pre-paradigmatic stage. Hence, the question of integration is timely and important. This book should make a significant contribution towards achieving the worthy goal of deeper integration, at the right time in the field's steady evolution.

Acknowledgements

Roch Parayre is thanked for his helpful comments, as are the participants of the McKinsey Strategy Forum of which the author is a member along with other academics and McKinsey partners.

PART III

THE BOUNDARY SCHOOL: STRATEGY AS A BOUNDARY DECISION

9

The Boundary School

Nicolai J. Foss

The boundary school, we are told by the editors of this volume, is a serious candidate for playing the role of a synthesizing school in strategic management. It bears promise of being able to organize crucial strategic issues and to draw on complementary insights.

As indicated by its name, the boundary school may be understood as a compilation of theories that are all concerned with analysing what economists (and some organization theorists) refer to as 'the boundaries of the firm'. (Strictly speaking, we might as well talk of, for example, 'the boundaries of the market'.) In economics, the boundaries of the firm are normally defined in terms of ownership (Hart, 1995): if firm A has ownership rights over asset *a* and firm B does not, asset *a* is inside the boundaries of firm A and outside the boundaries of firm B. More generally, the boundaries of firm A are defined by those assets that firm A owns. This has implications for the way that the boundaries issue is normally understood in management studies, namely as the organization of transactions, for assets and transactions are usually bundled. For example, internalizing a transaction means obtaining ownership rights to the equipment that support the transaction.

Therefore, an aspect of the boundaries of the firm is the issue of which activities or transactions should be undertaken in firms (hierarchies), which should take place in various intermediate forms (such as franchising, licensing arrangements, long-term supplier contracts, joint ventures, etc.), and which should be handled in 'anonymous' markets. These are the issues that are treated in different ways by the various approaches that may be seen as constituting the boundary school.

Evidently, they are of great strategic significance. For example, the issues of diversification, outsourcing, partnering, strategic alliances, virtual corporations, how foreign markets should be serviced, etc. all directly involve the issue of the boundaries of the firm.

From a mainstream strategy perspective (for example, the resource-based perspective), the boundaries of the firm would seem to derive their importance from the fact that they determine the firm's sourcing of resources (in-house or market sourcing), co-determine the terms at which resources may be acquired, influence the extent to which rents may be appropriated from, for example, valuable knowledge, etc. Thus, in such a scheme, the boundaries issue is seen to be directly relevant to the issue of sustained competitive advantage, arguably the key issue in strategy (content) research. This is because knowing something about a firm's boundaries and, therefore, its contracts, also tells us something about how efficiently strategic resources are organized. However, there is more to it than this, because a firm's boundaries, including in a wider reading, its relations to outside suppliers, for example, may in themselves constitute strategic resources.

From both a scientific and a normative perspective, we wish to know which entities and mechanisms determine observed boundary choices. Innovation? Production costs? Knowledge accumulation? Dependence considerations? Transaction costs? Intuitively, these all seem relevant to some degree, but which factors are the most important, which may legitimately be kept in the background or abstracted from, and how is the mix between causal factors constituted in different situations? Should we rely on a power perspective or on an efficiency perspective for answering these questions? And so on.

Thus, there are many and difficult questions that have a bearing on the issue under consideration here – questions that are addressed and answered in different ways by different approaches in economics and sociological organization theory. It should be recognized from the outset that talking about 'the boundary school' is what doctrinal historians call a 'rational reconstruction'. To put it more bluntly, there may not be such a thing as a distinct boundary school in existence. However, there are undeniably a number of related theories that share an interest in a well-defined set of issues, which may overlap or be complementary. From a practical point of view, it may therefore make sense to talk about a 'school' in the sense of a box of tools that may be applied to problem solving in practice. Discussion of this is one of the purposes of this chapter.

Among the theories that may be seen as constituting the boundary school are various manifestations of transaction cost economics, most notably Williamson's (1985, 1996) brand, the resource-dependency approach originally developed by Pfeffer and Salancik (1978), various approaches to industrial networks (for example, Axelsson and Easton, 1992) and also the capabilities approach to firms (Langlois and Foss, 1997; Langlois and Robertson, 1995; Penrose, 1959; Richardson, 1972).

Of course, the issue of the boundaries of the firm has always been centre stage in the more explicitly managerial literature. For example, the make or buy decision is one of the classics of strategy, and has continuously received attention from management writers, as it has done recently in the guise of 'outsourcing'. Similarly, the issue of the boundaries of the firm has emerged in all sorts of managerial discussions on, for example, diversification. However, it is characteristic of the more managerial literature that the discussion is not explicitly founded in theory, and that this produces ambiguities.[1] I shall therefore consider only the four theories identified above.

I shall argue that some of these theories are related in various ways; ways that will then be examined in more detail. For example, there are some parallels between the (sociological) resource-dependency approach and transaction cost economics, many networks arguments can be given a straightforward transaction cost interpretation, and capabilities and transaction cost resasoning may be fruitfully combined, etc.

The main purpose of this chapter is to emphasize further the strategic importance of the issue of the boundaries of the firm, to present a map of sorts of the boundary school, and to speculate on how the diverse constituent theories of this school are connected. More specifically, I shall put forward and defend the following propositions.

- The issue of the boundaries of the firm is a crucial strategic issue; it goes right to the heart of corporate strategy and also involves business and functional strategy (see The Strategic Importance of Firm Boundaries, below).
- There are a number of theoretical approaches, from different underlying disciplines, that have approached the issue. To some extent these approaches can be harmonized, but in some ways they are in conflict (see Alternative Theories of the Boundaries of the Firm and Implications, below).
- Because of this, and other difficulties, such as the lack of clarity as to what exactly constitutes the boundaries of the firm, the strategic implications of the boundary school are not entirely clear. Further research and attempts to clarify and synthesize are needed (see Implications and Concluding comments).

As these issues individually warrant separate chapters, this chapter is necessarily brief in places.

The Strategic Importance of Firm Boundaries

Strategizing and Economizing

Oliver Williamson (1994) – the flagbearer of the arguably most important economic approach belonging to the boundary school, namely the transaction cost approach – recently argued that there is a sharp distinction between 'economizing' (on transaction and production costs) and 'strategizing' (by engaging in various clever ploys against other players in product markets). An important aspect of 'economizing' is to choose the boundaries of the firm correctly; if this is not done, the firm may suffer severe transaction and production cost penalties. Moreover, Williamson argued that economizing is superior to strategizing.

> ... economizing is much more fundamental than strategizing. This is because strategizing is relevant principally to firms that possess market power – which are a small

fraction of the total ... I advance the argument that ... *economy is the best strategy*. That is the central and unchanging message of the transaction cost economics perspective ... To be sure, economizing and strategizing are not mutually exclusive. Strategic ploys are sometimes used to disguise economic weaknesses. (Williamson, 1994: 362; emphasis in original)

In contrast, I argue that Williamson confuses strategy in general with a very specific model of strategy, namely the one derived from industrial economics (for example, Porter, 1980). Admittedly, this model does emphasize tactical ploys, threats, and so on. However, the strategy field in general is not at all committed to this specific model; for example, it is questioned by the recent resource-based school in strategy research (Foss, 1997a). This misunderstanding leads Williamson to portray a false relation between strategizing and economizing. Not only is economizing often an important aspect of strategizing, but strategizing considerations sometimes over-rule economizing, and rightly so. For example, firms may engage in substantial knowledge exchange and learning from other firms, although this may expose them to serious transaction cost problems. However, the long-term benefits easily outweigh short-term transaction costs. (Similar points will be elaborated later.)

Strategizing decisions are concerned with the creation of rents through strategic and entrepreneurial initiative, whereas economizing is concerned with increasing rents through reducing inefficiencies. (For more on these distinctions, see Foss (1997b) and Langlois and Foss (1997).) But these are not in conflict; they are complementary aspects of the rent-creation process.

Williamson would presumably not disagree with the main point of this section – that the boundaries of the firm constitute a variable of paramount strategic importance. At any rate, principles relating to the boundaries of the firm are increasingly being translated into more managerial prose and are explicitly seen as being of strategic significance, as seen, for example, in the work of the highly respected transaction cost theorists, Milgrom and Roberts (1992) and Rubin (1990). Thus, economizing and strategizing are not opposed. On the contrary, economizing considerations will usually accompany strategizing considerations – the two perspectives complement each other. In the following section, I discuss a number of issues in which the boundaries of the firm are a crucial variable and in which an economizing orientation is also appropriate.

The Boundaries of the Firm as a Strategic Variable

Chandler on the Corporation

As a first illustration of the importance – indeed, the crucial importance – of the boundaries of the firm as a strategic variable, consider the work of Chandler (1962, 1990a, 1990b). His work is the standard reference on the emergence of the corporate form, and particularly on the emergence of the diversified company and the change in organizational structures that, at least in the USA, accompanied increasing diversification. Chandler's basic theory can be summarized as follows.

Technological change, particularly the telegraph, the railroad, the steamship and the cable allowed a tremendous increase in the extent of the market – one that opened up a huge potential for scale-based mass-production with an emphasis on 'economies of speed' (Chandler, 1962). This created a strong need for co-ordination. The organizational and technological innovations required for taking advantage of the new opportunities were complementary, in the sense that doing more of one of the activities increased the returns from doing more of another activity (Milgrom and Roberts, 1992). Moreover, the relevant innovations were often 'systemic' in nature, that is, they required simultaneous changes in adjacent stages of production. Finally, large geographical distances were involved. All of this required intensive co-ordinative efforts.

The institution that arose to take advantage of the opportunities presented by the technologically induced widening of markets and to solve the accompanying co-ordination problems was the modern corporation. This institution possessed the co-ordinative capability not possessed by the market organization under the specific regime of economic change then prevailing in the American economy. Or, to be more precise, the corporation mobilized the required co-ordinative capability that would have been prohibitively costly to organize in the context of market relations. (Thus, strategizing and economizing join forces). In fact, Lazonick (1991) seems to sharpen Chandler's argument into the proposition that undertaking the massive, systemic innovations in processes and organization that were undertaken by the early American corporations is something the market is inherently incapable of doing.[2]

Chandler's (and certainly Lazonick's) argument may sometimes read as a ringing endorsement of the merits of vertical integration. Indeed, according to Chandler (1990b), being big and heavily vertically integrated is a necessary condition for successful performance, at least in the global arena; this makes it most possible to stimulate efficient throughput, innovation and development of capabilities. The highly vertically integrated company is currently out of fashion and, at any rate, Chandler's views are flatly contradicted by those who advocate 'the virtual corporation', that is, the relatively short-lived but very flexible partnering that develops in order to reap gains from temporary technological opportunities, as the organizational form of the future, by various advocates of 'networking', of 'industrial districts' and so on.

The point here is that these disagreements stem from different understandings of the strategic implications of the boundary choice. For example, there is an underlying disagreement whether or not productive and innovative capabilities can be created and nurtured across the boundaries of several networked firms.

Outsourcing

Another, related, example has to do with the highly topical debate on outsourcing (as summarized in Bettis et al., 1992). Outsourcing simply means letting suppliers take over activities that were once undertaken in house. It is, therefore, an example of vertical disintegration, and because it allows the firm to get access to the high-powered incentives of market supply (rather than the dulled incentives of internal procurement) and to eliminate some fixed costs, outsourcing may be an attractive strategy, particularly for flagging business units. Moreover, a clever outsourcing strategy frees financial resources that can be used for expanding core business.

However, unless it is carefully executed, outsourcing may be associated with serious perils. In fact, the critics of outsourcing, such as Bettis et al. (1992), have (unknowingly) taken a Chandlerian position and argued that excessive outsourcing on the part of western firms to Japanese and South-east Asian firms has led to a loss of ability to upgrade capabilities on the part of western firms in many industries. Thus, myopic economizing considerations can harm longer-run strategizing considerations. This is because western firms have not understood the strategic intentions of their Asian suppliers (namely to learn from the relation rather than simply to supply), who have later emerged as vigorous competitors. It is also because western firms have allowed Asian supplier firms to get 'too close' to core capabilities (for example, by outsourcing core products) and have lost track of important technological developments in components and the manufacture of components, etc.

Again the point is that a boundary choice – whether or not to disintegrate vertically – strongly influences longer-run strategic considerations, whether or not management is aware of this. For example, outsourcing activities that are close to the corporate core to partners whose intentions are ill understood seriously risks harming longer-run knowledge-building efforts.

Implications and Desiderata

The upshot of this section is that the boundary choice relates to a number of crucial strategic issues. Extrapolating somewhat from the examples given, the boundary choice may be seen to be directly relevant to decisions relating to diversification, make and buy, outsourcing, participation in business networks, strategic alliances, joint ventures, franchising, etc. To put it briefly, virtually all issues of corporate strategy involve the boundaries of the firm.

As traditionally understood, corporate strategy involves the twin issues of, first, which markets the firm should operate in and, second, how divisions should be managed. Obviously, the boundaries of the firm are directly relevant to the first issue, since this can be reformulated as a matter of where the firm's efficient boundaries should lie. However, the second issue is also relevant, for managing a division from a corporate headquarters is only justified to the extent that the headquarters adds more value to the operation of the division; otherwise, it would be more efficient to let the division stand alone (as a separate legal entity) or perhaps let it be owned by another firm. Obviously, these considerations again involve the boundaries issue, since they raise the issue of who should own (and control) the division (i.e. the assets of the division).

The boundaries issue also relates to business strategy, since choosing the right boundaries may be conducive both to a low-cost or a quality strategy. For example, both strategies may require some vertical integration, albeit for different reasons (controlling throughput versus controlling the quality of inputs). Moreover, where the boundaries are drawn may also relate to the issue of appropriability, because a higher degree of vertical integration may help keep would-be imitators at bay (by making the firm more complex and hence more difficult to imitate and by more control over knowledge flows).

Indeed, to the extent that one views strategy as a matter of accumulating and deploying valuable bundles of knowledge assets – such as capabilities or core competencies – and appropriating the rents from these assets, the boundaries issue is crucial. For example, collaboration between firms – a specific way of drawing the boundaries of the firm – may provide opportunities for firms to internalize the skills of their partners (Hamel, 1991). The boundary choice therefore influences the possibilities of reaping rents from the firms' scarce resources and capabilities, not only because it influences appropriability (knowledge protection), but also because it is a mechanism for knowledge acquisition.

As a general matter, we suggest therefore that the boundaries of the firm (in both the vertical and the horizontal dimensions) should be chosen so that rents are maximized.[3] Clearly, a specific consideration is that we would like to know more about the connection between the boundary choice and the accumulation of capabilities. We have substantial relevant empirical evidence, for example, from the debate on outsourcing, from business history, etc., but it is more doubtful that we have theorizing that is adequate to allow us to approach the issue in all its complexities. The following section addresses theories of the boundaries of the firm in more detail.

Alternative Theories of the Boundaries of the Firm

Theories of the boundaries of the firm are many and diverse. They identify different aspects of the boundaries of the firm and different explanatory mechanisms behind these, they are drawn from different disciplines and, not surprisingly, they have different managerial implications. One partial reason for the plurality of theories is that they are, at least in economics, derived from more general theories of the firm. And economics has witnessed a virtual explosion of work on the theory of the firm over the last 15 to 20 years. In this section, I review what I see as the most important theories, beginning with the arguably most highly developed theory[4] or, rather, theories, namely transaction cost theories.

Transaction Cost Theories: Coase, Williamson and Hart

Transaction cost theories of the boundaries of the firm include, most notably, the edifice that Williamson has been constructing over the last three decades.[5] However, the story begins with Ronald Coase. What Coase observed was that, in the world of standard neoclassical economics, firms have no reason to exist. According to economics textbooks, the decentralized price system is the ideal structure for carrying out economic co-ordination. Why then are some transactions removed from the price system to the interior of organizations called firms? The answer, Coase reasoned, must be that there is a 'cost to using the price mechanism' (Coase, 1937: 390). Thus was born the idea of transaction costs: costs that stand separate from and in addition to ordinary production costs. In his 1937 article, Coase lists several sources of those 'costs of using the price mechanism' that give rise to the institution of the firm. In part, these are the costs of writing contracts. The 'most obvious cost of "organising" production through the price mechanism is that of discovering what the relevant prices are' (Coase, 1937: 390). A second type of cost is that of executing separate contracts for each of the many market transactions necessary for co-ordinating complex production activity. These costs can be avoided by firm organization.

However, Coase's basic insights were essentially neglected until the beginning of the 1970s. Since then the economics of transaction costs as applied to organization has burgeoned into a major subfield in the economics discipline, and has had a strong influence in the organization and strategy departments of business schools, no doubt because the theory addresses core issues in organization and strategy in a precise and convincing manner.[6] An early development was Alchian and Demsetz (1972) and Jensen and Meckling (1976), two seminal and founding contributions of that brand of transaction cost economics that is often referred to as 'nexus of contracts' theory. However, it is characteristic of this brand that the very notion of the boundaries of the firm is elusive. It is not really clear what is 'inside' and what is 'outside' the firm.[7] Because these theories essentially deny the central phenomenon under discussion here, I shall disregard them in the following pages and proceed instead to the other dominant branch of transaction cost economics, namely that associated with Williamson.

Building on Coasian foundations and mixing these with essential ideas of the Carnegie–Mellon school in organization theory (notably bounded rationality) and his own ideas (such as that of opportunism), Williamson has, over more than three decades, constructed an impressive, if sometimes unnecessarily complicated, theoretical structure. Perhaps most notably, he has been instrumental in extending the traditional concern with the theory of the firm to a much broader concern with economic organization in general.

Williamson (1985, 1996) has increasingly focused on what has become perhaps the central concept in the present-day economics of organization: asset specificity. It is a concept that has apparently come to crowd out all others in the explanatory pantheon. The logic is basically simple. Assets are highly specific when they have value within the context of a particular transaction but have relatively little value outside the transaction. This opens the door to opportunism, particularly under circumstances where the relevant contract between the parties is incomplete, that is, it does not cover all future contingencies. Once the contract is signed and the assets deployed, one of the parties may use some unforeseen contingency (for example, changing demand or technology) to effect a 'hold-up'. For instance, one party may demand a price reduction and support this by threatening to pull out of the arrangement – thereby reducing the value of the specific assets – unless a greater share of the quasi-rents of joint production find their way into the threat-maker's pockets.

Fear of such 'hold up' will affect investment choices. In the absence of appropriate contractual safeguards, the transacting parties may choose less specific – and therefore less specialized and less productive – technology. If, by contrast, the transacting parties were to pool their capital into a single enterprise in whose profits they jointly shared or if one of the parties were given all ownership rights to the relevant assets, the incentives for unproductive rent-seeking would be attenuated and the more productive specialized technology would be chosen.

With asset specificity as his central explanatory component, Williamson has constructed an impressive and rich theory not only of firms but of all sorts of contractual organization, and has explicitly tied this to contract law. For example, he has increasingly emphasized the importance of what he calls 'hybrids' (Williamson, 1996: Chapter 4), that is to say, those governance structures[8] that are intermediate between markets and hierarchies. These are seen as arising under conditions of medium asset specificity and to be supported by their own kind of implicit contract law.

The work of Hart and others (Grossman and Hart, 1986; Hart, 1995) – known as the incomplete contracts literature – is in many ways a formal continuation and formalization of Williamsonian insights. The literature distinguishes two types of rights under contract: specific rights and residual rights. The latter are generic rights to make production decisions in circumstances not spelled out in the contract. The choice between contract and internal organization may be reduced to a question of the efficient allocation of the residual rights of control when contracts are incomplete and assets highly specific. Suppose there are two parties co-operating in production, each bringing to the arrangement a bundle of assets. If none of the assets is highly specific, opportunism is impossible (all things being equal) as either party can liquidate at no or low cost as soon as troublesome unforeseen contingencies arise. If, however, assets are specific, or if opportunism becomes possible for other reasons, it may be efficient to place the residual rights of control in the hands of only one of the parties by giving that party ownership of both sets of assets. In general, the owner ought to be the party whose possession of the residual right minimizes rent-seeking costs, which typically means the party whose contribution to the quasi-rents of co-operation is greater.

Thus, the incomplete contracts literature allows us to say who should (efficiently) own which assets (that is, who integrates whom). Moreover, it does something few have been able to do before: it defines the boundaries of the firm in a consistent and unambiguous way. Thus, a firm is defined by the bundle of assets under common ownership. This 'formal' definition of the firm and its boundaries is somewhat at variance with the next approach to be considered.

The Resource-Dependence Approach

The (largely sociological) resource-dependence approach was launched with a number of publications during the 1970s by Pfeffer and Salancik, either separately or jointly, and culminated with the publication in 1978 of their joint book, *The External Control of Organizations: a Resource Dependence Perspective*. In the context of organization theory, the approach is perhaps best thought of as an important correction to structural contingency theory. Where the theory asserted that firms had to adapt internal structure to external contingencies, Pfeffer and Salancik elaborated the essentially simple point that firms may as well try to influence these contingencies and environments rather than passively responding to them. Although others have made contributions and the approach has been extended somewhat, I shall refer to this classic contribution exclusively.[9]

Pfeffer and Salancik essentially follow Cyert and March (1963) in assuming that firms try to accumulate slack resources and profits, and that they will actively influence their environments in order to reach this end. One way of accomplishing this is to reduce dependence on external factors, such as other firms.[10] Dependence is conceptualized as follows.

> Concentration of the control over discretion over resources and the importance of the resources to the organization together determine the focal organization's dependence on any given other group or organization. Dependence can then be defined as the product of the importance of a given input or output to the organization and the extent to which it is controlled by relatively few organizations. (Pfeffer and Salancik, 1978: 51)

Now, reducing dependence may take place through strategies that involve direct changes to the boundaries of the firm, that is, the transferring of ownership titles to various assets. This is essentially the type of case mainly examined in transaction cost economics, and includes vertical integration, diversification and horizontal integration. In fact, the resource-dependence approach sometimes reads as a sort of sociological version of transaction cost economics, among other things, because of the distinction between various sorts of interdependencies. For example, the distinction between 'reciprocal' and 'asymmetric' interdependence (Pfeffer and Salancik, 1978: 52–3) is comparable to the concepts of 'complementary' and 'specific assets' of transaction cost economics.

However, it would clearly be wrong to say that the resource-dependence approach is no more than a sociological version of transaction cost economics. One view is, of course, that the approach is not an efficiency approach, but is based on power considerations and on reduction of uncertainty (rather than the maximization of rents) as over-riding motives for economic actors. More to the point, however, Pfeffer and Salancik forcefully argue that reduction of dependence may also be accomplished through other, less formal, means than direct ownership, such as the formation of cartels, business associations, social norms, interlocking boards of directors, and so on.

In other words, they introduce the important distinction (popularized by sociology) between 'real' and 'formal' control, a distinction that has not been recognized in economics until very recently (Hart, 1995). These strategies make the firm's environment a negotiated environment (Grandori, 1987: 61), and will sometimes be chosen because they confer co-ordination and, particularly, flexibility benefits that direct ownership may not confer. As Pfeffer and Salancik argue, anticipating recent ideas on the virtual corporation: 'Relationships established through communication and consensus can be established, renegotiated, and reestablished with more ease than the integration of organizations by merger can be altered' (Pfeffer and Salancik, 1978: 145). That 'informal' co-operative strategies may sometimes be more flexible than direct ownership is also a theme of the next approach to be considered.

Network Approaches

During the last two decades, many scholars have written about firm networks, particularly in an industrial marketing context, and several distinct groups of network theorists may be distinguished in the UK and in Sweden to name some examples (Axelsson and Easton, 1992). Moreover, 'network' has increasingly become a strategic management buzzword, and has now lost its earlier almost exclusive affiliation to industrial marketing. Finally, contributors to the network approach appear to draw on a diversity of different disciplines, insights and contributions, for example, exchange sociology, organizational economics, the resource-dependency approach, sociological work on networks and embeddedness, etc. Accordingly, it is not easy to reconstruct a set of well-defined themes that run through the various contributions to 'the' network approach. However, the following related broad ideas may perhaps be singled out as common themes.

First, there is a view that networks of co-operating firms are quite pervasive social institutions. (This is an idea that is strongly supported by the new economic sociology (for example, Granovetter, 1985).) As Thorelli (1986) says 'The point taken here is that the entire economy may be viewed as a network of organizations with a vast hierarchy of sub-ordinate, criss-crossing networks' (Thorelli, 1986: 38).

Second, networks are seen as structuring exchange relations on a par with hierarchies and markets, and to be just as worthy of scientific inquiry. The firm's 'environment' is a complex context consisting of heterogeneous competitors and co-operating firms who condition the firm's behavior. Therefore, proponents of the network approach are often highly critical of those theories and approaches that they take to portray firms as confronting an anonymous environment (such as mainstream strategic management or industrial organization) (Håkansson and Snehota, 1989).

Third, trust is seen as a much more descriptively accurate assumption about firm interaction than, in particular, opportunism (Johansson and Mattson, 1987), as empirical research has revealed many cases of firms willingly putting themselves in the position of risking being held-up opportunistically. (For an extended critique of this argument, see Foss and Koch (1996).) Trust is gradually built in long-term business relationships. (See also Koenig and van Wijk, Chapter 10, this volume.) Indeed, the typical and interesting kind of interaction envisaged as taking place between the firms in the network is that of informal contacts made by actors with close interpersonal relations.

Fourth, as in the resource-dependence perspective, on which many contributors to the network approach draw, power and its distribution among the actors of the network are assumed to be important. Underlying the distributions of power between actors are, in turn, dependent relationships between participants. As noted by Johanson and Mattsson (1987: 36), there is 'A basic assumption in the network model ... that the individual firm is dependent on resources controlled by other firms', but the drama associated with this condition in the resource-dependence perspective is not shared.

Fifth, long-term, trust-based network relations are seen as supporting individual firms' processes of accumulation of resources and capabilities (Jarillo, 1993). Firms engage themselves in repeated interaction with other firms in order to obtain access to the complementary but dissimilar resources and capabilities of other firms, and to ease their own accumulation processes. Moreover, firms may obtain the benefits of diversity (including diversity in technological experimentation) from participation in broad networks (Foss, 1999).

As noted by Johanson and Mattsson (1993: 3), 'Much work is needed before the network approach can be considered a coherent theory.' In line with this view, it seems that a considerable part of what counts as the theoretical part of the literature on networks should be considered as collections of 'stylized facts', and attempts to proceed from these in a more or less inductive manner, rather than fully-fledged theoretical components. It is, therefore, tempting to paraphrase what Coase once said of the institutional economics of Veblen, Commons, and Ayres, namely that the network approach is essentially a mass of empirical data in need of a theory – or a bonfire!

This would be wrong, however, for there are valuable insights associated with the approach that are, if not entirely neglected in other approaches, then certainly more strongly emphasized in network approach. These include, for example, the ideas that networks are organized to increase access to information, that 'transactions' are far from being homogenous and are rather multi-faceted and dense, that trust is a critical contingency, and that social embeddedness matters – these points are particularly emphasized by the network approach.

However, I think that it is fair to say that the network approach is not a theory about the boundaries of the firm proper. At least, it does not at all match the transaction cost approach (which its proponents so often criticize) in terms of precise insights into this issue. However, network ideas are certainly relevant for understanding, for example, the connection between information acquisition and the boundaries of the firm, or how social embeddedness may influence where these boundaries are located. Thus, the network approach is, in the end, more a theory of firm learning and of the firm's embeddedness than an approach directed at understanding firm boundaries. Something similar may also be said of the next approach to be considered.

The Capabilities Approach

How can firms make the best use of their distinctive capabilities? How have they done this in the past? How can they go on developing new valuable capabilities? Such questions have been central in the strategy field since its inception at the end of the 1950s. According to the editors of this book (Chapter 1), the capabilities perspective (or 'school'), which is a collection of resource-based and evolutionary perspectives on the firm, is in fact one of the important candidates for playing the role of a synthesizing school in the context of strategic management research. However, as I briefly argue here, there is some overlap between the boundary school and the capabilities school, since the latter also contains insights of relevance for the issue of the boundaries of the firm (see also Stiles, Chapter 11).

Briefly, the capabilities school may be said to be founded on the common-sense recognition that individuals and organizations are necessarily limited in what they know how to do well. Indeed, the main interest of the capabilities view is to understand what is distinctive about firms as unitary, historical organizations of co-operating individuals. The conceptualization of the firm that underlies much work on capabilities was perhaps best expressed in the late Edith Penrose's *The Theory of the Growth of the Firm* (1959). 'The firm', Penrose says, 'is ... a collection of productive resources the disposal of which between different uses and over time is determined by administrative decision' (Penrose, 1959: 24).

Now, resources in Penrose's view yield services, and it is these services – clearly a theoretical precursor to the concept of capabilities – that interest her most. Although resources/services are firm specific, they are nevertheless somewhat replaceable inside the firm, and, when in excess, provide a stepping-stone for diversifying into new markets. Clearly, this is a first stab at a theory of firm boundaries based on capabilities considerations. Later research (for example, Teece, 1982) has further refined Penrose's theory. In fact, Penrose's notion of deploying excess capabilities to neighbouring markets, combined with transaction cost considerations, is perhaps the dominant mode of explanation in diversification studies (Montgomery, 1994).

Roughly speaking, the theory is this. As firms carry on their normal business, they are likely to accumulate excess resources, for example, excess managerial capabilities. In principle, rents from these resources may be captured in different ways, for example, through market exchange, long-term contracts, or in-house use. Because of transaction cost problems, which may be particularly severe when the excess resources involved are knowledge resources, in-house use is more efficient, and the firm will accordingly apply the excess resources to related markets.

A few years after Penrose, British economist George Richardson (1972) tied together the issues of capabilities and the boundaries of the firm even more explicitly. In Richardson's terminology, production can be broken down into various stages or activities (à la Porter, 1985). Some activities are similar, in that they draw on the same general capabilities. Activities can also be complementary in that they are connected in the chain of production and therefore need to be co-ordinated with one another. Juxtaposing different degrees of similarity against different degrees of complementarity produces a matrix that maps different types of economic organization. For example, closely complementary and similar activities may be best undertaken under unified governance. Closely complementary, but dissimilar, activities, on the other hand, are best undertaken in some sort of interfirm arrangement.

As the examples of Penrose and Richardson demonstrate, the capabilities perspective clearly has important implications for the boundaries of the firm. In fact, a number of writers have recently suggested that it is a perspective on this issue that is distinct from the transaction cost approach(es) (Foss, 1993; Langlois and Foss, 1997; Langlois and Robertson, 1995). They argue that – as a quite general matter – capabilities are determinants of the boundaries of the firm on a par with asset specificity. To be more exact, problems of economic organization may crucially reflect the possibility that a firm may control production knowledge that is, in important dimensions, significantly different from what others control, i.e. that the underlying capabilities are highly dissimilar. Thus members of one firm may quite literally not understand what another firm wants from them (for example, in supplier contracts) or is offering them (for example, in license contracts).

TABLE 9.1   *A taxonomy of approaches constituting the boundary school*

	Transaction cost economics	The resource-dependency approach	The network approach	The capabilities approach
Main thrust	The efficient organization of transactions and assets	The control over and dependence on resources	Networks as informational structures	Competitive advantage; knowledge accumulation
Unit of analysis	The transaction	The dependence relation	The relation	Capabilities
Timeframe	Static (comparative statics)	Static	Dynamic	Dynamic
Disciplinary orientation	Neoclassical economics	Mainly sociology	Mainly sociology	Evolutionary economics
Understanding of boundaries	Asset specificity is key; efficient boundaries understood in terms of incentives and transaction costs	Reflect attempts to reduce dependence; contrast between formal ownership and control	Not well developed, has but implications for boundaries	Depends on the degree of complementarity important and similarity of capabilities
Relevance to strategic management	Connection between ownership and investment incentives	Not necessary to own assets to control them	The importance of trust and interfirm learning	Connection between competitive advantage and firm boundaries

Because of the extreme specificity and tacitness of much productive knowledge, one firm may have difficulties understanding another firm's capabilities, and both firms separately and together may know more than their contracts can. In this setting, the costs of making contacts with potential partners, of educating potential licensees and franchisees, of teaching suppliers what it is one needs from them, etc. become very real factors in determining where the boundaries of firms will be placed.[11]

Summing Up

Given what has been said in the preceding pages about the possible constituent theories of the boundary school, we may now sum up their main characteristics in a more synoptic form, as shown in Table 9.1.

Implications

Differences and Ambiguities

As Table 9.1 reveals, there are many and deep differences between the various constituent approaches of the boundary school. Some emphasize static incentive alignment issues and a basic efficiency orientation (the transaction cost approach), while other approaches put the emphasis on power considerations (the resource-dependence approach) and still other approaches put more of an emphasis on knowledge accumulation issues (the network approach and the capabilities approach). The approaches are founded on different disciplines (economics, sociology), on different orientations (power, effiency), use different units of analysis, and would seem to have different implications for managerial practice.

In other words, the various approaches utilize what may be called different 'explanatory languages' for addressing the boundaries of the firm. For example, do the boundaries of the firm primarily matter because they influence the costs of aligning incentives and creating efficient investment levels or because they may reduce uncertainty and dependence or because they reflect various aspects of capabilities? The very notion of the boundaries of the firm seems ambigious in the context of the four approaches. In fact, only two of them, namely the transaction cost and the resource-dependence approach, are clear on this issue, while the remaining two relate to it more indirectly. Transaction cost theories of the firm tell us that ownership of assets and the boundaries of the firm coincide, while the resource-dependence perspective holds that formal ownership does not necessarily coincide with effective control (real ownership?).

Thus, the differences seem to be more pronounced than the similarities. In a general sense, this threatens the whole idea of a boundary school. Evidently, it is rather meaningless to claim a school exists simply because a diversity of theories share some ideas, particularly if the theories are rivals; instead, we should talk about a multiplicity of schools. Of course, there will be no clear managerial implications from what is merely a collection of heterogeneous, and perhaps even conflicting, theories. Therefore, what is really at stake here is the relationship between the theories that we take to constitute the boundary school. I examine this issue in the following pages.

Relationships between the Theories of the Boundary School

The methodological comparison of different theories is a notoriously difficult area (see, for example, Krajewski, 1977) and I will not go into all the philosophical difficulties here, but just make a few suggestions.[12]

As a starting point, we may ask whether the theories are equal in the sense that they share a domain of application. Since all the theories under consideration are about, or have direct implications for, the boundaries of the firm, this clearly is the case. The next thing to inquire into is what I earlier called their 'theoretical language', that is, the central concepts, explanatory mechanisms, mode of analysis, degree of formalization, etc. that the theories employ. As we have seen already, there is very substantial divergence here. As a result, the theories cannot be equivalent in any sense.

This leaves us with a number of other possibilities with respect to the four theories. For example, are they competitive and perhaps in contradiction to each other? Is it possible to establish some sort of correspondence between them? Is it perhaps even possible to break down one of the theories into another one? (see Krajewski, 1977).

Theories may be competitive in the sense that they address the same object of explanation. The hypotheses underlying the relevant alternative theories have some implications where they are in opposition and where it is, therefore, possible to discriminate between them. It would indeed seem reasonable to argue that the theories under consideration are, in fact, competitive. For example, the capabilities perspective and the transaction cost perspective may have rival implications as to where the boundaries of the firm should optimally be drawn, because the first perspective explicitly incorporates long-term knowledge accumulation issues whereas the latter does not.

However, it is generally accepted that one way in which science makes progress is through demonstration that seemingly opposed theories are actually closer to each other than was first thought. Such a demonstration may be accomplished in many ways. For instance, it may be demonstrated that one of the theories under consideration can be reduced to resemble or match another theory. Or one may build a more general theory that incorporates the seemingly rival theories as special cases. Or one may pursue a pragmatic research strategy in which one eclectically combines those key insights of the relevant theories that can be combined. It is this last strategy that I shall briefly discuss here.

A Pragmatic Research Strategy

Although it is undeniably the case that there are many and deep-seated differences between the explanatory methods employed by the four approaches, some of these may do more to differentiate the approaches from each other than others. For example, it may be argued that the fact that the network, resource-dependence and capabilities approaches do not make substantial use of the incentive alignment arguments of transaction cost economics is a relatively unimportant difference, since these arguments can be integrated with the core ideas of the first three approaches. We may ask, given that we wish to engage ourselves in learning through network interaction, are the right incentives in place? That is, is there a sufficient number of credible commitments (cf. Williamson, 1985) and are relations of trust sufficiently widespread (cf. Williamson, 1996: Chapter 10) that we dare take the risk of, for example, making some of our critical knowledge visible to network partners?

Thus, a pragmatic research strategy may be to combine those aspects of the four approaches that can usefully be aligned, and side-step the more troublesome aspects. This is in line with the approach taken to synthesizing schools by Elfring and Volberda (Chapter 1), who basically take the stance that it is possible to align approaches in a practical dimension, where the practical problem statements with which managers are confronted serve as the synthesizing mechanisms. The real goal is to solve the problem and it is legitimate to draw on many perspectives. What counts is the ability of a combination of theories to bring new and real insights. Obviously, such an eclectic approach is not threatened by arguments that underlying assumptions are in conflict.

To continue this reasoning, there may be practical problem areas where the theories under consideration complement each other in the sense that one of the theories is made richer by including some insights and propositions of another theory. Consider the following points as impressionistic examples of this.

- The resource-dependence approach points to the importance of non-formal mechanisms of control and dependence reduction and to the flexibility advantages this may sometimes confer. This clearly complements the formal perspective on control (ownership) in transaction cost theories.
- The network and capabilities approaches point to the importance of the boundaries of the firm for building knowledge assets. This is again a complement to transaction cost theories.
- Transaction cost theories, on the other hand, provide an understanding of the economic mechanisms (for example, hostages and other credible commitments) that underlie the long-term trust relationship, discussed in the network approach.
- The network approach adds a conceptualization of being embedded in a web of co-operating and competing firms that complements the rather 'introspective' stance of the capabilities approach.
- The network approach also helps theorize market transaction costs by pointing to the importance of trust relationships, etc.
- The focus on the longer-term issue of knowledge building that characterizes the capabilities and the network approach complement the shorter-term focus on transaction minimization and power and dependence that characterize the transaction cost and resource-dependence approaches. In fact, these are considerations that should be balanced against each other; arguably, there is a trade-off between them, akin to the one between static and dynamic efficiency. At any rate, pursuing a myopic 'economizing' strategy exclusively is a guaranteed recipe for long-term suboptimization.

As the above points indicate, there is a large potential for integrating selected insights from the four approaches, and in many practical situations it will no doubt be advantageous to rely on more than one perspective. But the integrative potential is not only a matter of practical concerns, it is increasingly becoming a theoretical issue.

In fact, there is a growing number of contributions that are founded on the conviction that combining key ideas of some of the above approaches is a fruitful research strategy. For example, Teece (1982) suggested combining capabilities and transaction cost considerations to aid understanding of efficient diversification, and he later used the same set of ideas for discussing the firm's innovation boundaries (Teece, 1987). Kay (1993) and Reve (1990) also used transaction cost ideas and capabilities ideas to construct a strategic theory of the firm, while Foss and Koch (1996) argued that network ideas and transaction costs did overlap to some extent, and where this was not the case the two approaches were complementary rather than contradictory. These integrative efforts imply that it may, after all, be increasingly meaningful to talk about 'a boundary school' (see Langlois and Foss, 1997 for further discussion).

Conclusions

This chapter has been concerned with analysing the boundary school within contemporary strategic management. The main conclusions can be summarized as follows.

There is no conflict between economizing (on transaction and production costs) and strategizing (creating new sources of rents); rather the two perspectives relate to different aspects of the rent-creation process. Moreover, both may involve the boundaries of the firm. They are, therefore, complementary.

The boundaries of the firm is a central strategic issue, as evidenced both by business history (Chandler, 1962) and more topical issues in strategic management (for example, the debate on outsourcing), and relates directly to issues such as diversification, vertical integration, joint ventures, strategic alliances, etc.

The approaches that may be seen as composing the boundary school – the transaction cost approach, the resource-dependence approach, the network approach and the capabilities approach – differ in a number of ways, such as the disciplines they draw on. Some emphasize static incentive alignment (the transaction cost approach) or power considerations (the resource-dependence approach), while others put more of an emphasis on knowledge accumulation issues (the network approach and the capabilities approach).

However, it has been argued that these different approaches are complementary, and that their essential insights might, and indeed should, be combined in an integrated model. Thus, it may, after all, be possible to begin to speak meaningfully of a boundary school.

Notes

1 For example, it has often been asserted that vertical integration may arise because a downstream firm may wish to have timely delivery or a certain quality level of its inputs. Or, vertical integration is seen as a means to break 'bottlenecks' in the value chain. While all these motives may be real motives, and quite legitimate ones, we would still like to know why, for example, a long-term contract cannot handle these problems of delivery, quality, etc. and why vertical integration is required.

2 Langlois and Robertson (1995), on the other hand, argue that the market is capable of accomplishing a great deal more than Lazonick claims – innovative capability does not rest solely with the corporate form of organization. For example, the development of the PC is an example of the strong innovative capabilities that may reside in a network of competing and co-operating relatively small firms.

3 As we shall see, transaction cost economics formally allows us to say where the boundaries should be drawn so that quasi-rents (joint surplus) on assets are maximized. But this theory does not say anything about maximizing rents from knowledge acquisition that is brought about in, for example, a joint venture (although it may not be incapable of doing this). The theory is essentially about how the boundaries of the firm connect with the appropriability question rather than about how the boundaries of the firm connect with asset-building.

4 This is, of course, a controversial point of view. However, I think that it would be generally agreed that at least in terms of criteria such as formalization, precision and falsifiable predictions, transaction cost economics is more highly developed than the other approaches under consideration here.

5 Principal/agent theory is sometimes interpreted as a transaction cost theory of the boundaries of the firm. It is not. First, principal/agent theory abstracts from the costs of writing contracts (if not of enforcing them). Second, the theory does not allow discrimination between, for example, an employment relation and a relation between a firm and its supplier. Arguably, this is because the category of ownership cannot be treated adequately in the comprehensive contracting set-up used in principal/agent models. For further discussion, see Hart (1995).

6 However, it has met with steadfast resistance and criticism from more traditionally minded organization scholars. The most recent and probably most sophisticated attack on organizational economics (in the guise of Williamson's transaction cost theory) is Ghoshal and Moran (1996).

7 For a particularly explicit statement, see Cheung (1983). It should be mentioned that the inability of nexus of contracts theorists to identify something called 'the boundaries of the firm' is seen by them as a virtue rather than a vice.

8 This is Williamson's term for the contractual institutions that regulate transactions and contracts, namely firms, hybrids and markets. They should not be confused with the actual contracts themselves, but are rather to be thought of as supporting frameworks, specifically frameworks that embody mechanisms for conflict resolution.

9 In contrast to the other parts of the boundary school under consideration here, it is doubtful whether there really still is a viable resource-dependence approach. In 1982, Pfeffer assimilated the approach with the population ecology perspective (Pfeffer, 1982). The justification for including it here is that Pfeffer and Salancik's book is still a standard reference in much organization theory on firm boundaries.

10 In other words, it is seen as desirable to reduce the 'power' of other firms over one's own firm. There is a presumption in the resource-dependency perspective that dependence is 'bad' and that firms will actively seek to avoid this. From a transaction cost perspective, this does not necessarily make sense if contracting is 'seen in its entirety' (Williamson, 1996). This is because even relations that are characterized by a high degree of dependence may be effective, efficient, desirable, etc. because they are supported by the appropriate governance mechanisms (for example, hostages).

11 Note that these 'dynamic transaction costs' (Langlois and Robertson, 1995) are in a different category from the transaction costs usually considered in the modern economics of organization. Transacting difficulties are not a matter of incentive problems within an otherwise well-defined and well-understood exchange context, but a matter of basic co-ordination problems. For evidence of this view, see Chandler (1962) and Langlois and Robertson (1995).

12 Foss (2000) makes an extended analysis of the relation between transaction cost theories and capabilities theories of the firm, based on Krajewski (1977).

10

Managing Beyond Boundaries:
The Dynamics of Trust in Alliances

Christian Koenig and Gilles van Wijk

Various disciplines have advocated the extension of the boundaries of the firm by the development of interfirm co-operation as an efficient way of addressing issues such as technological and institutional uncertainty, international development or even sustainable development. But the majority of the work on the extension of the boundaries of the firm by alliances, partnerships, joint ventures and other forms of collaboration has tended to focus on rather narrow issues such as the welfare aspects of restrictions to competition (Jacquemin, 1988), the appropriate governance structures or the relationship between co-operative strategy and performance.

Generally speaking, the focus of current research on the outcome of collaboration does not recognize the relationship between the process and outcome of co-operation (Hébert and Geringer, 1993) and tends to underestimate key elements of the dynamics of collaboration, in particular the role of informal processes, trust and power. This chapter aims to contribute to the 'boundary' school (see Elfring and Volberda, Chapter 1), by combining transaction cost and game theory approaches with a dynamic process perspective. Trust is a key concept, which will be used to link the formal part represented by contracts with informal processes.

The purpose of this chapter is to present a new perspective on the dynamics of co-operation, by emphasizing the role of trust as a learning process and outlining its evolving, recursive relationship with contracts. Trust is what allows co-operation and contracts to emerge, but it is also the result of interactions governed by contracts and is itself secured by those same contracts. The stance taken is that co-operation, although sought after, cannot be fully planned out. Instead it emerges from the interaction between partners, and is framed by contractual or formal control mechanisms or structural arrangements. Trust is not excluded by formal mechanisms and structure. On the contrary, it grows out of interaction, and structure and contracts only appear as a way to secure it. The blending and mutual enhancement of trust and structure may vary with the type of co-operation, such as that between industrial districts (Inzerilli, 1990), research and development partnerships, business groups or strategic alliances (Powell, 1996). But the point is that trust is neither solely traceable to shared norms and values nor derived exclusively from strategy and calculation: it is a learning process. This perspective on the dynamics of trust and co-operation is still developing and is shared by authors from various disciplines, from organization theory to economics (for example, Powell, 1996; Sabel, 1993).

The actual emergence of co-operation is what is at stake in alliances. Although these have indeed developed at rapid rates, both in numbers and in scope, their performance seems to have generated dissatisfaction; co-operation is perceived as needed or obvious as a strategy, yet the management and governance of collaborative organizations pose numerous problems. Alliances are sometimes presented as a learning race (Hamel, 1991; Hamel et al., 1989) with winners and losers or appear to be eminently unstable (Kogut, 1989). But students of alliances have also suggested that partner firms spend an inordinate amount of time elaborating sophisticated contracts and incentive schemes at the expense of flexibility, learning and actual creation of co-operation between firms (Koenig and van Wijk, 1991). It has thus been suggested that trust, and not (or not only) contracts, is a precondition to the success of alliances of all forms, allowing the boundaries of co-operation to evolve over time (Barney and Hansen, 1994; Ernst and Bleeke, 1993; Houghton, 1990; Lynch, 1989; Mohr and Spekman, 1994; Zaheer and Venkatraman, 1995). More generally, trust has become a favourite item on the list of necessary ingredients for fruitful co-operation between individuals or between firms (see, for example, Gambetta, 1988; Kramer and Tyler, 1996), if not for economic development in general (Fukuyama, 1995).

In order to introduce this notion of emerging trust and co-operation, we will look first at the relationship between trust and co-operation and between trust and contracts, which will be interpreted as sets of interaction process rules that first enable the emergence of trust and then are determined by it.

The Problem of Co-operation and the Limits of Contracts

The Problem of Co-operation

Co-ordination and co-operation have long been crucial problems for economics as well as organizational studies (see in particular Schelling, 1960). The traditional approach of economics has been based on the two basic postulates of individual rationality and the market as the social interaction device that ensures the compatibility of individual actions and decisions. These postulates are usually extended to non-market situations. Dating back to Arrow (1974), Leibenstein (1966, 1976) or Simon (1976), among others, it has long been established that organizations should not be treated as 'black boxes'. But the recognition of the importance of institutional forms, of non-market social forms, has often been achieved by economics at the expense of comprehensiveness or relevance. In an effort to make economics the 'universal grammar of social sciences' (Hirshleifer, 1985), institutional approaches, in particular, have focused on organizational behaviour as issues of agency costs, opportunistic behaviour, incentive mechanisms or transaction costs. The boundaries of the standard theory of the firm have been extended, but the issues it focuses on remain largely at the boundary of the firm, thus ignoring non-contractual forms of social relationships or interaction, based on power and authority, co-ordination and co-operation (see, for example, Bradach and Eccles, 1989; Favereau, 1993).

All forms of co-operation generate problems that are unknown to independent or central actors: ambiguity in communication, opportunism of the parties involved and uncertainty linked to the ultimate autonomy of the actors. Among the means available (power, rules, norms and values) to solve these problems in a dyadic relationship, formal rules and contractual mechanisms are often presented as efficient approaches, since they are supposed to act as incentives and control systems that should maintain the actions of partners within mutually agreed bounds.

Contracts, Incentives and Co-operation

Whether these incentives are formalized in rules or emerge from interaction and reputation mechanisms, agency and incentives theory as well as game theory and transaction cost economics all insist on basically calculative behaviour on the part of rational agents. In these approaches, the attempts to resolve the co-operation/ competition dilemma lead to the introduction of ad hoc exchange structures such as the exchange of hostages, to extensive formal contracts, and to an overemphasis on the benefits of increasing interdependence among the firms. Still, this is not sufficient to allow for opportunistic behaviour. Strictly rational behaviour, informed by transaction cost analysis and game theory, will lead markets or hierarchies to prevail, whereas alliances are presented as unstable, costly and risky governance structures (Kogut, 1989). Thus, from this perspective, co-operation appears to be the fortuitous complementarity of maximizing strategies (Sabel, 1993), a representation that does not account for the proliferation and viability of many alliances.

Let us turn to the classic example of the basic dilemma of co-operation in game theory: the prisoner's dilemma. In this game, two players interact in a way that leads them to a Nash-equilibrium situation where each finds it more advantageous not to co-operate.

Why is it, then, that we do observe stable equilibria in which firms do co-operate over time when the prisoner's dilemma is repeated? The time horizon of the game is crucial. If the game is to be repeated a finite number of times, each party has an incentive to co-operate until the last time, where each has an incentive to defect. Knowing this, each party will defect in the previous game. Taking this reasoning to its logical conclusion, each party will defect from the first game on, and the two players will, therefore, never co-operate.

A major result of game theory, however, is that the incentive to co-operate increases with the length of the time horizon. If, at any period, there is a probability that the game will be played in the next period, then an efficient strategy is to co-operate in the first period and then do whatever the other party does. This 'tit for tat' strategy and the role of the 'shadow of the future' were first analysed by Axelrod (1984) as an example of a robust strategy when playing repeated prisoners' dilemmas. Game theorists have since confirmed that when the time horizon is sufficiently long and when there is a slight probability that one player is 'crazy', that is to say, that he will always co-operate in the first period, then the other player should co-operate too. But the co-operation lasts only until the expected (small) gains of co-operating in the first few periods and the (large) gain of the defection period outweigh the prospective loss of not co-operating in subsequent periods (see Tirole, 1988).

Kreps (1990) and Kreps et al. (1982) elaborated on this situation and formulated it in terms of trust, trustworthiness and reputation. A tells B, for instance, that he will begin by trusting him, hoping that he will honour that trust, and will keep trusting B as long as that trust is not abused. If B believes A's statement, and if they interact repeatedly, then the trust arrangement is self-enforcing. Dasgupta (1988: 59) puts it like this.

> For trust to be developed between individuals they must have repeated encounters, and they must have some memory of previous experiences. Moreover, for honesty to have potency as a concept, there must be some cost involved in honest behaviour. And finally, trust is linked with reputation, and reputation has to be acquired.

But, in that case, can trust be distinguished from calculatedness? Williamson (1993b) points out that 'calculative assessments of the efficacy of reputation effects are ... properly included' in efficient contracting devices. 'Reference to trust adds nothing' and the use of trust in game theory as in many other contexts, according to Williamson, obscures rather than illuminates the interaction mechanisms between exchanging parties. For Williamson, most of what is ascribed to trust can actually be drawn from traditional calculated behaviour.

Williamson's position is interesting to the extent that he spells out a sort of gradation of trust, from trust as a risk-reducing mechanism to trust as an informal control mechanism in an interpersonal relationship. In this relationship, for instance between X and Y, there are conditions for trust to exist.

1   X must consciously refuse to monitor Y
2   X is predisposed to ascribe good intentions to Y when things go wrong
3   X treats Y in a discrete structural way (Williamson, 1993b: 483).

One should add reciprocity to these conditions. Therefore, personal trust or nearly calculative trust, is informal, in the sense that no contractual mechanisms are used to monitor the behaviour, and condition 3 indicates that change dynamics are based on discrete modifications, on mutually admitted reforms. Since 'calculative trust is a contradiction in terms' (Williamson, 1993b: 463), trust exists only in very special cases of interpersonal relationships, such as love or friendship, which Williamson calls 'nearly non-calculative trust'. Thus, instead of examining the impact of trust on a dynamic relationship, Williamson limits its role to close interpersonal relationships and claims the concept plays no role in trade relationships.

A major limitation of Williamson's approach, as well as that of game theory, is that the games and transactions are 'disembedded' from their social context

(Granovetter, 1985), from the personal relationships between organizations (Ring and van de Ven, 1989, 1993) and that there is an infinite number of equilibria (Dasgupta, 1988; Fudenberg and Maskin, 1986). As much as we concur with Williamson's implicit proposition that trust is not instrumental, we must admit that trade relationships involve more than calculative risk taking; individuals and groups who need co-operative co-ordination use numerous value references outside the realm of economic calculus (Boltanski and Thévenot, 1991). It has been shown, for example, that a tit for tat interaction à la Axelrod between anonymous people with no neighbourhood or familiarity relationship, interacting on a random basis, does not lead to stable co-operation (Boyer and Orléan, 1995). More generally, what is at stake in trust and co-operation is a plurality of individual social links with respect to which economic strategizing appears too restrictive.

Moreover, as stated above, Williamson's approach is static. Yet, an interesting result of studies on alliances is that repeated interaction is conducive to trust, and thus allows partner firms to avoid many of the costs associated with formal, equity alliances (Gulati, 1995).

The Limits of Contracts

In game theory as in transaction cost analysis, the current behaviour of partners in a co-operation derives from backward deductions from an anticipated series of risky interactions. Expectations may be governed by a system of formal rules or contracts, thus the problem for partner firms becomes the elaboration of efficient contracts. But contracts, or reputation effects, need to be secured, so that each party is able to evaluate whether deviations from prescribed behaviour will be sanctioned. Formal or implicit contracts require a third party to ensure that formal or implicit obligations are met and rules enforced. As Shapiro (1987) suggested in the case of impersonal relations or March and Olsen (1989) in the case of democratic systems, institutions may act as substitutes of trust in the sense that they transform interaction and co-operation problems into issues of risk analysis, but then the question is of knowing who guards the guardians of trust. Answering this question ultimately requires a system of references, values and behaviours outside the realm of economic analysis and calculative behaviour.

Contracts and incentives have other limits. They are essentially conceived to reduce the impact of opportunism, seen as the key driver of interfirm relationship. It is not only a pessimistic view, but also a static approach; by focusing on appropriate contractual mechanisms, transaction cost analysis, in particular, neglects how relationships may evolve, how interaction can modify expectations and how rules can change over time. Similarly, game theory focuses on backward deduction, at the expense of possible 'forward induction' (Ponssard, 1994) and of learning from ongoing interaction.

Considering the evolution of co-operative relationships and the learning process they generate, we suggest a different interpretation of the role of contracts. They should be seen not only as interaction process rules that allow commitments to be made and expectations to be formed, but also as the framework within which adaptation and learning can take place, allowing the scope of co-operation to evolve from individuals to institutions as a whole, from limited tasks to full-blown projects and from one-shot deals to long-term alliances. As we shall see, trust that develops outside the realm of interest and calculus then becomes a key ingredient in making co-operation a success.

Trust: Within and Beyond Contract

The Role of Trust: Perspectives

There are numerous definitions of trust, in various streams of academic traditions ranging from interpersonal relationships to economic exchanges and ethical principles (for a review of different fields, see Hosmer, 1995). One common trait found in numerous fields, however, is the relationship between trust and vulnerability and dependence. Vulnerability exists when social exchange involves unspecified obligations for which no binding contracts can be written, and the decision to trust is dependent on the action of the other party. This is the view shared by many authors, including Blau (1964), Gambetta (1988) and Luhmann (1973, 1988). The vulnerability argument is also found in Sabel (1993) for whom 'when parties to an exchange trust each other, they share mutual confidence that others will not exploit any adverse selection, moral hazard, hold-up or any other vulnerabilities that might exist in a particular exchange'. Therefore, trust is always a risky investment (Mayer et al., 1995).

Neo-institutionalists have focused on the role of institutions in reducing this risk. In this perspective, social systems emerge from interactions between actors, which rely on social mechanisms that channel social actors' expectations and actions, and where trust reduces the complexity of social interaction, enabling actors to establish specific expectations about their future behaviour (Lane and Bachmann, 1995, 1996; Luhmann, 1973; Powell and DiMaggio, 1991). Following a long tradition dating back to Durkheim, Simmel and Douglas, trust is thus based on shared interpretations; on conventional rather than formal mechanisms. It cannot develop solely from the realms of interest and calculus.

There are several ways of achieving this, as proposed by Zucker (1986). She distinguishes between process-based trust, characteristic-based trust and institutionally based trust. Process-based trust emerges out of experience and interaction between actors (trust is an investment in signals of trustworthiness), while characteristic-based trust is tied to the similarity (culture, education, etc.) of backgrounds of people involved in interaction or exchange (trust is free or is taken for granted) and institutionally based trust is tied to formal structures, depending on individual or firm-specific attributes such as certified competencies, legal status, membership of trade associations and so forth (trust can be purchased). The evolution towards institutionally based trust, or system trust is, for Giddens (1990) and Luhmann (1973), an attribute of modern societies.

Trust is produced among social actors when they hold shared beliefs and hence build up mutual expectations. This view is not different from the conventionalist perspective, where conventions allow actors to develop mutual expectations about the competencies and behaviour of others, thus relieving actors from the need to speculate about others' intentions (Salais, 1994). As such, it does not require altruistic behaviour. Institutions, contract law or business associations provide such shared norms or knowledge, making the risk of trust bearable in the institutionalist perspective, while the conventionalists would argue that rules, seen as heuristics or cognitive devices, fulfil this function of collectively acknowledged reference for interaction. For Luhmann, institutions, contracts or rules can reduce the risks of interaction without eliminating them, yet they provide shared meanings rather than a basis for calculation, whereas for Coleman (1990) the decision to trust is based upon calculation of the gains and losses from the risk of trust.

Trust is an informal mode of control governing mutually identified actors (Koenig and van Wijk, 1991; van Wijk, 1985). It reduces uncertainty regarding mutual behaviour through a process of self-control. Trust is a belief of one actor about his/her relationship to another actor. This belief leads each party to act in mutually relevant situations in order to enhance the other party's interest with the implicit expectation that the other will reciprocate in kind, acknowledging his/her obligation to the first actor. The trusting party develops mostly implicit anticipations regarding the trusted party's behaviour. Aware of the anticipations regarding its general conduct, the trusted party becomes trustworthy if it feels the obligation to fulfil these anticipations. Obligation is a sense of duty not necessarily related to material sanctions. The combination of anticipation and obligation yields an effective informal mode of co-ordination. In addition, the existence of trust in a relationship gives the co-operation a flexibility not available in formal transactions; it makes possible initiatives that are outside the agenda. This entails one actor drawing upon a form of credit while the other forbears, with the expectation that ultimately both will be better off (Buckley and Casson, 1988).

Trust generates a sense of predictability of others' behaviour, thus reducing sources of uncertainty (Luhmann, 1973, 1988). It makes incomplete contracts workable (Macaulay, 1963) and it economizes on transaction costs. 'Trust is one resource that, by diminishing contract uncertainty, lowers the cost of exchanges in the economy' (Brenner, 1983: 95). This argument is also made by Bromiley and Cummings (1995). More generally, as Arrow (1974: 23) states, 'Trust is an important lubricant of a social system'. This point of view is shared by numerous authors who explain that trust is indispensable in social relationships (see Blau, 1964; Lewis and Weigert, 1985; Zucker, 1986) or, more specifically, in sustaining manufacturer–distributor relationships (Anderson and Narus, 1990; Anderson and Weitz, 1989).

The process of anticipation in effect leads to the implicit recognition of the parties' actual characteristics, for example, technical capacity, punctuality, way of doing things and relative power. Moreover, trust helps the emergence of a single locus of control at the alliance level.

Trust as Predictability

Trust as predictability of other parties' behaviour prevails in much of the literature cited above. As stated by Lewis and Weigert, 'Trust exists in a social system insofar as the members of that system act according to and are secure in the expected futures constituted by the presence of each other or their symbolic representation' (1985: 968). This does not require, however, that the parties have common interests. Actually, if they did have common interests, the question of trust would not arise. As pointed out by Zucker, there can be some collective orientation at the beginning of the interaction, 'but self-interest is often expected and legitimate at subsequent stages of the exchange'. Heide and John (1988) have suggested that when partners are not equal in power or relative dependence, the more dependent firm seeks to protect its transaction-specific assets by taking various dependence-balancing actions. Trust between parties may reduce this need to offset dependence. But it can also be said that trust may be supported by unequivocal power relationships, as has been suggested regarding alliances with Japanese firms (Hamel, 1991).

In this context, the creation of trust may only be a manifestation of possibly unobtrusive power, which can occur through the institution of relevant procedures with compliance obligations or by displaying the appropriate symbolic representation, which may be acquired, as in the case of degrees and competencies (Lewis and Weigert, 1985). Trust is, therefore, like power, instrumental. It can be consciously built to serve or protect the interest of a specific party, without the necessary reciprocity. Both serve the purpose of reducing the complexity of social interaction and are therefore sometimes presented as functional equivalents (Luhmann, 1973). This does not mean that expectations cannot be built, with the obligation to fulfil them, but it means that a concept that cannot clearly distinguish between the manipulation of meaning and symbols and a genuine attempt to create shared meaning is not very useful. It is, to paraphrase Gambetta (1988), difficult to believe in a concept of trust that runs the risk of considering trust as illusory or manipulated, thereby referring to subordination mechanisms.

It follows from this discussion that instrumental visions of trust have two significant shortcomings. From an analytical point of view they do not provide more insight than power. Rather, the two concepts tend to be, respectively, a soft and a hard version of otherwise functionally equivalent notions leading to co-ordination and reduction of uncertainty. By itself, the analytical perspective is, however, a very narrow approach to concepts of the significance of trust and power. Indeed, a deeper insight is to be gained from the ontological perspective. In essence, trust appears to be outside the scope of instrumentality. It can exist only on the basis of its own merits: it can be learned, it can evolve, and it can be broken, without there being any practical need for it. It is a by-product of relationships; it survives as long as it is not being broken, i.e. when trust is instrumentalized. Indeed, the instrumental vision stems from a paradox. Trust cannot be programmed but, paradoxically, as long as it prevails it is a wonderful facilitator, providing opportunities for flexible and creative behaviour. Power stands in sharp contrast, because it is purely instrumental and central to all relationships, but also critically limited to the existing social system. Power's only creativity is tied to the astute use made of the people, the processes and the organizational structures. Trust reaches beyond this, and enables new collective arrangements to emerge in the anticipation/obligation learning dynamic.

Initiation of Boundary Transactions

The initiation of boundary transactions is a challenge to the parties in as much as there is no a priori structure ensuring convergence of the firms' actions. Even if objectives are broadly shared, the mutual adjustment required for successful transactions involves reciprocal actions that soon reveal differences in specific objectives, and that are not checked by either a detailed contract, or a single locus of control. Yet firms manage to set up co-ordinated actions and even to collaborate intensively.

The broader legal structures governing the firms' behaviour in their environment, as well as 'normal business practice' are not sufficient either to achieve boundary exchanges without serious risks of genuine misunderstanding or of opportunism, hence Williamson's (1975) argument for hierarchies. The question therefore remains of how substantial exchanges are achieved even among competing firms. Once the first arrangements take shape, they create a precedent and, therefore, have a referential quality. They determine future developments to a large extent in a stage-setting process (Bettenhausen and Murnighan, 1985). The importance of understanding the initiation process is further reinforced by the fact that it sets the stage in a definitive way.

This crucial process can only take place when there is trust among the parties. Defined as a process of anticipation and obligation, it enables the creative, flexible and idiosyncratic adjustment that is not possible with rules, values and norms.

The Role of Trust

Deutsch (1962) suggested that trust was a preliminary, necessary, ingredient for people to start a relationship. The particular importance of trust during the initiation phase of interfirm relations is due to the expectation of competent action, heeding mutual interests, in the give and take process. Competent action is defined on the basis of each party's expertise and resources in general and, as such, is radically different from rational expectation. Rational expectation relates specifically to the contents of action, while expectation of competent action leaves it to the other party to decide (creatively) upon the appropriate course of action in the mutual interest of both parties.

We should emphasize that this departure of the orthodox rational expectation has far reaching consequences with respect to theoretical underpinnings. Indeed, the 'invisible hand' paradigm suggests that if everybody optimizes locally, the market forces will ensure a collective progress. Instead, the present argument proposes that individuals can and, occasionally, do forego their immediate interest to achieve a collective purpose. The collective achievement may be superior, but it entails an individual exposure to risk and breach of trust, so a dynamic balance must be maintained continuously between the level of the achievement and the level of risk.

Development of Boundary Transactions

The role of experience in the development and maintenance of trust has often been mentioned (Gulati, 1995; Sabel, 1993). If it is not considered here to be a source of trust, it nevertheless plays a significant role in the development of boundary transactions and in the reinforcement of trust. Indeed, trust fills out a number of blanks in the analysis of existing boundary relationships in alliances. It explains the process of working together, as opposed to working side by side, independently, but in a complementary fashion.

Working together refers typically to the creative collaboration of an advertising agency with its customer, whereas working side by side refers to situations of formal co-ordination, for instance customer–supplier relations in a competitive market. The nature of exchanges varies from well-defined predictable co-ordination, to intensive ad hoc emerging and creative collaboration. Co-ordination and collaboration are fundamentally different, in terms of process and of outcomes.

Co-ordination

Co-ordination can be planned and programmed ahead of time leading to a formal arrangement and high efficiency. On either side of the boundary the relevant contributions are integrated in the overall processes of organization without any disruption of each firms' objectives. The decision to continue or to interrupt is based on the balance between resources committed and returns.

The efficiency of co-ordination does not depend on trust. Only the initiating process requires trust in order for formal arrangements to be defined jointly. Afterwards, market forces and the firms' private interests ensure efficient transactions.

Collaboration

Collaboration entails a mutual commitment of resources in an open-ended process. These situations of co-operation are not formally planned, but are defined by their objectives. Collaborating firms need to trust each other to achieve the level of creative, mutual adjustment required. Collaboration is distinguished from co-ordination by the shift in objectives and in locus of control.

Objectives are more than just shared. The intensive collaboration leads to a fusion into an alliance that appropriates the objectives. The alliance becomes an organization in its own right, identified and defined by its objectives. As soon as the fusion of objectives becomes effective, thanks to mutual trust, the alliance becomes efficient. Conversely, when opportunism of the collaboration is called into question, and formal control is imposed, then efficiency achieved by the alliance collapses. Intensive collaboration for flexibility and creativity requires a single locus of control, otherwise expectations of competent action and responsiveness through heeding resulting obligations cannot be achieved.

Mutual Enhancement between Trust and Rules

The preceding discussion suggests that, depending on the nature of the transactions, trust or rules are more likely to ensure efficiency of the boundary transactions. When flexible and creative exchanges are necessary, building upon mutual contributions, trust actually leads to a transformation of boundary transactions into a new entity, the alliance. This should not imply, however, that once trust or rules have generated a transaction mode this mode will prevail indefinitely. Indeed, there appears to be instead a strong mutual enhancement between trust and rules.

Formalization in Collaborations

The process of 'learning each other' in a trust relationship makes it possible to achieve a very productive relationship in terms of taking advantage of mutual competencies in a creative fashion. However, pragmatism and efficiency soon lead to the need to formalize at some level that which has been successfully experimented and can be exploited advantageously in a systematic fashion – for example, a production technology, an organizational arrangement or a more generic research method or strategy.

Formalizing provides a variety of advantages and safeguards. First, it ensures a reproducibility in time and space that renders wider exploitation possible. Second, it leads to control. Based upon the initial formalization, some idea of relative performance can be derived, and incremental improvements can be tested and implemented. Third, formalization leads to the legitimation of an existing mode of transaction. The stakes can get very high in collaborations and unless some formalization is implemented, failure can be extremely damaging, if it turns out afterwards that no formal controls existed to monitor the exchanges of competence or capital assets.

Even intensive collaborations based on trust are therefore expected to evolve into a level of formalization. This avoids overextending trust and actually provides a basis for further trust-based developments.

Conclusion

Managing beyond boundaries requires trust. However, trust cannot be instrumentalized, unlike power. Indeed, as a dialectical process between actors, trust achieves co-ordination through anticipation and obligation in a dynamic learning process. Trust is more aptly described as a by-product of exchanges. There is no cost associated with the development of trust, except when there is manipulation, but trust has clear benefits, even if they remain mostly hidden and intangible, such as reducing uncertainty, obviating monitoring costs typical for formal arrangements, and creation of value in the exchange processes.

This chapter has contributed to the boundary school by combining theories dealing with the formal side of co-operation with theories focusing on the informal aspects of co-operative arrangements. The interaction and dynamics between the formal arrangements as represented by contracts and trust as an informal learning process is a central issue in our understanding of the emergence and maintenance of co-operative arrangements. In this chapter some observations have been made concerning the interaction and dynamics between contracts and trust.

More research is needed to validate the conclusions made here. But the research strategy should not be to associate simply positive alliance outcomes with the presence of trust. This chapter suggests, rather, that the dynamics of the learning process should be better understood.

11

Strategic Alliances

Janine Stiles

This chapter focuses upon aspects of the development and stability of relationships with business partners as part of the boundary school in strategy. Specifically it identifies the need to measure and assess the capabilities of partner firms both when entering, and while operating within, the lifetime of an alliance arrangement in an effort to understand how these might be used to influence the relationship. Management of these traditionally 'fuzzy' boundaries between partner organizations, which lack the traditional control mechanisms associated with ownership, has proven frequently in the past to be a minefield of problems, made more difficult by the relative complexity and dynamism that this organizational form represents. This chapter looks to address one aspect of this problem, that of what influences a firm to act in a co-operative or a competitive way within a partnership, and how this has an influence, therefore, upon the ultimate organizational arrangement created.

Background

The popularity of working in partnership in business has exploded over the past few years with current estimates of growth averaging between 27% and 30% per annum in the industrialized countries (Anderson and Narus, 1990; Bleeke and Ernst, 1991). This surge in interest has been fuelled by the characteristics of the current business environment. Growing competitiveness, the emergence of new markets, technological developments and the maturity and homogeneity of markets have all helped to push back industrial boundaries and have facilitated the globalization of markets within the world economy. Within this new and volatile environment, partnership can offer a low-cost and flexible opportunity for the firm to maintain or improve its competitive position while allowing it to keep its options open with respect to which technologies to pursue or which markets to target. It can even allow the flexibility of multiple options to be explored as opposed to the high cost and restrictions of an acquisition or merger (Doz, 1992).

As the concept has developed over time, partnering arrangements have grown to become increasingly complex, often resulting in multiple collaborative arrangements with both vertical and horizontal links (Hamel, 1990; Harrigan, 1986; Wheatcroft and Lipman, 1990). As a result, this is now seen as one of the most flexible and important competitive tools for businesses operating in today's global environment (Geringer, 1988; Geringer, 1991; Goldenberg, 1988; Harrigan, 1986; Jones and Shill, 1991; Lewis, 1990; Lorange and Roos, 1992). Many businesses now perceive collaborative ventures as critical in their plans to establish strategic business networks and as valuable strategic weapons with which to battle in the increasingly competitive business environment (Geringer, 1991; Harrigan, 1987; Joynt, 1990; Lei and Slocum, 1992; Lei, 1993; Takec and Singh, 1992).

Various terms have been used to describe forms of strategic partnering. These include 'international coalitions' (Porter and Fuller, 1986), 'strategic networks' (Jarillo, 1988) and, most commonly, 'strategic alliances'. Definitions are equally varied. An alliance may be seen as the 'joining of forces and resources, for a specified or indefinite period, to achieve a common objective' (Takec and Singh, 1992). This definition reflects the traditional view of partnerships being based upon creating value for the participant firms. Other definitions, however, identify a more competitive aspect to the relationship. Lei and Slocum (1992) define alliances as 'coalignments between two or more firms in which the partners hope to learn and acquire from each other the technologies, products, skills and knowledge that are not otherwise available to their competitors'. If this is the case, the alliance, far from being an advantageous co-operative arrangement as the previous definition suggests, may increase the competitive pressure on an individual partner. This aspect of the strategic alliance has been termed 'collaborative competition' and has the distinctive aim of value appropriation (Hamel, 1990, 1991).

Co-operative Aspects of Strategic Alliances

Research suggests that one of the benefits that may be attributed to a partner relationship stems from the pooling of resources and/or capabilities, and the mutual dependence aspects of the relationship that can be used for strategic advantage (Lorange and Roos, 1992; Lynch, 1990; Mohr and Nevin, 1990; Mohr and Spekman, 1994). Without this mutual sharing of resources, strategic alliances can at worst be an inefficient and ineffective means of operation. As an illustration of this, Harrigan and Dalmia (1991) cite the example of an American firm with three joint ventures in Asia and demonstrate that 'without this foundation for sharing information and co-ordinating activities, no communications were occurring in activities that needed substantial co-ordination to meet developmental deadlines'. It may further be argued that where one partner begins to operate for its own benefit within the relationship 'the relationship will suffer and *both* will feel the negative consequences' (original emphasis, Mohr and Spekman, 1994). Thus, research suggests that benefits to be gained through the pooling of resources in this form of operation necessitates a co-operative approach to the partnership as a prerequisite to success.

Over time depreciation of resources and capabilities through imitation by rivals may result in an individual firm's competitive advantage, and its consequent returns, being eroded. Co-operation then also provides the opportunity to upgrade both firms' positions, comparatively more rapidly than could be achieved individually, through the pooling of their resources and capabilities (Grant, 1991; Mahoney and Pandian, 1992). This pooling has the potential to result in a greater degree of benefit than the proportional result expected. (For a discussion on the overlap between the capabilities perspective and boundary school theories, see Foss, Chapter 9.) It may be argued, therefore, that the synergy created by mutual co-operation is a further driver of strategic advantage within a partnership.

Interorganizational co-operation can also result in a reduction in transaction costs and, therefore, enable competitive advantage through increased economic efficiency (Hennart, 1988; Kogut, 1988; Williamson, 1975). These costs may include financial costs, but also extend to non-financial costs such as the loss of specific knowledge, and costs associated with uncertainty or supplier/buyer power. Co-operative partnerships may, therefore, be seen as providing protection or security to firms where the option of using the market system is viewed as a high risk and, therefore, problematic solution. From this perspective alliances may be viewed as allowing evasion of small-number bargaining and, consequently, an enhancement of competitive positioning (Kogut, 1988; Lyons, 1991).

Co-operation within partnerships can also be viewed as aiding replication of experiential knowledge such as complex organizational routines that may not easily be transferred through the market. An alliance partnership can allow a firm to replicate effectively a particular process within the partner firm and thus efficiently transfer know-how which may be otherwise encumbered by the hazards surrounding the pricing of information (Kogut, 1988). The advantages associated with this stem from the expanded market/capacity/efficiency potential, which an alliance partnership can offer once both firms involved gain the benefits associated with the particular process transferred (Berg et al., 1981; Kogut, 1988; Mohr and Spekman, 1994). From this perspective it may be argued that strategic alliances designed to exploit each player's unique characteristics to maximum effect will produce the greatest competitive advantage (Grant, 1991; Mahoney and Pandian, 1992).

Competitive Aspects of Strategic Alliances

The concept of skill building as a key explicit goal can, however, also be viewed from the competitive perspective. The subsequent loss of the core competence or capabilities that provide a firm with its individual competitive advantage, as exclusive knowledge or expertise is passed on to the partner firm, can result in the removal of the reason behind the partnership, and ultimately in termination of the relationship (Hamel, 1990, 1991; Lyons, 1991). It may further result in a loss of market positioning for the weaker firm as the stronger partner uses the skills/resources appropriated from its partner to advance its position (Badaracco, 1991; Hamel, 1990, 1991). Thus, although there are perceived benefits in the alliance as a mechanism for transfer of organizational knowledge, this 'must be evaluated within the context of the competitive incentives among the partners and the competitive rivalry within the industry' (Kogut, 1988). The need for each partner to protect its strategic resources therefore needs to be recognized (Jones and Shill, 1991; Lorange and Roos, 1992).

Competitive tactics used by a partner firm can also induce a level of dependency in a weaker firm. This can skew influence and control within the relationship and is often a precursor to a merger or acquisition attempt by the dominant player (Devlin and Bleackley, 1988; Hamel, 1990, 1991; Lyons, 1991).

The strategic alliance relationship may encourage a partner firm to concentrate its resources on a specific section of production or service in which it can develop a particular expertise that will benefit the partnership. The consequent focusing of skills and resources can result in an effective de-skilling of competencies or processes crucial to the overall process, creating an external dependence for things such as components, supplies, designs, skills and technologies (Lei and Slocum, 1992). While the alliance partnership continues, this alliance dependency can encourage distortions in the control of the partnership and may again speed the decline, and possible take-over of the partnership by the dominant party (Hamel, 1990, 1991; Lorange and Roos, 1992; Lorange et al., 1992).

As a further corollary to the de-skilling characteristics that can accompany an alliance, the partnership arrangement may also instil an element of inertia within the individual organizations involved. As explicit competition within the market is reduced through alliance formation, 'development inertia' can occur within the industry as lower levels of competition in the market reduce the incentive for innovation (Lei and Slocum, 1992). Thus the implicit impact of the alliance partnership may be evidenced in generally lower levels of development within the industry. The ultimate implications of this may be a reduction in the ability to prolong the product's lifecycle within the industry or restrictions in the development of a new product lifecycle prior to decline.

A further competitive reason for entering an alliance has been highlighted by Hamel (1990, 1991). He identifies the use of the alliance relationship as a means of more accurately calibrating a partner's strength and weaknesses than would otherwise be possible. As a consequence, the competitive risk in future collisions with the partner may be significantly altered. In this respect the alliance may, again, be viewed as an internally competitive, rather than co-operative, tool.

Thus, the co-operative and competitive aspects of the strategic alliance can have major implications both for the individual partners and for the future of the alliance relationship. From the co-operative perspective they can facilitate rapid upgrade in resources and create synergistic benefits from the pooling of resources/capabilities. They can also help to reduce costs and encourage efficiency through the transfer of knowledge and capabilities that might otherwise not be effectively transferable through the market system. From the competitive perspective, however, the alliance may result in a loss of core competencies and capabilities, encourage alliance dependency and loss of control, and introduce a form of development inertia into the industry. This may ultimately have implications for the potential product lifecycle and for the balance of future competition within the industry.

The influence of these different perspectives, therefore, has significant implications for firms considering entering a partnership. As Lei and Slocum (1992) state 'although collaboration and competition do go hand-in-hand, how managers approach this duality will significantly affect the firm's propensity for learning and developing new skills'. The co-operative/competitive distinction does not, therefore, necessarily denote alternative forms of alliance arrangements. It may be argued that this simply reflects different combinations of alliance 'drivers' in each participating firm, and the consequent motivational differences that these induce.

Although co-operative and competitive intents or abilities may co-exist for each partner within a relationship, how these are emphasized or operationalized together will, therefore, dictate the overall potential and character the alliance will ultimately adopt. It is important to examine these two perspectives further to try to develop a better understanding of which characteristics either of the firm or of the particular relationship can influence the degree of co-operative and/or competitive intent within a partnership.

Evaluating the Theories

Six major theoretical streams used to interpret alliance management and behaviour may be identified. These include strategic choice or positioning (Harrigan, 1988), international business theory (Berg et al., 1981), negotiations theory (Gray and Yan, 1992), transaction cost theory (Hennart, 1988; Kogut, 1988; Williamson, 1975), game theory (von Neumann and Morgenstern, 1944) and resource-dependency theory (Hamel, 1990; Hansen and Wernerfelt, 1989; Penrose, 1985). Each has contributed towards a further understanding of the influences upon the strategic alliance arrangement. However, although these theories share some commonalities, the objectives they attribute to firms are fundamentally different (Kogut, 1988) and each have specific limitations that need to be considered.

Strategic choice or behaviour theory stems from the concept that a firm will choose a particular strategy based upon profit maximization through competitive advantage in the market place in relation to its rivals (Harrigan, 1988). Although useful, therefore, in evaluating aspects of the alliance associated with strategic symmetry (Gray and Yan, 1992; Harrigan, 1988; Vickers, 1985), the perspective appears firmly focused on the achievement of value creation and less directly on the competitive aspects of collaboration. Thus the application of this theory alone to research of this type would seem to require significant compensatory weightings and re-interpretation to reduce the inherent bias in the approach.

International business theorists perceive the role of the strategic alliance as one of achieving global competitive advantage, a role which is viewed primarily as a transitional state, operating as a vehicle for total ownership (Gray and Yan, 1992). Although not biased towards a competitive or a co-operative view, the theory does not appear to take into account the more stable forms of partnerships that may now be identified. It appears, therefore, to be somewhat limited in the scope of the alliance operations that can be encompassed by this theoretical approach.

Transaction cost theory focuses upon the increase in economic efficiency that may be attained through interorganizational co-operation (Williamson, 1975). From this view firms will choose to co-operate and internalize their transactions, rather than use the market system if that option will result in a lower transaction cost to the company than the market can offer. It is, therefore, useful in distinguishing between different forms of entry mode into international markets (Gray and Yan, 1992). It also acknowledges both competitive and co-operative aspects of a collaborative partnership. However, as it focuses upon the formation process of alliances rather than the subsequent development, it lacks a dynamic aspect pertinent to alliance behaviour.

Game theory (von Neumann and Morgenstern, 1944) considers the operation of the firm in terms of anticipating or predicting competitors' reactions to any movement a firm might make (Hay and Williamson, 1991). This may be viewed in terms of zero sum, positive sum (co-operative), or negative sum (competitive) results. The theory is therefore useful in providing an initial framework for analysis in terms of incorporating both a co-operative and a competitive dimension. It also highlights the interdependency aspect of the alliance relationship. Although criticized by some authors for over-simplifying the situation, it is a useful starting point for consideration of alliance research.

The resource-based theory focuses upon the resources and capabilities of the firm as providing the foundation for its long-term strategy (Grant, 1991). An underlying characteristic of this view is that resources and capabilities are heterogeneous and, as a consequence of this, each firm develops its own unique character, resulting in sustainable performance differences (Penrose, 1985). This theory usefully draws upon the benefits of transaction cost theory by considering the alliance in terms of transaction options. Further, econometric studies appear to support the theory that firm-specific resources and capabilities act as a driving force for the firm's diversification strategy, as they underline the firm's emphasis on growth in its attempts to transfer intangible capital between related activities. It appears, therefore, to have a recognized application to alliance operations as a key diversification/growth strategy that should provide a contribution not only to the formation process, but also throughout the continuing process of the alliance relationship (Mahoney and Pandian, 1992), thus incorporating the ability to compliment the dynamic element that characterizes this form of business operation. A further strength of this paradigm is its ability to fit comfortably within the context of organizational economics while remaining complementary to industrial organization theory. Thus, it may be argued that it provides a unifying theory within business management research. Finally, the theory appears to provide an unbiased basis from which to view the co-operative/competitive aspects of intent.

It may be suggested, therefore, that the simple sum game approach to evaluating the strategic alliance identified in game theory provides a useful basis to begin study of this form of organizational behaviour. However, in order to consider the factors influencing choice within this study, the resource-based theory can help to provide further insights relevant to this form of investigation.

Towards an Initial Framework
of Competitive/Co-operative Intent

Previous research on alliances has tended to bias investigations towards either the co-operative or the competitive aspects of the phenomenon. It is argued here, however, that prior identification of the factors that influence the degree of competitive and/or co-operative intent in an alliance relationship would enhance understanding of alliance formulation and operation and enable managers to plan their strategic partnerships more effectively.

The theoretical evaluation above can be used to assist in the identification of factors that are likely to influence the extent to which firms adopt a co-operative and/or a competitive intent. These include:

- the level of mobility
- the level of imitability
- the level of uniqueness
- value to the partner firm.

The Level of Mobility

The level of mobility of the key resources and/or capabilities of the firm from one partner to the other may be seen as a factor influencing intent within a strategic partnership. Not all resources are easily or equally transferable (Grant, 1991; Peteraf, 1993). At one extreme mobility may be high, at the other extreme things such as tacit knowledge, encompassing specific market knowledge, politics, skills and experience of operations, may prove much more difficult to transfer (Hennart, 1988; Kogut, 1988; Teece, 1986). Thus the 'capture' of some key capabilities or resources can prove more difficult than others and may necessitate the transfer of key personnel with the implicit knowledge required. It may be argued, therefore, that the level of mobility of a partner's key resources or capabilities may have an influence upon the intent with which a firm enters an alliance partnership. This begs the formulation of a research question around the mobility factor considering this question: to what extent does the mobility of the resources or competencies of a partner firm key to the relationship influence the co-operative or competitive emphasis within the intent of an entrant firm?[1]

The Level of Imitability

Where the key resources and/or capabilities of a partner firm are perceived as highly immobile, an alternative approach may be to adopt a policy of replication or imitation (Grant, 1991). However, the emphasis here will be significantly influenced by the cost/benefit involved – both in financial and temporal terms – and the ease of imitation, as some capabilities are more easily imitated than others, particularly those based on highly complex organizational routines or those fused into the firm's corporate culture. Where there are many obstacles or a high cost associated with imitation it may be argued that firms will be less likely to enter a partnership with a competitive intent. The research question associated with this aspect is, therefore: to what extent does the ease of imitability of key resources or capabilities of a partner firm influence the competitive or co-operative intent of an entrant firm?

The Level of Uniqueness

It has been argued previously that all resources and capabilities are, to varying extents, unique in that the productive value of the resources and capabilities are basically heterogeneous. This heterogeneity can result in varying levels of efficiency, superiority and utility for the firm concerned (Barney, 1991; Penrose, 1985; Peteraf, 1993). As superior resources are also limited in supply, this level of uniqueness can act as a driving force for alliance partnerships, as the more unique a key capability or resource appears to be, the more value it is likely to add (Mahoney and Pandian, 1992; Peteraf, 1993). It may, therefore, be suggested that the level of uniqueness must have an influence upon the intent with which firms enter and operate an alliance partnership. Thus a further research question stemming from this is: to what extent does the level of uniqueness of key resources or capabilities of a partner firm influence the intent with which the entrant firm enters and operates within the alliance partnership?

Value to the Partner Firm

The concept of value needs, however, to be considered further. Although the resources and capabilities have a value, different values may be implied for the same capabilities and resources between different firms. This may be due to the different supporting resources of an individual firm. It may also stem from the different forms and ways in which these resources or capabilities may be applied by an individual firm. Differences will, therefore, exist in the perceived value to be gained from acquisition of a particular resource or capability (Hennart, 1988; Peteraf, 1983). This value may be measured in terms of current or long-term sustainable value (Grant, 1991). It may, therefore, be suggested that a further question in respect of this research is: to what extent will the perceived value of a partner firm's key resources and capabilities induce a competitive or a co-operative intent on the part of an entrant firm?

The four key factors above appear to encompass the main aspects that influence the co-operative/competitive intent of an entrant firm. However, it may be argued that these simply form a theoretical intent which would not be realizable without a positive evaluation of an additional four factors:

- the level of transparency of the partner firm
- the level of complexity
- the level of cultural compatibility
- the level of experience.

The Level of Transparency of the Partner Firm

The extent to which a partner firm allows the entrant firm access to its key resources or capabilities has been defined as transparency (Grant, 1991; Hamel, 1990, 1991). There has to be a degree of sharing in any partnership; even those who are characteristically protective need to offer enough to provide an incentive for the partnership to occur. However, the level of openness assumed by each partner may differ. Where the level of transparency is high, either due to agreement, ineptitude or inability by the partner firm to protect itself, access to information and information sharing is relatively straightforward. In consequence, a higher transfer of skills or competencies than was either agreed or wanted may occur (Hamel, 1990). On the other hand, where access is very restricted, either due to deliberate mistrust of the partner firm or due to environmental restrictions, such as regulatory barriers or political disagreement, transference of even highly valued or imitable skills may prove problematic to the entrant firm. In consequence a further question which may be posed is: to what extent does the level of transparency of a partner firm support the competitive or co-operative intent of an entrant firm?

The Level of Complexity

The level of complexity or involvement by one partner with another may vary significantly. At one extreme partnerships may be simple marketing agreements that operate at arms' length with little additional involvement between the two parties concerned, and at the other extreme the partners may be tied firmly together in a wide-ranging alliance or joint venture with possibly cross-equity investment, a sharing of resources, functions and interlinking systems. The latter form of partnership can impose a high level of interdependence within the relationship, thus making it more difficult for either partner to terminate the arrangement (Stiles, 1994). Additionally, many organizations today may be part of larger, highly complex multiple systems or 'spiders' webs' of alliances (Harrigan, 1986). In this respect firms may not only be tied to the direct partner, but also into a larger network, departure from which could result in significant losses. In these circumstances the level of complexity may be seen as influencing the behaviour of the partnership. As such, a further research question to consider is: to what extent does the complexity of the alliance influence the pursuit of a co-operative or competitive intent by the entrant firm?

The Level of Cultural Compatibility

Cultural differences have been noted in the past as being one of the major reasons why partnerships disintegrate (Alcar Group, 1989; Ross, 1994). Different ways of working, different systems and approaches, and different perspectives can all create tensions within an alliance and add to the complex management issues induced by this type of organizational arrangement. Where cultural dissimilarities exist in either a corporate or a national context it may be argued that partner firms will be less likely to feel committed to ensuring the partnership continues and may, therefore, be encouraged to take the opportunity to adopt a value appropriation view to the partnership. In contrast, where a high level of cultural compatibility exists, commitment to the partnership is likely to be high and a long-term relationship, encouraging a co-operative emphasis, is more likely to be preferred. This may be considered in respect of the research with the question: to what extent does the cultural compatibility of the partners encourage a more co-operative or a more competitive view of the relationship?

The Level of Experience

As experience of working within the alliance develops, confidence tends to increase, as do the particular skills and flexibility necessary for influencing and manipulating the relationship. Previous research has also revealed that this has a direct and positive effect upon the success rate of the venture (Pekar and Allio, 1994). In comparison, relatively inexperienced firms demonstrate weak alliance strategy development (Pekar and Allio, 1994). It may, therefore, be suggested that as firms develop their expertise and management skills in alliance partnerships, this increases their abilities and success rates in this form of operation. It may be further argued that this level of experience is, therefore, an influencing factor in the extent to which firms are able to drive a competitive intent within the relationship. In terms of the research it is therefore important to consider the question: to what extent does the level of experience of partnering relationships influence the ability of an entrant firm to exercise a competitive rather than a co-operative intent?

The framework outlined above can be demonstrated on a three dimensional axis, which brings together the co-operative, competitive and realizable aspects of the alliance partnership (see Figure 11.1).

Figure 11.1 demonstrates the impact of the co-operative/competitive argument when combined with the context of realizability.

Where an entrant firm has low co-operative and low competitive intent, regardless of whether realizability is high or low, the relationship is likely at best to prove static with little value added or gained, and at worst the entrant firm is at risk of being taken over (Boxes 1 and 5).

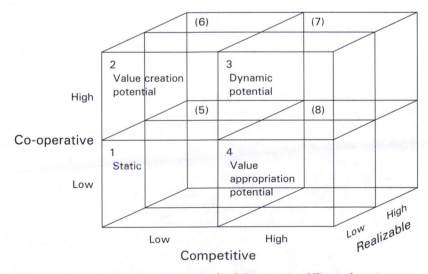

FIGURE 11.1   *Co-operative/competitive/realizability matrix (NB numbers in brackets refer to boxes at the rear of the matrix)*

Where the characteristics of the partner firm encourage a highly co-operative approach to the relationship with few competitive elements present (Boxes 2 and 6), this suggests a high level of value creation potential by the entrant firm. This will be more likely to occur, however, if realizability is high (Box 6), while in Box 2 the potential for value creation could remain largely unrealized. This could be due to factors such as the partner firm's reluctance to communicate or be open with the entrant firm, lack of experience or cultural incompatibility.

If an entrant firm enters a relationship where a high level of competitive intent and a low level of co-operative intention is engendered (Boxes 4 and 8) this would suggest a strong emphasis towards value appropriation by the entrant firm. This could be in the context of intending to learn from the partner particular processes or technologies it has, or in terms of trying to gain access to the partner firm's markets. Where there is a low level of realizability this remains a dormant risk to the other partner. However, where realizability is high the other partner will risk loss of skills, markets and possibly ultimate extinction or acquisition of the firm (Box 8).

Where both co-operative and competitive intents are identified within the entrant firm the relationship is likely to reflect strong complex, dynamic and volatile characteristics (Boxes 3 and 7). In this situation the entrant firm will actively work with the partner firm to generate growth and synergy. It will also, however, be actively seeking to gain from the relationship for its own ends. Under these circumstances, changes in the development of the alliance are potentially most likely and the dynamics of the relationship may be expected to push the alliance either towards increasing emphasis upon value creation or value appropriation. This will depend upon the comparable strength and ability of the partner either to defend itself or to continue to bring a sufficient level of recognized value to the partnership, and upon the external dynamics of the business environment. It will also depend upon the realizability aspects, thus only those firms that qualify to fit within the high realizability box would be able to implement this (Box 7).

Summary and Conclusions

Increasing amounts of research into strategic alliances have identified that both a competitive and a co-operative intent can exist within a partnership, the implications of which can influence both the success and the ultimate destiny of the relationship. This co-operative and/or competitive intent of an individual partner firm should not, however, be viewed simply in terms of opposing options, but rather as a combination of characteristics which, together, can help to explain the motivation of the partners involved and, consequently, the ultimate form, duration and level of success a particular alliance is likely to enjoy.

It has been argued here that the theoretical intent of each partner can be clarified by considering the relationship in terms of specific criteria, including the level of mobility, imitability, uniqueness and value of the key skills or competencies that each partner brings into the relationship. Further, the realizability of the co-operative/competitive intent requires additional factors relating to the level of transparency, complexity, cultural compatibility and experience of previous alliance partnering to be taken into account in order to operationalize the theoretical intent identified.

The framework for evaluating realizable co-operative/competitive intent within a relationship is aimed at assisting firms in their evaluation and management of a partner within an alliance arrangement. The ability to understand the aims and objectives of both partners, to ensure the relationship is continually used to its best advantage, and the pitfalls avoided or at least identified and weighed constantly against the benefits of the partnership are of paramount importance for the ultimate success of the relationship. It is argued here that the framework outlined above provides a means of considering and re-evaluating these factors in a structured and evaluative form within this type of organizational behaviour.

Note

1 The term 'partner firm' is applied to the 'other' partner in the alliance. In contrast, the term 'entrant firm' refers to the firm from which the perspective of the research question is being approached within the alliance arrangement.

12

The Boundary Decision in Strategy

Charles Baden-Fuller

Innocuous questions are often the most difficult to answer, as they typically contain traps and pitfalls for the unwary. The implied questions asked by the boundary school, 'Where should an organization draw its boundaries and how should it manage across this divide?'are two difficult questions. One difficulty arises because organizations are organic and constantly changing both their boundaries and ways of managing them. For example, joint ventures, alliances and networks are becoming more popular now than ever before, and new approaches to management across boundaries on account of new technology are changing the way management can be undertaken.

To begin, I step backwards and ask if there are any universal laws about organizational size and hence about their boundaries. A glance at the industrial landscape suggests that there is unlikely to be a single answer to this question. Take any industry, and we see myriad firms operating differently. Some firms are deeply integrated upstream towards sources of supply, others are integrated downstream towards markets and some are not integrated at all but remain as specialists. Size, too, differs. Although many industries are dominated by large firms, often there are small players that co-exist. Certainly, the performance of firms differs greatly within an industry, but no single strategy dominates completely (Rumelt, 1991). Where cross-sectional data are paradoxical, time series data can often help. Yet time trends are not clear cut. Chandler (1962) has argued that over the last century there has been a trend towards vertical integration and horizontal expansion, but he is careful to acknowledge that there is no universal law. Now, in the last decade, there has been a rapid reversal of Chandler's observed trend as organizations downsize and spin off activities (Markides, 1995). Along the dimension of internationalization, we also see ambiguity. The general trend has been increased expansion, yet the work of Baden-Fuller and Stopford (1991) makes us cautious of any universality.

The lack of universal rules or laws suggests that we need to consider a contingency approach, and these should be predictive or explanatory. Optimal boundary decisions appear to be highly context specific. Firms often pay substantial premiums to purchase rivals and almost as large a set of premiums subsequently to divest them. In both cases, the stock market seems willing to bid up the value of most of the new combinations. This suggests that there is value to be created in locally optimizing the firm structure. Work on organizational renewal lends support to the notion that optimal boundaries are dynamic, for the theories suggest that redrawing the firm's boundaries can play a vital part in the process of revitalizing organizations and achieving long-term success (Volberda, 1998).

Nicolai Foss' contribution is valuable to those seeking a contingency explanation. He spells out where we stand at present. Transaction cost economics provides one approach: it claims that it is the nature of the assets that a firm owns which determine the boundary choice. Where assets are highly specific, they should be owned and controlled internally, but non-specific assets can be outsourced. Transaction cost economics, for all its appearance of certainty and confidence, has long been accused of claiming both too much and too little. Foss (Chapter 9) takes some care to show that the claims of transaction cost economics are really rather empty. In contrast, he points out that while the competence and capability approach is seemingly more prosaic, it has greater potential. This school focuses attention on complementarity and similarity of internal organizational capabilities. Firms should take control, i.e. expand their boundaries, where new capabilities are needed to build competitive advantage, and outsource less critical requirements. Foss likes the capability approach, for this perspective sees strategizing everywhere, whereas transaction cost economics sees only economizing.

Foss' claim that the resource-based view provides a different explanation from the transaction cost approach needs validating. Unfortunately, it is a difficult matter to test. Retrospective examination of any decision could prove problematic. Take an example of a boundary choice, such as the decision of an oil company to undertake its own refining: the economists would find data to argue that it minimizes transactions costs, the capability school that it can be the basis for exploiting knowledge and building future competitive positions. Good managers would not see the two theories as competing, but rather as complementary and claim that the purpose of co-ownership is to do both. However, if we examine a decision before it takes place we may find differences. Before, managers may be choosing one course of action because it emphasizes long-term knowledge accumulation issues whereas another course of action may be chosen to minimize transaction costs. So Foss' contribution must await further testing, for until there is a series of formal tests that set out predictions, it is hard to be precise about where we stand.

My opening question had a second part: how should firms manage across the divide? There is no doubt that some consider this to be the more important question. Many have noted that organizational boundaries are so blurred that it is irrelevant to ask where the boundary should be. For example, while some large computer industry firms use ownership to span many countries, others create networks of partners. Similarly, in restaurants there are some large co-owned chains but others, such as McDonald's, are a network of franchises that are not co-owned, yet they have closely connected strategies and share specific assets, such as the brand. That both work well is a clear tribute to the potential power of adopting the right management style to overcome structural differences.

Stiles (Chapter 11) addresses this question by pointing out that the old dichotomy of co-operative and competitive relationships are not 'either or' choices, but dimensions that can be in tension or resolution. Stiles' chapter is clearly rooted in the capabilities perspective, for she sees the process of resource building as a dynamic one, allowing the partnering firms to 'out-race' rivals in the quest for advantage. Those who build the quickest can win (Prahalad and Hamel, 1990). By seeing the relationships as taking many possible forms, she raises the question of whether the boundary per se is as important as the way in which firms manage across it.

It is with regard to this management issue that I turn to Koenig and Wijk's contribution (Chapter 10). Here, we have a discourse that carefully stakes out the differences between the schools of thought. Traditional economic approaches' have provided models that limit the potential from human relationships, stressing downside risk. But many take the more optimistic view that human agency is not guided by such depressing rules. They believe and show that trust plays a very positive role in bridging the gap. Contributions that can be seen as coming from the network school show how managers can resolve the challenges they face. Healthy competition can exist in collaborative races.

In conclusion, these three chapters shed light on some age old questions. Although they cannot precisely tell us where the firm should draw its boundary, they give us a perspective from which to appreciate the relevant issues. There are emerging ideas that potentially give rise to different contingencies, but the authors also point out that good management style may overcome many hurdles. Correctly choosing the style may be the real question that needs attention.

PART IV

THE DYNAMIC CAPABILITIES SCHOOL: STRATEGY AS A COLLECTIVE LEARNING PROCESS TO DEVELOP DISTINCTIVE COMPETENCES

13

Building Blocks for Strategy Theory: Resources, Dynamic Capabilities and Competences

Ron Sanchez

Given the diversity of disciplinary approaches to strategy, it has often been remarked that strategic management as a field of study can be more clearly defined by the issues it addresses than by the theoretical foundations and research methodologies it uses. Whether strategic management's openness to diverse approaches makes the field a 'fast train to nowhere' (Daft and Buenger, 1990) for researchers attracted to the issues it studies or, alternatively, a fertile ground for the 'actual minds' of researchers to participate in creating the 'possible worlds' of tomorrow's management theory and practice (Bowman, 1990), will remain an open question for some time. As the editors of this volume and others have argued, however, synthesis of the many insights that are being generated by diverse approaches to strategic management is clearly a precondition for the field that will eventually deliver a coherent, cogent framework for better management of organizations (Elfring and Volberda, Chapter 1).

This volume identifies three perspectives on strategic management that offer some promise for integrating the diverse theoretical approaches now motivating the field. The boundary school offers potential for synthesis of strategy theory by simultaneously considering multiple approaches that offer insights into strategic decisions affecting the boundaries of organizations. The configurational school offers potential for synthesis by drawing on insights developed within any of Mintzberg's (1990b) nine strategy schools of thought in order to understand the episodic and situational fit of alternative strategies in various environmental contexts. In this sense, the boundary school perspective reflects strategic management's asserted character as an issue-based field, while the configurational school reflects the field's theoretical eclecticism.

This chapter introduces a third synthesizing perspective, which the editors of this volume have named the dynamic capabilities school. In discussing this third perspective, I have taken the liberty of expanding the name of the school to 'resources, dynamic capabilities and competence' to emphasize that the perspective discussed here rests upon a progression of concepts, each of which significantly extends the ability of this evolving perspective to achieve integration of diverse approaches to strategy theory.

The discussion of the resources, dynamic capabilities and competence perspective is organized in the following way. First, I review the introduction of resources as a pivotal concept for integrating ideas about firms and their competitive environments. The discussion summarizes the progressive elaboration of the concept of resources and their role in firm strategies developed in the work of Barney (1986a, 1991), Dierickx and Cool (1989), Penrose (1959) and Wernerfelt (1984). While the body of work developing what has come to be known as the resource-based view of the firm (Wernerfelt, 1984) is large and continues to grow, the papers considered here constitute a key set of important elaborations on the concept of resources as a foundational building block for strategy theory.

Following this is a summary of the concept of dynamic capabilities, which extends the concept of resources by addressing aspects of the dynamics of resource creation and use within organizations. Elements of dynamic capabilities concepts appeared in many sources in the strategic management and economics literatures in the 1970s and 1980s. This discussion considers representative aspects of dynamic capabilities concepts developed by Amit and Schoemaker (1993), Nelson and Winter (1982) and Teece et al. (1990, 1997).

The concept of competence is then considered, with an explanation of ways in which it builds on and extends concepts of resources and dynamic capabilities. The discussion considers the notion of core competences advanced by Hamel (1991, 1994) and Prahalad and Hamel (1990, 1993). The notion of core competence found a broad resonance (Rumelt, 1994) with many researchers and practitioners and precipitated various initiatives to elaborate a competence-based theory of strategic management (Hamel and Heene, 1994; Heene and Sanchez, 1997; Sanchez and Heene, 1997a, 1997b; Sanchez et al., 1996). Since the competence perspective is presented here as the most recent and comprehensive extension of the concepts of resources and dynamic capabilities, I take a more detailed look at efforts to elaborate the concept of competence and to build a derived theory of competence-based competition. A discussion of how these concepts enable synthesis follows, and then I review the concepts of strategic flexibility and organizational learning (which are examined in more detail in Chapters 14 and 15).

A conclusions section provides final comments on the ways in which the resources, dynamic capabilities and competences perspective provides a means for achieving integration with current approaches to the study of strategic management.

To illustrate the progressive conceptual development within the resources, dynamic capabilities and competence perspective, Table 13.1 provides a summary of the key conceptual building blocks (concepts, focal issues and basic propositions) contributed by the papers on resources, dynamic capabilities and competences considered in this chapter.

Resources

While most economic theory of the day was content to treat firms as atomistic entities and to study their interactions at various levels of aggregation within economies, economist Edith Penrose (1959) investigated how firms' internal management processes affected their behaviour. Treating a firm as a collection of productive resources, Penrose focused on the issue of why and how firms grow. Through her close observation of British firms in the 1950s, Penrose developed a theory of the growth of firms in which the availability of slack physical and human resources within a firm stimulates a search by managers for opportunities to expand a firm's activities – first through expansion within the firm's current product markets (for example, by opening new branches in geographical expansion), but perhaps eventually through expansion outside the firm's current product markets.

In Penrose's study, the key determinant of both modes of the growth of firms was the ability to use the 'services' of a firm's current resources to take advantage of perceived 'productive opportunities' in a product market. Penrose proposed that three aspects of a firm's management limited its growth:

1 management's ability to recognize market demand that presented the firm with opportunities suited to the services the firm's available resources could provide
2 management's ability to combine the firm's available resources with new resources needed to compete in a new geographic or product market
3 management's willingness to accept the risk inherent in trying to use new combinations of resources to serve new market demands.

Adopting a definition of resources as tangible and intangible assets that 'are tied semipermanently to the firm', Wernerfelt (1984) introduces the concept of resource position barriers, which are higher costs faced by firms acquiring a new resource compared to the costs enjoyed by firms that were first movers in creating and using a given resource. In essence, Wernerfelt adds to the characterization of resources the possibility that lower costs of using a resource may result when a firm has developed experience in using that resource. Resources that are subject to experience curve effects and can thereby create resource position barriers are termed 'attractive resources' because they are 'types of resources that can lead to high profits'.

TABLE 13.1 *Key concepts and propositions in the resources, dynamic capabilities and competences perspective*

Resources perspective

Concepts	Reference	Focal issue(s)	Basic proposition(s)

• Resources
• Services of resources
• Productive opportunities
	Penrose, 1959	Why and how firms grow	• Firm growth is motivated by availability of firm resources
			• Firm growth is limited by management's
			  1 recognition of productive opportunities suited to the firm's available resources
			  2 ability to combine existing and new resources
			  3 willingness to accept the risk of using new resource combinations to meet new market demands

• Resource position barriers • Attractive resources • Imperfect markets for resources	Wernerfelt, 1984	• Resources that lead to profits • Motive for diversification	• Resource position barriers can be created when experience in using resources lowers costs for incumbents and imposes higher costs on imitators • Diversification is an attempt to extend a firm's resource position barrier into new markets by combining a firm's current resources with new resources • Mergers and acquisitions are attempts to acquire groups of resources that include attractive resources
• Heterogeneous and imperfectly mobile resources • Firm resource endowments	Barney, 1986a, 1991	Sources of sustained competitive advantage	• Firms cannot create a sustained competitive advantage in markets with homogeneous and perfectly mobile resources • Creating a sustained competitive advantage depends on control of a firm resource endowment that includes resources that are heterogeneous, imperfectly mobile, valuable, rare, imperfectly imitable and non-substitutable
• Asset stocks and flows • Asset mass efficiencies • Asset stock interconnectedness • Time-compression diseconomies	Dierickx and Cool, 1989	Sources of rent-earning potential of resources	• The rent-earning potential of resources results from properties of resources that create asset mass efficiencies, asset mass interconnectedness and time compression diseconomies in firms' efforts to accumulate assets stocks and to create assets

Table 13.1 (*continued*)

Table 13.1 (*continued*)

Concepts	Reference	Focal issue(s)	Basic proposition(s)
Dynamic capabilities perspective			
• Organizational routines • Natural trajectories of skill development	Nelson and Winter, 1982	Sources of economic change	• Change in economic activities results from the learning and embedding of new skills in new organizational routines • Skill development in organizations follows natural trajectories determined by the organization's existing skill base and routines
• Dynamic capabilities • Path dependencies	Teece et al., 1997	Impacts of path dependencies on the formation of capabilities and of capabilities on wealth creation and capture	• Competitive advantage arises from a firm's current distinctive ways of co-ordinating and combining its difficult-to-trade and complementary assets and, from the evolutionary path, a firm follows in advancing its resulting capabilities
• Strategic assets • Strategic industry factors	Amit and Schoemaker, 1993	How firm processes and market uncertainties affect the ability of firms to acquire and use assets to generate organizational rents	• At any point in time, certain assets will be important determinants of a firm's ability to earn rents in a given market, i.e. they will be strategic industry factors, but these assets will be imperfectly predictable and subject to market failure • The cognitive and social processes of managers will determine the assets a firm acquires and thus its potential for generating organizational rents
Competences perspective			
• Core competences • Knowledge resources • Strategic architecture	Hamel, 1991, 1994 Prahalad and Hamel, 1990, 1993 Rumelt, 1994	• Exploitation of competences • Collective learning • Knowledge sharing	• Firms have certain 'core' competences that span across products and businesses, change more slowly than products, and arise from collective learning; firms compete and achieve competitive advantage through creating and using their core competences • Knowledge resources are key sources of competitive advantage; a firm's strategic architecture influences its use of resources

Table 13.1 (*continued*)

Table 13.1 (*continued*)

Concepts	Reference	Focal issue(s)	Basic proposition(s)
Competences perspective			
• Firm-addressable assets • Competence • Competence building • Competence leveraging • Organizational knowledge • Strategic goals • Strategic logic • Competence groups • Competence-based competition	• Sanchez et al., 1996 • Heene and Sanchez, 1997 • Sanchez and Heene, 1997a, 1997b	• Nature of competence • Processes of competence building and leveraging • Organizational sense making • Managerial cognition	• Knowledge, applying knowledge in action and learning are the foundations of skills, capabilities and firm competences • Firms function as open systems of resource flows motivated by managers' perceptions of strategic gaps a firm must close to achieve an acceptable level of goal attainment; firms have distinctive strategic goals that lead to unique patterns of resource flows and competence building and leveraging activities • Competence leveraging drives short-term competitive dynamics, while competence building drives long-term competitive dynamics • The complexity and uncertainty inherent in managing resource flows in a dynamic environment makes the 'contest between managerial cognitions' in devising strategic logics a primary feature of competence-based competition • Firms rely on the use of both firm-specific and firm-addressable resources, and competition occurs in markets for key resources as well as in markets for products • Competence-based competition includes forms of co-operation (as well as competition) with providers of key resources • Firms' differing abilities in co-ordinating resources and resource flows and in managing their systemic interdependencies greatly influence competitive outcomes in dynamic environments • Creating a systemic organizational capacity for strategic flexibility may be the dominant logic for competence-based strategic management in dynamic environments

Wernerfelt also argues that diversification can be viewed as a process in which a firm combines one or more attractive resources in which it enjoys a resource position barrier with new resources to enter new product markets. By doing so it can extend the cost advantages of its resource position barrier. Adding the notion that markets for attractive resources will be imperfect, Wernerfelt characterizes mergers and acquisitions as processes by which firms often try to acquire bundles of attractive resources in highly imperfect markets for resources.

Barney (1986a, 1991) invokes the concept of firm resources in investigating the sources of sustained competitive advantage. Using a very broad definition of firm resources as including 'all assets, capabilities, organizational processes, firm attributes, information, knowledge, etc. [*sic*] controlled by a firm that enable the firm to conceive of and implement strategies that improve its efficiency and effectiveness', Barney suggests that firm resources can be classified into three categories: physical capital resources, human capital resources and organizational capital resources. A firm achieves sustained competitive advantage in its use of its firm resources when it implements a 'value creating strategy' that cannot be implemented by current or potential competitors and when other firms cannot duplicate the benefits of the strategy.

Arguing that no firm could conceive and implement a strategy that would lead to a sustained competitive advantage in an industry with 'homogeneous and perfectly mobile resources', Barney (1991) proposes that only firm resources that are heterogeneous and imperfectly mobile could serve as the basis for a strategy that could lead to a sustained competitive advantage. In addition, these hetero-geneous and imperfectly mobile firm resources would have to meet four conditions to be a source of sustained competitive advantage.

1   The firm resources must be valuable in the sense that they can be used to exploit opportunities or neutralize threats.
2   The firm resources must be rare in the sense that they are not possessed by large numbers of competing or potentially competing firms.
3   The firm resources must be imperfectly imitable by competitors or would-be competitors. Imperfect imitability can result when firm resources have been created or acquired through unique historical conditions (their place in time and space), are subject to causal ambiguity (competing firms cannot under-stand how the firm's resources lead to sustained competitive advantage) or arise from a social complexity that it is beyond the ability of firms systemati-cally to manage and influence.
4   The firm resources must not be substitutable in the sense that there are no strategically equivalent valuable, rare and imperfectly imitable resources that firms can use instead of the firm's resources.

Barney concludes that firm resource endowments of valuable, rare, imper-fectly imitable and non-substitutable heterogeneous and imperfectly immobile resources greatly determine firms' relative abilities to achieve sustained competi-tive advantage.

The implications of imperfect markets for strategically important resources are probed by Dierickx and Cool (1989), who investigate ways in which the 'rent earning potential' of a firm's resources depend on the properties of a firm's asset stocks and flows. Characterizing the process for formation of firm resource endowments as an accumulation of asset stocks, Dierickx and Cool argue that four dynamic properties of the accumulation of asset stocks prevent perfect imitation of a firm's endowment of non-tradeable resources by other firms.

1   Time compression 'dis-economies' raise the costs to competitors who would try to duplicate an asset stock quickly by increasing the flow of resources allocated to building up that stock. For example, raising the rate of investment in research and development (R and D) will lead to higher unit costs in adding R and D assets and thus to lower marginal gains from accelerating investments.
2   Asset mass efficiencies 'facilitate' processes for increasing stocks of assets as the current stock of an asset increases. Thus, firms that already have significant R and D asset stocks may more readily add to their stocks of R and D than firms that have low initial levels of R and D assets.
3   Asset stock interconnectedness reduces the difficulty of increasing one stock when stocks of other assets are high. Firms that have high stocks of customer suggestions for improving products, for example, may be able to identify and improve stocks of product quality more readily than firms with low stocks of customer suggestions.
4   Causal ambiguity makes it difficult for competitors to identify and control the variables that drive the accumulation of specific asset stocks.

Barney (1986a, 1986b, 1991), Dierickx and Cool (1989), Penrose (1959), Wernerfelt (1984) and others not mentioned here have made an important contribution to the eventual integration of strategy theory by providing useful conceptualizations of strategically important resources and the ways in which those resources may stimulate firm growth and diversification, support the creation of sustainable competitive advantage and enable the earning of economic profits.

Dynamic Capabilities

Paralleling the recognition of the role of resources in both enabling and constraining the strategic behaviour of firms in the 1980s was a growing awareness of the importance of firms' relative abilities to use current resources, to create new resources and to devise new ways of using current or new resources. Key characterizations of the dynamic capabilities of firms to create and use resources are developed in representative works by Amit and Schoemaker (1993), Nelson and Winter (1982) and Teece et al. (1997).

Investigating the ways in which firms innovate and thereby precipitate changes in economic activity, Nelson and Winter (1982) proposed that a firm's skills are embedded in organizational routines, which are the repetitive activities a firm develops in its use of specific resources. Because much of a firm's learning is enabled by its current skills and is therefore centred on seeking improvements to existing skills, a firm's current skill-based routines bind much of the firm's learning and create natural trajectories of skill development within the firm.

Teece et al. (1997) developed a notion of dynamic capabilities as a firm's ability to 'integrate, build, and reconfigure' internal and external routines composed of distinctive activities in the use of firm-specific resources. They address the ways in which organizational and managerial processes (co-ordination and integration, and reconfiguration and transformation) combined with a firm's current resource positions create path dependencies that constrain a firm's ability to make short-term adjustments in current routines and to develop new kinds of routines and resources. These conceptualizations closely reflect Nelson and Winter's notion of natural trajectories in the development of a firm's patterns of resource use.

Although a firm's path dependencies constrain the ways the firm can respond to or shape its competitive environment, Teece et al. point out that the path dependencies of competing firms also limit their ability to replicate or imitate a valuable capability already developed by another firm. This view of path dependencies essentially combines Wernerfelt's notion of resource position barriers and Dierickx and Cool's (1989) proposition that the assets already included in a firm's resource position may facilitate the firm's processes of accumulating new asset stocks and, thereby, impose relative disadvantages on firms that do not already have comparable asset stocks. Teece et al., in effect, propose that the path dependency created by a firm's existing routines in using resources may facilitate the firm's ability to extend its current routines, while the path dependencies induced by other firms' established routines in using resources make it more difficult for them to replicate any value-creating routines the firm manages to develop.

Combining concepts of resources and dynamic capabilities, Amit and Schoemaker (1993: 36) use the term 'strategic assets' to refer to 'the set of difficult to trade and imitate, scarce, appropriable, and specialized resources and capabilities that bestow a firm's competitive advantage'. They propose that certain strategic assets will, at any point in time, be subject to market failures and will therefore become the 'prime determinants of organizational rents' in an industry, where organizational rents refer to the economic rents that can be captured by the organization rather than by the owner of the resources and capabilities the organization uses. Amit and Schoemaker (1993: 36) refer to such strategic assets as strategic industry factors and emphasize that 'the relevant set of strategic industry factors changes and cannot be predicted with certainty ex ante.'

The inability to predict with certainty the strategic industry factors a firm will need in order to generate organizational rents leads to uncertainty, complexity and social conflict in managerial processes for anticipating possible futures, for assessing competitive interactions within alternative futures and for overcoming organizational inertia and disputes in seeking to change a firm's set of strategic assets. Thus, Amit and Schoemaker extend the conceptualization of the processes firms use to build resources and capabilities by incorporating important cognitive and social dimensions of the managerial decision making process.

The three views of the dynamics of capability development and use mentioned here are representative of important extensions of the concept of resources made in the 1980s and 1990s to include consideration of organizational capabilities through which organizations identify, develop and use resources, and the ways in which those capabilities affect a firm's ability to obtain competitive advantage and generate economic profits from the control and use of resources.

Competences

The early 1990s saw the emergence of a new emphasis on organizational competences that incorporated concepts of resources and dynamic capabilities developed throughout the 1980s. The competence perspective on strategy adds new conceptual dimensions that capture further aspects of the complex interplay of resources, capabilities, organizational processes, managerial cognitions and social interactions within and between firms. In this section, I consider the original idea of core competences introduced by Hamel and Prahalad, then take a more detailed look at subsequent efforts to develop the concept of competence and to build a derived theory of competence-based competition. I consider a number of ways in which the conceptual extensions achieved through the competence perspective make some significant synthesis of diverse approaches to strategy theory possible.

The Idea of Core Competences

Interest in an integrative concept of organizational competence was stimulated by a series of articles on core competences by Hamel (1991, 1994) and Prahalad and Hamel (1990, 1993). In summarizing the ideas put forward by Hamel and Prahalad, Rumelt (1994: xv–xvi) suggested that a core competence is distinguished by four characteristics.

1 Core competences are capabilities of organizations that can 'span' across, i.e. be used in, products or businesses.
2 An organization's core competences change more slowly than the products they make possible.
3 Core competences arise through the 'collective learning' of the firm as it co-ordinates diverse production skills, integrates multiple streams of technologies and learns through use of its resources and capabilities.
4 The 'competitive locus' of competence-based competition is a contest for acquisition of skills, while competition in product markets is 'merely a superficial expression' of the underlying competition in developing competences.

Hamel and Heene (1994) identify several aspirations for a more integrative theory of strategic management founded on new notions of organizational competence. They suggested that the concept of competence may provide a theoretical lens for obtaining new insights into how creating and sustaining competitive advantage depends on firm capabilities in managing the creation and use of knowledge resources. Developing the notion of competence should also illuminate the characteristics of a firm's 'strategic architecture' and associated concepts, tools, techniques and models that can help a firm be more effective in combining resources and capabilities to build and leverage organizational competences. They also emphasized the potential usefulness of competence ideas in understanding how firms may think and act systemically in creating strategic and operational flexibility, including management processes that can create an explicit shared vision of the future to guide a firm in identifying and creating new competences.

Elaborating the Competence Perspective

The ambitious improvements in strategy theory that Hamel and Heene proposed may be obtainable through a competence perspective, has stimulated a broad effort to elaborate a theory of competence-based competition that incorporates prior concepts of resources and dynamic capabilities, as well as new elements suggested by core competence ideas. Setting out to develop clear, coherent conceptualizations of resources, capabilities and competences that could serve as the foundation for a theory of competence-based competition, Sanchez et al. (1996) proposed concepts, definitions and vocabulary for a new integrative framework for describing competitive phenomena. Among the key concepts and definitions they propose are the following.

- Assets – anything tangible or intangible the firm can use in its processes for creating, producing and/or offering its products (goods or services) to a market.
- Firm-specific assets – assets that a firm owns or tightly controls.
- Firm-addressable assets – assets that a firm does not own or tightly control, but that it can arrange to access and use from time to time.
- Capabilities – repeatable patterns of action in the use of assets to create, produce and/or offer products to a market. Capabilities are regarded as an important special category of intangible assets because they determine the way a firm uses its tangible assets and other kinds of intangible assets.
- Resources – assets that are available and useful to a firm in detecting and responding to market opportunities or threats.
- Competence – the ability of a firm to sustain the co-ordinated deployment of assets in ways that help a firm achieve its goals. Thus, to be recognized as a competence, a firm activity in using resources and capabilities must meet three conditions of organization (implicit in the notion of co-ordination), intention (implicit in the notion of deployment) and the potential for goal attainment.
- Competence maintenance – Sanchez et al. incorporate a notion of organizational entropy by proposing that in a dynamic environment, simply maintaining a firm's current competences requires continuous adaptation of current resources and capabilities to changing environmental conditions.
- Competence building – any process by which a firm achieves qualitative changes in its existing stocks of assets and capabilities, including new abilities to co-ordinate and deploy new or existing assets and capabilities, in ways that help a firm achieve its goals. Competence building is characterized as creating new strategic options for future action by a firm in pursuit of its goals.

- Competence leveraging – applying a firm's existing competences to current or new market opportunities in ways that do not require qualitative changes in the firm's assets or capabilities. Competence leveraging may draw on the firm's existing stocks of assets and capabilities or may require quantitative changes in stocks of like-kind assets similar to those the firm already uses. Competence leveraging is characterized as the exercise of existing options for action created by the firm's prior competence building (Sanchez et al., 1996: 7–11).

Enabling Synthesis and Integration

The foregoing concepts of competence and competence-based competition may provide the foundation for integrating a number of approaches to strategy theory that thus far have remained unconnected theoretical domains. Sanchez and Heene (1997a) suggest some of the synthesis of strategy theory that the theory of competence-based competition and its concepts of resources, dynamic capabilities and competences appears to facilitate.

1 *Integrating 'process' and 'content' approaches.* Competence theory suggests that the potential uses, and thus the strategic value of, a resource depend on the way a firm combines, co-ordinates and deploys the resource with other firm-specific and firm-addressable resources. Thus, a competence perspective jointly examines the effects of a firm's processes for co-ordinating deployments of resources (a 'process' variable) on the strategic advantages that the firm can obtain from specific endowments of resources (a 'content' variable).

2 *Integrating 'industry structures' and 'competitive dynamics' approaches.* Some approaches to strategy theory have regarded industry structures as exogenously determined, while some approaches have emphasized (endogenous) firm processes that can bring about changes in industry structures by 'changing the rules of competition'. Competence theory suggests that firms' competence-building activities create assets, capabilities and knowledge structures within industries that both support and constrain subsequent competence leveraging and building. Thus, in the competence perspective, managerial cognition and organizational capacities for learning are considered the engines of strategic change that determine the resource endowments of firms that in turn collectively constitute industry structures.

3 *Integrating competitive and co-operative views of firm interactions.* By characterizing firms as open systems that depend on inputs of many kinds of resources from other firms, as well as on access to markets for their products, competence theory recognizes that firms both compete for critical resources and product markets and, at the same time, co-operate in many ways to create new resources and markets. This view allows competition and co-operation between firms to be seen as complementary and thus interdependent processes, rather than mutually exclusive possibilities.

4 *Integrating processes of cognition and co-ordination.* Competence theory suggests that endowments of resources and capabilities alone are not adequate

to create competitive advantage, since a firm with unique resource endowments (for example, superior technology) may fail to develop distinctive competences and competitive advantages because its managers are not effective in co-ordinating or targeting the firm's resources and capabilities. Further, when a firm's managers have a superior ability to co-ordinate or deploy resources and capabilities, it may even be possible for a firm to create distinctive competences by using resources that are similar to those used by other firms. Thus, in the competence perspective, creating competitive advantage requires the joint operation of managerial cognitive processes and organizational co-ordination processes, as well as endowments of and/or access to resources and capabilities.

5 *An integrative view of the systemic interdependencies in a firm's competences.* In the competence perspective, the complex interactions among a firm's assets, capabilities and cognitive and co-ordination processes are considered to result in complex interdependencies that often make it problematical to determine the relative importance to a firm of specific resources and capabilities. Competence theory therefore suggests that understanding the sources of a firm's competences may require an intrinsically integrative view of the many elements that make up the firm as a system.

6 *Integrating 'internal' and 'external' approaches to understanding competitive dynamics.* Viewing firms as open systems that depend on resource flows from other firms to build and leverage competences helps to explain the growing use of networks and alliances in dynamic markets. By linking resources in networks, co-operating firms may jointly realize the benefits of asset mass efficiencies, asset interconnectedness and reduced time-compression 'diseconomies' (Dierickx and Cool, 1989) that would not be available to the stand-alone firm.

Chapters on Strategic Flexibility and Organizational Learning Management

The resources, dynamic capabilities and competence perspective gives rise to a number of important collateral concepts that have gained prominence in recent discussions of strategy theory. I now briefly consider the concepts of strategic flexibility and organizational learning, developed within the resources, dynamic capabilities and competence perspective. These concepts are briefly explained to introduce Chapter 14 by Sanchez and Mahoney and Chapter 15 by Kirjavainen and to suggest the contributions these chapters make to the integration of strategy theory within the resources, dynamic capabilities and competences perspective.

Strategic Flexibility

Creating and maintaining competences in dynamic market environments requires the flexibility to acquire and deploy assets in new ways appropriate to changing circumstances. Thus, in dynamic product or resource markets, strategic flexibility – the ability to change a firm's strategic uses of resources and capabilities – becomes critical to a firm's success in competence-based competition. Strategic flexibility has been characterized as depending jointly on a firm's resource flexibilities and the co-ordination flexibilities of a firm's managers in imagining new configurations and uses for current and new resources (Sanchez, 1995a). In this view, the flexibilities of a firm's resources and managerial co-ordination increase with the number of alternative uses to which a firm can apply its resources and capabilities, and decrease with the cost and time required to change from one alternative use to another. Taking a related view, Volberda (1996a, 1998) proposes that a firm's organizational flexibility increases with the variety of actual and potential managerial capabilities the firm has, and with the rapidity with which the firm can activate its alternative managerial capabilities.

Chapter 14 explains how using modularity in an organization's product and process architectures can create important forms of strategic flexibilities and improve organizational learning. Creating modular product architectures enables firms to substitute component variations into modular product designs, thereby increasing the variety of products a firm can develop, the speed with which it can upgrade products and, thus, the flexibility of the firm in product market competition. Modular product architectures create a form of embedded co-ordination that makes possible the autonomous and concurrent development of components by loosely coupled development organizations. Sanchez and Mahoney explain how modular product and organization designs thereby enable more efficient techno- logical learning processes and accelerated market learning (Chapter 14). By reduc- ing the costs, time and managerial co-ordination required to develop and deploy new capabilities, modular architectures may provide a 'strategic architecture' (Hamel and Heene, 1994) capable of reducing path-dependency effects in dynamic capabilities formations by improving organizational capacities for learning.

Sanchez and Mahoney also suggest that creating modularity in product and organization designs enables a new conceptual integration of intended (flexibility-building) and emergent (flexibility-deploying) strategies for manag- ing the uncertainty of dynamic environments (Chapter 14).

Organizational Learning

Competence-based competition may be likened to a state of perpetual corporate entrepreneurialism based on continuous learning about how to build new compe- tences and leverage existing competences. Organizational learning may, therefore, be thought of as the engine of competence building (Sanchez and Heene, 1997b). Chapter 15 undertakes to develop an empirically grounded theory of organizational learning, with particular reference to strategic learning in knowledge-intensive firms. Strategic learning is characterized as a learning processes through which a firm develops its portfolio of competences. Kirjavainen's empirical study suggests that strategic learning in knowledge-intensive firms is likely to be a cyclical process involving a complex interplay between three identifiable dimensions of learning: paradigmatic learning, organizational learning and meta-learning (Chapter 15). This expanded conceptualization of strategic learning thus suggests the need for and possibility of integrating three levels of analysis of learning processes within organizations.

Conclusions

As the title of this chapter indicates, this discussion has suggested that the resources, dynamic capabilities and competences perspective provides important conceptual building blocks for integrating diverse approaches to theory building in strategic management. In this regard, it may be useful to revisit the two views mentioned in the introduction that strategic management is an issue-focused field and that the field is theoretically eclectic and lacks a coherent theory base.

Although the resources, dynamic capabilities and competence perspective could conceivably be characterized as issue focused, like the boundary school, it is 'focused' on the issue of organizational adaptation and performance under dynamic environmental uncertainty. This concern engages a broad and fundamentally important set of inter-related issues that include not just decisions about organizational boundaries, but also about the design of process structures and dynamics within and across organizational boundaries.

Like the configurational school, the resources, dynamic capabilities and competence perspective draws on a number of theoretical perspectives, but it does so within a dynamic, systemic, cognitive and holistic representation of firms and their interactions, which provides an ample conceptual framework for achieving significant integrations of diverse approaches to strategy. This potential for theoretical integration is strongly suggested by the fact that many different concepts for characterizing organizations in competitive environments can be understood as special cases in a larger scheme of possibilities recognized by the competence perspective (Sanchez, 1997). For example, while one approach to strategy posits commitment as the essential 'dynamic of strategy' (Ghemawat, 1991), in competence theory strategic commitment is understood as a final step in a more comprehensive dynamic process of creating and exercising strategic options to make commitments (see also van den Bosch, Chapter 6, this volume). Given its more comprehensive view of key aspects of the strategic management process, the resources, dynamic capabilities and competences perspective appears to provide a promising new conceptual vehicle for redefining, expanding and ultimately integrating diverse theoretical approaches to strategic management.

14

Modularity and Dynamic Capabilities

Ron Sanchez and Joseph T. Mahoney

In this chapter we explain how using modularity to create flexibilities in both product and organization designs (Sanchez, 1995a; Sanchez and Mahoney, 1996) can enhance dynamic capabilities development (Teece et al., 1997). We explain the concept of modularity in products and organizations, and we suggest ways in which modularity provides a framework for strategically managing learning processes that can be effective both in developing capabilities and applying capabilities to external market opportunities and requirements. In this manner, we suggest that modular product and organization designs provide a fundamental framework for improving the adaptive co-ordination of firms in dynamic environments.

The first step in creating modularity in product designs is standardizing input and output interfaces between the functional components that make up a product. Standardizing interfaces allows the decomposition of an overall product design into a nearly independent (Simon, 1962) or loosely coupled (Orton and Weick, 1990) system of functional components. Modularity in product designs is achieved when standardized interfaces between components are specified to allow for a range of component variations to be substituted into a product design without having to change designs of other components (Garud and Kumaraswamy, 1993).

The use of modularity in product designs may have important consequences for product market strategies, organization designs and organizational learning. The ability to substitute component variations into modular product designs increases the variety of products a firm can develop and the speed with which it can upgrade products, increasing the strategic flexibility of the firm in product market competition (Sanchez, 1991, 1993, 1995a). Decomposition of a product design into modular components also allows the autonomous and concurrent development of components by loosely coupled development organizations, making possible modular organization designs for creating and producing products (Sanchez and Mahoney, 1996). Modularity in product designs creates, in essence, a form of *embedded co-ordination* – hierarchical co-ordination that functions without continuous exercise of managerial authority – that lowers the cost and difficulty of organizing and managing complex processes. In ways that we explain below, modular product and organization designs provide a framework for more efficient technological learning processes both at architectural and component levels of technology (Sanchez, 1996a; Sanchez and Mahoney, 1996) and for accelerated market learning through processes such as real-time market research (Sanchez and Sudharshan, 1993). By reducing the costs, difficulty and required managerial co-ordination for developing and deploying new capabilities, modularity can improve the overall strategic flexibility of a firm to respond to and initiate strategic change at several levels within the organization.

Analogously, we suggest that standardized communication interfaces and procedural protocols of computer-assisted design and development (CADD), computer integrated manufacturing (CIM) and electronic data interchange (EDI) systems create 'quick-connect' capabilities between firms that further facilitate the modularization of organization structures and processes (Sanchez, 1996b). These quick-connect technologies may further extend the embedded co-ordination of modularity to include widely dispersed processes of technological and market learning in global networks of loosely coupled firms engaged in developing, producing, distributing and servicing products.

By improving a firm's own technology and market learning processes, and by extending the ability of a firm to co-ordinate and benefit from learning processes undertaken within networks of firms, modularity may provide a framework for improved and expanded organizational learning that reduces path-dependency effects in dynamic capabilities formation (Teece et al., 1997). We suggest that appropriate use of modularity may lead to improved capacities for learning in creating and applying know-how, know-why, and know-what forms of knowledge within organizations (Sanchez, 1996b, 1996c).

We also suggest that achieving improved strategic flexibility through modularity in product and organization designs enables a new conceptual fusion of intended (flexibility-building) and emergent (flexibility-deploying) strategies for managing the uncertainty of dynamic markets. The conceptual fusion of intended and emergent strategies through modularity concepts may constitute a fundamental and promising new approach to improving the integration and coherence of strategy formulation and implementation processes (Itami, 1987; Leonard-Barton, 1988, 1992; Mahoney, 1995) and thus to the more effective identification, building and leveraging of new capabilities on which a firm's ability to survive in dynamic environments ultimately depends.

Our discussion is organized in the following way. First, we discuss modularity as a framework for developing and deploying strategic capabilities in product market competition. Reflecting the view that 'products design organizations' (Sanchez and Mahoney, 1996), we then explain how modularity in product designs can create embedded co-ordination that enables the modular design of organizations. We go on to explain how modularity in product and organization designs can provide a framework for improving processes for organizational learning and capabilities development. Following this, we suggest how modular product and organization designs facilitate the fusion of intended and emergent strategies in dynamic environments. We conclude by suggesting implications for strategy theory of the feasibility of achieving new forms of strategic flexibility and dynamic capabilities development through modularity in product and organization designs.

Modularity and Strategic Capabilities in Product Market Competition

Complex systems, whether physical or social, exhibit structures and processes that consist, at least to some degree, of 'nearly decomposable subsystems' of components (Simon, 1962). A component in a product design performs a specific function or functions within a system of inter-related components whose collective functioning creates the overall functionality of a product.

A system – whether physical, organizational or technical – may be distinguished as loosely coupled or tightly coupled (Orton and Weick, 1990) by the degree to which its component parts tend to be independent or interdependent in relation to each other. A product design can therefore be distinguished fundamentally by the degree to which the overall product design has been decomposed into 'loosely coupled' versus 'tightly coupled' component designs. The degree to which component designs are tightly or loosely coupled in a product design is determined by the interface specifications, which define the input and output relationships between components and thereby determine how dependent one component's design will be on the designs of other components with which it interacts. Interface specifications define, for example, the way in which components are physically fitted to each other, the way in which power is transferred between components and the way in which communication and control signals are exchanged between components.

Modularity in product designs is created by a special form of standardized component interface specifications. Interface specifications become standardized when they are not allowed to change during a given period of time – for example, during a product development period and perhaps even during the commercial lifetime of a 'generation' of products. Modularity in product designs is created when standardized interfaces are specified in order to permit the introduction of a range of design variations for each type of component in the overall product design. Modular product design therefore creates a loosely coupled system of component designs (Sanchez and Mahoney, 1996), because introducing design variations in one component will not require compensating changes in the designs of other components, so long as all component designs used in a modular product design remain within the range of variations allowed by the standardized interfaces.

Modularity becomes an important source of strategic flexibility in product market competition when a number of different versions of modular components can be readily substituted (Garud and Kumaraswamy, 1993) or 'mixed and matched' (Sanderson and Uzumeri, 1990) in a modular product design to generate a potentially large number of product variations distinguished by different combinations of component-based features, functionalities and/or performance levels (Sanchez, 1991, 1995b). Modular product designs may therefore provide a platform (Wheelwright and Sasser, 1989) for achieving greater product variety at lower design costs, creating the potential for more extensive product differentiation. Modular designs also facilitate both more rapid upgrading and accelerated cost reductions of products by allowing the direct substitution of technologically improved and/or less costly modular components as soon as they become available. These flexibilities derived from modular product designs may improve a firm's capabilities to respond to changing markets and technologies by introducing more product variations more rapidly and at lower cost (Volberda, 1996a).

We suggest that these strategic flexibilities and resultant competitive benefits of modularity, as well as other strategic benefits that we discuss below, are stimulating the increasingly widespread use of modular product designs in markets as diverse as jet aircraft, automobiles, consumer electronics, household appliances, machinery, personal computers, software, test instruments, financial services and power tools (Langlois and Robertson, 1992; Sanchez and Mahoney, 1996; Sanchez and Sudharshan, 1993; Sanderson and Uzumeri, 1990).

Embedded Co-ordination and Modularity in Organization Designs

Traditional engineering design typically follows a methodology of constrained optimization, which results in (production) cost or performance 'optimized' product designs based on functional subsystems of highly integrated, tightly coupled components. In such product designs, the interfaces specified between tightly coupled components must reflect the specific design characteristics of each inter-related component. As a consequence, since even a small change in the design of one component may require extensive compensating changes in designs of many other components, processes for developing products composed of tightly coupled component designs are likely to require intensive communication and co-ordination between component development units. Thus, creating product designs composed of tightly coupled components will require organization designs consisting of tightly coupled development processes in which continuous exercise of managerial attention and authority must be used to co-ordinate highly interdependent component development processes. The close and continuous exercise of managerial co-ordination, in turn, usually requires an authority hierarchy that is typically achieved only within the boundaries of a single firm or within a dominant firm and its quasi-integrated component suppliers (see Nishiguchi, 1994). This fundamentally causal relationship between tightly coupled product designs and tightly coupled organization designs is illustrated in Figure 14.1.

Creating modular product designs based on loosely coupled component designs, on the other hand, has far-reaching impacts on feasible organization designs. The standardized interfaces in modular product designs create an information structure (Sanchez and Mahoney, 1996) that defines the required outputs of component development processes. As long as the design created by a component development organization conforms to the standardized input and output interfaces specified for that component by the modular product design, the

Tight coupling of component designs requires tight coupling of component development processes and continuous exercise of managerial authority, resulting in tightly coupled organizational structures within an authority-based hierarchy (e.g. one firm)

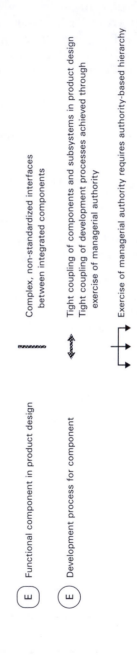

Organization design with tightly coupled development processes

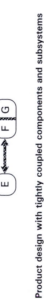

Requires

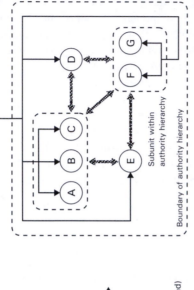

Product design with tightly coupled components and subsystems
(many components are highly integrated; component interfaces are not standardized)

(E) Functional component in product design

(E) Development process for component

Complex, non-standardized interfaces between integrated components

Tight coupling of components and subsystems in product design
Tight coupling of development processes achieved through exercise of managerial authority

Exercise of managerial authority requires authority-based hierarchy

FIGURE 14.1 *Tightly coupled component designs require tightly coupled component development processes*

processes of individual component developers do not need to be managed directly or monitored (except for timeliness) by the firm co-ordinating overall product development. Thus, individual component developers can perform modular component development tasks autonomously, because the essential task of co-ordinating the overall product development process becomes, in effect, embedded in the information structure of required development outputs provided by the standardized interface specifications of the modular product design (Sanchez, 1995a). Moreover, once component interfaces are standardized, thereby establishing the essential features of the required outputs of all component development processes, all component development processes can be carried out concurrently. Thus, modular product design provides a means to achieve hierarchical co-ordination of autonomous and concurrent development processes without the need for continuous exercise of managerial authority, a form of embedded co-ordination that can result from modularity in product designs (Sanchez and Mahoney, 1996).

Firms developing different component variations for modular product designs may therefore be organized into a network of loosely coupled development processes, enabling a loose coupling or modularization of organizational designs for creating and producing products. The enabling relationship between loosely coupled modular product designs and loosely coupled modular organization designs is shown in Figure 14.2.

More generally, we suggest that the degree and nature of the decomposition of a product design fundamentally determines the degree and nature of the decomposition of feasible organization designs for developing that product. Thus, while organizations ostensibly design products, at a more fundamental level it can be argued that products design organization, in the sense that the development (and other) tasks implicit in a given product design largely determine feasible organization designs for developing (and perhaps producing, distributing and servicing) that product (Sanchez and Mahoney, 1996).

Computer-assisted design and development (CADD), computer-integrated manufacturing (CIM) and electronic data interchange (EDI) are recent developments in computer systems that provide standardized information processing interfaces and procedural protocols that further enhance the ability of firms using modular designs to 'quick connect' (Sanchez, 1996b) with other firms using similar information systems. The quick-connectivity between firms made possible by information systems with standardized interfaces can stimulate the formation of 'electronic hierarchies' (Malone et al., 1987) of firms that can be rapidly configured into electronically mediated resource chains to develop, produce, distribute, market and service products (Sanchez, 1995a). As suggested in Figure 14.2, creating standardized interfaces between components in modular product designs, combined with using standardized quick-connect electronic interfaces between firms, may provide the 'interoperability' (Hald and Konsynski, 1993) among firms that enables a global network (Kogut and Kulatilaka, 1994) or 'constellation' (Normann and Ramirez, 1993) of developers and suppliers to create component variations for a wide and changing array of products.

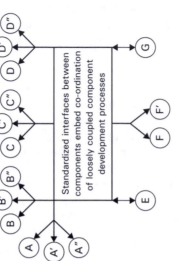

Loose coupling of component development processes made possible by embedded co-ordination achieved through the information structure of standardized component interface specifications that define required outputs of component development processes

Standardized interfaces between components embed co-ordination of loosely coupled component development processes

Modular organization design with loosely coupled development processes

Standardized component interface specifications create loose coupling of component designs in modular product designs

Loose coupling between component development processes achieved through embedded co-ordination made possible by information structure of standardized component interface specifications

Enables

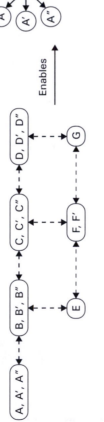

Modular product design with loosely coupled components

(product design is well decomposed into components with standardized interfaces that allow for a range of variations in individual modular components, e.g., A, A', and A'')

Range of component design variations allowed by component interface specifications in modular product design

Loosely coupled component development processes achieved for modular components

FIGURE 14.2 *Modular product designs enable loosely coupled (modular) development processes*

IKEA's computer-based co-ordination of more than 1800 loosely coupled suppliers of modular ready-to-assemble furniture components is an example of a modular organization for product creation, production and distribution that spans more than 50 countries (Normann and Ramirez, 1993). Boeing's 777 assembly process in Seattle is another example of modularity in product design used to create and co-ordinate a global organization design. Parts of the modular plane's fuselage and passenger doors are made in Japan; parts of the tail and rudder assembly come from Australia; nose cones and flaps are made in Italy; engines come from any of three manufacturers in the USA and England; landing gears come from Canada, France and the USA; some of the electrical systems are made in England; the nose landing gear door comes from Ireland; and parts of the tail, wings and nose sections are produced by the Boeing Company itself in various locations in the USA and Canada. The modular design of the 777, coupled with the standardized interfaces in the information system linking Boeing and its suppliers, makes possible the modular organization of the development, production and delivery processes for this complex aircraft requiring over 3 000 000 parts (Woolsey, 1994).

Modular organization designs made possible by modular product designs and quick-connect interfaces between information systems thus appear to provide a new means to achieve superior speed of competitive response through faster, more diverse and more extensive adaptive co-ordination. The strategic flexibilities to be derived from such quick-response capabilities may substantially increase the ability of an organization to respond to or initiate new product opportunities in dynamic markets (Volberda, 1996b, 1998).

Modularity as a Framework for Organizational Learning and Capabilities Development

The decomposition of a product design into functional components and the information structure represented by the specifications of input and output interfaces between components jointly define a product architecture (Abernathy and Clark, 1985; Clark, 1985; Henderson and Clark, 1990; Sanchez and Mahoney, 1996). We now suggest that modular product architectures may provide a framework both for improving organizational learning processes and for more strategic focusing of capabilities development.

Traditional sequential or 'overlapping problem-solving' approaches to creating new products (Clark and Fujimoto, 1991) typically mix the development of new technologies and new products in a sequential process for developing tightly coupled components. In these approaches, technological uncertainties are resolved progressively through an iterative process of design and redesign of inter-related components until an acceptable product architecture finally emerges from the product development process. In these processes, however, tightly coupled upstream component designs must often be reworked when unanticipated component interactions are discovered during downstream component development processes. Thus, product development by sequential or overlapping component development processes becomes a complex, highly recursive and consequently time-consuming process in which technological learning at both the component level (understanding how components function) and the product architectural level (understanding how components interact) may be stymied by the complex inter-dependency of architectural and component level learning processes. Tightly coupled processes for joint development of new technologies and new component designs may, therefore, lead to significant inefficiencies in both kinds of learning processes.

Modular product architectures enable a different approach to technological learning in which learning processes at architectural and component levels may be intentionally decoupled and managed as loosely coupled processes (Sanchez and Mahoney, 1996). Fully specifying the standardized component interfaces in a modular product design requires a high level of architectural knowledge about how components will interact in a product design. Thus, modular product architectures must be based on technologies which are well understood at the architectural level before they are used in a product development project. As a result, in creating modular product architectures, technological learning processes at the architectural level must become decoupled from technological learning at the component level. In so doing, however, architectural level techno-logical learning may proceed unimpeded by complex interdependencies with component design processes in specific product development projects. At the same time, within the set of standardized input and output relationships between components established by a current modular product architecture, component level innovation and learning processes can proceed uninterrupted by repeated demands for component design changes that would be likely to occur if processes for developing new technologies and new components were tightly coupled.

The loose coupling of technological learning processes that becomes possible through the use of modular product architectures enables more efficient learning and innovation at the component level to occur within networks of widely dispersed, loosely coupled development organizations. Modularity thus provides a new framework for loose coupling of architectural and component level learn-ing that may reduce path-dependency effects by increasing the resources and organizational forms available to firms in developing new technological capabili-ties at both architectural and component levels.

Modular product architectures also provide a framework for integrating techno-logical learning at both architectural and component levels with market learning about both long-term trends and current opportunities (Sanchez, 1995b), as shown in Figure 14.3. Long-term planning for product architectures that may serve as platforms for future generations of products provides a structured frame-work for conceptualizing and evaluating possible future product strategies. Defining the essential characteristics and desired flexibilities of future product architectures provides a process for integrating perceived long-term techno-logical and market trends, as well as identifying possibilities for the firm's own initiatives to influence both trends. Periodic creation of new product architectures provides a structured framework for applying a firm's own or other-wise addressable technological and marketing capabilities to medium-term market opportunities. The flexibility to leverage product variations by mixing and matching

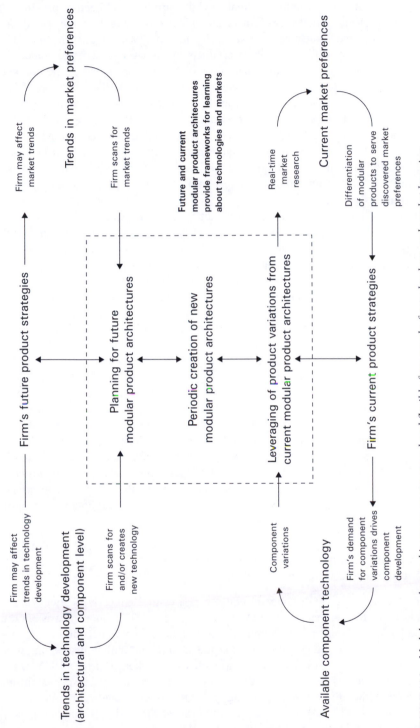

FIGURE 14.3 *Modular product architectures as structured and flexible frameworks for technology and market learning*

component variations within a current modular product architecture provides a framework for intensified short-term technological and market learning. The flexibility to mix and match component variations facilitates market learning by enabling extensive differentiation of products to discover market preferences – a process Sanchez and Sudharshan (1993) have termed 'real-time market research'. At the same time, developing new component variations to serve the demand for product variations that can be leveraged from a current modular product architecture provides a framework for focused technological learning and innovation at the component level. Thus, modular product architectures can provide both a more structured and a more flexible framework for building and linking the firm's technological capabilities at several levels with improved capabilities for learning about and responding to market trends and current opportunities.

It might seem that using modular product architectures intentionally to decouple organizational learning processes, especially those carried out through global networks of firms, might obstruct sharing of learning between organizations and, consequently, limit the combinative capabilities that may be derived from cumulative knowledge (Bartlett, 1993; Kogut and Bowman, 1994; Kogut and Zander, 1992). When modular product architectures are effectively combined with quick-connect information systems, however, modularity appears to facilitate an evolutionary process of technology development and market testing that supports accelerated knowledge building and capabilities development within networks of firms (Baldwin and Clark, 1994; Sanchez, 1996a). CADD's standardized interfaces and protocols for co-ordinating design, communications, scheduling and documentation, for example, ensure that all participants in a product creation process can, in effect, analyse problems and document decisions in ways that are visible to all participants. Accessible archives of design decisions and feedback on product performance provide an audit trail of the lessons learned in development projects, which can contribute to a growing organizational memory (Walsh and Ungson, 1991) within the network of linked firms. Modular product architectures and quick-connect information systems may, therefore, join to create platforms for sharing structured and detailed knowledge throughout networks of participating organizations.

Modularity as a means to Achieve the Fusion of Intended and Emergent Strategies

Effective and efficient organization design is a central concern of organization theory and strategic management (Williamson, 1993a). This concern was anticipated by the early debate in economics between proponents of economic organization by planning (Lange, 1936), who argued that co-ordination by planning was both possible and workable, and proponents of markets (Hayek, 1945) who argued that markets have superior efficiency in handling rich and dispersed information and, therefore, in co-ordinating intricately inter-related economic activities. Hayek (1978: 183), for example, emphasized the notion of 'human action without human design', resulting in an emerging 'spontaneous order'.

The Lange–Hayek debate over planning versus spontaneous ordering in economies at large has counterparts in the field of strategic management, including the Ansoff–Mintzberg debate over the merits of strategic planning versus emergent strategies at the firm level (Ansoff, 1988, 1991; Mintzberg, 1990a, 1991). Mintzberg's (1978) emergent strategies, for example, are reminiscent of Hayek's (1978) 'spontaneous ordering' in asserting that specific, coherent patterns of action cannot be delineated adequately by any one mind ex ante, but may only emerge and be apprehended by many participants ex post.

Williamson (1991) adds a further perspective by suggesting that the 'institutions of capitalism' allow for adaptation within an institutional framework and can thus be seen as supporting both planned and spontaneous ordering. In a similar vein, we suggest here that modular product and organization designs offer strategic management a new framework for the conceptual synthesis of planning and emergence. More specifically, the creation of modular product architectures and the use of quick-connect information systems to enact modular organizations appear to be powerful new means for achieving an intended (planned) strategy of providing a range of flexible (emergent) responses to an uncertain environment. In essence, emergent configurations and deployments of specific product and organization variations derived from the flexibilities of planned modular product and organization designs enable the playing out of a range of emergent strategies in response to environmental change. Strategic flexibility achieved through creating modular product and organization designs may, therefore, be an overarching strategy that allows the coherent conceptual fusion of intended and emergent strategies.

Williamson, elaborating on Simon's (1962) notion of hierarchies in complex systems, also proposed a hierarchical decomposition principle for organizational structure, stipulating that:

> ... internal organization should be designed in such a way as to effect *quasi-independence* between the parts, the high-frequency dynamics (*operating activities*) and low-frequency dynamics (*strategic planning*) should be clearly distinguished, and incentives should be aligned within and between components ... (1986: 146; our emphasis)

In this regard, we suggest here that under dynamic conditions in product markets, the most viable organizational form may be a strategically flexible firm capable of exercising a range of emergent product market initiatives (high-frequency dynamics) made possible by the planned creation of modular product architectures (low-frequency dynamics). Moreover, the embedded co-ordination that can be achieved through the standardized interfaces of modular product designs may enable extension of the hierarchical decomposition principle beyond the boundaries of one organization to include a potentially large number of loosely coupled organizations. In essence, the embedded co-ordination of modular product architectures may provide a fundamental means of achieving flexible hierarchical organization both within individual organizations and through networks of loosely coupled modular organizations.

Implications for Strategy Theory

A useful tool for strategic management and organization science is to make use of the world's failure to describe the complexity of our world as simply as possible (Simon, 1981: 222). Better understanding of the potential decomposability of complex organizational phenomena into loosely coupled subsystems may be a key to gaining new insights into the fluid structures and new organizational dynamics of many contemporary product markets.

Simon further notes that, '... design is concerned with the discovery and elaboration of alternatives' (1982: 419). Modularity in product and organization designs may provide strategic managers in dynamic markets with a new means to create strategic flexibilities that make possible a broader range of strategic alternatives. Growing use of modular product designs may also explain at least in part the accelerating de-integration of both product creation and production processes and the resulting rise of both networks of organizations and increasingly dynamic markets in the 2000s.

Apprehending the dominant logic for successfully competing in current markets is a primary goal of strategic management (Prahalad and Bettis, 1986). While commitment has often been invoked in strategy theory as a key concept for ex post explanations of economic rents (for example, Ghemawat, 1991), strategic flexibility now appears to be a key concept for understanding successful ex ante strategizing under uncertainty (Sanchez, 1993, 1995a). In effect, strategic flexibility may be thought of as the condition of having options for managing the evolving uncertainties of the present and future, while commitment can be seen as the condition of having exercised one or more strategic options in the past. Further, while it is common in the resource-based view within strategy to argue that a firm's commitments provide isolating mechanisms that deter entry by would-be competitors (Mahoney and Pandian, 1992; Rumelt, 1984), it is now becoming apparent that superior product design flexibility and manufacturing flexibility may also deter entry, especially in dynamic product markets (Chang, 1993). Thus, we suggest that strategic flexibility achieved through modular product and organization designs may be a new dominant logic for successful product-based competition in dynamic markets (Sanchez, 1995a).

Strategic flexibility achieved through modularity in products and organizations may also permit a synthesis of intended strategy (wherein modular product and organization designs are intendedly created as flexible vehicles for accommodating change) and emergent strategy (wherein firms leverage modular product variations and reconfigure resource chains as technologies evolve and new market preferences are discovered). The recent growth of real-time market research by Sony and other firms, for example, suggests how the flexibility of modular product designs can be used to achieve rapid product adaptation as evolving preferences are discovered in new product markets (Sanchez and Sudharshan, 1993; Sanderson and Uzumeri, 1990). Moreover, strategic flexibility can enable more than just a dynamically efficient adaptive response to the uncertainty of turbulent markets. Superior flexibility achieved through modular designs can also be used proactively to create turbulence and uncertainty in product markets that less flexible competitors may not be able to respond to readily (Gerwin, 1993).

In investigating the strategic impact of modularity in product and organization designs, we are heeding Williamson's (1976: 102) advice to investigate 'transactional phenomena [at] ... the semi-microanalytic level of detail'. This perspective has led us to suggest some extensions to concepts of dynamic capabilities in current strategy theory, including:

1   extending the resource-based view's emphasis on commitment to specific-use resources and capabilities to include recognition of the strategic value of flexible resources and capabilities in dynamic markets, e.g. modular product and organization designs
2   explaining new forms of competitive product strategies in which use of modularity to achieve embedded co-ordination of modular organizations may create new levels of strategic flexibility
3   suggesting ways in which modularity provides a framework for more effective learning and development of organizational capabilities
4   proposing that the perceived dichotomy of intended and emergent strategies in strategy theory can be resolved through a concept of strategic flexibility (obtained through modular product and organization designs) that enables a fusion of planning and emergence.

15

Strategic Learning in a Knowledge-intensive Organization

Paula Kirjavainen

During the past few years, the competitive value of learning has been emphasized both by consultants and researchers in the field of strategic management. According to a popular slogan, the ability to learn faster than competitors may well be the only sustainable competitive advantage. Firms are believed to compete for core competencies and strategic capabilities that are embedded in the organization and develop in time through collective learning processes. Yet, learning as a strategic and/or organizational phenomenon remains poorly understood.

This chapter brings the notion of learning into the context of long-term competence development by exploring the processes through which (individual) learning affects strategic change in knowledge-intensive firms (KIFs). The identification of the kind of learning and organizational knowledge formation that are strategically significant in a KIF results in a conceptual framework that integrates some well-known American and Scandinavian theoretical views on (organizational) learning. On the basis of empirical data, strategic learning is argued to be a cyclical process that occurs on two levels – learning and meta-learning – and involves intertwined changes in the paradigm and the organizational knowledge base. Although this framework depicts the collective paradigmatic development within the group of significant actors as the primary driver of a KIF's strategic learning, it also underlines the roles that learning by individual managers and key experts play in the process.

The chapter begins by examining the multifaceted nature of organizational learning and by discussing the importance of the competence-based approach for understanding the KIF's strategic challenges. The empirical study on which the theoretical ideas are based is also described. Implications for research and management are drawn at the end.

The Multifaceted Nature of Organizational Learning

There is no common understanding of how learning relates to the long-term development of an organization. The number of different conceptualizations reflects the divergence between strategic management and organization theory as well as the multiplicity of perspectives within them.

The researchers within the traditions of behavioural organization theory emphasize the importance of behavioural change and the role of organizational routines. According to them, organizations learn experientially as they encode inferences from history into routines that guide behaviour (Cyert and March, 1963; Levitt and March, 1988). Other researchers, in turn, build their views on the theories of social cognition. They stress the importance of cognitive change and the role of management in scanning and interpreting the organizational environment. They relate learning to the development of knowledge about action outcome relationships and to the processes of putting the cognitive theories into action (Daft and Weick, 1984; Hedberg and Jönsson, 1977). The notion of learning has been introduced to the field of strategic management by researchers who criticize the clear-cut distinction between strategy formulation and implementation. They consider learning as an incremental approach to strategy making, where the strategic actors, while experimenting and discovering, learn by doing (Mintzberg and Waters, 1985; Normann, 1977; Quinn, 1980a).

Despite the differences, there appears to be some consensus regarding a theory for strategic learning in an organization. First, it is widely accepted that individual learning is a necessary but not a sufficient condition for collective learning and that collective learning is more than the cumulative result of individual learning (Dodgson, 1993; Hedberg, 1981; Huber, 1991). Second, while behavioural changes may be a part of strategically significant learning, the essence of strategic learning relates to the development of cognitive insight (Fiol and Lyles, 1985; Friedlander, 1983). Third, learning bridges past actions, the outcome of those actions and intentions about future actions (Argyris and Schön, 1978; Fiol and Lyles, 1985; Mintzberg and Waters, 1985).

So far the strategy and organization theorists have, however, merely borrowed the notion of learning from other sciences such as psychology and, accordingly, conceptualized it in a wide variety of ways. It is likely that none of these conceptualizations alone grasp the complexity of the processes that actually link (individual) learning to strategic change in an organization.

In this chapter, these processes are investigated from the perspective of empirical reality. It is, however, beyond the scope of this chapter to dwell on the subject of individual learning. Individual learning is here defined as the process through which the meaning of a certain experience is re-interpreted in such a way that the new interpretation guides future understanding, valuing and action (see Kolb, 1984; Mezirow, 1990). By 'action learning' (Argyris and Schön, 1974) we mean learning aimed at problem solving that combines individual responsibility as a member of the work organization with the reflection of personal experience. Strategic learning, in turn, refers to the combination of processes through which (individual) learning can initiate, advance, restrain or inhibit changes in the KIF's strategy.

Strategy and Strategic Change in KIFs

Rationale for a Competence-based Approach

KIFs are, by definition, strategically dependent on one resource: knowledge. This is important for them as raw material, means of production and capital (Lehtimäki, 1993; Sveiby and Lloyd, 1987). As a consequence, the resource-based approach to strategy (Wernerfelt, 1984, 1995) seems to suit these organizations well.

The KIF's resource base consists of two types of knowledge resource: knowledge that is bound to individuals and knowledge that is assimilated in the organization. Both individual and organizational knowledge can concern issues that are either managerial or professional, i.e. expert, and both can be either 'tacit' or 'explicit' (see Bonora and Revang, 1991; Sveiby and Lloyd, 1987). The knowledge resource that is the most characteristic of KIFs is the expertise of individuals and their 'social capital', i.e. mutual trust with clients or customers. The organization may also have physical knowledge capital, for example, in the form of capital goods such as computer programs (Starbuck, 1992). Most of the organizational knowledge, however, resides in organizational routines, that is, in the structure of the organization, in the statements of organizational policies and procedures and in the organization's socio-cultural norms (Hedberg, 1981: 6–7; Huber, 1991: 105–7; Shrivastava, 1983: 17–18).

Organizational knowledge is strategically significant for a KIF, in the sense that it balances the KIF's dependence on its individual-bound knowledge resources (see, for example, Åkerberg, 1993; Bonora and Revang, 1991). Still, none of the knowledge resources alone, or even jointly, explain the success and survival of a KIF. Rather, it is the KIF's ability to deploy its diverse knowledge resources on the market, in other words, its strategic capabilities (Stalk et al., 1992) or core competencies (Prahalad and Hamel, 1990) that is crucial. (In the following, the terms 'core competence' and 'strategic capabilities' will be used interchangeably.)

Being products of an organization's history (Teece, 1986) and inextricably built into its actions (Amit and Schoemaker, 1993), dynamic capabilities, unlike strategic knowledge resources, are difficult to imitate. Even if technologies change or key experts resign unexpectedly, the strategic significance of organizational capabilities does not disappear all at once. They can, at least to some extent, always be renewed by complementing or changing the resources that underlie them. Furthermore, KIFs may also develop strategic capabilities that are based on the ability to deploy knowledge resources owned and controlled by their collaborators.

The above discussion stresses two conceptual distinctions. First, while individuals may possess personal competencies, competence in the strategic sense refers only to corporate competence that is embedded in the organization.

Corporate competence spans a number of business units and products within a corporation (Rumelt, 1994). Individual products and services are but momentary expressions of a corporation's core competencies (Prahalad and Hamel, 1990). Second, distinction is made between resources and capabilities. Resources are defined as stocks of available factors owned or controlled by the firm (Amit and Schoemaker, 1993). Capability, on the other hand, refers to the capacity for a team of resources to perform some task or activity (Grant, 1991). Capabilities are firm specific, and developed over time, through complex interactions among resources (Amit and Schoemaker, 1993; Bogaert et al., 1994; see also Sanchez, Chapter 13, this volume).

While most authors assert that firms do not have just one core competence but a whole portfolio of competencies and capabilities, there is no common conception of how these link to each other. Turner and Crawford (1994: 243) distinguish between management competencies and technical competencies. In the case of the former, we are concerned primarily with the technological aspects of the creation, production and delivery of the organization's products and services. In the case of the latter, in turn, we are referring to the 'direction, development, motivation, control and integration of the organization's performance'. Tampoe (1994: 69) argues that competencies are often hierarchical. A holding company, for example, may have core competencies that make it successful in managing a diversified business while the different companies within the group will have specific core competencies that are alien to the holding company.

On the basis of the above, it can be concluded that the management of the firm's competencies is a critical competence per se (Prahalad and Hamel, 1990: 81; Roos and von Krogh, 1992: 425). The competencies of the individual managers as well as the organizational practices of strategic management constitute the firm's 'strategic management capability' (see Normann, 1985) that may also be considered a meta-level of the firm's competence portfolio. Consequently, in order to feature the core of a KIF's strategy, both the firm's competencies and its capabilities of managing its competence portfolio must be investigated.

Rationale for a Holistic Approach

Recent case studies on KIFs have suggested that the process of strategy development in these organizations is very different from what the conventional literature on strategy assumes (see, for example, Burgelman, 1991; Mintzberg and McHugh, 1985). Strategy in a knowledge-intensive organization typically takes shape, to a large extent, emergently – either independent of the (ex-ante) intended strategies or in spite of them (Mintzberg and Waters, 1985). Moreover, the top management cannot be regarded as the sole strategic actor in KIFs. Strategic action becomes dispersed to all levels of the organization as the knowledge workers make quite independent choices about what kind of clients to work with, what kind of projects to undertake, which methods to use and so on. This kind of strategic behaviour alters the KIF's pattern of action in small, incremental steps, sometimes also producing 'strategic runners' (Mintzberg and McHugh, 1985).

Some researchers, as well as many practitioners, have been very sceptical about whether there can be deliberate strategic plans in KIFs. This is another way of asking whether KIFs can formulate strategies and then gather the resources needed for their implementation or whether they are merely destined to gather the best possible (human) resources in the hope that successful strategies will emerge from the resource base (Lahdenpää, 1991). Most authors, however, admit that KIFs are likely to have 'umbrella strategies' (Mintzberg and Waters, 1985) or 'perspectives' (Mintzberg, 1987b), in other words, broad guidelines for organizational behaviour that are often also rooted in the organizational culture (Mintzberg and McHugh, 1985).

In conclusion, it can be argued that understanding the KIF's strategic processes calls for a holistic approach. We need to view strategy as an outcome of complexly intertwined cognitive, cultural and political processes and to acknowledge the ambiguity of the line between strategy and operations.

Description of the Case Study

The theoretical ideas developed in this article are based on a comparative case study of strategy formation and strategic change in two KIFs. The purpose of the study was to develop a conceptual framework that would increase our understanding of how learning relates to strategic change in a knowledge-intensive organization.

Two Finnish KIFs were selected as the target companies. One is SAMI, a group of management consultants that specializes in strategic development and operates in six areas of expertise: strategic analysis, marketing, organizational development, production and logistics, information technology and human resources. The other target company is Elomatic, a group of design engineers that provides consulting services in four areas of technology: shipbuilding, industrial, pulp and paper and CAD. In the Finnish market, both companies hold a solid position in their respective industries.

Both target companies are representative KIFs. In fact, they were chosen to fill a theoretical category of knowledge-intensive organizations, in which the knowledge intensivity appears in its purest form (see Lehtimäki, 1993). Apart from their knowledge-intensive character, however, the target firms are very different. They differ in the size of their organization, structure of ownership and the nature of their business. These differences were sought to build a comparative research setting in which it would become possible to examine how the knowledge-intensive context influences the process of interest and, accordingly, to contribute to the development of organizational theory.

The case material includes data concerning the target firms' 'intended and realized strategies' over their whole history. It was collected in the period between 1991 and 1995 by applying a wide variety of qualitative data collection methods: participative observation, personal interviews and archival analysis. Thus, the study was conducted partly in retrospect and partly by following the events in real time.

This article reports part of the research results. A preliminary framework of strategic learning, describing the subprocesses and linkages between them, is put forward. The framework was inductively derived from the empirical case study evidence but theoretical literature and research results were used to identify a priori constructs as well as to shape and sharpen hypotheses (for building theories from case studies see, for example, Eisenhardt, 1989a; Pettigrew, 1990).

Identifying the a priori Constructs

A number of potentially important constructs were identified from the literature on learning in organizations. The recent debate on the subject was found to fall into three categories.

Within the first category (managerial or organizational), learning is viewed as development of collective cognitive structures. The managerial frames for interpretation and action are described using concepts such as 'myth' (Hedberg and Jönsson, 1977), 'dominating ideas' (Normann, 1977), 'interpretative scheme' (Bartunek, 1984), 'dominant logic' (Prahalad and Bettis, 1986) and 'paradigm' (Johnson, 1987, 1990). Most descriptions of cognitive structure change dynamics or sequences have been influenced by Lewin's (1947) way of characterizing the learning process into three phases: unfreezing, change and refreezing (Barr et al., 1992; Bartunek, 1984; Grinyer and Spender, 1979b; Hedberg and Jönsson, 1977; Johnson, 1990).

Within the second category (organizational), learning is viewed as a process of organizational knowledge creation that either incorporates or is closely related to the processes through which an organization acquires, distributes, stores and retrieves information (Huber, 1991). This research has produced typologies of knowledge coupled with conceptualizations of the conversion processes between individual/organizational and tacit/explicit knowledge (Bonora and Revang, 1991; Nonaka, 1991, 1994; Starbuck, 1992).

The third category entails the debate on learning organizations, which has focused on identifying structures, systems and management practices that would enhance information processing and knowledge creation in an organization (Garvin, 1993; Pedler et al., 1991; Senge, 1990). These authors view meta-learning, that is, the development of the entity's ability to learn, as a normative goal or as a property of an ideal organization. The notion of meta-learning aligns with what Bateson (1972) has called 'deutero learning' and what psychologists term meta-cognitive learning. All refer to processes where an entity first reflects upon its previous learning experiences and then, on the basis of this reflection, enhances its capacity for future learning (Argyris and Schön, 1978: 26–9). In the context of strategic development, meta-learning has been understood as a quest for strategic management capability (Normann, 1985). The term 'strategic management capability' refers to the firm's ability to achieve good strategic action on a longer term, repeated basis. There is, however, no common understanding of what constitutes such capabilities.

Altogether, the three categories of learning literature contribute to the preliminary understanding of the target phenomenon by specifying two potentially important domains of learning (paradigmatic and organizational) as well as two levels (learning and meta-learning).

Discussion of the Case Study Findings

Both target firms progressed through three stages of strategic development punctuated by two periods of strategic change. The first one of the changes was an anticipative adjustment in the company's competitive strategy, whereas the second represents a frame-breaking redefinition of business (Nadler and Tushman, 1989). In addition, a transformation from one KIF configuration to another (Miller and Friesen, 1984) could be detected in both firms: SAMI started operations as an 'expertise-based bunch of professionals' but was gradually developed to an 'experience-based team of professionals'. Elomatic, in turn, started as an 'efficiency-based factory of professionals' but is now best described as an 'experience-based team of independent KIFs' (Maister, 1993).

In the following section, the target companies' overall process of strategic change is first described from the perspective of paradigmatic development. After that, the processes of organizational knowledge creation and the development of strategic management capability are discussed in relation to the paradigmatic changes.

Paradigmatic Learning by the Two Target Firms

The target firms' paradigms turned out to be relatively stable, yet continuously changing cognitive–affective frames that prevailed in the 'group of significant actors' (Normann, 1977). With regard to the functions of paradigm, the findings align with Johnson's (1987: 271) definition of a paradigm as 'a relatively homogenous approach to the interpretation of the complexity that the organization faces [that] also provides a repertoire of action and responses to the interpretations of signals that are experienced by managers and seen by them as demonstrably relevant'. Yet, the target firms' strategic behaviour was affected by two categories of interactively connected assumptions. (See, for example, Bougon et al., 1977; Fiol and Huff, 1992; Lyles and Schwenk, 1992 for a discussion on different aspects of cognitive structures).

The causal argumentative assumptions, also known as 'scripts' (Gioia, 1986) or 'schemas' (Normann, 1977) are the simplifications of complex reality that permit strategic actors to analyse enormous amounts of information rapidly and efficiently and, more importantly, to act on the basis of their analysis. This part of the paradigm represents 'a network of expectations that is learned from experience, stored in memory and devoted to the guidance of action' (Gioia, 1986: 54–7). Core assumptions, in turn, are more like cultural values (Schein, 1985): they are not necessarily as directly tied to action but they provide the point of self-reference needed to utilize causal argumentative assumptions (Fiol and Huff, 1992: 278) and, accordingly, give meaning to strategic action.

Interactions between these two categories of assumptions play a central role in the target firms' overall process of paradigmatic development, including the following phases: the birth of the early years' paradigm, refreezing of that paradigm, the gradual questioning of it, paradigm shift and the refreezing of the new paradigm.

The origins of the target organizations could be traced to their founders' professional and personal interests, which laid a particular foundation for their later developments. SAMI started operations in the early 1980s to become an organization in which a couple of distinguished experts could realize themselves and develop their expertise in the area of strategic management. The founding partners decided to start a business of their own because they thought that their former employers had very little to offer them in terms of personal development. Elomatic, in turn, specialized in designing for shipbuilders as the founder, in his own words, 'had fallen in love with ships some thirty years before'.

The target firms' founding business ideas were so innovative and their know-how level so high that more and more customers demanded their services. The organic growth (Sveiby and Lloyd, 1987: 153), however, did not satisfy the companies' owners. In the mid-1980s, the founding business ideas in both companies were displaced by new competitive strategies. The changes were initiated by the companies' innovative and ambitious owner-managers who sought alternative avenues of growth as they anticipated that the founding business idea alone could not result in satisfactory development.

As their new paradigmatic assumptions directed them to enlarge the knowledge resource base, both SAMI and Elomatic faced a period of extensive growth and diversification. During the second half of the 1980s the target companies' excellent performance in terms of volume growth and returns 'froze' these assumptions (see Hedberg and Jönsson, 1977). The target companies, during their intensive growth periods, entered a 'paradigmatic state' in which they adjusted marginally within the prevailing paradigmatic assumptions but ceased to adapt to changes in their environment (Johnson, 1990). Although their 'strategic drift' (Johnson, 1987) did not last very long, it resulted in deteriorating performance. This is explained by the content of the prevailing paradigms: the redefinition of the target firms' competitive strategies had changed only a part of their paradigmatic assumptions. Many of the value-like assumptions associated with the organizations' early years still guided managerial behaviour (Schein, 1985). Organizational development in the target firms provides illustrative examples.

SAMI's business expanded fast and a number of new consultants were recruited. Although all of them were skilful professionals, they were not 'famous' like the distinguished experts who had founded the company. The client companies demanded their services because of their experience of solving particular types of problem, not because of their expertise. In fact SAMI, which had entered the market as 'a bunch of gurus', was incrementally turning into an 'experience-based practise' (Maister, 1993). The founding partners, however, still viewed the organization as an 'unbureaucratic home of experts' – a true adhocracy (Mintzberg, 1983) – where all standardization should be kept to a minimum. In a continuously growing company, this, of course, led to considerable inefficiency of operative action.

Elomatic's management acquired several small companies but gave hardly any consideration to integrating them to the group as a whole. In fact, the companies acquired were treated as if they had been portfolio investments. The motive behind this was the management's strong belief in the efficiency of small independent units and, even more importantly, the founder's respect for entrepreneurship as the driving force of any business. In the late 1980s, the cultural diversity and the overlapping functions, however, began to hamper Elomatic's business.

In both target firms, the management's initial response to the emerging problems drew on the now inappropriate but still current paradigm, which of course provoked a deepening of the problems (Prahalad and Bettis, 1986: 498). The mismatch between the prevailing paradigmatic assumptions and the requirements of their strategic conditions persisted in the target firms until they culminated in a crisis (Bartunek, 1984; Hedberg, 1981). Unlike under favourable conditions, the strategic situation which the significant actors perceived as coercive led to a more thorough reflection of the strategic choices. That is to say the target companies' management not only carefully reconsidered the content of their strategies but also explicitly reflected upon the background of their previous choices as well as the outcome of those choices. The new strategies were formulated on the basis of the insights developed in these discussions (Fiol and Lyles, 1985).

In the course of the target firms' business redefinition and systematically managed change processes, the value-like paradigmatic assumptions of the early years were finally unlearned, new paradigmatic assumptions were specified and the paradigm as a whole received a more coherent and consistent form. More importantly, as a result of the explicit discussions and, sometimes, heated debate, the significant actors were now more conscious of their paradigmatic assumptions.

Organizational Knowledge Creation and the Dynamics of Paradigmatic Change

Two categories of learning processes appear to be particulary important for understanding the relationship between paradigmatic development and organizational knowledge creation in the target firms. First, that of co-ordinated learning of the firm's operative core, which occurs along the lines of intended strategies and, second, that of individual learning or learning by small groups of organizational members, which occurs independent of the intended strategies. The former makes it possible for the organization to exploit the opportunities associated with its current domain while the latter may encourage organizational renewal (Burgelman, 1991; Mintzberg and Waters, 1985).

In their early years, both target companies managed to transform the combinations of their knowledge resources and organizational processes into strategic capabilities that consistently provided superior value to their client firms

(Stalk et al., 1992). In SAMI, this value was based on the uniqueness of the company's services, while in Elomatic the value was related to the cost-effectiveness of the company's designing process.

SAMI's consultants converted their (individual-bound) knowledge of strategic management to a process model that was actively used as a basis for client work. The same model also gave the company status within the profession and provided a framework for the consultants' future 'learning by doing'. Organizational features such as the continuous and lively interaction between the members and the shared vision characterized by excitement and professional ambition enhanced and co-ordinated the individuals' learning (Normann, 1985; Senge, 1990).

In Elomatic, the experientially gained knowledge was used to develop designing tools and methods in order to make the firm's production process as cost-effective as possible. The owner of the company also invented a laser camera, which at the time increased both the quality and the efficiency of designing, as well as brought fame and glory to the company. The appropriately structured and systematically managed organization, together with the organizational climate typical for a family business, provided the basis for effective individual learning.

The target firms' strategic capabilities were based on organizational knowledge – unique service concepts, proprietary technology and organizational routines that gave a concrete form to the management's intended strategies by enhancing and co-ordinating experiential learning of many individuals in the 'operative core' (Mintzberg, 1983). Thus, it can be said, that organizational learning within the intended strategies led to the volume growth of the target firms' early years and, subsequently, 'froze' their initial paradigms.

During the target firms' second period of development, the same strategic capabilities, however, broke down, as their management devoted most of their attention to expanding the business. On the other hand, new capabilities that would have realized the intended organizational synergy were not developed. Thus, it can be said that the target firms' failure to learn as organizations caused problems that subsequently triggered the paradigm shifts.

The target firms' experiences illustrate three types of learning failure (Kim, 1993). In the first type, learning was opportunistic. The target companies' entrepreneurial management acquired new high-standard knowledge resources, got licences for new consulting tools and recruited more experts, but failed to develop organizational routines to support the utilization of those resources in the company's established business processes. As a result, the new knowledge did not increase but rather decreased the effectiveness of the organization as a whole. In the second type, learning was fragmented. The individual members of the organization learned experientially and the independent units accumulated new knowledge. Yet, the organization as a whole did not learn. In the absence of organizational routines that would have supported interunit collaboration the new knowledge was not diffused over the unit boundaries. Situational learning, the third type, occurred as the individual experts and teams of experts encountered novel problems, improvised on the spot, solved the problems and moved on to the next task. In other words, new knowledge was created but in a manner that made it situation specific. In SAMI, situational learning was mainly caused by the over-emphasized avoidance of standardization. The organizational storage of client data, for example, was unsystematic, and different consultants serving the same client company often gathered the same base material instead of retrieving it from their own organization. Elomatic also suffered from situational learning because of its bureaucratic organization and occasionally authoritarian leadership style, both results of a rapid but poorly managed growth. Such conditions did not encourage organizational members, especially junior experts, to process new ideas.

All strategically significant learning, however, is not organizational. Neither does it occur within the firm's current concept of strategy. The target companies' third phase of development illustrates how episodes of individual learning that occur independent of the intended strategies may accumulate and, later on, contribute significantly to paradigmatic renewal.

In both target firms, many of the new experts that the management recruited to implement the intended strategies caused unexpected changes in the organization's actual pattern of action, as the firms' offerings were shaped by these individuals' competence, client contacts and personal interests (Mintzberg and McHugh, 1985). New knowledge was created by the experts' experiential learning occurring in projects that differed from the ordinary with regard to the nature of the client problem, the type of client company or the methods of solution. Furthermore, a large part of all knowledge acquisitions in the target firms could be characterized as the entrepreneurial managers' opportunistic moves driven by their personal learning.

While the target companies grew extensively and diversified their businesses, their management paid little or no attention to the changes that 'autonomous strategy formation' and 'entrepreneurial leaps' brought to the organizational knowledge base, thus allowing the changes to accumulate. In the course of the systematic strategic reorientation process, the target companies' managers, however, had to reflect upon the actual content of the company's competence portfolio and to decide which of the strategic runners deserved additional attention and investment. As the emergent changes in the knowledge base were formalized (Mintzberg and Waters, 1985) and integrated into the current concept of strategy (Burgelman, 1991) the target companies developed a new understanding of their strategic direction. The autonomous changes in the knowledge base had thus provided the basis from which the new paradigmatic assumptions were derived.

More importantly, the 'strategic runners' were not only integrated to the strategic intentions but also to the organizations' actual pattern of behaviour. The target firms' management implemented their new competitive strategies by developing organizational routines that would enhance and co-ordinate additional learning and, thus, transform the new knowledge into strategic capabilities. These capabilities, in turn, generated positive feedback, profitability and competitive success that established the target companies' new paradigms.

The role of industry-specific knowledge in SAMI's range provides an illustrative example of the above.

Although SAMI's specialized subunits had their 'natural markets', i.e. target groups for whom the benefits of their services were the most obvious, industry-specific knowledge was never planned to be an important part of SAMI's consulting services. On the contrary, it was considered unethical to provide strategic consulting to client companies that were competing with each other. For a consulting company that operated on the relatively small Finnish market, development of industry-specific knowledge was not believed to be a worthwhile pursuit. In the early 1990s SAMI's subunit that specialized in strategic marketing, however, recruited a consultant who, in addition to his other qualifications, happened to have expertise in trade. The new recruit turned out to be very successful. He developed new consulting concepts on the basis of his knowledge about trade and encouraged other organizational members to reconsider the issue of industry-specific knowledge. They concluded that strategy consulting within an industry was unethical only when it concerned the determination of the client's strategic direction, but that strategic development – and the typical projects SAMI took on – involved a great deal more. Nowadays SAMI's articulated goal is to provide high-quality consultancy services on the basis of three types of expertise: processual, function related and industry specific. In 1995, SAMI adopted a team-based organizational structure in which one group of teams was assigned to maintain and develop the firm's industry-specific knowledge.

Altogether, the most important one of a KIF's organizational knowledge creation processes seems to be the process that converts diverse knowledge resources into organizational capabilities. In such a process organizational routines developed to concretize the management's strategic vision and co-ordinate experiential learning of the organization's operational core. By emphasizing the role of organizational routines and broadly based individual learning in the development of strategic capabilities, the case findings reinforce the view that only knowledge that is noted by the strategic management can give a firm a sustainable competitive advantage (Andreu and Ciborra, 1994; Hamel, 1994; Leonard-Barton, 1992). On the other hand, the findings also imply a new interpretation of the path dependence of knowledge (Andreu and Ciborra, 1994; Dierickx and Cool, 1989). The sustainability of competitive advantages produced by a certain knowledge base does not depend on whether it was developed within the organization or was acquired from outside, but depends on what the management does to knowledge that already is in the organization. Although added professional knowledge acquired externally or through an individual expert's development can give a KIF competitive advantage, the sustainability of it depends on how the management interprets the significance of new knowledge and succeeds in integrating it into its intended strategies and making it a part of the organization's operational model.

Strategic Management Capability: a Contextual Factor and an Outcome of Learning

The process of strategic management is the arena in which the new paradigmatic assumptions – in a more or less conscious manner – emerge, become sharpened and established. Accordingly, it is only natural to assume that organizational strategic management practices have an important influence on paradigmatic learning. The case study results show clearly that the extent to which the management becomes conscious of its paradigmatic assumptions depends on how analytically, in which forums and by whom, strategic issues are dealt with in the organization. Three features of the KIF's strategic management appeared to be of particular importance: the team of top management in which the individual members' knowledge and inclinations complement each other, the discursive process of strategy making that involves members from all levels of the organizational hierarchy, and analytical language (Normann, 1985), which is conceptually advanced. These can be paralleled with the abilities of self-diagnosis and the skills of reflection that have been considered necessary for an entity's meta-learning capacity (Argyris and Schön, 1978; Senge, 1990).

With the increase in the target firms' size and age, the firm-specific features of their strategic management were replaced by more general features of KIF management (see, for example, Maister, 1993; Sveiby and Lloyd, 1987). This development represents 'professionalization of management', a process that is also implicit in the findings of organizational lifecycle research (Greiner, 1972; Miller and Friesen, 1984). Very few of the observed changes resulted from systematic assessment of the firm's strategic management capability and/or the managers' conscious efforts to improve the quality of its strategic management. Rather, the structural and systemic context of the target firms' strategic management had to be viewed as an expression of their given paradigms and managerial choices that grew out of it.

The case study evidence provides two types of illustration of how paradigms influence strategic management. First, the paradigm creates a particular power setting. A paradigm that builds mainly on professional values and on the realities of the knowledge-intensive production does not direct the strategic actors' attention to the problems of general management. In SAMI, the managing partners were experts in strategic development and, accordingly, constantly overlooked the problems of operative management. In Elomatic, the top management consisted of former experts, who instead of devoting their attention to strategic issues, often became too intrigued by the operative details. Second, the paradigm may bias individual decisions that are critical to strategic management capability. During its 25 years of development, Elomatic, for example, recruited two managing directors who both represented the shipbuilding industry, i.e. the area of technology that was preferred by the founder of the company. Yet, especially at the time of the second recruitment, designing in shipbuilding actually accounted for less than 15% of the group's total sales.

The experiences of both target companies suggest that managerial influences from outside the organization have a significant impact on both paradigmatic renewal and the development of strategic management capability. In SAMI, the tools of strategic thinking seemed to follow the fashion: developments in strategy theory were applied quickly in order to analyse their own business/organization. Elomatic, in turn, acquired 'strategic dissidents' by recruiting managers from other industries.

Furthermore, it became evident that experiential learning by individual managers may increase the firm's managerial knowledge in a way that supports the development of both the paradigm and strategic management capability. In fact, the founders of both target companies stated that they had progressed from 'confusion to comprehension' (Brytting, 1991: 178) in managing their knowledge-intensive businesses. Especially in Elomatic, however, the paradigm shift became concrete as a quantum change (Miller and Friesen, 1984) of strategic management practices.

> After recruiting a new managing director the top management became conscious of the problems that the inappropriate paradigm had caused the organization during its intensive growth. On the basis of this observation the strategic management practices were developed in order to provide more opportunities, arenas and tools for discussing the background assumptions of the strategic choices. They decided to have a more broadly based board and systematically to train the key expert managers in strategic thinking. The process of strategic planning was reorganized to encourage dialogue and participation.

Summary of the Emerging Framework

On the basis of the case study, a heuristic model of strategic learning in a KIF can be presented (see Figure 15.1). The results show clearly, that paradigmatic learning is the core process of strategic learning in KIFs. The dynamics of a KIF's strategic learning can be understood in relation to how the developments in the organizational knowledge base and in the strategic management capability affect the process of paradigmatic change.

Strategic decisions are made on the basis of the prevailing paradigm (see arrow A in Figure 15.1). Some of them shape and modify the organizational knowledge base while others affect the firm's strategic management capability (arrows B1 and B2).

The prevailing paradigm determines how the KIF management succeeds in developing organizational routines that co-ordinate the learning of the operative core and, thus, gradually transform the diverse individual and organizational knowledge resources into strategic capabilities. It is also crucial in determining whether the KIF is able to exploit the experiential learning of its individual experts to renew the organizational strategy or whether such learning as well as other autonomous knowledge creation processes merely disrupt the organizational knowledge base (see* symbols in Figure 15.1).

The KIF's strategic management capability constitutes two elements: individual-bound management knowledge and organizational strategic management practices, i.e. structures, systems and behavioural routines that could also be defined as organization-bound management knowledge. The KIF's strategic management capability constitutes the context of paradigmatic learning (arrow C in Figure 15.1). For example, changes in individual-bound management knowledge may contribute to paradigmatic change. The firm's individual-bound managerial knowledge may, for example, increase because of new recruits or as a result of experiential learning by individual managers.

Paradigmatic development itself is continuously driven by two factors (arrows E1 and E2 in Figure 15.1): changes in the organizational environment and changes in the personal interest of significant actors. The process of paradigmatic change is characterized by three phases: the gradual questioning of the prevailing assumptions and the rise of novel ones, paradigm shift and the refreezing of the paradigm (Barr et al., 1992; Bartunek, 1984; Hedberg and Jönsson, 1977; Johnson, 1990).

The results suggest a conception of paradigmatic change that is somewhat different from the previous ones. First of all, the phases of paradigmatic change are not necessarily so clearly separable and in sequence as most of the literature (at least implicitly) suggests. The first phase of paradigmatic change is characterized by gradual questioning of the prevailing assumptions and by a simultaneous rise of candidates for new assumptions. Thus, the first phase of paradigmatic change is more about increasing incoherency of the paradigm than about abandoning assumptions. The 'unlearning' seems to take place in the next phase and interactively with the crystallization of the new assumptions. The paradigm shift is therefore best described as the integration of old and new assumptions.

Moreover, there is always some kind of stir among the prevailing paradigmatic assumptions. This is encouraged by problems and opportunities as well as new people (Hedberg, 1981). The paradigmatic change, however, should be viewed as a complex process that needs special circumstances to be complete. The case study evidence suggests a perceived crisis to be the most important catalyst, because it may trigger a collective in-depth reflection that drives the paradigmatic change through all three phases. In contrast, key executive changes and other outside managerial influences, for example, may support the paradigmatic change by explicating and questioning unconscious assumptions. Yet, they are not likely to lead to a wide modification and reorganization of the paradigmatic assumptions (paradigm shift) nor to concrete actions of which the performance outcome would in time refreeze to become the new paradigm.

By 'collective in-depth reflection' we refer to a process that is analogous to what Mezirow (1990) has termed 'critical reflection'. In the process of critical reflection, the strategic actors not only become conscious of the action–outcome relationships of their choices but also of the pre-assumptions on which these choices were based. In the course of the process, these assumptions become modified and organized in such a manner that they enable a more resolving and coherent paradigm ('perspective' in Mezirow's terminology) to emerge. Finally, the process of critical reflection also includes decisions or other behavioural changes that make the new paradigm concrete.

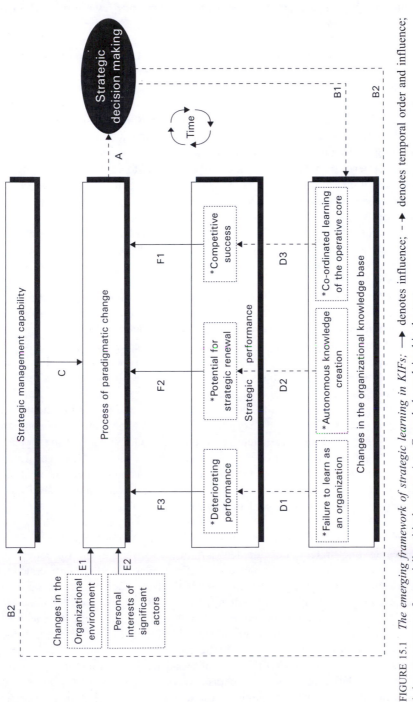

FIGURE 15.1 *The emerging framework of strategic learning in KIFs*; → denotes influence; -- → denotes temporal order and influence; * denotes sources of potentially critical events; A to G symbols explained in the text

The case study evidence suggests that there are at least four important linkages between organizational knowledge creation and paradigmatic developments, and that they all go through 'perceived strategic performance' (see arrows D1–D3 and F1–F3 in Figure 15.1).

1   Co-ordinated learning of the KIF's operative core is required to realize strategies. This type of organizational learning along the lines of intended strategies (Mintzberg, 1978) creates positive feedback that establishes the paradigm (arrows D3 and F1 in Figure 15.1). It is important to note, however, that accidental and/or misinterpreted business success may also more or less unconsciously give paradigmatic character to strategic choices that the significant actors imagine explain the success.
2   A weak performance, in turn, is more likely to lead to a reflection of strategic choices. It may also occasionally surface and question the assumptions behind the choices as well as raise challenging assumptions (arrows D1 and F3 in Figure 15.1).
3   A continued failure to learn as an organization is likely to cause problems that ultimately accumulate into a crisis. A perceived crisis, in turn, as explained above, encourages critical reflection and may thus trigger a process of complete paradigmatic change.
4   After an organization has entered a 'period of flux' (Mintzberg, 1978) during which there is a lack of clarity about the strategic direction of the organization, autonomous changes of the organizational knowledge base may contribute to paradigmatic renewal as they become noted and subsequently formalized by the strategic management (Burgelman, 1991; Mintzberg and Waters, 1985). In the target firms, such changes were provoked by the management's opportunistic knowledge acquisitions and by the experts' experiential learning occurring in projects that differed from the ordinary with regard to the nature of the client problem, the type of client company or the methods of solution (arrow D2 in Figure 15.1). New paradigmatic assumptions became crystallized and some of the old ones were finally abandoned, as the target firms' management went deeply into the critical evaluation and reorganization of the organizational knowledge base and developed new competence-based conceptions of their corporate strategies (arrow F2 in Figure 15.1).

A novel feature of the framework in relation to previous conceptions of learning in the context of strategic development is that it incorporates both a collective cognitive process within the group of significant actors and a more concrete structural and behavioural process that affects the firm's core competencies and strategic management capability (Hedberg, 1981). This requisite is made concrete in the idea of collective remembrance as a method of critical reflection as well as in the Mezirow's (1990) definition of critical reflection, which also entails the deployment of the insights developed in the process.

There are several grounds for this type of broad and integrating view of strategic learning in KIFs. In KIFs there seems always to be a relatively small group of significant actors whose thinking and acting guides the firm's strategic future. The composition of this group is not determined by the formal management hierarchy and it may also vary in the course of the company's history. Nevertheless, this group of significant actors is always there and, therefore, the greater the centralization of power, the more important it becomes to understand the psychosocial reality prevailing in it (Normann, 1977: 32).

KIFs are, by nature, very individualistic organizations. Individual key experts and other powerful organizational members are likely to have a more visible role in influencing the content of the firm's strategy than their colleagues in more traditional and bureaucratic manufacturing organizations (Mintzberg and McHugh, 1985). Therefore, the framework also aims at understanding how learning by individual managers and key experts is linked to the overall process of strategic learning.

Despite their tendency to depend on the individual-bound expert knowledge, the KIF's strategic performance hinges on its management's capability of increasing the value of the organization. In the long run, this is measured by how the KIF succeeds in developing strategic capabilities, i.e. organizational routines that consistently deploy the diverse knowledge resources to provide superior value to clients or customers. It is logical to include these behavioural aspects in the framework of strategic learning because only in the form of routine changes is learning in the organizational context most likely to have effects that are more than transient (Levitt and March, 1988). Altogether, it is the process of complete paradigmatic change and the deployment of the insights developed during this process that make strategic learning cumulative.

Conclusions

This chapter reports a preliminary attempt to describe the diversity of processes that relate learning to strategic change in a particular group of organizations that are termed 'knowledge intensive'. Despite their inherent dependence on knowledge, KIFs do not constitute ideal learning organizations any more than organizations of some other type would. Yet, they are interesting laboratories for studying the development of dynamic capabilities, as the process of interest is 'transparently observable' in them (Pettigrew, 1990).

On the basis of the results, it can be argued that more holistic approaches and interdisciplinary collaboration are needed to understand strategic learning. The strategic learning approach developed here fits Elfring and Volberda's definition of a synthesizing school (connecting theory and practice of strategic management) as discussed in Chapter 1. Moreover, it seems to be closely related to the dynamic capabilities school of strategic management. The strategic learning perspective developed in this chapter provides the dynamic capabilities school with conceptual language that describes the processes through which core competencies and strategic capabilities develop. It bridges strategy and organization theory but, at the same time, adds psychology and educational sciences to the list of base disciplines by emphasizing phenomena that relate to cognitive processes, values and emotions. The strategic learning approach also adds two clusters of problem areas to the dynamic capabilities school: first, how can we develop an organizational design that would enhance and co-ordinate individual learning for the benefit of the whole and, second, how can we manage the development of collective cognitive structures?

A number of managerial implications can be drawn from the case study results. First, both the management's definition of strategy and the measures taken to implement it are important for the development of strategic capabilities. Defining strategy as an idea for strategic capability might be an appropriate way to give a concrete form to the intended competitive advantage. To define its idea for a strategic capability the management must make an explicit and clear decision on the logic of its competitive edge and, moreover, identify the concrete knowledge resources, business processes and organizational routines that realize this logic. Second, the development of strategic capabilities in a KIF involves the challenge of maintaining the delicate balance between 'creative chaos' and systematic management. Diversity and autonomy make the emergence of new knowledge possible. Yet, effective learning calls for repetition ensured by direction and standardization. As the KIF managers strive to develop flexible structures that permit autonomous changes in the knowledge base, they must stay alert to notice and critically evaluate the emerging new competencies. A part of these strategic runners will (and should) always be rejected, but those with the most potential for a strategic capability must be integrated into the firm's current concept of strategy and be consistently supported by the development of organizational routines that will co-ordinate the learning of the operative core. Third, the best way to enhance strategic learning, however, is to manage the core of this process, that is, paradigmatic learning. This is done by developing conceptual tools and organizational arenas for collective self-diagnosis and reflection.

16

The State of Art of the Dynamic Capabilities School

Howard Thomas

Overview

Over the past 20 years one basic question which has occupied the attention of both strategy researchers and practitioners alike is 'With whom, and how, do firms compete and how do they sustain their competitive advantage over time?' This question has become even more complex given the increasing pace of technological change and global competition in the business environment. How research in competitive strategy has attempted to answer this question is the subject of this reflective commentary.

I comment first on the nature of the three schools of strategic thought, the lite-rature review provided by Sanchez on the dynamic capabilities school and the chapters by Sanchez and Mahoney and Kirjavainan. Since Sanchez's review sets the context of the discussion and covers much ground, this commentary provides an alternative viewpoint on the subject of theory development.

Comments on Chapters 13, 14 and 15

In Chapter 13, Sanchez (and Elfring and Volberda, Chapter 1) notes the existence of three schools of thought in the strategy field, namely the boundary school, the configurational school and the dynamic capabilities school. Each of these is described as a synthesizing approach for enhancing theory development in strategy yet each seems to be presented as a relatively separate school of thought. My pref-erence is to see much more overlap between the schools, which should, therefore, provide a basis for theory dialogue, discussion and debate in the spirit of Bowman's (1990) call for 'theoretical pluralism' in the development of the strategy field.

Sanchez provides a review of many of the main themes in the dynamic capa-bilities school, which he defines as including the concepts of the resource-based view and competence-based competition. While the review is thorough and measured, I view it as a relatively narrow treatment since it largely excludes treatment of the economic, cognitive and behavioural approaches including strategic groups and managerial cognition, which have led to the evolution of the research stream in competitive strategy. It also seems to ignore two very significant papers in the evolution of the resource-based view of the firm, namely Rumelt's (1984) paper on the strategic theory of the firm and Lippman and Rumelt's (1982) paper on the concept of uncertain imitability, which underlie much of Barney and Prahalad and Hamel's theoretical framework.

Sanchez positions the contributions of Chapter 14 by Sanchez and Mahoney and Chapter 15 by Kirjavainan in the areas of strategic flexibility and organizational learning, respectively. I agree with this assessment and, therefore, will complement his commentary by providing a number of observations and questions about each chapter.

Sanchez and Mahoney (Chapter 14) propose that modularity in product designs can 'improve the overall strategic flexibility of a firm to respond to and initiate strategic change at several levels within the organization'. It is argued that modularity in product designs can, inter alia, increase the firm's product variety, speed in upgrading products and make possible modular organization designs for creating and producing products. While the concept of modularity and platform designs is well entrenched in the Clark–Wheelwright Harvard school (1995) of operations management, the chapter's general thesis evokes the following observations and questions. Is strategic flexibility (see also Kathryn Harrigan's (1985b) early book on the subject) a resource, a competence or a capability or is it simply a form of organizational slack, using March and Simon's (1958) term? Similarly, is modularity a dynamic capability or a competence? Will modular product organizations survive as viable organizational forms? The studies on the workings of Ford's Team Taurus and Chrysler's LH platforms in the automobile area suggest that platform teams are temporary or transient organizational forms that may not fit easily into corporate organizational structures.

Kirjavainan's discussion (Chapter 15), focused on organizational learning, follows the European tradition of processual research in strategy (Pettigrew, 1985), i.e. the use of fine-grained, case study research to develop insights into research issues. Her comparative study of knowledge and learning in a consulting and a design team suggests that individual learning and knowledge can be transformed into organizational learning through a series of cyclical adaptive processes that may, in turn, force changes in organizational structures. As the competitive process evolves, the strategic learning processes may result in the development of organizational, team and knowledge-based core competences. Clearly, the strength of this research approach is the fine-grained organizational detail and the potential for framing research hypotheses based on the data. The clear weakness is the self-selection of the two case study research sites and the attendant lack of generalizability to the class of knowledge intensive firms (KIFs) as a whole. For example, what types of firms would be described as KIFs? Do consultants and designers differ from software and biotechnology engineers in their learning frameworks and in developing team-embodied competences?

Both chapters suggest areas of firm competence such as modularity, strategic flexibility, organizational learning and team-based skills, which can affect how firms can, and do, perform in the market place.

In the following sections I attempt to build upon these research papers both to frame the question of how firms compete and to tie together future strategy research under the umbrella of the resource-based view of the firm.

The Evolution of Competitive Strategy Research

To answer the questions of who competes with whom and how firms compete, it is clearly required that researchers adopt a unit of analysis more fine grained than the industry level of analysis, but at a level of aggregation often greater than the firm level alone. This question has been addressed from several different theoretical perspectives. How these perspectives are integrated and moulded to develop a multidimensional theoretical framework for understanding basic issues of competition and rivalry, is important for the field of strategy. Economic, cognitive and social forces can all influence the ways firms define competitors, the strategies adopted by those firms in pursuing their interests and the outcomes of both their contests and collaborations.

Beginning with the earliest theories regarding spatial competition, competitive strategy research gained its early inspiration largely from the literature on industrial organizational (I-O) economics (Bain, 1968), examining how the economic characteristics of firms within an industry have been used to place firms within strategic groups (McGee and Thomas, 1986). Drawing from the literature on managerial cognition, other researchers (Porac et al., 1989; Reger and Huff, 1993) have attempted to identify cognitive communities within an industry based upon the shared mental models and 'maps' that executives use to evaluate their environment and identify their rivals, as well as the dimensions along which they compete. As research has evolved, the methods and perspectives of social network analysis have also been used to examine issues both of interorganizational rivalry and co-operation within industries. Finally, the more recent literature on the resource-based view of the firm (Penrose, 1959) and competence-based competition (Prahalad and Hamel, 1990) can provide a basis for integration of the economic, cognitive and social approaches to competition, and for developing a set of questions to guide future research in this area.

Tying it All Together

Notions of competitive space are discussed within competence-based competition. In their book *Competing for the Future*, Hamel and Prahalad (1994) suggest that rather than behaving reactively by identifying how to compete within their existing competitive space, those firms which will be most successful in the future strive not only to reshape their existing competitive space, but to create new competitive spaces for themselves as well. The resource-based view encompasses elements of both the strategic groups and the management cognition literatures. The resource configurations identified by strategic groups researchers interact with the cognitive recipes or mental models which managers possess to shape the ways in which growth strategies are developed and implemented. Each can influence the other, and the degree to which management correctly identifies and leverages its resources impacts the firm's potential for developing a sustained competitive advantage. Firms do not develop these cognitive recipes (Spender, 1989) in isolation, however. As Porac and his colleagues have shown (1995), networks of relationships among competitors can help to shape individual mental models and develop stable, commonly shared beliefs regarding firm capabilities and patterns of competition within an industry. Powell and his colleagues (1996) have demonstrated that networks can be used for co-operative as well as competitive purposes, and that networks of relationships can be used to develop and leverage a firm's core competences. Further, the ability to develop and manage network relationships can be a core competence in itself.

Where do we go from Here? Future Directions in Competitive Strategy Research

The resource-based view and competence-based competition possess a number of qualities that can be used to direct competitive strategy research. First, this theoretical perspective places substantial emphasis on performance, specifically the ability to develop and maintain sustainable competitive advantage. Questions regarding why some firms outperform others are the province of strategy researchers alone.

Second, this perspective is dynamic, rather than static in nature. Much of the past research in strategy has attempted to answer the question 'What do firms do?' A more useful question is 'How do firms do what they do?' The dynamic systems and routines through which competences or resources are developed and leveraged are then considered explicitly, rather than just assumed to occur.

Third, this perspective encourages a focus upon longitudinal evaluations of strategic activity. Much past and current strategy research is cross-sectional rather than longitudinal in design (Lewin and Volberda, 1999). The temporal and path-dependent nature of longitudinal process examinations is significant in developing a greater understanding of firm strategy development and should be included in future research.

Finally, this perspective is process, not just outcome, oriented. Resources alone are not the key. The implementation of strategy is integral to the understanding of strategy itself; the two cannot be separated. Studying assets alone is not useful because tangible assets themselves become relatively insignificant in comparison to the ways in which they are deployed.

I would like to propose six issues, which I think should drive future competitive strategy research. They are:

1   definitional issues
2   measurement issues
3   the unit of analysis considered
4   the study of processes, not states
5   the examination of organizational failures, as well as successes
6   a greater consideration of microanalytic data from within the organization.

Definitional Issues

To date we as a field have not reached consensus on precise definitions (Camerer, 1985). Although a certain amount of imprecision is to be expected given the relative newness of competence-based research, hair splitting over the definitions of key constructs will become counterproductive if it continues for much longer. For example, what is the real difference between resources, capabilities and competences and how does the qualifier 'dynamic' help? One way to answer that question is to ask, 'Are these distinctions empirically tractable?' In other words, can we measure them and, if so, does each construct really measure different things? If the answer to these questions is no, then the construct should be discarded or redefined in a more tractable and useful way. The same tests may be applied to discussions of competence building versus competence leveraging, and the relationship between goals and performance. It is unlikely that the question, 'Are competence building and leveraging distinct activities?' has a simple yes or no answer. Whether, through a given activity, a firm is building or leveraging a competence may be a matter of degree, and may also be somewhat context dependent. Issues regarding how we define what constitutes firm performance, and how different performance measures are related to the firm's goals, also need to be revisited. Accounting measures such as return on investment (ROI) and return on assets (ROA), while convenient, are imperfect, may be subject to manipulation, and may or may not be related to the firm's true strategic goals and objectives.

Measurement Issues

Developing consistent definitions of constructs such as competences, competence building or leverage and performance is only half the battle. In order to be useful, these definitions must also be measurable. If a construct is conceptually clear but empirically impossible to measure, then it is of limited use in advancing our quest for knowledge. This does not necessarily mean that measurement must be easy, but it must be possible. Alternative – and, in some cases, less quantitative – measures of the key constructs mentioned above need to be considered (Sanchez and Thomas, 1996).

Unit of Analysis

Strategy research has at one point or another considered the business unit, the firm, the group, the product market, the process market and the industry as appropriate units of analysis. All of these units of analysis are helpful in framing competition. However, the identification and leveraging of core competences is a concept that can span all units of analysis. In determining a firm's core competences and how they affect firm performance, it may be useful in future research to consider their impact at two or more of these units of analysis simultaneously. Such an approach provides necessary triangulation and enhances the value of the concept of competence.

Study Processes, not just States

The longitudinal study of processes suggests a change in focus away from the absolute values of measures and towards the change in value of a measure or measures over time, as well as the rate at which they change. Many traditional measures used in strategy research, which to date have only been examined cross-sectionally, could be examined from this perspective as well, providing new insights (Thomas et al., 1996).

Examine Organizational Failures

In a cross-sectional study of existing firms in an industry, firms that have failed are by definition excluded from the study. By taking a longitudinal approach, researchers may more easily examine the causes of organizational under-performance and failure, as well as success. It is important to remember, however, that asking why firms fail is not simply the converse of asking why firms succeed. These factors need not be opposite ends of a single continuum. They may, in fact, reflect two separate continua that interact. A firm that takes actions which lead to failure, but that also takes other actions which lead to success, may continue to exist, but in a chronic state of under-performance. Such a firm is different from a firm that sits in the middle range of both continua. Firms that simultaneously occupy the extremes of both continua may have a greater potential for superior performance if they can learn how to reduce those factors which, all else being equal, would lead to failure. Researchers also need to make a greater effort to study outliers in an industry – both good and bad. By focusing on these extreme cases, researchers are more likely to learn about those factors which determine success and failure. Thus, researchers should endeavour to break with the analytical approach that currently dominates strategy research, i.e. focusing on those factors which result in convergence and identifying central tendencies within the data.

Consider Microanalytic Data

There is a need to get inside the firm and study processes at the individual – or perhaps more appropriately – the team level. Network approaches to studying the decision-making processes within teams, especially top management teams within an organization, and the interactions and dynamics between teams within an organization may be especially useful. Such research would provide us with a greater understanding of how the firm works and where its true competences may lie. This microlevel behavioural data may then be linked to organizational behavioural data, thus linking individuals (or teams) to organizational processes. It is through these linkages that organizational competences may be identified and highlighted.

Conclusion

Attempting to answer the question 'With whom and how do firms compete and how do they sustain their advantage?' has been at the centre of much of my research over the last 15 years. What started out as an analytical convenience, the notion that firms could be arranged into strategic groups, was discovered to be a phenomena with significant implications for the structure and function of corporate competition and performance. Over the years I, and others, have applied a variety of theoretical perspectives in this area of enquiry, and have raised as many questions as we have answered. In this commentary, I have attempted to use aspects of my own research stream to reflect on the work that has been done in this area, and to suggest an integrative theoretical perspective and set of issues that may be used to guide future competitive strategy research. The use of multiple lenses for viewing phenomena, increased precision in the definitions of constructs and the measures used to test them, the adoption of dynamic longitudinal designs and a focus on multiple units of analysis will all continue to further our understanding of the ways companies co-operate and compete for sustained advantage.

PART V

THE CONFIGURATIONAL SCHOOL: STRATEGY AS A DECISION OF TRANSITION FROM ONE ARCHETYPE TO ANOTHER

17

Researching Configuration

Henry Mintzberg, Bruce Ahlstrand and Joseph Lampel[1]

In this volume, the configurational school is considered to be one of the options for synthesis in strategic management. What are the antecedents of this school? In this chapter we begin with a discussion of the work on configuration with some of the early research carried out by the management policy group at McGill University. We follow this with discussion of the work of Danny Miller, the first person to receive his doctorate from that group, who has been particularly prolific in the configuration school. We then turn to a review of other research of this nature.

Configuration Studies at McGill University

The arrival of Pradip Khandwalla at McGill University's Faculty of Management in the early 1970s stimulated interest there in the configuration approach. In his doctoral thesis at Carnegie-Mellon University, Khandwalla (1970) uncovered what amounted to an empirical justification for this approach. Effectiveness in the organizations he studied related not to the use of any particular attribute, such as the decentralization of power or a particular approach to planning, but to the intercorrelations between several attributes. In other words, organizations functioned effectively because they put different characteristics together in complementary ways – for example, a certain kind of planning with a certain form of structuring with a certain style of leading.

This finding stimulated the interest of one of us in the concept of configuration, reflected especially in two books that categorized organizations, one in terms of their structures (Mintzberg, 1979), the other in terms of their power relationships (Mintzberg, 1983). Taking these two together, organizations were described as being entrepreneurial, machine, professional, adhocracy, diversified, political and missionary.

A major research project began at McGill in 1971 to track the strategies of various organizations over long periods of time, typically 30 to 50 or more years. The approach was therefore historical, designed to identify periods of stable strategy and of transformation, and then to address a number of broad questions – for example, how do different strategies connect to each other, what forces drive strategic change, when are strategies imposed deliberately and when and how do they emerge?

Strategies were identified as patterns in action that sustained themselves for identifiable periods of time, for example, with regard to aircraft purchase at Air Canada or store openings at Steinbergs (Mintzberg et al., 1998). These strategies were then lined up against one another along a common time scale to identify distinct stages in the history of the organization. Among the types of stages identified were:

- stage of development (hiring people, establishing systems, firming up strategic positions, etc.)
- stage of stability (fine tuning the strategies and structures, etc. in place)
- stage of adaptation (marginal changes in structures and strategic positions)
- stage of struggle (groping for a new sense of direction, whether in limbo, in flux or by experimentation)
- stage of revolution (rapid transformation of many characteristics concurrently).

Also of interest was how such stages tend to sequence themselves over time. Four main patterns were recognized:

- *periodic bumps*, which were common, especially in conventional organizations; long periods of stability interrupted by occasional periods of revolution
- oscillating shifts, when stages of adaptive convergence toward stability were followed by ones of divergent struggle for change, sometimes in surprisingly regular cycles
- lifecycles, where a stage of development was followed by one of stability or maturity, etc.
- regular progress, in which the organization engaged in more or less steady adaptation.

Clearly the first three of these are more compatible with the premises of the configuration school than the fourth.

These patterns seem to map rather well on to the forms of organization discussed earlier. Periodic bumps may be especially characteristic of the machine organization, which tends to change by occasional revolutions, known as 'turnaround'. The adhocracy, in contrast, seems to prefer the oscillating shifts, alternately diverging to allow for maximum creativity in its projects and then converging after too much variety to 'get some order around here'. The professional organization seems to favour regular progress, which means almost perpetual adaptation at the operating level with rarely any dramatic transformation overall. Lifecycles may be characteristic of all organizations, in some sense, except that some live longer than others (perhaps through repeated mid-life crises). The entrepreneurial organization is obviously favoured in the earliest stage of this cycle, but it also appears during the turnaround of the mature organization, when a strong leader tends to exercise decisive control.

Miller's Contribution to Configuration

Danny Miller, affiliated initially with McGill University and then the École des Hautes Etudes Commerciales of Montreal, has been prolific in this area. His work has been especially ambitious in its integration across different attributes of organizations, and in its combination of breadth (large samples) with depth (probes into specific organizations). While some of Miller's research reflects traditional contingency theory, most fits squarely into the configuration school of strategic management. It deals with what Miller (1982, 1996) likes to call archetypes, that is, states of strategy, structure, situation and process, with transitions between archetypes, and with strategic and structural change as quantum rather than incremental.

Archetypes

Miller's doctoral dissertation (Miller, 1976; see also 1979) used published studies of companies to construct 10 archetypes of strategy formation: four of failure and six of success. For example, in the 'stagnant bureaucracy' 'a previously placid and simple environment has lulled the firm to sleep. The top management is emotionally committed to the old strategies, and the information systems are too feeble to provide it with evidence of the need to change ...' (Miller and Friesen, 1984: 94). Other failure archetypes include the the 'headless giant' (a set of businesses with weak central authority) and the 'aftermath' (where a new team is trying to effect a turnaround with scarce resources and inadequate experience), while among the success archetypes are the 'dominant firm' (well established, generally immune from serious challenge, with key patents, centralized structures and traditional strategies), the 'entrepreneurial conglomerate' (an extension of the rather bold and ingenious person who built and continues to run the organization) and the 'innovator' (generally, a smaller firm with niche strategies, a simple structure and an undiversified product line, with much product innovation).

A Quantum View of Change

In later work, Miller and Friesen (1980, 1982; Miller, 1982) described change in organizations as quantum, an idea that goes to the very heart of the configuration school. Quantum change means the changing of many elements concurrently, in contrast to piecemeal change – one element at a time, say strategy first, then structure, then systems, etc. Such change may be rapid – revolutionary, to use their word – although it can also unfold gradually.

This view suggests that organizations resolve the opposing forces for change and continuity by attending first to one and then to the other. While some strategy or other may always be changing at the margins it seems equally true that major shifts in strategic perspective occur only rarely. For example, in the Steinberg study, only two important reorientations were found in 60 years, while at Air Canada, no major shift was found over the airline's first four decades, following its initial positioning (Mintzberg et al., 1998). Otherwise, organizations spend most of their time pursuing given strategic orientations (perfecting a particular retailing formula, for example). This suggests that success is achieved not by changing strategies, but by exploiting those already in place.

While this goes on, however, the world changes, sometimes slowly, occasionally in a dramatic shift. Thus, at some point the configuration falls out of synchronization with its environment. Then what Miller and Friesen call a strategic revolution has to take place, during which many things change at once. In effect, the organization tries to leap to a new stability to re-establish as quickly as possible an integrated posture among a new set of strategies, structures and culture – in other words, a new configuration.

But what about all the emergent strategies that grow like weeds around the organization? What the quantum theory suggests is that the really novel ones are generally held in check in some corner of the organization until a strategic revolution becomes necessary. Then, instead of having to develop new strategies from scratch or having to copy those of competitors, the organization can find its new deliberate direction within its own emerging patterns.

The quantum theory of change seems to apply particularly well to large, established, mass-production organizations – the machines. Because they are so reliant on standardized procedures, they tend to resist serious strategic change fiercely. So here is where we tend to find the long periods of stability punctured by the short bouts of transformation. Adhocracies, in contrast, seem to follow a more balanced pattern of change and stability, earlier labelled oscillating shifts (see Mintzberg and McHugh, 1985 on a film making company). Organizations in the business of producing novel outputs apparently need to fly off in all directions for periods of time to sustain their creativity, then settle down to find some order in the resulting chaos.

Change as Revolutionary or Incremental?

Miller's notion of change as revolutionary in the configuration school is countered by Quinn's notion of change as incremental in the learning school. This, in fact, has become one of the debates of strategic management, paralleled by the great debate in biology between Stephen Jay Gould's claims about punctuated equilibrium and Charles Darwin's concept of change as evolutionary. Of course, which it is depends on how closely you look, and from which vantage point. (Gould, for example, has described a million years as barely a moment in his perception of time.) Thus, change that appears incremental to one observer may seem revolutionary to another.

Different researchers in strategic management have, in fact, focused on different types of organizations and different episodes in their development. They have also studied different phenomena. For example, whereas Quinn interviewed individual executives about their thought processes (namely their intentions and perceptions), Miller tracked the recorded behaviours of organizations (namely their actions and outcomes). So the two might, in fact, have been describing two sequential stages in the same process: strategists may learn incrementally and then drive strategic change in revolutionary fashion. In other words, organizations may bide their time until they figure out where they have to go, and then, when a strategic window opens, they leap.

Excellence and the Perils of Excellence

In an early article, Miller together with Mintzberg (1983) argued that the approach of configuration – what they called 'the perspective of synthesis' – offers a rich basis for describing organizations. Many factors can be taken into account in describing various forms. Moreover, configuration might well be a natural state of affairs; Darwinian forces could drive organizations to seek some kind of coherence among their different parts, which can be synergistic and, so, efficient. Indeed, such coherence could also make these organizations easier to understand and, therefore, to manage, for example, by enabling managers to apply only those techniques appropriate for a given configuration (matrix structures in adhocracies, quality circles in machine-type organizations, etc.).

In a more recent article, Miller (1993: 130) went further. He suggested that configuration may be 'the essence of strategy': since strategy is pattern, no coherence or consistency over time implies no overall strategy. Miller also elaborated upon the advantages of configuration, for example, that it makes imitation more difficult and allows the organization to react more quickly. But it may have a serious downside as well, making things too simple for the manager: '... simplicity is dangerous because it can blind managers and tether their organizations to a confining set of skills, concerns, and environmental states.' Thus, while writers such as Peters and Waterman (1982) and Porter (1980) have conveyed the message that outstanding performance often *demands* dedicated, even passionate, single-mindedness, that may become the very problem. The very things that make an organization excellent can breed subsequent failure.

Miller, in fact, elaborated upon this in a book called *The Icarus Paradox* (1990b), drawing on the legend of the Greek figure whose ability to fly drew him close to the sun, which melted the wax holding together the feathers of his wings and sent him tumbling to his death. In a similar vein, Miller described four main 'trajectories' he uncovered in his research that lead from success to failure.

- The focusing trajectory takes punctilious, quality-driven craftsmen – organizations with masterful engineers and airtight operations – and turns them into rigidly controlled, detail-obsessed tinkerers – firms whose insular, technocratic cultures alienate customers with perfect but irrelevant offerings.

- The venturing trajectory converts growth-driven, entrepreneurial builders – companies managed by imaginative leaders and creative planning and financial staffs – into impulsive, greedy imperialists, who severely overtax their resources by expanding helter-skelter into businesses they know nothing about.
- The inventing trajectory takes pioneers with unexcelled R and D departments, flexible think-tank operations, and state-of-the-art products, and transforms them into utopian escapists, run by cults of chaos-loving scientists who squander resources in the pursuit of hopelessly grandiose and futuristic inventions.
- Finally, the decoupling trajectory transforms salesmen – organizations with unparalleled marketing skills, prominent brand names and broad markets, into aimless, bureaucratic drifters, whose sales fetish obscures design issues, and who produce a stale and disjointed line of 'me-too' offerings (Miller, 1990b: 4–5).

Notice how constructive configurations become destructive ones, yet remain configurations nonetheless. Indeed, configuration becomes the very problem. Lest anyone be inclined to doubt Miller's argument, the firms he names as having been 'trapped' by these trajectories include IBM, Procter & Gamble, Texas Instruments, Chrysler, General Motors, Apple Computer and Walt Disney Productions among many others. Maybe we simply have to put up with cycles of success and failure, growth and decline (which is, of course, the 'natural' human condition).

Probes into Configuration

Research work on configuration as well as transformation has hardly been absent from the discussions of our other schools, for example, on strategic groups in the positioning school, on reframing in the cognitive school, turnaround in the entrepreneurial school and stagnation in the cultural school (as the absence of transformation). Here we consider several intense research probes into configuration and, in the next section, ones into transition.

Strategy and Structure

In turning to other studies about configuration that have had wide circulation in strategic management, we must begin with Chandler's (1962) work on strategy and structure. As noted earlier, in studying the evolution of 'the large American industrial enterprise', Chandler identified four 'chapters' in their history, which, in sequence, represent stages in their lifecycles. First was the initial acquisition of resources of plant, equipment and people or of the purchase and consolidation of smaller firms that had already done this (as in the origins of General Motors). Marketing and distribution channels were built and control was obtained over supplies (which came to be known as vertical integration). Second, the executives turned to the more efficient use of these resources, with the establishment of functional structures (production, sales, etc.) to co-ordinate the throughput. Third, there followed another period of growth, as limits were met in the initial markets; the firms diversified into new markets or new lines of business related to the existing ones and, fourth, that required a second shift in structure too. This came to be known as the divisionalized form, pioneered by Dupont, so that each business could be managed by a particular unit, reporting for overall financial control to a central headquarters.

Chandler, of course, completed his study long ago. Were he to update it today, he might be inclined to add a stage of consolidation of business and outsourcing of certain activities, reversing the earlier moves toward diversification and vertical integration. Large firms now typically concentrate on key businesses and core competences, while shedding many of their activities in favour of an extended network of associates. This, together with Chandler's four stages, suggests oscillating cycles of control and release.

Chandler's work was extended particularly by a string of doctoral theses at the Harvard Business School. These were not, however, done as his kind of deep probe into specific companies, rather as larger sample surveys of many firms, to understand better the relationships between the strategies of diversification and the structures of divisionalization. Probably best known is the study by Rumelt (published as a book in 1974), who found that although some 70% of the firms in the Fortune 500 were in a single or a dominant business in 1949, by 1969 over half of these firms had diversified, many into categories he called related or unrelated (namely conglomerate) businesses (or else had been acquired and so had their places usually taken by other, more diversified firms). In parallel with this, much as Chandler had found, they matched their new strategies with new structures of product-based diversification (from 20% of the firms in 1949 to 75% in 1969). While there has been some backtracking since, a broader conclusion that Rumelt drew may now hold even more strongly: besides strategy, 'structure also follows fashion' (Rumelt, 1974: 149).

Prospectors and Defenders

A very different study of configuration, but no less popular among academics as well as some practitioners, has been that of Miles and Snow (1978; Miles et al., 1978). Based on a study of firms in four industries (textbook publishing, electronics, food processing and health care), they classified corporate behaviours into four broad categories, which they labelled defenders, prospectors, analysers and reactors, each with 'its own unique strategy for relating to its chosen market(s)', as well as its related 'particular configuration of technology, structure, and process' (Miles et al., 1978: 550–7).

- The defender is concerned with stability, namely how to 'seal off a portion of the market in order to create a stable domain ... a limited set of products [is] directed into a narrow segment of the total market'. There, to keep out competitors, the defender prices competitively or concentrates on quality. Technological efficiency is important, as is strict control of the organization.
- The prospector, in contrast, actively searches out innovative new product and market opportunities (sometimes even at the expense of profitability). The key here is to maintain flexibility, in both technology and administrative arrangements.

- The analyser sits between the defenders and the prospectors, seeking to 'minimize risk while maximizing the opportunity for profit', so that the approach is best described as 'balanced'.
- The reactor, unlike the other three, reacts to its environment. This is a failure; 'inconsistent and unstable'. In other words, here we have a 'residual' strategy, arising when one of the other three strategies is inappropriately pursued.

Hence, the Miles and Snow typology reduces to two basic forms, which seem to correspond to the machine and adhocracy organizations, with the third a hybrid form and the fourth really a collection of inappropriate responses.

Rational, Bureaucratic and Political Actors

Graham Allison's (1971) celebrated study of the behaviour of the Soviet and American decision makers during the Cuban Missile Crisis is another excellent example of configurational work, linking dimensions of strategy (or 'policy' in government), structure and managerial style, etc. Allison claimed that people 'think about problems of foreign and military policy in terms of largely implicit conceptual models that have significant consequences for the content of their thought'. He outlined three in particular.

The rational actor model sees government actions 'as the more or less purposive acts of unified national governments'. Goals are clear, choices are made, actions follow. 'Predictions about what a nation will do or would have done are generated by calculating the rational thing to do in a certain situation, given specified objectives.'

Allison called this model 'useful' but in need of being 'supplemented, if not supplanted', by the two other 'frames of reference that focus on the government machine'. The organizational process model focuses on the internal systemic process of government – 'the strengths, standard operating procedures, and repertoires' of the various parts of the organization as a bureaucratic system. The key is to understand the patterns of behaviours among the relevant units – as gears and levers in decision making. The governmental politics model concentrates on the politics of government: '... what happens is characterized as a *resultant* of various bargaining games among players in the national government'. The focus is on the 'perceptions, motivations, power, and maneuvers of the players'. The events are explained by understanding 'who did what to whom', based on the relative power and skills of the different players (Allison, 1971: 3–7).

Probes into Periods of Transition

Another body of configuration research probes deeply into the periods of major change in organizations. A good example of this is Pettigrew's (1985, 1987) study of transformation at ICI, which integrates the material of a number of schools. Pettigrew viewed such change, not as an episode, but as a series of episodes. To understand such change, Pettigrew argued for the need to go beyond rational–linear theories. There is a need to examine:

... the juxtaposition of the rational and the political, the quest for efficiency and power, the role of exceptional [people] and extreme circumstances, the untidiness of chance, forces in the environment, and to explore some of the conditions in which mixtures of these occur. (Pettigrew, 1985: 24)

Pettigrew drew the following conclusions about the change process at ICI from 1969 to 1986.

1   Change did not occur as a continuous incremental process.
2   The pattern of change was for radical eras of change to occur at periodic intervals. Of the three periods of high levers of change activity, two, the ones between 1960 and 1964 and 1980 to 1986 could be sensibly labeled as revolutionary in that they featured substantial ideological, structural, and business strategy change ... The periods between these packages of changes were occasions for implementing and stabilizing changes, and ... eras of organizational learning when ideological justification was prepared for the revolutionary break.
3   Each of these periods of high levers of change activity was associated with world economic recessions, with their associated effects on ... ICI's relative business performance. In other words, ICI made substantial changes only when it was in severe economic difficulties. However, a critical facet of these change periods was ... also the active strategies by managers to construct a climate for change around the performance difficulties.
4   The revolutionary periods of change were also connected with changes in leadership and power in ICI.
5   Finally, within the eras of revolutionary change there was little evidence to support Chandler's ... dictum that structure follows strategy. Rather, the pattern of change in ICI was a complex mixture of adjustment in core beliefs of the top decision-makers, followed by changes in structure, systems, and rewards, with the business strategy changes emerging and being implemented rather more slowly after [these] changes ... had been legitimated and implemented (Pettigrew, 1987: 664–5).

Notice how Pettigrew's conclusions support Miller's notion of quantum change. Notice, too, how he has woven the notions of a number of the strategy schools around distinct periods in the life of this organization.

Another probe of a similar nature was carried out by Johnson (1987) into a British clothing retailer. His conclusions tend to focus on the interpretative view of strategy, but woven together with a rationalistic and adaptive (or incremental) view. Johnson concluded that the managers he studied 'saw themselves as logical incrementalists, and believed that this was a sensible way to manage'. However, they were driven by a set of core beliefs that determined how they interpreted and acted upon the complexity they faced. This set up barriers to change against which challenges had to be seen as 'political and cultural actions rather than a master of intellectual debate'. But as 'strategic drift' occurred and performance declined, incremental adjustments had to be replaced by fundamental change: 'there is a need to 'unfreeze' the paradigm ... [to] break up ... political alliances and [challenge and change] rituals and routines', with outsiders perhaps playing a key role in introducing new perspectives and ideas.

> It is likely that the change process that occurs will be, relatively speaking, ill defined and general. Members of the organization will know that change is occurring but may not be that clear about where it is leading or what it signifies. However, it may be that this process of change is a necessary precursor to the introduction of specific strategies. (Johnson, 1987)

That may require the sorts of analytical and planning approaches more usually identified with rationalistic, scientific management. But these 'cannot be effective unless the change processes to break down the [old beliefs] are already in process' (Johnson, 1987: 270–4).

Returning to more typology-type findings, Doz and Prahalad, in a study of 16 companies, described the change process in four stages, of the incubation of a new vision followed by variety generation as 'newly appointed key managers started working toward providing legitimacy to their vision and undermining the legitimacy of the prevalent conventional wisdom' (Doz and Prahalad, 1987: 72). Then, at least in the successful cases, power shifts occurred – not formal organizational change, but 'a series of relatively minor reallocations of decision and implementation authority' that made a difference (Doz and Prahalad, 1987: 73–4). Finally, in the refocusing stage, the true meaning of the changes was communicated, the formal management systems modified, and key managers moved. So the transformation was really a sequence of relatively minor steps over time, in which the cognitive perspective had to change in order for there to be strategic redirection, which, in turn, necessitated a shift of power allocation.

Finally, in a fascinating recent book by Hurst (1995), based on his own experiences as an executive rather than empirical research, organizational change is described through an 'ecocycle' model of crisis and renewal. The model consists of two loops that intersect to form the symbol of infinity. The ecocycle of a forest runs through phases of growth and exploitation: 'the rapid colonization of any available space' (Hurst, 1995: 98), then conservation, namely stable relationships among established organisms, followed by creative destruction, a role played by natural forest fires, which leads to renewal, etc. So, too, do human organizations cycle around similar phases, between emergent and constrained actions. Entrepreneurial action leads to conservation, or settling down to established procedure, much as Chandler described, which eventually provokes crisis and confusion, which stimulates creative response, and so a new cycle begins (see Figure 17.1).

The 'front' half or 'performance loop' of the model, shown as a solid line, is the 'conventional lifecycle'. This, according to Hurst, is where strategic management is found. The back half, or 'learning loop', shown as a dotted line, represents 'a less familiar, renewal cycle of "death" and reconception'. This is the realm of charismatic leadership (Hurst, 1995: 104).

In sharp contrast to the linear lifecycle, as supported by Chandler, this model describes an unending loop between crisis and renewal, in which the approaches

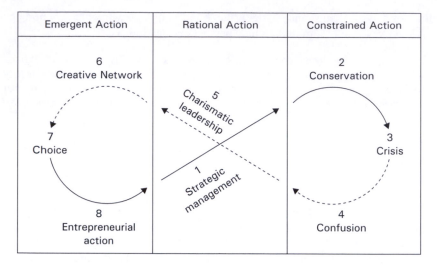

FIGURE 17.1   *Organizational change described through an 'ecocycle' model of crisis and renewal (Hurst, 1995)*

of many other schools can be seen in sequence. Sometimes the connections between the stages are smooth and almost linear (in other words, imperceptible or 'seamless', more in the spirit of splitting), while at other times, they tend to be rapid and nonlinear (namely lumpy).

Hurst also notes that the model goes beyond the organization, to describe how 'unconnected elements *become* organizations' and organizations are themselves broken back down into their 'elements' (Hurst, 1995: 105). 'Renewal requires destruction' (Hurst, 1995: 102). Also 'healthy human organizations should, like natural forests, consist of "patches" at different stages of development' (Hurst, 1995: 105).

Critique of the Configuration School

McGillomania

The most pointed criticism of the configuration school has been mounted by Donaldson (1996), who once described it as 'McGillomania'. Donaldson argues that configurations represent a flawed approach to theorizing, precisely because they are so easy to understand and teach.

> Few real organizations are simple structures or machine bureaucracies: almost all organizations lie somewhere in the middle. Students, be they MBA or executives, mostly come from organizations which have intermediary levers of size, standardization, organicness and so on. Managers are involved in managing change, usually of degree: some growth in size, a little more innovation, maturing of this product line but not that product line and so on. They need a framework on to which they can map their

experience and which yields highly differentiated and gradated prescriptive advice. In configurations they find stark, but simplistic caricature: simple structures, machine bureaucracy, innovating adhocracies. These models provide scant help. (Donaldson, 1996: 127)

Organizations come in 'many shades of gray and not just black and white', he added. These 'ideal types' therefore provide a vocabulary, but this vocabulary is relatively crude when it comes to describing the diversity of the organizational world. 'Each configuration has problems' (Donaldson, 1996). For example, multi-divisional firms may have units with different structures that pursue different strategies. To tackle these issues, Lawless (Chapter 19, this volume) attempts to underpin some of the contributions in the configuration school with a more rigorous theoretical basis.

Donaldson reserves the brunt of his criticism for the other major plank of the configuration school: quantum change. It is empirically and conceptually erroneous, he argues, to maintain that firms are either static or changing rapidly. 'Most organizations, most of the time, are changing incrementally' (Donaldson, 1996: 122). Furthermore, to say that organizations at intermediate points between different configurations are in disequilibrium – whose strategies are non-viable until they reach a more stable configuration – begs the question of how they manage to make this transition at all.

Donaldson's criticism is based on the one criterion of accuracy: if theories are true or not. But all theories are false; they are just words or pictures on pieces of paper. Reality is always more complex. (The world may not be flat, for example, but neither is it round. It bulges at the equator and has all kinds of bumps, called mountains.) So usefulness becomes a key criterion, especially for practising managers. (The flat Earth theory is particularly useful for building airport runways in Holland.) In the contribution by Bailey and Johnson (Chapter 18, this volume) it is exactly the perception of managers that is addressed. Configuration of strategy development as perceived by management is explored.

This does not negate Donaldson's criticisms – the world seen as configurations is flawed, too – but it does raise at least equally important questions about his preferred alternative, which is in the spirit of contingency theory. In other words, managers have to choose from among flawed theories.

As we have tried to show in this chapter, configuration can often be very helpful, even as a vocabulary by which to understand how different forms of organizations combine in the ways Donaldson describes. Moreover, theories, as tools, evolve. It took a long time for biological taxonomists to evolve today's highly complex and powerful classification. They would have got nowhere if they had thrown the entire enterprise overboard because it was not sufficient to encompass all the variety of species they could observe.

As for the pace of change, the jury is out on this one, as it is likely always to be, since there is plenty of obvious evidence for both incremental and quantum, or revolutionary, change, and plenty of usefulness of both views as well. Of course, one is more compatible with contingency theory, the other with configuration theory, so we had better be careful who we believe in this debate.

Lumping

Because pattern is in the eye of the beholder, all lumping must be considered somewhat arbitrary. To describe by configuration is to distort in order to explain. But that is true of every concept, every theory, indeed every word (which is just a category). All simplify in one way or another. So the issue really amounts to how serious this form of distortion is compared with some other. Like it or not, we need categories to help us understand our complex world. (Imagine a world without words.) And so we need lumping, even though we are aware of its limitations.

To take one visible example, we all find useful the categorization of the continents. Australia is one such continent: it sits geographically distinct, even the character of its people can be distinguished (with regard to language and accent, for example). But Greenland fits these criteria too, maybe even more so, although this 'island' is not quite so large. So why is it excluded? Africa is included: it is huge, although rather more diverse in language, etc. But why is Europe considered a continent? It has a huge diversity of languages and no evident boundary to the east. Is Europe a continent simply because it was Europeans who designated the continents?

We conclude that categories, including configurations, are figments of our imagination (or lack of it) at least as much as they are identifiable things.

The Edges

The configurational approach should not, therefore, allow us to ignore the nuances of our messy world. We need fine-grained work that exposes the complex inter-relationships between things. As Raphael (1976) has pointed out, the richest forms of life exist on the edges, between sea and land, forest and field, etc. That is where much of the exciting innovation takes place in the world of organizations, too, outside the pat categories, beyond the neat configurations. In one sense, then, while we cannot specify a context for this school – it is, after all, the school of contexts – we can draw attention to the contexts it misses: nuanced ones, those not (or not yet) categorized, those that are perhaps not categorizable.

Similarly, at the same time that organizations benefit from configuration, they can also suffer from it. This came out clearly in Miller's work in *The Icarus Paradox*: the very consistency that promotes success can lead to failure. 'Selecting the right degree of configuration is a complex balancing act. Managers must avoid the blandness or chaos of too little configuration while skirting the obsessionality of too much. Excellent wines have complexity and nuance, blending together different tastes into a harmonious balance' (Miller, 1996: 511).

Overall, the contribution of the configuration school has been evident in strategic management. It brings order to the messy world of strategy formation, particularly to its huge, diverse literature and practice. Bear in mind what you have just been through in this volume: various strategy directions imagined out of a single world that is not nearly as lumpy as suggested. But if you have stayed with it this far, then you must have some appreciation for all these lumps. Just bear in mind Whitehead's admonition: 'Seek simplicity and distrust it.'

Note

1 Adapted from Mintzberg, H., Lampel, J. and Ahlstrand, B.W. (1998) *Strategy Safari: A Guided Tour through the Wilds of Strategic Management*, New York: Free Press, Chapter 11.

18

A Framework for a Managerial Understanding of Strategy Development

Andy Bailey and Gerry Johnson

This chapter is concerned with the process by which strategy develops in organizations. It builds on research that aims to develop a clearer understanding of the strategy development process as perceived by the actors involved within that process – the managers themselves. It takes as its starting point the assertion that the strategy development process is multidimensional in nature and that organizations are open to an array of influences both from inside and outside when developing strategy and, therefore, an integrated framework for its interpretation is required.

   The research reported here is positioned within the strategy process research tradition, which focuses on 'the actions that lead to and support strategy' (Huff and Reger, 1987: 212), is concerned with how an organization, through its systems and processes, deliberate or unintentional, achieves or maintains its position (Chakravarthy and Doz, 1992), and in so doing adopts a configurational approach (Mintzberg, 1990b; Meyer et al., 1993). The research aims, first, to develop an empirically based framework for understanding strategy development processes, second, to assess the applicability of existing explanations of strategy development and, third, to provide a clearer understanding of strategy development processes for managers and management researchers. The chapter presents the theoretical framework on which the research is based; the methodology employed is explained and an integrated framework relating to processes of strategy development constructed. This framework is subsequently used to illustrate propositions that inform our understanding of strategy development in organizations.

The Strategy Development Process in Organizations

In normative management literature the process by which organizations determine strategy is often presented as an analytical, systematic and deliberate process of planning. However, it has been shown that processes of strategy development cannot typically be explained in such ways; managerial deliberations, decisions and actions take place within, and are influenced by, the political and cultural context of an organization as well as by external pressures (Johnson, 1987; Pettigrew, 1973, 1985).

A variety of explanations of strategy development have been postulated, however, they are characterized by a number of limitations. The first limitation concerns the scope of explanation used through the application of unitary frameworks for understanding the process of strategy development, such as the planning perspective (Ansoff, 1965; Steiner, 1969) and the ecological perspective (Hannan and Freeman, 1984, 1989). The strategy development process is more likely to be multifaceted (Derkinderen and Crum, 1988; Eisenhardt and Zbaracki, 1992; Fredrickson, 1983). Indeed, studies that have sought to understand strategy development in context have demonstrated as much (Hickson et al., 1986; Johnson, 1987; Pettigrew, 1985; Pettigrew and Whipp, 1991).

A second limitation relates to a lack of generalizability of these contextual studies due to the methodological approach followed. The case studies of Johnson (1987), Mintzberg and Waters (1982), Pettigrew (1973, 1985) and Quinn (1980a), and the historical studies by Boswell (1983) and Grinyer and Spender (1979a, 1979b) have provided rich insights into the process of strategy development. However, given their context specificity, generalizability is problematic.

An area of growing importance has been the conceptual development of more integrated frameworks to explain the strategy development process. This has been accomplished on a theoretical basis (Chaffee, 1985; Eisenhart and Zbaracki, 1992; Hart, 1992; Mintzberg, 1990b; Rajagopalan et al., 1993; Schwenk, 1988a) by applying theoretical perspectives to case studies (Allison, 1971; Johnson, 1987), through interviews (Shrivastava and Grant, 1985) or in a structured form to managers (Hart and Banbury, 1994; Hickson et al., 1986). Such research has demonstrated that through the use of an integrated framework a clearer understanding of the strategy development process and its complexity can be achieved.

The multidimensional nature of strategy development means, as with other multidimensional phenomena, that the possible combinations of attributes that could exist is infinite. This variety of combination is likely, though, to be 'limited by the attributes' tendency to fall into coherent patterns' (Meyer et al., 1993: 1176) and, therefore, common patterns or configurations of strategy development processes are likely. The management process then 'is best understood in terms of overall patterns rather than in terms of analyses on narrowly drawn sets of organisational properties' (Meyer et al., 1993: 1181).

In understanding the strategy development process there is an argument for the adoption of a research approach that is configurational in nature, employs multiple perspectives of explanation and utilizes these explanations concurrently in a complementary rather than a competitive manner. The remainder of this chapter builds on such an integrated framework of explanation and demonstrates the application of this framework to understanding strategy development processes.

The Development of the Theoretical Model

It is acknowledged that the development of a meaningful, integrated framework to explain strategy development processes should build upon prior theory and empirical research. Six theoretical perspectives or archetypal explanations of strategy development processes may be derived from the literature. There is considerable similarity between these six perspectives and Mintzberg's nine schools of thought (Chapter 1). While the explanations are not presented as definitive, they represent meaningful classifications of current theory and a basis for further empirical investigation. It is important to stress that it is most unlikely that any one of the explanations given accounts entirely for the processes at work in an organization; strategy development needs to be understood in terms of a mix of processes. The six explanations are summarized below.

The Planning Perspective

Building on the writings of Ansoff (1965), Steiner (1969) and others, the planning perspective suggests that strategy formulation is an intentional process involving a logical, sequential, analytical set of procedures. Well-defined strategic goals and objectives are set by the senior members of the organization. The organization and its environment, both internal and external, are systematically analysed. Strategic options are generated and systematically evaluated. Based on this assessment the option judged to maximize the value of outcomes in relation to organizational goals and which best fits the selection criteria is chosen. The selected option is subsequently detailed in the form of precise implementation plans, and systems for monitoring and controlling the strategy are determined.

The Incremental Perspective

The notion of logical incrementalism (Quinn, 1980a) holds that strategy formulation is purposeful and intentional but that, given its complexity, managers cannot analyse all aspects of the environment or establish precise objectives. Rather, strategic choice takes place through what Lindblom (1959) refers to as 'successive limited comparisons'. Managers have a view of where they want the organization to be and try to move towards this in an evolutionary way by attempting to secure a strong core business and at the same time experiment with side bet ventures (Quinn, 1980b).

Strategy is developed in an iterative manner, encompassing feedback loops to previous phases where problem and solution may be redefined or redeveloped (Lyles, 1981). Managers accept the uncertainty of their environment as they realize they are not able to know how it will change; rather they attempt to be sensitive to it through constant scanning, evaluation and 'learning by doing'. Strategic goals are kept vague and general in nature (Quinn, 1980b) so as not to stifle ideas or prevent experimentation. Strategic options then develop and are assessed through a managed process of experimentation and partial implementation (Johnson, 1987) with commitment to a strategic option remaining tentative during the early stages of its development.

Over time successful strategies are retained by the organization while inappropriate strategies are eliminated. In this way the strengths of the organization are maintained as changes in the environment are matched with changes in strategy.

The Political Perspective

Organizations are political entities and, as such, strategies are susceptible to influence from stakeholders. These stakeholders or interest groups are likely to have different concerns (Pfeffer and Salancik, 1978) and attempt to achieve their own ends (Cyert and March, 1963). Coalitions form to pursue shared objectives and to sponsor different strategic options (Narayanan and Fahey, 1982). These options are fought for, not only on the basis of their benefit to the organization, but also because they have implications for the status or influence of different stakeholders. These differences and conflicts are resolved through bargaining, negotiation and compromise with the result that goals and objectives, strategic issues and strategies themselves, are derived from this process rather than from an analytically neutral assessment and evaluation.

The level of influence these stakeholders are able to exercise differs (Heller et al., 1988) and is often conditional upon the organization's dependency upon such groups for resources (Pfeffer and Salancik, 1978) and the potential difficulty in replacing the present stakeholder as the source of that resource (Hinings et al., 1974). The power and influence of a stakeholder can also be acquired by other groups. For example, those internal groups or 'boundary spanners' who deal with the external environment can attain greater influence over strategy (Jemison, 1981a) by virtue of the organization's dependency on the external group with which they deal. Similarly, stakeholder influence is not constant from decision to decision (Hickson et al., 1986). The decision situation determines the level of stakeholder involvement and both their level of influence and the dynamics of that influence throughout the process.

Influence is also gained through information, information is not politically neutral, but rather it is a source of power for those who control it. This influence is achieved through the ability to resolve, reduce and manage uncertainty (Schwenk, 1989) or by filtering information to reflect the priorities of the group providing that information.

The Cultural Perspective

The strategy an organization adopts can also be attributed to cultural influences. Shared frames of reference, which are the organization's beliefs, enable the organization and the world in which it operates to be understood. Organizational frames of reference or paradigms (Johnson, 1987) enable new situations to be perceived in ways that are not unique (Schön, 1983). These frames of reference exist at the organizational level, but also on an industry wide basis (Spender, 1989) in the form of commonly accepted 'recipes' and within institutional types (DiMaggio and Powell, 1983). Managers, then, are influenced by a number of frames of reference when determining strategy.

These frames operate to simplify dealings with the complexity of situations, provide a ready-made frame for the interpretation of new situations (Weick, 1979), enable decisions to be made in a way that makes sense and provide a guide to appropriate behaviour (Gioia and Poole, 1984). Their usefulness increases as situations become more ambiguous and as the efficiency of formal decision making processes decreases (Beyer, 1981).

The values and assumptions of a group are, in turn, underpinned by routines (Walsh and Ungson, 1991), rituals (Meyer and Rowan, 1977; Trice and Beyer, 1986), stories (Schank and Abelson, 1977) and other symbolic artefacts, which represent and reinforce a 'way of doing things around here' (Deal and Kennedy, 1982). These frames of reference are embedded in organizational activities (Johnson, 1990) and provide a repertoire for action, albeit one that is likely to be resistant to change (Greenwood and Hinings, 1993; Johnson, 1990).

The Visionary Perspective

The strategy an organization adopts can also be seen as emerging from a vision that represents the desired future state of the organization (Ackoff, 1993; Jaques and Clement, 1991). This vision, which is primarily associated with an individual (for example, an organization's leader or a past leader) or small group, directs the strategy and provides a framework for strategic decision making.

This vision may emerge from the intuition and innovation of a founder or it might be based on radical ideas that challenge accepted norms, contradict established principles and paradigms (Trice and Beyer, 1986). It may confront shared reality (Smith, 1994) or go beyond familiar experience and knowledge (Trice and Beyer, 1986). More mundanely, it may come about because a new executive applies his or her existing frame of reference from another context to a new organization.

Whether visionary status is achieved through the generation of a vision, the synthesis of existing visions, the communication of a vision or through the organization's history, it places control and power in the hands of the visionary who gains the capacity to translate intention into reality and sustain it (Bennis and Nanus, 1985).

The Enforced Choice Perspective

It can also be argued that managers in organizations have little or no control over the choice of strategies they use. Factors in the environment impinge on the organization in such a way as to encourage – and even determine – the adoption of organizational structures and activities suited to that environment (Hannan and Freeman, 1989). These external constraints and barriers in the environment operate to restrict and prescribe the strategy that can be followed, reduce the level of intentional strategic choice and limit the role played by organizational members in strategy selection (Aldrich, 1979).

The strategic change that does occur is likely to be instigated from outside the organization and to be developed in a responsive rather than proactive manner. While strategic change and variation in an organization's processes, structures and systems may occur as an intentional response to the environment, they may occur unintentionally (Aldrich, 1979) through conflict over control of resources, ambiguity of organizational reality, accident, errors, tactical moves or luck (Aldrich and Mueller, 1982). Those variations that fit changes in the environment and provide advantage are retained and disseminated throughout the organization and across its generations through culture, symbols, socialization, administration and training.

Methodology

A variety of research approaches have been utilized in examining the strategy development process. This research adopts a large scale survey methodology, focusing on the managerial perception of the strategy development process. Indeed, managerial input has played an integral part across the duration of this research project, including the critique of theoretical perspectives and the validation and assessment of the integrated framework. The methodology is summarized below (for a full discussion of the development of the research instrument see Bailey and Johnson, 1993).

Each of the six theoretical perspectives described above were operationalized by identifying singularly attributable characteristics. From these characteristics a pool of items or statements suitable for a self-completion questionnaire were developed.

To ensure content validity, the item pool was presented to an expert panel of ten academics active in the field of strategy process research. This panel assessed each item to determine which of the six perspectives, if any, it was characteristic of, and the extent to which it characterized that perspective. Their responses were analysed to identify those items which were allocated to the same perspective at a level of interjudge agreement of 70% or higher. A mean score was computed for each selected item in terms of the extent to which it characterized the perspective; items were then ranked based on these scores. Those items consistently attributed to the same perspective and which were seen to be most characteristic of that perspective formed the basis of the questionnaire items.

Face validity was established through two forms of managerial assessment. The first involved face-to-face interviews with five senior managers concerning strategy development in their respective organizations. The second form of managerial assessment utilized data collected through pilot research (Bailey and Johnson, 1992). Based on these data, strategy development profiles (a pictorial representation of the strategy development process) were developed and subsequently presented, along with the underlying theoretical perspectives, to managers. Managers were typically able to distinguish unidentified profiles of their own organization from profiles of other organizations.

By combining the results from the expert panel with those from the managerial assessment the final selection of items for inclusion in the strategy development questionnaire were identified.

Forty-seven items resulted from this procedure: eight relating to the planning perspective, eight to the incremental perspective, seven to the political perspective, nine to the cultural perspective, eight to the visionary perspective and seven to the enforced choice perspective. The items were randomly located within a larger questionnaire concerning strategy development and its broader issues. This questionnaire was administered to a large sample of executives. Respondents were asked to respond to each item using a 7-point Likert scale ranging from 1 (you strongly disagree with the item in relation to your organization) to 7 (you strongly agree with the item in relation to your organization).

Data Source

A limitation of previous research in this field has been the reliance on a single respondent, usually a chief executive or another senior executive, as the source of information pertaining to the strategy development process. The use of single respondents as the source of data has been questioned by a number of researchers (Phillips, 1981; Venkatraman and Grant, 1986). Indeed, awareness of issues pertaining to strategy has been seen to differ with organizational level (Hambrick, 1981). One individual, even a chief executive, cannot be assumed to be able to judge accurately all components of an organization, particularly aspects of a complex nature. To gain a fuller understanding of the process of strategy development and reduce the potential for bias due to a reliance on a single viewpoint, multiple respondents (all of whom had a detailed knowledge of the strategy development process) were used in this research.

Results

Completed questionnaires were received from 1174 managers in 141 organizations. The organizations surveyed were drawn from the manufacturing, service, financial service and public sectors across the UK. The size of the organizations ranged from four to 100 000 employees. Turnover ranged from less than £1M (3.3% of responding organizations), £1–10M (14.8%), £11–100M (33.0%), £101–500M (23.6%), £501–1000M (8.7%) to over £1000M (16.6%).

An Empirical Test of Perspectives of Strategy Development

A principal components analysis (PCA) was performed on the responses to the 47 strategy development items in order to identify the underlying structure of responses. Oblique rotation was employed as it was expected that the perspectives would account for the process in combination and, therefore, the factors would be correlated. For inclusion of items in the factor model an item factor loading (on basis of the structure matrix loading) of 0.45 or above was required, a level indicated to be 'fair' by Comrey (1973).

The number of factors for extraction was estimated using Cattell's scree plot (Cattell, 1966), which indicated a six factor solution (accounting for 48.9% of the variance). Further, a six factor solution would be expected, based on the theoretical underpinnings of the research and from which the item pool was derived.[1]

To assess the stability of the factor solution a split-half procedure was employed. The two solutions were highly similar. The results reported here are based on the data set as a whole.

The reliability of the six components was examined using Cronbach's alpha. Five of the scales produced an acceptable level of internal reliability of greater than 0.7, while the incremental scale attained an alpha of 0.64. However, given the factor structure and the theoretical underpinnings of this scale it was retained in the study.

Managerial Understanding of the Strategy Development Process

Central to this research was the evaluation of existing explanations of strategy development, grounded in theory and prior research, through exposure to managers. The PCA provided an indication of this. Given the operationalization of the perspectives, the grouping of items through PCA was hypothesized a priori. Consequently, a solution that matches the hypothesized groupings provides evidence of factorial validity (Comrey, 1988) and lends support to the applicability of the six perspectives.

A general fit was identified between the hypothesized items grouping and the grouping of items based on managerial response, however, six items theorized to be associated with particular perspectives failed to load at a significant level on their hypothesized perspectives. All items used to operationalize the planning, political and enforced choice perspectives loaded as hypothesized.

On the cultural perspective two items relating to commonly shared organizational values and beliefs directing strategy did not associate with the other items used to operationalize this perspective. The cultural perspective as captured here reflects established ways of doing things, with historical influences and experience built up over time and explicit reference to organizational culture.

The incremental perspective included characteristics relating to the notion of 'logical incrementalism' presented by Quinn (1980a), but also characteristics more attributable to 'muddling through' as described by Lindblom (1959). The component derived through PCA represented a more, rather than less, purposive process. Characteristics reflecting continued delay in strategic response and a solely reactive managerial process failed to load with the other items.

The perspective operationalized from the literature that deviated most was the visionary perspective. Here the items loading on this component focused on the influence of a senior figure over the organization's strategic direction and two items solely related to a 'vision', without reference to an individual or group, did not load at the required level. The perspective is, therefore, reconceptualized to reflect a notion of strategy development associated with a central powerful figure (for example, the chief executive or a similar figure with institutionalized authority). Therefore it is more to do with 'command' – similar to the mode identified by Hart (1992) – and is amended as such. In so far as a vision is relevant here, it is associated with an individual such that the individual represents strategy.

While it is argued that these six perspectives identified through the PCA represent components of the strategy development process, they are not presented here as definitive. Indeed, other accounts of the process may exist. This is illustrated with the 'vision' items, as discussed above. While these items were not seen to relate to the process as characterized by the measurement of strategy development presented here, there are accounts of strategy being developed based on vision (Westley and Mintzberg, 1989). However, this framework does provide a basis upon which strategy development can be examined.

The characteristics associated with the six perspectives, post PCA, utilized in the remainder of this chapter are summarized in Appendix 18.1.

TABLE 18.1 *Multidimensionality of strategy development*

Perspective	% of respondents (0.25 sd above mean)	% of respondents (using mean)	% of organizations (0.25 sd above mean)	% of organizations (using mean)
Planning	7.9	5.8	7.3	3.9
Incremental	2.7	1.3	1.7	0.3
Cultural	0.9	0.3	1.7	1.1
Political	1.7	0.9	1.9	0.6
Command	2.5	1.7	2.2	0.6
Enforced				
choice	1.9	0.7	2.2	0.6
Total	17.6	10.6	17	7.1

Using the Perspectives to Explore Strategy Development

In this section a series of propositions are explored, which aim to advance our understanding of strategy development processes and to provide a basis for further research. The data is used in an illustrative manner.

Multidimensional Explanations of Strategy Development

On the basis of both theory and empirical evidence, a number of writers (Derkinderen and Crum, 1988; Eisenhardt and Zbaracki, 1992; Fredrickson, 1983) have argued that unidimensional explanations of strategy development are unrealistic. We recognize that it is unlikely that the sort of explanations advanced earlier are mutually exclusive but that they occur in combination, giving rise to the following proposition.

Proposition 1   The strategy development process will typically be characterized by an inter-relationship between perspectives.

Table 18.1 shows the percentage of respondents that consider the strategy development process in their organization to be unidimensional. Using a cut-off point of 0.25 of a standard deviation (SD) above the mean on any perspective, this represents only 17.6% of the sample, which falls to 10.6% if the mean score on any perspective is taken as the cut-off point.

If the data is examined at the organizational level then 17% of the organizations (cut-off point of 0.25 SD) and 7.1% (at the mean) are seen to be represented by unidimensionality. In short, unidimensional perceptions of the strategy development process are not typical among managers, rather the strategy development process is described by the managers in two or more perspectives in terms of this framework.

Configurations of Strategy Development Processes

Given the multidimensional nature of strategy development and the tendency of such phenomena to fall into coherent groupings (Meyer et al., 1993), common patterns or configurations of the strategy development process are likely. Certainly, there are theoretical grounds on which such patterns might be expected to exist. Arguably, there are at least three meta-theories of strategy development in organizations. The first suggests that strategy is developed intentionally and through deliberate rational processes. At its extreme this is represented by the strategic planners (Ansoff, 1965; Steiner, 1969), but the notion of logical incrementalism (Quinn, 1980a) also proposes that managers deliberately manage the external and internal context within which strategy is built. A second meta-theory, building on notions of bounded rationality, suggests that actors in organizations understand their organizational world and its context through cognitive schema (Schwenk, 1988b) and, in turn, enact their organizational world (Weick, 1979). Therefore strategy development is better seen as the outcome of such cognitive processes within an organizationally or institutionally specific domain (Johnson, 1988). A third meta-theory is that the extent of managerial choice is limited; managers are essentially responsive to an intrusive environment that effectively determines the strategy the organization follows. This is the ecologists' argument (Aldrich, 1979; Hannan and Freeman, 1989). We might expect these meta-theories to be reflected in the ways in which managers perceive strategy development in their organizations or, more formally, that which is stated in our second proposition.

Proposition 2   There will be discernible configurations of strategy development processes.

Pettigrew (1985) has emphasized the importance of seeking to understand strategy development processes within context because context will influence the way in which strategies come about. While identifying the possibility of configurations of the strategy development process is, in itself, of interest, a search for explanation of different patterns must, therefore, seek to place these differences in context.

The Industry Level
Spender (1989) has shown how recipes, which contribute to the development of strategy, differ by industry. These recipes are culturally bound and it has been shown that, while there are differences of culture at the organizational level, there is greater similarity of cultures within industries than across them (Chatman and Jehn, 1994). We might, then, expect to find evidence of differences in patterns of strategy development at the industry level. Certainly, writers on management have argued, for example, that the context of public sector organizations (Bryson, 1993), local government, (Greenwood et al., 1980), service sector organizations (Normann, 1984) and high technology firms (Eisenhardt and Bourgeois, 1988) influences the way in which their strategy development takes place. This gives rise to our next proposition.

Proposition 2a   Configurations of strategy development exist at the industry level.

If the unit of analysis is taken to be the industry sector, then underlying differences in the perceived processes of strategy development exist. For example, differences between the public and professional service sectors exist around the enforced choice and cultural perspectives (see Figure 18.1).[2] Each of these

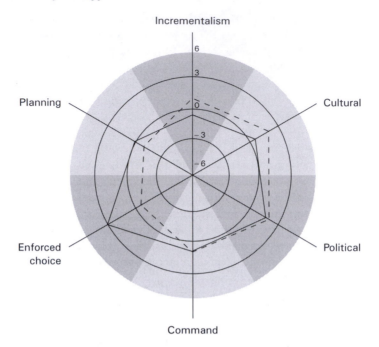

FIGURE 18.1   *Differences between the public sector (—) and the professional service sector (– – –) around the enforced choice and cultural perspectives*

perspectives tends to influence strategy development processes more in one sector than the other.

In the public sector the enforced choice and political perspectives characterize the strategy development process. Strategic choice is seen to be limited, with strategy being driven by external forces. While the primary determinant of strategy is external, internal political activity occurs around the prioritization of strategic issues, though involvement and influence is dependent on power and position. Those groups who deal with the external environment and who control externally derived resources or information, much of which is likely to relate to externally defined imperatives, attain greater influence over strategy. Influence is also attained by senior figures by virtue of their position and access to the external environment.

Within the professional service sector, while similarly characterized by the political perspective, the cultural perspective also characterizes the process. The enforced choice perspective, of greatest influence in the public sector, is uncharacteristic of the process. Within this context, strategic direction is determined by powerful organizational members, rather than being driven by external forces. The power of members, which is internally established and linked to culture, is enhanced by access to resources and through personal status, with strategic direction emerging as a result of bargaining and compromise between these individuals. A common culture derived from the common training and past experiences

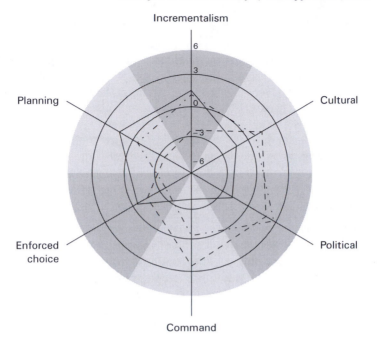

FIGURE 18.2 *Differences between three financial service organizations;*
— *organization A;* – – – *organization B;* – ·· – *organization C*

of individuals and 'a way of doing things' influences strategic direction. Strategy
that does not sit well with the culture or with the preferences of the powerful will
be resisted.

The Organizational Level
We might also expect differences to exist within sectors at the level of the organi-
zation (Hart and Banbury, 1994; Pettigrew and Whipp, 1991; Shrivastava and
Grant, 1985). Hence our next proposition.

Proposition 2b   Configurations of the strategy development process exist at the
organizational level.

Three financial service organization's operating in the UK home insurance market
are used as illustrations. Organizations A and B are seen to differ substantially on
all perspectives except that of enforced choice. Differences also exist between
organizations A and C and B and C (see Figure 18.2).

Organization A   The perceived process of strategy development in organization A
emphasizes the planning process within an incremental stance. The process
centres on the systematic collection and assessment of data and the definition of
strategic objectives, though under influence from an iterative, adaptive approach
to the environment. Strategy is then adjusted to match changes in the market
place sensed through constant analysis. This iterative approach to the environment, with planning activities moderated by a pragmatic resistance to the early

commitment to strategy, suggests the notion of logical incrementalism (Quinn, 1980a).

Organization B In contrast, organization B has a process of strategy development characterized by political and cultural influences with a senior organizational figure exerting a high level of control over strategy. Here, the strategy development process is not characterized by planning or an adaptive approach. Rather, the strategy reflects and accommodates the vested and conflicting interests of particular groups that are likely to attempt to advance their own priorities and may block or restrict implementation of an unfavourable strategy.

Strategy is not solely related to the exercise of power and influence but also reflects 'a way of doing things' and the influence of history and past experience in the development and assessment of strategic options.

Organization C The process of strategy development for organization C is also characterized by a political, cultural and incremental approach. The strongest of these perspectives is the political. Negotiation over strategic direction occurs between interest groups with differing strategic priorities. This political process is moderated by a cultural influence from past experience and a 'way of doing things', such that the political and cultural influences are closely intertwined with the culture supporting the political process and the political process supporting culture. In this configuration strategy emerges as an incremental response to a need for change, with strategy developing through an ongoing process of adjustment.

Our illustrations of differences at the organizational level point to the need for a more structured examination of such patterns through a more fine-grained understanding of organizational context.

The Managerial Level

The relationship between context and the strategy development process can, of course, also be considered at the individual level – it may be that individual circumstances or experience affect the way in which managers perceive processes. Elsewhere, researchers interested in the study of managerial demographics have argued the extent to which managerial level (Hambrick, 1981; Ireland et al., 1987), function (Ashmos et al., 1990; Bowman and Daniels, 1995) and tenure (Michel and Hambrick, 1992; Wiersema and Bantel, 1992) affect issue perception and organizational consensus. Still others have examined the roles and behaviour of different levels of management in relation to strategy development, for example, in terms of managerial elites (Pettigrew, 1992b) and middle-level managers (Floyd and Wooldridge, 1992). The underlying point is that we should not assume that there is a homogeneity of perceptions about strategy development processes, but that there could be systematic differences worthy of study according to managerial demographics or other managerial characteristics. This leads to the next proposition.

Proposition 2c Configurations of the strategy development process exist at the managerial level.

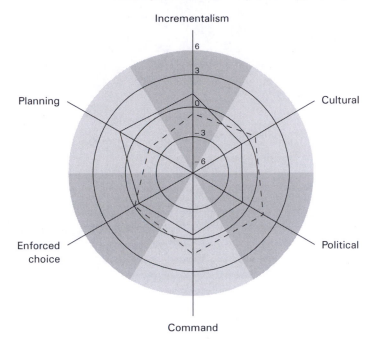

FIGURE 18.3 *Differences between a matched sample of CEDs/MDs (——) and senior managers (– – –) with a direct reporting relationship to the board regarding the strategy development process*

To examine patterns at this level it would be necessary to use extensive demographic data, which is beyond the scope of this chapter. However, an illustration of patterns between levels of management demonstrates differences between a matched sample of chief executives/managing directors (CEOs) and senior managers with a direct reporting relationship to the board, regarding the strategy development process (see Figure 18.3). While CEOs view the process as one of planned incrementalism this is not the situation as perceived by those below. Indeed, significant differences in opinion about the process in operation are seen between the CEOs and senior managers. The CEOs see the process to be characterized more by the planning process and significantly more by the incremental perspective than do senior managers. Similarly, CEOs are significantly less likely to perceive the process to be driven by external forces. The senior managers, in contrast, perceive the process to be characterized more by the command perspective, with the process being driven to some degree by internal political activity.

While the above illustrates configurations based on the managerial level, there is, of course, the possibility that other such configurations are discernible, for example, by function, external or internal focus, tenure, involvement in strategy debate and personality measures.

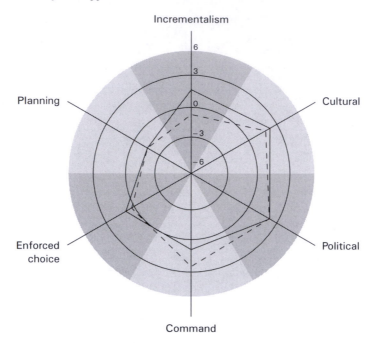

FIGURE 18.4 *The strategy development process at the time of commencement, T1 (—) and after implementation of changes, T2 (– – –) at a professional service firm*

Temporal Patterns of Strategy Development

There have been pleas to observe process over time and if possible in real time (van de Ven, 1992). The application of a framework such as the one developed here may permit more ready access to organizations over time. Since environmental context, organizational strategy and the management of organizations change over time, in the terms of this research we might expect the following proposition to be true.

Proposition 3 Patterns of strategy development will change over time.

As an illustration, consider a professional service firm which, over a period of three years, has undergone a major strategy review to address an increasingly competitive market, changed its managing partner and restructured its organization. Figure 18.4 depicts the strategy development process at the commencement of and after these changes, as seen by the firm's partners.

Unlike many corporations where an individual's involvement in decision making at an operational level may be strongly influenced by role and function, partnerships operate less rigidly. Decision outcomes are more likely to reflect the influence and desires of various individuals and interest groups, the strength of which may change given different issues or projects. Not surprisingly, the process of strategy development in the partnership before change (T1) is primarily driven by political and cultural processes and, arguably as a consequence, an adaptive or incremental response to an influential environment.

Processes of negotiation, debate and compromise around particular issues characterize how strategic problems are defined and strategies developed. The firm's long professional history and culture also influence the identification of issues and options and mediate the choice of strategy. Common assumptions are likely to allow the various power groups to relate to each other within routines that are taken for granted. In this context, the strategies pursued emerge in an adaptive manner through a series of continual small scale changes and steps.

The appointment of a new managing partner to oversee changes in strategy and structure appears to have changed this situation (T2). An adaptive approach no longer characterizes the strategy development process. Rather, strategy is seen to relate primarily to the power of the 'big man' and his aspirations for the firm's future.

Although influence over strategy development is still closely related to processes associated with the possession and utilization of power, the importance of the political perspective has diminished. The cultural influences on strategy development also appear to be less strong and might be associated with a programme of 'culture change' initiated by the managing partner. However, the relationship between political and cultural perspectives and command is, in itself, of significance. The professional ethos that permeates the firm and its members provides a common understanding and an established power structure through which political activity can be exercised. Indeed, the command figure has emerged from this structure. Thus, even though the managing partner is seen to have ultimate control, his power is moderated. In addition, as this individual has developed and progressed through the same professional and organizational structure as his colleagues, he is likely to hold a similar view of the world and the strategic issues faced.

Discussion

The research has demonstrated that there is a reasonable fit between managerial understanding of the strategy development process and the theoretical explanations developed to explain it. Where differences are identified the perspectives have been modified to account for these differences.

While the shortcomings of a questionnaire research methodology are acknowledged, the methodology employed is appropriate for assessing and quantifying the strategy development processes perceived to be operating in organizations. Moreover, the approach has provided access to a number of organizations operating in different contexts and has, therefore, enabled the development of an integrated framework of strategy development that is not context specific. As a result, the spread of organizational contexts surveyed addresses concerns regarding the concentration on specific industry sectors for research into the strategy development process (Eisenhardt and Zbaracki, 1992). Further, as suggested by Rajagopalan et al. (1993) the measurement of the perspectives has employed the use of multi-item scales, and their validity and reliability have been assessed.

From the exploration of the propositions, it is clear that the strategy development is not necessarily captured by a single perspective in isolation. Consequently, the use of unitary perspectives in understanding strategy development is ineffective in conveying the complexity of the processes seen to exist. Further, while the strategy development process is seen to be multidimensional, a singularly common configuration of strategy development processes is not seen. Nonetheless, there is evidence that systematic patterns of similarity and difference, in effect configurations of strategy development, are discernible by context whether at the level of the industry, the organization or the manager.

This contingency notion of strategy development may be explored further by being more specific about the nature of these contexts. For example, managers in different industry sectors are faced with different environmental contexts – differences might be expected to relate to the competitive intensity of markets, the extent of industry growth or the stages of the industry lifecycle. There are also different types of organization within the same industry in terms of size, ownership structure, market share, scope, etc. At the individual level, it may be that individual circumstances or personality affect the way in which managers perceive processes. Again, it might be expected that differences could relate to such factors.

Any consideration of contingent explanations of processual variations quickly runs into the risk of exponential complexity. It is not the suggestion here that we should build a contingency model sophisticated enough to account for all variations. However, it is recognized that if strategy development processes are to be understood, then there must be sufficient questioning of the relationship of process and context to provide meaningful explanation. Until now, this has been difficult to do using limited case based examples, whereas this framework provides a relatively sensitive instrument by which the relationship can be explored.

In presenting the propositions, this chapter has been descriptive and not prescriptive. There is no suggestion here that because such processes exist, this is how strategy should be managed. However, it is important to understand the reality of strategy making in organizations, not least because those who seek to influence the strategy of organizations do so within that reality. There is little point in formulating strategies that may be elegant analytically if there is no understanding of the processes that are actually at work. Rather than attempting to determine which perspective or combination of perspectives is 'right', a more useful approach may be to explore how the process is best described under differing conditions.

Building on a theoretical base, our research has used managerial perceptions of strategy development processes in organizations to build an analytical framework and research instrument, which has been used to profile such processes within and across organizations. This chapter has set out the framework, shown its application and used results from the work so far to examine and discuss a number of propositions derived from prior work in the field. In so doing it has demonstrated a methodology that is both sensitive to context and yet allows for generalizability of findings.

Notes

1 Details of the principal component analysis are available from the authors on request.
2 Interpretation of the strategy development profile is based on distance from the mid-point ring (highlighted in bold). This mid-point represents the standardized mean of all 1174 respondents. Points moving away from this ring towards the outside of the profile (accompanied by a positive score) represent the degree to which the perspective is seen to be characteristic of the strategy development process. Points moving inwards towards the centre (accompanied by a negative score) represent the degree to which the perspective is seen to be uncharacteristic of the process.

Acknowledgements

This work was sponsored by ESRC grant no. R000235100. We would also like to thank Kevin Daniels, J.-C. Spender and Cliff Bowman for their useful comments on various stages of the research.

Appendix 18.1 Characteristics of the six perspectives

Planning
- Strategies are the outcome of rational, sequential, planned and methodical procedures.
- Strategic goals are set by senior organizational figures.
- The organization and environment are analysed.
- Definite and precise objectives are set.
- Precise plans for implementation are developed.
- The strategy is made explicit in the form of detailed plans.

Incrementalism
- Strategy is continually adjusted to match changes in the operating environment.
- Strategic options are continually assessed for fit.
- Early commitment to a strategy is tentative and subject to review.
- Strategy develops through experimentation and gradual implementation.
- Successful options gain additional resources.
- Strategy develops through small scale changes.

Cultural
- A 'way of doing things' in the organization impacts on strategic direction.
- Strategies are evolved in accordance with a set of shared assumptions that exist in the organization.
- A core set of shared assumptions based on past experience and history guide strategic actions.
- Organizational history directs the search for and selection of strategic options.
- Strategy that does not fit with the culture is resisted.

Political
- Strategies are developed by negotiation and bargaining between interest groups.
- The interest groups seek to realize their own desired objectives.
- Their influence on strategy formulation increases with power.
- Power comes from the ability to create or control the flow of scarce resources.
- Interest groups form coalitions to further their desired strategy.

- The control and provision of information is also a source of power.
- A strategy acceptable to the most powerful interest groups is developed.

Command
- An individual is the driving force behind the organization's strategy.
- Strategy is primarily associated with the institutional power of an individual or small group.
- The strategy represents this individual's aspirations for the organization's future.
- The individual becomes the representation of the strategy for the organization.
- An individual has a high degree of control over strategy.
- A 'vision' belonging to the whole organization is not seen.

Enforced choice
- Strategies are prescribed by the operating environment.
- Strategic choice is limited by external forces that the organization is unable to control.
- Strategic change is instigated from outside the organization.
- Organizations are not able to influence their operating environments.
- Barriers in the environment severely restrict strategic mobility.

19

Strategy Configurations
in the Evolution of Markets

Michael W. Lawless

Market evolution offers a simple, specific explanation for configurations in a population of firms. It also supports new propositions concerning competition between these similar firms, and their tendencies to persist in unsuccessful conduct or absorb costs to change strategies. A configuration is a set of capabilities and strategies common to a particular group of firms in a market over time. In the 'rugged landscape' of any imperfect market, firms co-evolve with local conditions, converging on strategies suited to survival in their niche and investing in complementary capabilities. A market that contains different ecological niches is more likely to have diverse configurations. The more different the conduct to survive in each different niche and the greater the costs of deviation, the more distinct are the configurations from each other. However, configurations are not a priori discrete, since some capabilities and strategies may suit – at least partially – more than one set of local market conditions. Configurations are thus explained in terms of the co-evolution of firms and markets and lead to propositions concerning firms' performance, survival and adaptation.

Configurations are an attractive construct to many organizational scholars. They align remarkably well with our intuitions, experience and empirical findings about behaviour patterns of firms. It is widely believed that a few general patterns of conduct and structure can describe the essential characteristics of classes of companies, differentiate groups of firms from each other and help explain their success or failure (see also Chapter 17). Categorizations as diverse as strategic groups (Caves and Porter, 1977) and archetypes (Miller and Friesen, 1984) relate multivariate firm types to individual firm performance. (Not everyone would include strategic groups in a discussion of configurations, since they represent the thinking in two different schools of strategy research. However, it is no stretch to describe strategic groups with the characteristics I have already outlined for configurations. Since strategic groups are a coherent story for discrete intra-industry patterns of conduct, they are part of the context for my theoretical argument.)

There is an intuitive appeal in recognizing that many forces influence firms' consistency, synergy and fit, and that their effect on performance could be modelled as multivariate gestalts. Miller and Friesen (1984) find configurations improve on the bivariate models of earlier management literature, which are linear, cross-sectional, and concentrate on unidirectional relations. It was a welcome turn in research to recognize both the complexity of competitive strategy and the low power of the previous generation of empirical models.

The perspective lowers a barrier that separates much of the strategy research from related subfields in economics. Within strategy studies, it helps bridge theory development between idiosyncratic firms in case studies and the long-run homogeneity of firms of efficient market theory. Classification is an early step in theory development and the language of strategy types (for example, 'prospector' and 'defender', or 'focus' and 'differentiation') bridges the gap between academics and managers.

Still, we have made relatively little progress toward a persuasive theory for configurations, especially considering the rigour applied to other strategy research – for example, on valuation, value chain analysis and real options. The fact that they exist at all is still based mostly on empirical findings that are themselves suspect. There is little theoretical justification for patterns of similar conduct to occur in firms in a market or for an impact on the performance of their members. Miller and Friesen (1984) state that developing their configurations was mainly a 'theory-free search for patterns'. Such exploration is difficult to justify years later under the accumulation of research. Theory-based research and more reliable findings should be expected by now.

Configurations Frameworks

I divide the received configurations literature into two schools of thought on dimensions of provenance and state of theory development. This lets me describe much of the research parsimoniously and set the context for proposing an evolutionary model. A more comprehensive review of the literature is available in Chapter 17.

The organizations school, associated with the early work of Miles and Snow (1978) and Miller and Friesen (1984), models effects of a variety of organizational and environmental variables. Firms' strategies and performance are the dependent variables. The model draws methods and constructs from an earlier tradition that framed organizational structure as the outcome of environmental, technological and other forces. Describing configurations, Hinings and Greenwood (1988) propose that firms are caught up in contextual settings and that organizational designs are constrained by size, technology and environment. Miller and Friesen (1984) ultimately use a similar contingency construct to explain why some archetypes are successful and others are not. Diverse, fine-grained contingencies have been tested – for example, performance outcomes of fit between a mode of technology management and strategy types (Miller, 1988). Much of the work is grounded in theory. With little theory on which to base the choice of independent variables, the literature casts a wide net. Many diverse effects have been identified over time, but integration is elusive.

I use the label 'economics school' for structural analysis of firm groups rooted in industrial organization economics. Most of this is strategic groups research, starting before Caves and Porter's landmark study (1977). Here, the market is still the basic unit of analysis. The intention is to decompose it into firm aggregates that describe intra-industry structure. Decomposition is framed in terms of barriers to entry within markets, which make it costly to shift from one distinct pattern of strategy to another. The resulting strategic groups are a structural explanation for differences in conduct within a market.

These strategic groups greatly increased the value of IO economics for strategists. However, the model is not perfect, given the different traditions of strategic groups and configurations. The original argument for strategic groups (Caves and Porter, 1977) is that subsets of the firms in a market with similar strategies also share an outlook. Short 'strategic distance' leads to affinity among like firms. Mobility barriers are perceived as a shared advantage for the firms in each group, protecting them all from the threat of entry. Shared incentives and tacit collusion therefore underlie the received proposition that strategic groups are related to performance. In retrospect, both assumptions appear presumptuous and it seems unnecessary for there to be configurations. However, the impact is minimal since much of the empirical work has ignored the theory, concentrating instead on the groupings themselves. The assertion that any configurations that define strategic groups are only artifacts of methods such as cluster analysis remains open to criticism. Both the theory and methods are persistent problems and the research tends to create additional categories in new settings using different measures (Daems and Thomas, 1994).

Evolutionary Model

A theoretical explanation for configurations would fill a gap in strategy theory and lead to stronger evaluation of a growing body of empirical results. Even theory in early development would contribute, especially where it is supported by consistent findings. This is the state of the research presented here. I propose to model configurations as the outcome of market evolution. I look to technological change as the driving force that increases a market's complexity, but other forces and moderators apply, too, including regulation and mimetic conduct among firms. In markets where several generations of product technology are viable, firms can specialize or generalize in different ways. Configurations result where generational technological change affords a population of firms multiple alternative market positions, all of which are viable, even though they call for different strategies. Groups then emerge as similar firms adapt along a trajectory shaped by their existing capabilities. Shared characteristics in each cluster of firms determine the cluster's configuration, so that firms described by different capabilities and strategies belong to other configurations.

This model contrasts strongly with strategic group theory, but is consistent with evolutionary economics. It also relates to at least some thinking in the organizations school. Miller and Friesen (1984), for example, allude to an ecological process behind the development of configurations.

In the following sections, I outline the key elements in an evolutionary model and describe relationships with the emergence and behaviour of configurations and their members.

Initial Conditions

Market conditions are the 'landscape' on which evolution unfolds. Less intuitively, they are also one argument in the definition of niches, an antecedent to configurations (I explain this further below). Effects vary over the life of a market. Influences at the start of an evolutionary process continue to affect a population, often beyond the duration of effects of subsequent incremental events. Customer preferences, factor markets, logistical channels, capital requirements, customer base, institutional setting and other characteristics that affect configurations typically have greater impact very early on.

Initial conditions do not necessarily occur only once, however. An event that causes discontinuous change can effectively start a new evolutionary 'clock'. Deregulation in American telecommunications, diffusion of information technology in banking and commercial use of the internet are examples of this. In each instance, the landscape of the market changed discontinuously and the pattern of evolution after the event was substantially different from before. One could propose that the set of configurations in place before such change is subject to change through addition, attrition and adaptation.

Given the potential for idiosyncracy in initial conditions, the importance of configurations to explain performance is not certain a priori, but depends on market setting. One could imagine a market, for example, that closely resembles perfect competition. Market positions are undifferentiated, firms are alike and there is no basis for the emergence of distinctive configurations. An evolutionary model does not rule out the possibility that generic strategies can describe conduct in different industrial settings. However, it does recognize the limitations of that information to describe firms in specific markets.

It is more credible that markets are generally complex and that configurations help to describe diverse conduct in these commercial landscapes. Where conditions across a market vary, demands on firms' capabilities and strategies are irregularly distributed, too. A niche can be defined as a statement with two arguments: local market conditions and firms. It is the combination of market and firm characteristics that together make a favourable setting for some firms. Rather than describing a niche as a region in market space that is occupied, which may be more common, this ecological interpretation gives a defining role both to the environment and the population.

The niche construct is consistent with spatial models of markets and organizational environments from the organization theory and strategic management literatures. Blau (1977) models changes in social organizations in an n-space of dimensions describing the likelihood of association. Individuals with similar values on variables describing an n-dimensional space are more likely to share affiliation in social organizations. Aldrich (1979) describes environmental concentration/dispersion as the degree to which resources are evenly distributed over the range of the environment or concentrated in particular locations. Miller and Friesen (1984) expect that firms not only develop similar structures and asset bases, but that configuration members respond identically to environmental change. Harrigan (1985a) and others argue that strategic groups consist of firms located near each other and that common pressures impinge on the success of their strategies.

Specialization

A typology determined by specialism and generalism is traditional in the ecology literature. Specialist firms are suited to a narrow range of market conditions. For instance, there might be just a single product in the product line and a single price point, brand image, target customer group, etc. to which strategies and capabilities are aligned. Generalist firms are identified not only by a broader market presence, multiple products, diverse customer base, etc. but also by an organizational infrastructure to manage their several different points of market presence. They are differentiated from specialists by their corporate, multi-unit (M-form) structure. Differences in capabilities and strategies between generalists and specialists are readily deduced.

These are the basic categories in the evolutionary model of configurations. The only elaboration is still important: further division into types of specialist and generalist. So, disaggregated configurations have greater resemblance to those in the recent literature. For instance, a market might have both high and low price specialists.

Where a set of capabilities, adapted to a set of market conditions, is poorly matched to others, firms must specialize in ways that are difficult to reverse. The value of their capabilities in other market positions is longer, and firms incur a penalty in relocating to a different cluster of resources where specialized strategies and capabilities are less efficient or effective. Firms that change configurations incur a penalty consisting of three different types of costs: lost value from current capabilities that are not useful in the new setting, uncertainty absorption in the transition and investment to develop new strategies and capabilities. Evolution of configurations then casts some doubt on the efficacy of flexible strategies that downplay the commitment firms make to configurations. It also places greater importance on firms' ability to develop specific capabilities for adaptation and learning.

Generational Technological Change and Configurations

The incidence of market niches is not sufficient to imply the presence of configurations. They evolve only where niches also require specialized capabilities with little alternative use value. Members of any particular configuration are identified by their common capabilities and are distinguished from other configurations by capability differences. If identical capabilities suit firms equally in several different niches or if firms with different capabilities can meet the constraints of the same niche, then there is no theoretical reason to expect configurations.

The microcomputer industry is a fast-changing environment where one might not expect to see configurations. Technological change shortens lifecycles, and now many hardware and software products have less than a year in the market before a new version or release appears. If firms cannot forecast where the market is

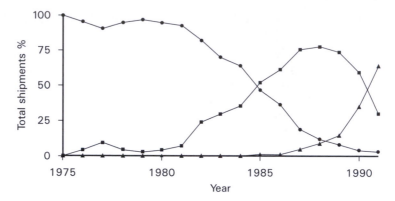

FIGURE 19.1 *Generations of personal computers in the USA, 1975–1991 (shares of PCs by microprocessors; ▪ 8-bit; ● 16-bit; ▲ 32-bit)*

going, one might expect them to rely on generic capabilities that do not commit them to a particular market location, whose future is difficult to anticipate. In this case, there would be little reason to presume that incumbents and entrants would become partitioned into discrete archetypes. Instead, most firms would resemble each other, possessing highly similar capability sets broadly applicable to many types of niches. Lawless and Anderson (1996) demonstrate that this is not what happens, even where the pace of change is as fast as it is in microcomputer manufacture. They identify a pattern of market change where older generations of product technology endure even while newer technology is in the market. An alternative to the Schumpeterian model (1934) of instantaneous and complete displacement of older technology, generational change occurs where multiple generations hold viable market share at the same time. Figure 19.1 shows this pattern in the American microcomputer market. It shows that personal computers based on 8, 16, and 32 bit chips all claimed market share in the same years. The implications for configurations are significant. In a market with only one technology (in the late 1970s), firms had the choice of specializing or staying out of the market. As soon as there are two generations (8 and 16 bit), the potential diversity of configurations is tripled. Firms can specialize in the older generation or specialize in the newer generation. (Note that different prices, target markets, production efficiency and more are called for between the two.) Alternatively, firms can generalize by broadening their product lines to span both generations. In this way, diversity of configurations increases with the number of technology generations.

Lawless and Anderson (1996) observe patterns of both generational technological change and proliferation in their study of the American computer industry study. First, computer manufacturers cluster into configurations instead of retaining similar flexible capabilities, because markets reward specialization of firm resources to niche requirements. When different niches impose sharply different requirements for survival and profitability, it is difficult for the generalist to span them. Instead, the flexible generalist is out-competed at every turn by rivals whose capabilities are tailored to the demands of a particular location in the market place. Each niche imposes similar constraints on all firms that occupy it and diversity among members is limited to the range of capabilities that can produce a profit under the same conditions. Consequently, firms become specialized to their positions in the market and configurations prevail because specialists outperform generalists where environmental resources are unevenly distributed. Second, capabilities are 'sticky'. Constructing and maintaining a capability must involve a strategic commitment. Imagine that niches are specialized, so that each niche requires the firm to adopt a different configuration of resources, but that a firm could, in each period, draw the resources needed to compete from a pool of capabilities without incurring any costs. Any firm could then compete on equal terms with firms specialized to that niche. The partitioning of a market into niches leads to specialized firm configurations only when it is difficult and/or costly for a firm to reverse its commitment to the asset pattern best suited to a particular position in the market space.

This is not to say that firms never change. Rather, it suggests that capabilities can be difficult to create, imitate and abandon. Ghemawat (1991) defines specialized, durable and non-tradable factors as 'sticky'. Teece et al. (1997) argue that firms are locked into their capability endowments over a strategically relevant timeframe because of these characteristics.

Specialization and stickiness provide a theoretical underpinning that explains why firms within an industry congregate into a discrete number of differentiated groupings whose members share similar capabilities, which differ from those possessed by the members of other configurations. Further, it provides insight into the dynamics by which configurations emerge. First, where niches are discrete, the range of capabilities is constrained so that outliers that fail to fit the appropriate configuration perform badly. This is observed both by incumbents and new entrants, who learn that being an outlier is a poor strategy. Second, one might expect that specialization involves idiosyncratic learning. A firm that matches its capabilities to a particular market place acquires proprietary and, perhaps, tacit knowledge. This makes imitation difficult for firms that are not similarly configured (Rumelt, 1984). Third, the stronger the specialization and complementarity between market position and firm capabilities are, the stronger the selection pressures within a niche will be. Niches contain some firms that are very well suited to their demands and this places pressure on others in the niche to conform more closely to the highest fitting capability profile. In contrast, where niches are not very differentiated, several configurations of capabilities may be moderately well suited to several niches, exerting less selection pressure on firms to conform to a specific pattern characteristic to their niche.

Performance

The presence of niches in a market and the requirement of specialized capabilities are antecedents of performance of firms in configurations. This model leads to two hypotheses tested by Lawless (1998). First, he proposes that performance is positively related to firms' adaptation to the specialized requirements of their niches. The more distinctively firms' capabilities are associated with a niche, the better is their performance. Second, specialist firms – whose capabilities are predominantly suited to a particular niche – will perform better than generalist firms whose capabilities are likely to be associated with several different niches. Lawless tests the hypothesis that firms whose capabilities are distinctly associated with one niche will perform better than firms with capabilities common to more than one niche. Both of these propositions are supported, lending additional support to the integrity of configurations in a very dynamic market.

Discussion

Why do firms within an industry form into configurations characterized by capability profiles that are similar among members of the same group, but quite different from the profiles of firms in other groups? Until now, the prevailing explanation has been that firms must achieve internal fit: capabilities that are compatible with each other. In turn, the number of ways in which internal fit can be achieved is limited by the need for each configuration to fit the organization's environment. Thus we observe that there is no one best configuration, but neither are there an unlimited number of viable combinations (constrained equifinality).

Why do firms within an industry follow configurations or form into strategic groups? The prevailing explanation has been that firms erect mobility barriers – usually as the result of a conscious strategic analysis – that insulate them from rivals outside their group. Strategic groups are not configurations. There is nothing in the strategic groups literature that mandates that firms within the group share similar capabilities within a restricted range. Neither are firms belonging to the same archetype necessarily members of the same strategic group. One reason for this incommensurability is that configurations are often defined across industries while strategic groups are typically studied within a single industry.

Both the configurations and strategic group research programmes predict that an industry is not a homogeneous mass, but rather is partitioned into discrete clusters of firms. Neither provides strong theoretical justification for expecting such partitions and neither provides clear insight into the forces that would bring about such groupings. The linkage between configurations and strategic barriers is also left unclear, so that the two research programmes have been less able to draw upon one another than might be desired.

In this chapter, I propose a specific mechanism grounded in evolutionary economics to explain why industries come to be partitioned and how configurations might be related to barriers within a strategic resource-based view of the firm. When markets are lumpy, niches comprise markets. The capabilities required to satisfy one part of the market are not well suited to exploiting opportunities elsewhere in the market space. Because capabilities are sticky, firms must commit strategically to a set of endowments. That set of endowments must be both internally consistent and complementary to the needs of the market location of the firm.

In this view, configurations occur because it is not possible for one set of capabilities to span the barriers that separate market niches. It focuses less on the mobility barriers surrounding groups of firms than on the barriers between the market niches occupied by the firms. Configurations result because, once a firm has acquired a set of capabilities, it cannot alter the chosen pattern without incurring costs. In this sense, any commitment to any configuration carries with it a mobility penalty, if not necessarily a barrier. However, I place no restrictions on the firm's ability to choose a position among the variables we examine. To characterize configurations as strategic groups, I would have to proceed one step further, to identify capabilities that are inimitable.

I offer this chapter as exploratory research, subject to many limitations. I do not offer an alternative to remedy each of the difficulties of the configurations and strategic groups literatures. Resource allocation decisions are excluded from this analysis and I do not account completely for organizational structure. I do, however, offer a conceptual argument for the first time for the emergence of configurations and for their relationship with the performance of firms. In related work (Lawless and Anderson, 1996), I demonstrate empirically that, for a reasonably broad set of allocation decisions, the degree to which a firm's configuration matches the pattern characteristic of its market conditions significantly affects its performance.

Scholars in strategic management are concerned with the way that conduct affects performance. Consequently, when we observe that an industry is partitioned into clusters of firms whose conduct is similar within the group but different between groups, we must ask why. My aim here has been to move beyond simple appeals to fit and/or barriers and to set forth an explanatory mechanism that sheds light on the reasons why configurations emerge and persist. By basing the study of configurations in the evolutionary economics and resource-oriented strategy traditions, I hope to provide a foundation for further study of the way in which firms succeed by developing distinctive capabilities that fit the settings in which they compete.

20

Configurations and the Firm
in Current Strategic Management

Johannes M. Pennings

In this commentary, I shall review the current efforts to discern configurations in the structures and processes of decision making and behavioural routines as observed in and around organizations. The chapters in Part V concentrate on the architecture of organizations, their strategic choices and organizational arrangements. Organizations might reveal patterns that have inspired some authors to infer a particular configuration. The seemingly discernable types of architecture or design have led them to establish types – for example, the well-known Burns and Stalker (1961) organic and mechanistic systems of management or Likert's (1961) system I to system IV classification of organizations. In fact, the visibility of research efforts has been so extensive that the editors of this book have been tempted in their classification efforts to lump them together as yet another school of thought. Unfortunately, configurationists do not fit neatly into a paradigm and therefore lack the unity that we might attribute to a coherent school of writers. At this point, it might be useful to take stock of their efforts and to conclude whether their pursuit merits continued research. However, in view of their profound diversity, this school displays the very difficulties that one confronts when relying on typologies to bring order in the empirical reality of organizations. After all, typologies are created to reduce widespread variations in reality to manageable proportions. They amount to data reduction efforts so that the human mind can contemplate them without getting bogged down by distracting details.

Taxonomies used to play a major role in the framing of strategic management and organization design. Not unlike plant systematics and classification schemes in other fields of study, organization theorists and strategic management scholars have indulged in armchair theorizing about the types of strategies that one can conceive. Likewise, authors from Weber to Burns and Stalker, Likert and numerous others to Mintzberg have sought to bring order to the myriad forms that one could discern and have arrived at mental schemas to reduce them to a few meaningful categories. The categories derive from phenotypes with seemingly structural regularities to which one can attribute some architecture, design or configuration.

Art historians recognize Picasso's 'blue period', cytologists 'deciduous trees', strategic management writers 'focus' and organization theorists 'bureaucracy'. Such types amount to a form of data reduction such that our limited information processing capabilities can cope with myriad forms of the phenomena they observe. Typologies are usually of the armchair variety: the writer extracts some design in the variations by zeroing in on the figure and blanking out the background. Occasionally we also encounter empirical taxonomies in which the research employs actual statistical data reduction mechanisms such as cluster analysis and multidimensional scaling, followed by the naming of the types based on the attributes that are somehow correlated. Well-known examples are the taxonomy of the Aston group or the efforts to validate empirically the Porter types. Invariably, such empirically described typologies do not conform to a priori types. The statistical algorithm relies of the smallest sums of squares, while the armchair theorist depends on cognitive simplification and psychological closure.

In the contributions to Part V we clearly witness both types of data reduction. Mintzberg is the example of the armchair variety, with his well-known 'structures in five', which have proven to be a powerful pedagogical tool for teaching students of strategic management. Using the plant systematics metaphor, we might refer to these as typologies. In contrast, the chapter by Bailey and Johnson (Chapter 18) illustrates both a priori and empirical types, where the empirical types are nested within a priori types. For example, these authors classify organizations into public and professional service sectors and then perform a principal component analysis on managers' responses to 47 items in order to classify them into six types that are linked to prevailing perspectives in strategic management and organization theory. Of course, they could also have performed a principal component analysis of the managers to see whether they and their maps of strategy development lump them into public and private service sector firms. Given the divergence in the line diagrams that correspond to industry (or for that matter Organization, as in Figure 18.2), we might find clusters based on the responses of these managers – presumably, managerial perceptions vary by the industry in which they compete or in the organization they manage. It is not clear what such variations in perceptions imply for theory or practice. We encounter here the difficulty of treating typologies as tools for theory building; we have also already noticed that the configurational school is not a real school in the sense that its members hang together as a paradigmatic community.

Lawless writes in sharp contrast to the conventional inclusion of configurational types (Chapter 19). This chapter could more readily be lumped with evolutionary thinking about firms (Nelson and Winter, 1982) or with the resource-based view of the firm as articulated by Penrose (1959) and Wernerfelt (1984). The enquiry in this paper is informed by evolutionary and resource-based theory and attempts to develop theory further. So why is it included when it is such an outlier?

A possible reason might be Lawless' effort to present a conceptual framework against which the contributions of the literature so far may be evaluated and on which further enquiry may be based. His proposal is that configurations describe common patterns of conduct that are the product of firm–market co-evolution. The model allows for a dynamic view of configurations that is welcome in studies of today's markets. Further, history dependence in firms raises options for testing the viability of strategies. For example, a configuration based on irreversible commitments can be evaluated over time against an alternative based on agility and avoiding commitments.

Lawless' arguments are exploratory when applied to the study of configurations and further development is clearly indicated. In particular, the notion is unproven that environmental constructs can support valuable, rigorous empirical tests. This work, and any proof of its merit, lies ahead. Still, the literature is dominated by empirical work that only minimally discusses the theory behind the measurement models. It is not surprising to find relatively few signs of cumulative development. Theory is arguably now in a state very similar to the one it was in at the time of Miles and Snow's taxonomy and Porter's strategy typology. For example, most strategy configurations are cross-sectional. Arguments and findings from these studies describe dynamic markets and strategy transitions that themselves are part of configurations especially well.

The prevailing view in today's field of strategic management revolves around a firm's ability to sustain above average returns. Unlike the strategy–conduct–performance or industry structure view (Porter, 1990), the dominant paradigm of the 1960s, 1970s and 1980s, we are now firmly anchored in the tradition that is commonly labelled the resourced-based view (Barney, 1991; Wernerfelt, 1984). The former view holds that a firm's abnormal returns are a function of a firm's industry and the favourable position it holds there, based on attributes such as entry barriers, size distribution and product lifecycles. As we have witnessed in population ecology, industrial organization or industrial economics treats the firm largely as a black box. The firm as a configuration of attributes in the former school abounds with typologies that presumably underpin some pattern. As with the above typologies and taxonomies, many of those typologies have also disappeared into oblivion. Their disappearance might be due to their abstract and intangible nature, otherwise we still might admire them in the Smithsonian Institute or the British Museum. They include Porter's (1980) generic strategies: focus, differentiation and cost-leadership and, for misfits, stuck in the middle. Other configurations are those by Miles and Snow (1978), such as prospector, analyser, defender or Rumelt's diversifiers (1974). The Weber–Likert–Mintzberg typologies deal more with structural attributes, while the strategic types of Porter–Miles/Snow–Rumelt are more pertinent to the firms' modal strategy.

The resource-based view constitutes a newer perspective in which researchers seek to peek into the firm as a black box. The competitive advantage is inferred from the unique resources that reside within the firm. The paradigm amounts also to a fusion of strategic and organizational levels of analysis. The resources are embedded in the routines and arrangements that are the building blocks of organizations, but are also the platform that reflect the firm's path-dependent history of strategic choices. In a purely competitive environment firms cannot enjoy a unique advantage because these resources are perfectly tradable, substitutable or imitable. Some of these resources pertain to knowledge that is carried by the organizational membership. In the course of their existence, firms accumulate intangible assets that are embodied in equipment, patents and trade secrets, but that remain largely intangible. When knowledge becomes explicit, rather than tacit, it becomes more tradable and appropriable and, therefore, less amenable to the preservation of a firm's supremacy (Teece et al., 1997). Other resources are structural and less visible to the external environment. They include technologies in use that are relatively immune to appropriation, but also organizational routines such as budgeting, research and development arrangements, templates for organizing work and control and planning routines. We might also include culture and socialization processes that align members with the corporate strategy (Winter, 1987). Finally, we might identify bundles of assets that we can subsume under social capital (Pennings et al., 1998). The relational competencies allow firms to combine their unique resources with those of other firms, particularly firms that belong to the firm's value chain (Lorenzoni and Lipparini, 1999).

Lawless' chapter as representative of the resource-based view, dwells on the configuration of the firm's resources and generates something that amounts to a typology to determine whether cluster membership produces explanations for competitive advantage. This is quite a tour de force as the resource-based view holds that each firm's resource uniqueness resembles the results of gene mapping in which each one has a unique and distinct genetic code. The uniqueness might reside in modules or in configurations (compare Henderson and Clark, 1990). Lawless deals primarily with the configuration of resources. His chapter stands in the core of the resource-based view, which also happens to be the paradigm in vogue. It is useful to reflect a bit more closely on his train of thought to link cutting edge work to the configurational school.

Lawless' chapter echoes the current work on the firm's integrating role in bringing together diverse inputs and specialized areas of knowledge and combining them to perform a productive task. Such clusters of resources include both the manipulation of modular parts as well as architectural knowledge or networks of relationships (Black and Boal, 1994). Such clusters of resources can be equated with firm capabilities or competencies. Note that the clusters here represent bundles of resources, not clusters of clusters of bundles of resources. The punch line could be described as firm performance is negatively associated with 'despecialized' or platypus firms, i.e. firms whose bundles of resources are diluted over multiple clusters of resource configurations.

We should note some drawbacks against this chapter's approach, particularly if one were to treat it as an empirical–theoretical contribution to the configurational school. The study is bounded by time, industry (microcomputer) and firm – the first two highly arbitrary, and the third one problematic in view of the strategic alliances and other co-ordinative actions that extend a firm's resources into larger aggregates, like the value chain (Yoffie, 1996). While these constraints are dictated by practical considerations we need to consider the approach's serious shortcomings. In fact, when one considers a firm and its industry as a setting where both firm and industry boundaries are fractal (jagged and diffuse) – being linked with multiple industries amounts to the firm having acquired options to permit a random walk with a reasonable amount of positive luck – its resource configuration confers superior survival benefits, not diminished ones as Lawless implies. Being an outlier and residing at the fringes of the cluster would amount to exposure to somewhat unrelated resources, including market and technological resources that allow the firm a greater chance to escape its competency trap that is inimical to the core members of Lawless's clusters. Of course, Lawless might retort that he is agnostic about firm resources, that he covered only very general and strategically uninteresting ones (not industry idiosyncratic and hence non-comparable ones) so that comments on their specificity to the industry and firm are off the mark. Yet, when we focus on a firm's resource configuration, and especially in a high tech industry such as microcomputers where the landscape changes frequently and erratically, we need to consider a firm's technological, organizational and marketing resources and their configuration in order to antici-pate its readiness to survive in a landscape where the peaks are dancing (so that adaptation to a certain ruggedness has built-in obsolescence). Finally, the resource configuration today might have different performance value compared to the con-figuration of yesterday or tomorrow. So we have to trace the configurations longitudinally. These concerns raise issues around the nature of an industry, its boundaries and, if industry includes the firm, do industry boundaries also define firm boundaries or can firms reside in multiple industries, while still being clean members of a cluster? Consider Canon, which produces copiers, digital cameras, scanners and optical instruments. It spans multiple industries, yet is highly focused on digital imaging products that invoke multiple technologies (Galanic and Rodan, 1998). Its value network might include still other technologies, such as plastics and semiconductors.

Here we are again confronted with the fractal nature of firm boundaries, even if the focus is on firms, their resource configuration and the sort of typology that we generate with these bundles. The firms in Lawless' study are embedded in a value network and I am not the first to argue that we might treat the value network, or even the value chain, as the unit of analysis (Yoffie, 1996). Do the component manufacturers belong to the same group? Are the suppliers an inte-gral set of the data that we would subject to a cluster analysis to identify the purity of the clusters and the level of firm specialization in those clusters? The same comments apply more conclusively to the Bailey and Johnson study (Chapter 18).

The spirit of Lawless' study seems defensible, but the actual implementation leads to practical problems that remain hidden in the configurational school as a collection of descriptive efforts regarding organization and strategy. Lawless wants to be explanatory rather than descriptive, to link antecedents, i.e. degree of cluster membership, to consequences, i.e. performance. Yet, his study might open up interesting opportunities for quantifying a firm's combinative capabilities (Teece et al., 1997), including the performance implications of firms that stick to the knitting versus those that branch out to various extra-mural technologies and markets in order to retain their superior flexibility to move with the evolving landscape. On the other hand, such lines of research are a far cry from the armchair-based organizational types and strategy modes. These come and go and appear to have a good pedagogical value, but are too intangible to find their way into the British Museum or the Smithsonian Institute. After all, current biologists show little interest in Linneus' plant taxonomy, which can be found in museum display cases or other storage places. Does anyone know Weber's (1946) organizational types beyond the 'bureaucracy' class?

PART VI

NEW DIRECTIONS IN STRATEGY: WAYS TO SYNTHESIZE

21

Multiple Futures of Strategy Synthesis: Shifting Boundaries, Dynamic Capabilities and Strategy Configurations

Tom Elfring and Henk W. Volberda

Engines of Strategy Pluralism, Integration and Synthesis

What are the most promising new directions in strategy? Complexity theory, game theory, hypercompetition, knowledge theories, competence-based competition? Considering the turnover of these new theories and concepts, one might conclude that any continuity in strategy is lacking. Some even argue that strategy is a science of fashion (Camerer, 1985). In this book, however, we started with analysing the variety of perspectives in strategic management (Chapters 1 and 2). In pre-paradigmatic sciences such as strategic management, one should appreciate this kind of pluralism (Mahoney, 1993; Chapters 2, 7 and 16, this volume). Theories and concepts from various related and non-related disciplines really have expanded and enriched the knowledge base of strategic management.

Although we highly value the pluralism engine that has had a major impact on the development and evolution of strategic management, we agree with Schoemaker (Chapter 8) that the time is ripe to evaluate critically the added value of further fragmentation. In Pfeffer's terminology (1993), the strategy field is like a garden in which there are thousands of flowers blooming without any pruning or tending to the garden. The problems created by this lack of pruning permeate the meaning, methodology and research methods in strategic management. The field of strategic management is well beyond the classification stage (Hamel and Prahalad, 1994) and it is about the right time in the field's evolution for some focusing. In Part II we considered some fruitful efforts at integration of various complementary strategy perspectives by considering the role of the strategist (Chapter 5), time (Chapter 6) and multiple rationalities (Chapter 4).

Although we think that the drive toward integration should be propelled more vigorously from an academic standpoint, we think that real progress in the strategy field requires synthesis. Attempts at integration often lead to theoretical frameworks that are relatively disconnected from urgent problems in strategic management. In escaping this fragmentation–integration dilemma, we suggested an increased effort for synthesis. Synthesis does not attempt to develop a single paradigm consisting of universal concepts and laws covering the entire strategic management field. Instead, it is anchored in a few clusters of strategic management problems: drawing firm boundaries, developing dynamic capabilities and finding viable strategy configurations. We think these are the essential future directions in strategy synthesis. Parts III, IV and V of this book have contributed to our understanding of these three modes of strategy synthesis. In particular, they examined the key issues, concepts and theories constituting the domain of those schools. In the boundary school, strategy is a boundary decision and it basically concerns two issues: where to draw the boundary and how to manage across the divide. The dynamic capabilities school considers strategic management as a collective learning process aimed at developing distinctive capabilities that are difficult to imitate. Lastly, the configuration school conceptualizes strategy as the emergence, development and disintegration of strategy configurations, called strategy modes, archetypes and stages in particular organizational environments.

In this final chapter we will discuss the main issues for each of these schools of strategy synthesis, considering their contributing disciplines and problem-solving capacities. The contribution of the chapters to the synthesizing schools will be viewed in the context of some of the recent literature. One of the purposes of this chapter is to gain further insight into the domains of the three synthesizing schools by reviewing the contribution of each chapter to each of them. Furthermore, we want to evaluate how these synthesizing schools may alleviate the differentiation–integration dilemma discussed in Chapter 1. However, we do not view these schools as mutually exclusive; in fact, there is some overlap. This is inevitable, as we do not want to restrict in any way the development of the type of questions being addressed (Chapter 16). We should be open to new concepts and approaches in order to make progress. At the same time, however, accumulation of insight has been a serious concern not only in the field but also in this volume (Chapter 8). Our concept of strategy synthesis schools has been put forward to overcome differentiation–integration tension, and we will reflect on the capability of the synthesizing schools to do that. The field of strategy is diverse and divided into four core dimensions (see also Chapters 1 and 8):

- the domain of inquiry
- the contribution of base disciplines
- the methodological approach
- the purpose of the inquiry.

In the opening chapter we argued that focus and the issue of accumulation might be achieved by addressing a clear cluster of problems, or a well-defined domain, for each of the three specified schools. However, each of the synthesizing schools has a substantial variety of contributing disciplines. Some chapters have also shown that the methodological approaches within each of the three schools range from quantitative to qualitative methods, such as the case studies method. Furthermore, the purpose of the enquiry also shows differences, ranging from descriptive approaches to perspectives that aim to achieve normative outcomes. Thus, in the synthesizing schools the diversity is restricted for only one of the core dimensions and is captured in the three proposed schools.

For each of the schools of strategy synthesis, we will discuss the following topics: the key issues, the theoretical background, tools for practical problem solving, contribution of the chapters in this volume and new development. On the basis of these reviews, we will draw some conclusions about new directions in strategy and the research challenges that lie ahead of us. Finally, we will also reflect on the core hypothesis stated in Chapter 1, namely that the development of the strategy field along the lines of synthesizing schools makes the field less vulnerable to fragmentation and provides a solid foundation for the accumulation of new insights.

The Boundary School

Key Issues

The boundary school addresses two key questions: where should an organization draw its boundaries and how should it manage across the divide? (See Chapter 12.) The issue of the boundaries of the firm is intimately related to the challenge of strategy formulation. Shifts in the boundaries of the firm or strategies affecting these boundaries have an impact on the competitive position of the firm. The boundary school is concerned with the analysis and design of the boundaries of the firm, in order to create competitive advantage. As the firm can be seen as a bundle of activities, the organization of the transactions or activities is a main issue. In the boundary school, strategy is a boundary decision. One of the strategic questions is which activities should be undertaken within the boundaries of the firm, which should take place in various intermediate forms, such as franchising, partnering and alliances, and which should be handled in anonymous markets. Issues such as make or buy, outsourcing, vertical integration and partner selection are examples of recent debates in the popular press.

How should these transactions across the boundary be managed? Is single or multiple sourcing the preferred mode for market transactions and how does trust influence the dynamics of alliances between firms? These are all examples of questions dealing with boundary management. It may be productive to make a distinction between the content and the process aspects of boundary issues. The first question on the position of the boundary emphasizes the content. This type of strategic question focuses on the competitive and resource positions of the firm vis-à-vis its environment. In this approach the structural properties are emphasized. Input conditions, investments and the governance structure are important determinants of the boundary of the firm. For example, in the transaction theory the focus on structural elements, such as small numbers and asset specificity is evident.

The question of boundary management is concerned with the process aspects of the boundary school. It deals with the way the organization and decision-making processes influence the ability of the firm to achieve and maintain its strategic boundary choices. These processes are crucial in interorganizational relationships, such as partnerships and alliances. In these cases, the boundary is rather fuzzy and a substantial amount of managerial attention is needed to maintain the objectives of the boundary choices. The interactive processes among the parties of the alliance need to be examined in more detail to understand the dynamics in the relationship. The aim of the process approach is to shed light on the emergence, evolution and dissolution of partnerships (Ring and van de Ven, 1994). In this approach, the individual or agent of the firm is the central unit of analysis, as the agent plays an important role in the negotiation, execution and modification of the relationship. These processes are conceptualized as a repetitive sequence in which the parties create and claim value from the relationship (Zajac and Olsen, 1993). The processes that govern the management across the boundary of the firm are important for our understanding of the joint value creation in interorganizational relationships.

Theoretical Background

The chapters on the boundary school show the rich theoretical background and diversity in academic roots of this stream of research. Numerous disciplines address issues in the boundary school, ranging from economics to psychology and from sociology to history. The work of the business historian Chandler (1962) on vertical integration has proved to be an important empirical basis for the transaction cost economics as put forward by Williamson (1975, 1986, 1993a). An important contribution of transaction cost theory is the recognition that the boundaries of the firm are of paramount strategic importance. In addition, in this particular branch of economics, analytical concepts are developed to determine the 'correct' boundary of the firm. Concepts such as assets, asset specificity, incomplete contracts and ownership are central in transaction economics. The emphasis is on the formal side and in this approach the firm is defined by the bundle of assets under common ownership (see also Chapter 9).

In contrast to the formal view of transaction cost theory, the resource-dependency approach makes a distinction between real and formal control. This approach became well known through the work of Pfeffer and Salancik (1978) and is rooted very much in sociology. Power considerations and uncertainty reduction are the driving forces and are part of the firm's strategic repertoire. They represent efforts to influence the environment instead of passively responding to it. These strategies make the firm's environment a negotiated environment.

A formal distinction between internal and external is also difficult in the network approach. Relationships and co-operative strategies may have a powerful impact on the resource position of the firm despite its informal character. It is exactly these informal relationships that have attracted the attention of researchers. The various forms of co-operation can be positioned between the two ends of the continuum from internal to external. Underlying the research on co-operation is the idea that the boundary of the firm is not very clear cut: it can be seen as fuzzy and fleeting from one situation to another. In recent years we have witnessed a fast proliferation of co-operative arrangements. They range from strategic alliances and virtual corporations to international joint ventures and network companies. In the literature on interorganizational relationships, the individual and, consequently, psychology as a base discipline, plays an important role.

Tools for Practical Problem Solving

We have discussed the issues and research questions in the boundary school as well as the contribution of a variety of base disciplines. In our pragmatic approach to schools of thought the practical problem solving capacity is a central element of a synthesizing school. What tools or instruments have been developed to guide practitioners in their analysis of boundary problems? Porter's value chain (1985) can be seen as a blueprint for the analysis of whether firms should use internal production or contract out. The decision protocol integrated into the make or buy models of Quinn and Hilmer (1994) and Venkatesan (1992) is a more sophisticated method by which the most important questions as well as the pros and cons are made concrete. Venkatesan's strategic sourcing process (see Figure 21.1) and the value chain tool developed by Quinn and Hilmer builds on the knowledge derived from research into the outsourcing problem. The basic conclusion is that activities in the firm should be divided into strategic and non-strategic activities. The strategic activities should be kept in house and the non-core or commodity type of intermediate products be considered as candidates for outsourcing. Clearly, this insight has been inspired by such diverse backgrounds as transaction cost reasoning, theories concerning the benefits of specialization and economies of scale and organizational theories about control and co-ordination.

The tools discussed above fit into the so-called strategic versus commodity approach and reflect the more formal and content oriented perspectives in the boundary school. Some limitations of this approach have been put forward in the literature. Hendry (1995) argues that the costs of outsourcing, such as the reduced ability to learn, to be responsive to long-term changes and to co-ordinate are underestimated. His argument is that the reasoning in the strategic versus commodity approach is based on the formal side of the organization. To him the informal side is important as well, in particular the part that consists of conversations, personal interaction, inferences and intuition. This informal side cannot be analysed in terms of the strategic versus commodity approach. By moving certain parts of the organization from the inside to the outside, employees will not have the informal shared understanding and experience that goes with being an integral part of the organization. This shared understanding is important for transferring tacit knowledge, which is a key ingredient in learning (Boisot, 1998) and in realizing systemic innovations (Chesbrough and Teece, 1996).

Another problem is the lack of flexibility in the strategic versus commodity approach. Lacity et al. (1995) claim that, in turbulent environments, this approach

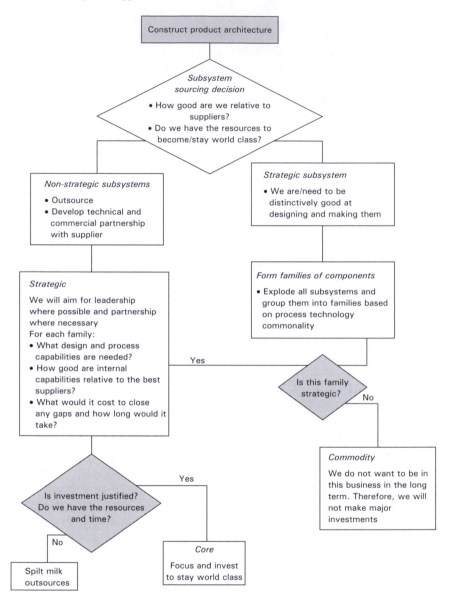

FIGURE 21.1   *A strategic framework for outsourcing (Venkatesan, 1992)*

leads to problems and disappointments. In turbulent environments activities that were once considered to be strategic can become standard commodities and vice versa. This became clear in their study concerning the outcomes of make or buy decisions of approximately 40 companies with respect to IT services (Lacity et al., 1995). The assumption underlying the decision of whether an activity is strategic or not is 'that managers can place big bets about their markets, future technologies, and suppliers' capabilities and motives with a great deal of

certainty. They cannot. The world is too turbulent, unpredictable and complex'
(Lacity et al., 1995: 84). They refer to a number of cases in which certain IT
services were deemed to be of strategic importance, whereas a few years later it
turned out they could be characterized as standard commodities, largely due to
technological changes. Consequently, it is preferable not to make a definitive
decision, thus creating more flexibility and learning opportunities. This is achieve-
able by promoting selective and partial outsourcing.

The problems with the strategic versus commodity approach underlying some
of the tools used to analyse make or buy decisions are concerned with both its
formal and its static characteristics. Recently, more dynamic tools have been
developed. In an article by Ring and van de Ven (1994) a conceptual framework
for analysing the dynamics of interfirm relationships was put forward. Zajac and
Olson (1993) have proposed a similar framework. In their stages model focusing
on the dynamics of co-operative relationships, they make suggestions for key
managerial questions for each of the three stages. This model can be helpful for
managers who are involved in the processes of building and shaping relationships
with important outside parties, such as suppliers.

Contribution of the Chapters
In his overview chapter on the boundary school Nicolai Foss reviews the contribution of four distinct theories to this synthesizing school (Chapter 9). An important achievement of the transaction cost theory is that the boundaries of the firm
have been defined in a consistent and unambiguous manner. The firm is defined
by the bundle of assets under common ownership. Assets and, in particular, asset
specificity and the incentive mechanism to keep opportunism at bay are the key
conceptual contributions to the boundary school. The emphasis of the formal side
and the appropriability of the assets is clearly an important aspect of the choice
of boundary. However, other aspects, such as the informal side, the context and
relationships to other parties and the issue of asset accumulation, are neglected in
transaction cost theory. One of the points put forward by Foss is that the other
aspects and the theories dealing with them are complementary to each other. The
other theories are the resource-dependency approach, the network perspective
and the resource-based view. The first two theories are widely recognized as
dealing with the boundary of the firm. The last one, the resource-based view or
capabilities perspective is, according to Foss, an important determinant of the
boundaries of the firm. Accumulation of productive knowledge across the boundaries of the firm appears to be rather difficult compared to internal development,
in particular when there is a high degree of tacitness.

Two observations can be made about the diversity of theoretical contributions
to the boundary school. First, including the capabilities perspective makes the
overlap with the dynamic capabilities school apparent. This perspective is relevant
to both the boundary and the dynamic capabilities school. Second, when some of
the theoretical contributions are complementary, which combinations are most
likely to improve our understanding of the boundary of the firm? What are potentially interesting routes for synthesis? Foss addresses these questions explicitly,
and his reflection on them adds to our conception of synthesizing schools.

There is huge potential for synthesis of the theories constituting the boundary school. Foss discusses a number of productive routes for synthesis. For example, he observes complementarities between the introspective stance of the capabilities approach and the network approach that defines the firm in terms of its being embedded in a web of co-operating and competing firms. But new insights may also be derived from combining the structural properties with the formal side of the transaction cost approach and the trust-based relationships in the network approach.

The two other chapters on the boundary school, on trust (Chapter 10) and alliances (Chapter 11), are further examples of a practical eclectic approach to the issue of synthesis. Koenig and van Wijk deal in more detail with the dynamics in co-operative relationships. Boundaries of co-operation evolve over time. They go beyond contracts, and emphasize the interplay between the formal and the informal, thus, combining the content perspective as put forward in the transaction cost approach with the process perspective as they see trust as a learning process.

Stiles also extends the content approach with process considerations. She puts the competitive and the co-operative perspectives into one framework and extends that with an analysis of the realizability of that strategy.

New Directions in the Boundary School

As the chapters on the boundary school have shown, exploiting complementarities between different theories in order to explain relatively novel phenomena, such as interfirm relationships, is a promising contribution to the development of this school. The challenges ahead of us are to make the analysis more dynamic and to introduce the element of time (Chapter 6). It becomes clear that the process perspective is important for a dynamic setting and is complementary to the content approach. This can be illustrated by the contribution of Koenig and van Wijk (Chapter 10). They conceptualized trust as part of interacting and dynamic processes. Trust is what allows co-operation and contracts to emerge. Contracts and formal arrangements grow out of interaction and structure and then act as a way to secure them. Even intensive collaboration based foremost on trust are expected to evolve to a level of formalization, as this avoids overextending trust and actually provides a basis for further trust-based developments. Consequently our understanding of interfirm relationships may have been improved by combining content and process based efforts.

More generally, combining informal and formal, or content and process approaches may create new insights. Elsewhere in the literature this pragmatic approach was used to study interfirm relationships. Ring and van de Ven (1994) tried to capture the dynamics of these relationships. They tried to operationalize these dynamic processes by looking at content and process factors that allow the relationship to evolve or dissolve over time. Zajac and Olson (1993), who proposed a stage model of co-operative relationships, took a similar eclectic approach.

These process approaches are a potentially interesting new development. They can be seen as complementary to the dominant content perspectives and consequently they promise to improve the explanatory power of the boundary school.

There are many processes that might have a bearing on the boundary of the firm. One can make a distinction between processes within the firm and processes across firms. It is the latter category in particular that we want to examine as the issue of co-operative relationships between firms has become a central domain of research in strategy.

The increasing importance of network organizations, various forms of alliances and co-operation in the supply chain is not fully understood in the strategy literature. This is especially true for some of the theories dealing with the boundary of the firm. This boundary becomes increasingly fuzzy and this lack of clarity creates all kinds of management problems. Certainly, in terms of the transaction cost theory, the transaction costs will tend to rise when the transactions across the boundary of the firm become more complex. However, as Foss observed in Chapter 9, the transaction cost approach is about economizing. In some cases the efficiency argument in the economizing perspective is over-ruled by strategy considerations. In other words, the benefits of strategizing may be greater than the additional costs associated with more complex transactions. The fundamental question is, therefore, to define the key processes to maximize the value derived from co-operative relationships. This question can be split into two parts. First, what processes can be distinguished to reduce the transaction costs? Second, what processes can be distinguished to create joint value for the exchange partners? In the emerging literature addressing these issues (Ring and van de Ven, 1994; Zajac and Olsen, 1993) the structural properties of the exchange relationship are used as a context for the analysis of the processes. In the following sections we discuss a number of recent studies that address these questions and present promising routes for further research.

New Frameworks Including Processes and Benefits

The aim of the studies by Ring and van de Ven (1994) and Zajac and Olsen (1993) was to develop a framework consisting of the key processes of the development of interorganizational exchange relationships. The two frameworks are different but overlap substantially. Both distinguish a number of stages to describe the development of the co-operative relationship. In each stage a number of characteristic processes are suggested to examine the development of the relationship and the adaptability of the relationship to creating the expected joint benefits. In the initial stage, the parties develop joint expectations about the motivations, perceptions of the parameters of exchange and benefits of this relationship over alternatives. In this first round of exchange different ways of communicating are explored and negotiations about the individual and mutual costs and benefits of the exchange take place.

The second stage deals with the execution of the commitments and rules of action as determined in the first stage. The repeated interactions and the distribution of the value created according to the deals made in the first round allow for a process of trust building. Trust can be developed as the parties live up to expectations. In this stage the repeated interaction may also lead to growing interpersonal relationships as the parties involved become more familiar with one another. The creation of relational norms concerning behaviour will develop.

These norms not only deal with the distribution of the additional value, but also allow mechanisms concerning conflict resolution to develop. Finally, learning about new ways to economize on production and transaction will accelerate as the parties are exposed to a greater variety of possibilities. Of course, the domain of learning will also encapsulate discovering new opportunities for the creation of benefits and joint value.

In the third stage the results of the relationship are evaluated and, when necessary, adjusted in order to improve transaction value. The assessment concerns both the performance of the co-operative relationship in terms of costs and benefits and the nature of the exchange process. Consequently, in this stage, the strategic objectives of the relationship may be adjusted, but the exchange processes themselves may also be subject to change.

The processes in the various stages are important for an understanding of the development of a co-operative relationship. They may give us new insights into how to manage across the divide. This process approach is complementary to the transaction cost approach as it includes the challenge of creating joint value from the relationship, such that it exceeds the additional costs associated with the transaction. Two processes are of particular interest: building trust and learning.

Building Trust

Building trust is seen as one of the key processes (see also Chapter 10) in the healthy development of co-operative relationships. However, it has not been spelled out how that key process of trust building is inter-related to the other processes and to the creation of joint value in the relationship. More research in this area is promising, as a recent study by Dyer (1997) shows. He developed a model of interfirm collaboration on the basis of the relationship between car manufacturers and their suppliers in Japan and in the USA. In this model the effect of trust went beyond the traditional impact of reducing the transaction costs. The main contribution was that trustworthiness also has a positive influence on investments in relation-specific assets and thereby has the potential to increase the joint value of the collaboration. Evidence was found that trustworthy partners engage in greater information sharing, a stronger commitment to future interaction and use self-employed safeguards to govern the relationship. As a result, the likelihood increases that the two parties will improve the joint value of the collaboration through relation-specific investments. The improved information sharing will contribute to the chances of discovering new joint investment opportunities. In addition, the commitment to a longer time horizon and the establishment of safeguards increases the number of joint investments that make economic sense as the payback period is extended.

A number of insights can be drawn from the results of the Dyer (1997) study. Building trust is an important process in the development of co-operative relationships. It is not cost free, it takes time and effort to agree on safeguards, to discuss commitments and to exchange information. However, the resulting trustworthiness is an important condition for relation-specific investments, which in turn are crucial for achieving the expected benefits. When the benefits of strategizing (Foss, Chapter 9) are greater than the costs associated with relationship building, it has been a worthwhile effort to develop a co-operative relationship as compared to a market transaction. This study has shown one particular case in which strategizing may over-rule economizing on transactions. Strategizing in this case is conceptualized by describing in detail the causality between certain relationship processes and some structural properties of the relationship. There are many potential inter-relations between the process approach and the structural perspective on the boundary of the firm. Detailed empirical studies are required to unravel the chain of causality and Dyer's (1997) study shows that such a route is promising. More insights may be expected from that route concerning the issue of how to manage across the divide.

Learning Processes
Another key process is that of learning in co-operative relationships. The main emphasis for future research on learning processes is on new ways to realize joint benefits from an alliance. The focus is again on the recognition and the realization of new combinations that add value to the alliance. Thus, also in the learning literature related to co-operative relationships, these new developments may put some meat on the bones of the concept of creating transaction value introduced by Zajac and Olsen (1993). This type of literature is complementary to the economizing perspective, which concentrates on minimizing transaction costs. We want to draw attention to two promising ways in which the learning processes perspective contributes to boundary management. First, conceptual advances are needed to improve our understanding of the dynamics of learning in alliances (Khanna et al., 1998). Second, firms increasingly rely on the knowledge of other firms to develop their competitive position. The ability of firms to interact and share knowledge with other firms may be seen as an organizational competence (Lorenzoni and Lipparini, 1999). This line of research uses some competence-based concepts to develop new insights into the issue of how to manage across the divide.

The study by Hamel (1991) on learning in alliances is well known. The context is the desire of the participants in the alliance to learn some of the partner's competencies. The benefits of the alliance can be gained by the party who is quickest to learn. The dynamics are all about learning the required competences as fast as possible. And the winner takes it all, because by that time the winner is not interested any more in investing in the relationship. Obviously, such opportunistic behaviour is not beneficial to the development of co-operative relationships. Efforts to curb such opportunistic behaviour hampers the learning process. In order to analyse the dynamics of learning alliances Khanna et al. (1998) introduced the concepts of private benefits, common benefits and the pay-off structure. Their main point is that the firms' incentives to learn are driven by their expected pay-off. In addition, they suggest that the pay-off structure is not fixed, but can be influenced by the partners' resource allocation decisions as the alliance evolves. It can be expected that the higher the ratio of private to common benefits the less likely it is that the partnership will flourish. Lack of commitment from one of the parties to invest resources in projects expected to lead to common benefits may jeopardize the alliance. However, in the negotiation process these imbalances may still be corrected. The ability to negotiate is an important capability for managing these learning alliances. The notion that sufficient resources should be committed to create common benefits instead of private benefits is helpful from a managerial perspective. The observation that the ability to negotiate is important in shaping the boundaries of the firm leads to the second contribution to the learning in alliances perspective.

The ability to manage across the boundary can be seen as a distinctive organizational capability according to Lorenzoni and Lipparini (1999). By using this perspective one can draw on the insights from the competence-based literature to improve our understanding of the key processes of learning across firms' boundaries. The challenge for a firm in a network is to be able to interact and share knowledge with partner firms in order to create common benefits. Lorenzoni and Lipparini review a number of concepts to enrich their core belief. One is the ability to absorb competences (Cohen and Levinthal, 1990) and the ability to combine existing competences in order to create new ones. One of Lorenzoni and Lipparini's key questions was how do these capabilities develop over time? The context of their longitudinal study was the leading firm networks in the packaging machine industry. They found that the leading firms have to undertake deliberate initiatives to create a network environment of trust and co-operation. Repeated interactions and early sharing of information on the part of the leading firm are required to build trust. Trust-based relationships can be extended to promote mechanisms for 'learning by interacting'. Suppliers are asked to help the leading firm to identify new technologies and opportunities. The leading firm, on the other hand, has to show that the committed resources lead to benefits for the entire network.

In the discussion above an increasing fuzziness of the boundary of the firm can be seen. The boundary has progressed from a simple buyer–supplier relationship to network structures. The work by Lorenzoni and Lipparini (1999) shows that the benefits can still outweigh the transaction costs in a leading firm network. However, it strongly depends on the relational capabilities of the leading firm to create sufficient joint benefits for others.

One of the challenges ahead is to examine the structures and processes in entrepreneurial networks. These are networks or clusters of activities in which a high number of start-ups originate: the recent surge of vibrant start-ups in Silicon Valley is a good example (Bahrami and Evans, 1995). In these networks there is no leading firm to co-ordinate the transactions and assure sufficient commitment of resources to common benefits. The start-ups are prime examples, however, of firms with excellent relational capabilities. They have little choice, as the option of doing everything in house is hardly feasible. They rely on their partners for a large number of competences, such as money, advice, marketing, managerial experience and legal advice. These complementary capabilities are usually not provided in a market-type transaction. Relationships are used and extended to obtain access to these complementary inputs. The added insights on trust, learning and creation of common benefits may run into difficulties when explaining the development of co-operative relationships in these entrepreneurial networks. In particular, the realization of common benefits remains very uncertain as the failure rate of start-ups is relatively high.

The focus in the boundary school has shifted from simple outsourcing decisions to co-operative relationships and networks. Recent contributions in the boundary school have emphasized the importance of strategizing over economizing. New concepts, such as private and common benefits, have been introduced to refine and operationalize the notion of creating transaction value instead of minimizing transaction costs. To improve our understanding of the creation of common benefits, processes have been examined that are important in shaping the boundaries of the firm. These recent advances are promising and we expect that further efforts to discover processes and chains of causation leading to the creation of joint value in transactions across boundaries to continue to contribute to the boundary school.

The Dynamic Capabilities School

Key Issues

The dynamic capabilities school addresses the question 'with whom and how do firms compete and how do they sustain their competitive advantage over time?' (Chapter 16) by emphasizing internal processes. The key issues in the capabilities approach are firms' relative abilities to use current resources, to create new resources and to devise new ways of using current or new resources (Chapter 13). Current resources could serve as a basis for a strategy that could lead to a sustainable competitive advantage (Barney, 1991). These resources have to meet four conditions to be a source of sustainable competitive advantage: they must be valuable, rare, difficult to imitate and difficult to substitute. There has been considerable debate about these conditions and the extent to which they must be met. For example, what does makes a resource valuable? The value of resources cannot be evaluated in isolation. The context is of importance; a resource that is valuable in a particular industry might be of no value in another industry. According to Collis and Montgomery (1995) the value of a resource or a capability is determined by the interplay of market forces, such as scarcity, demand and appropriability. For Grant (1991) the issue of appropriability concerns the allocation of returns on resources or capabilities where property rights are not fully defined. This is the case for intangible assets in particular, including brand names, copyrights and employee skills. Another hotly debated issue is the explanation of the origin of resources or capabilities that provide a firm with competitive advantage. There is always a prior explanation for the origin of a capability, i.e. the capability to develop that capability. This problem of infinite regression observed by Collis (1994) explains but also predicts the competitive implications of particular capabilities. These issues go beyond the more static analysis of the existing bundle of resources. Important research questions in this static or comparatively static perspective are how a firm can use this reservoir of resources to exploit a distinctive competence in different end markets and how such a strategy can contribute to the competitive position of the firm.

An increasing emphasis has been placed on examining a dynamic perspective of capabilities (Teece et al., 1997). In this perspective one of the objectives is to understand the trajectories for developing capabilities – understanding the managerial and organizational processes by which firms renew their capabilities and the forces that limit these processes. The ability to adjust the current routines and develop new kinds of capabilities is constrained by the firms' current resource positions, which create path dependencies. Learning processes play an important role in overcoming these path dependencies. Learning and exploring new knowledge and skills is important as a first step, but these new skills have to be recognized as valuable and they have to be integrated with the existing set of capabilities in order to build new ones. Two of the three chapters on the dynamic capability school address those organizational learning processes. Sanchez and Mahoney (Chapter 14) explain how using modularity in an organization's product and process architecture can improve organizational learning. Kirjavainen (Chapter 15) examines how different levels of learning interact and affect the processes of strategy formation.

Theoretical Background

The theoretical basis of the dynamic capability school is rather diverse. Insights, theories and concepts from economics (resource-based theory of the firm, theories of entrepreneurship and innovation), psychology (learning and cognition concepts) and biology, in particular population ecology (path dependencies, inertia), have been used to provide the building blocks to this synthesizing school. The resource-based theory of the firm (Learned et al., 1965; Penrose, 1959) is considered to be a starting point for theory building. A chosen strategy is only viable when it leads to a distinctive competence (Selznick, 1957). This novel approach attempts to open up the black box by conceptualizing the firm as a bundle of firm-specific resources that can lead to superior performance. Although this approach originally only considered purely physical resources, a shift can be seen towards more interest in intangible resources and tacit knowledge (Itami, 1987; Quinn, 1992). Besides the resourced-based theory of the firm, theories of entrepreneurship and innovation have also contributed to this school (Kirzner, 1973; Schumpeter, 1934). A unique competence requires the proliferation of existing skills within the firm (Kirzner, 1973). On the other hand, the development of a new core competence goes hand in hand with the 'creative destruction' of existing skills (Schumpeter, 1934). In the same way, innovation theories like Nelson and Winter's (1982) evolutionary theory of economic change state that the development of skills is based on making routines of existing activities and leads to so-called 'natural trajectories'. This implies that the development of skills is an incremental process. The factors that determine these incremental learning processes, such as the organization's history, prior investments and cognitive structures, are sometimes called path dependencies in the dynamic capabilities school. In addition to innovation theories, the synthesizing school discussed here is firmly anchored in learning theories derived from psychology. The development of distinctive competencies demands the accentuation and profiling of routines, which is also referred to as 'single-loop learning' (Argyris and Schön, 1978). A core competence can, however, lead to a core rigidity (Leonard-Barton, 1992). For this reason, firms must be able to break the habit of existing routines and develop entirely new ones, that is to say they must embark upon 'double-loop learning'. Cognition theories also play a role in this process of developing new capabilities. New opportunities must be recognized and different levels of learning must be distinguished. Individual and collective learning and the linkages between them are important for our understanding of the ability of firms to renew their capabilities. This synthesizing school is also partly based on biology in the sense that only those skills selected by the environment are developed.

Tools for Practical Problem Solving

How can firms identify core capabilities and then develop and use them? While the speed of change in today's turbulent environment weakens the sustainability of specialized routines, it increases the importance of the advantage provided by dynamic capabilities, which remain valuable as long as competitive change persists. Firms still need specialized routines, but these routines have a dysfunctional flipside as rapidly changing environments render them obsolete. For instance, in the 1980s, American car manufacturers found that a simple high-volume, standardized production repertoire appeared to be insufficient to cope with the many challenges posed by the changing environment. Rather, these challenges required a willingness to invest heavily in extremely dynamic capabilities, often far beyond that which may be utilized at any given point in time. Successful Japanese companies have shown these capabilities offer far more than the ability to make multiple products simultaneously – they also offer the benefits of reduced changeover costs across product generations and the ability to adjust the product mix in the face of uncertain demands, even at low volumes.

These days it may seem impossible for any manager to ignore changes in markets, products and technologies. Yet the popular business press is full of successful companies that focused too much on past routines, such as DEC, Wang computers and Sears. In other companies such as IBM, Kodak and Philips, which have recently undergone massive changes, existing or new managers are working on developing new capabilities (Volberda, 1998). But how can management create dynamic capabilities? What kind of dynamic capabilities are they? Most of the existing tools of the dynamic capabilities school are developed within functional areas and focus on functional capabilities, such as manufacturing, supplier relationships or human resource management. However, the more complex capabilities are more broadly based (Stalk et al., 1992), encompassing the entire value chain, such as short product development capabilities or fast product and process innovation capabilities.

The more tool-oriented work by Prahalad and Hamel (1990) is helpful for these more complex dynamic capabilities, which are more firm-specific and are developed over time through complex interactions among firms' resources (Amit and Schoemaker, 1993). They developed 'the roots of competitiveness', a conceptual model for formulating a number of core products and end markets on the basis of core competencies and capabilities (see Figure 21.2). Using the tree metaphor, the leaves and fruit represent the firm's end products and services, the branches constitute strategic business units which combine related products

End product

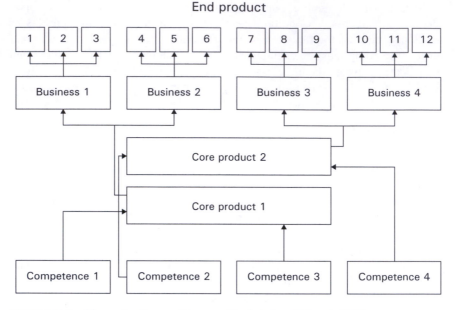

FIGURE 21.2   *The roots of competitiveness (Prahalad and Hamel, 1990)*

and services, the trunk denotes core products and, lastly, the roots represent capabilities or core competencies that enable the firm to sustain its existing branches and grow new ones.

To use this model, a core competence should:

- provide potential access to a wide variety of markets and application areas
- make a significant contribution to the perceived customer benefits of the end product
- be difficult to imitate, which is primarily achieved when complex combinations of skills and knowledge are formed.

Schoemaker (1992) also developed a capability matrix for the identification and development of core capabilities that are effective under different scenarios. The matrix is aimed at identifying and developing those core capabilities that are important in multiple segments under alternative scenarios (see Figure 21.3).

Schoemaker argues for a kind of renewed SWOT (strengths, weaknesses, opportunities, threats) analysis in which the strengths and weaknesses are related much more to invisible assets and core capabilities. His framework has four steps.

1   Generate broad scenarios of possible futures that your firm may encounter.
2   Conduct a competitive analysis of the industry and its strategic segments.
3   Analyse your company's and your competition's core capabilities.
4   Develop a strategic vision and identify your strategic options.

Scenarios

Strategic segments	Stagnation and saturation	Computer confusion	Computer cornucopia
Home	h.c.b.d	c.b.h.d	b.c.a.d
Education	c.h.d.e	c.d.h.a	d.c.e.b
Business	a.f.e.c	e.f.a.d	f.a.e.d
Workstations	g.d.e.a	d.g.h.e	d.f.g.b

Note: the top four capabilities are ranked within each cell in order of relative importance.

Legend for core capabilities	**Frequency of occurrence**
a. Highly knowledgeable salesforce	6
b. Access to distribution channels	5
c. User friendliness in product development	7
d. Availability of software and peripherals	11
e. Compatibility/integrative product line	7
f. Professional image – quality and reliability	4
g. Use of new and innovative technology	3
h. Low-cost position in manufacturing	5

FIGURE 21.3   *A core capabilities matrix for Apple (Schoemaker, 1992)*

While the concepts (resources, capabilities, core competence) of the dynamic capabilities school receive increasing attention from managers, the development of practical tools is still in its infancy. Although many tools have been developed for identifying functional capabilities, tools for analysing the more complex and strategic capabilities are sparse (Marino, 1996).

Contribution of the Chapters

Chapter 13 contributes to this volume in three ways. First, it gives an overview of the numerous studies and diverse theories and concepts that constitute the dynamic capability school as a synthesizing school. This chapter can serve as an advanced introduction to this perspective, as it carefully reviews the concepts, focal issues and basic propositions of the diverse set of research efforts in this field. Second, the development and transformation of the key concepts is placed in a historical context. Sanchez offers an interpretation of the development as a progression of concepts, each of which significantly extends the scope for understanding the main challenges in the strategy field. Third, this progressive conceptual development can be attributed, in his view, to its expanding ability to achieve integration of the many different concepts in the strategy field that, thus far, have been unconnected theoretical domains. Sanchez illustrates this potential for theoretical integration with a number of examples.

Chapter 14 adds insights to the discussion about strategic flexibility and organizational learning. Sanchez and Mahoney show how modularity in an organization's product and process architecture can enhance strategic flexibility. The creation of modular product architectures enables firms to substitute component variations into modular product designs, thereby increasing the variety of products a firm can develop and the speed with which it can upgrade products. Modularity can create a form of embedded co-ordination that facilitates the autonomous and concurrent development of components by loosely coupled organizations, thereby improving the strategic flexibility of the firm.

The main contribution of Chapter 15 is the improved understanding of how learning affects processes of strategy formation and change in knowledge-intensive firms. Kirjavainen's results are based on an in-depth case study and they can be characterized as theory building and not theory testing. Her work is highly integrative and therefore fits in very well to the tradition of this synthesizing school. She bridges strategy and organizational theory and integrates some of the well-known American and Scandinavian theoretical views on (organizational) learning. The result is a framework in which different levels of learning are recognized. In this framework collective learning is linked to individual learning. In her conceptualization of individual learning and linking mechanisms to collective learning, key experts and cognitive processes play a central role. This novel framework for strategic learning provides the dynamic capabilities school with the conceptual language to describe the processes through which capabilities develop.

New Research Directions: Co-evolution of Capabilities and Competition[1]

How dynamic are dynamic capabilities? Does managerial intention matter? Or are successful capabilities selected by the industry environment? These questions have occupied centre stage in research in the dynamic capabilities school (Lewin and Volberda, 1999; Volberda and Baden-Fuller, 1998). Notwithstanding the managerial relevance of these provocative questions, most of the research efforts in strategy are rooted in stability, not change. There has been relatively little focus on exactly how firms develop firm-specific competencies and how they renew them to follow shifts in the industry (Baden-Fuller and Volberda, 1997).

The theory of the firm addresses why firms exist and recent insights suggest that the answer lies in mechanisms that exploit unique competencies and knowledge (Barney, 1991; Nonaka, 1991). As explained by Conner and Prahalad (1996), this view contrasts with other views, such as those of minimizing transaction costs or resolving principal agent difficulties (Alchian and Demsetz, 1972; Williamson, 1975). The same literature, however, does not address how firms change. This has traditionally been the preserve of organizational theorists, with a long tradition stretching back to Barnard (1938), Chandler (1962), Pettigrew (1985) and van de Ven (1986). From the perspective of the dynamic capabilities school, these writers seem less concerned with the content of change. To answer these questions about the process and content of capability development, we need to return to dynamic theories.

Dynamic Theories

At one extreme, there are evolutionary theories emphasizing tight selection and path dependencies. They stress that organizations and their units accumulate know-how in the course of their existence and become repositories of skills that are unique and often difficult to separate. According to population ecology theory, these skills are the source of both inertia and distinctive competence

(Hannan and Freeman, 1977, 1984). The inertia is due to sunk costs in past investments and entrenched social structures, as well as to organization members becoming attached to cognitive styles, behavioural dispositions and decision heuristics. The accumulated skills that render firms and their units inert also provide opportunities for strengthening their unique advantages, and for further improving their know-how. The potential benefits include greater reliability in delivering sound and comprehensible products and many economies of efficiency and routine (Miller and Chen, 1994: 1). In a similar vein, institutional theories stress the coercive, normative and mimetic behaviour of organizations in the face of environmental forces for change. They, too, stress how difficult it is for existing firms to create new capabilities (DiMaggio and Powell, 1983; Greenwood and Hinings, 1988).

In their *Evolutionary Theory of Economic Change*, Nelson and Winter (1982) present firms as repositories of routines that endow them with a capacity to search. Yet the same routines suppress attention span and the capacity to absorb new information by spelling out behaviour that permits the search only for new ideas that are consistent with prior learning. According to this theory, capabilities are contingent on the proximity to tacit knowledge and to prior and commensurate skills. They have an inner logic of their own and give rise to natural trajectories. Given the tacit and cumulative nature of knowledge, experience with previous generations of a given technology is often essential for its future innovative success (Cohen and Levinthal, 1990). On the other hand, the switching costs or the costs of changing trajectories and acquiring knowledge unrelated to the asset base can be quite high (Henderson and Clark, 1990; Rosenberg, 1972). In a similar way, the firm in the resource-based theory is seen as a bundle of tangible and intangible resources and tacit know-how that must be identified, selected, developed and deployed to generate superior performance (Learned et al., 1965; Penrose, 1959; Wernerfelt, 1984). These scarce, firm-specific assets lead to unique capabilities that can hardly be changed; firms are stuck with what they have and have to live with their deficiencies (Teece et al., 1997).

In these selection and path dependent theories of capability development, firms do best by not trying to counter their history, but rather by allowing evolution to take its course. By contrast, other theories focusing more on adaptation and managerial intention argue that capability development is more versatile and less determined by tight selection and path dependencies. There is a large body of work that suggests that organizations can and do change, overcoming their own rigidities. For instance, Teece et al. (1997) have suggested it is not only the resources that matter, but also the mechanisms by which firms accumulate and dissipate new skills and new capabilities. They propose that dynamic capabilities represent the firm's latent abilities to renew its core competence over time. Moreover, the behavioural theory of the firm (Cyert and March, 1963) argues that a firm's ability to develop new capabilities is determined primarily by availability and control of organizational slack and by strategic intent to allocate this slack to renewal. The theory provides a process description of structural inertia and a justification for periodic renewal through restructuring and rationalization. In addition, the strategic choice perspective (Child, 1972, 1997; Miles and Snow,

1978, 1994; Thompson, 1967) argues that organizations are not always passive recipients of environmental influence but also have the opportunity and power to reshape the environment. Hrebiniak and Joyce (1985), Khandwalla (1977) and many other neocontingency theorists assert that capability development is a dynamic process subject both to managerial action and environmental forces. Finally, to align themselves with their environments, firms must have some unique capabilities for learning, unlearning or relearning on the basis of their past behaviour. Learning theories assume that capability development is both adaptive and manipulative, in the sense that organizations adjust defensively to reality and use the resulting knowledge offensively to improve their capabilities (Fiol and Lyles, 1985; Hedberg, 1981: 3).

Co-evolution

The theories discussed above seem to describe capability development as a process either of selection or adaptation (see Table 21.1). Certain theories, such as the behavioural theory of the firm, strategic choice and learning perspectives, attempt to elaborate the role of managerial intention further. Other theories, such as population ecology, institutionalism and, to some extent, evolutionary theories, discount the ability of organizations to self-consciously renew their capabilities significantly or repeatedly. Using variables such as resource scarcity, industry norms and shared logics, static routines and structural inertia, these selection perspectives argue that capability renewal is highly restricted. While these theories have shown us adaptive and selective routes to capability development, we think that future research will show much more pluralism (Lewin and Volberda, 1999).

TABLE 21.1   *Dynamic theories: selection versus adaptation*

Co-evolution of capabilities and competition	
Mainly selection	Mainly adaptation
• Population ecology: based on and limited to accumulation of structural and procedural baggage through retention processes (Aldrich and Pfeffer, 1976; Hannan and Freeman, 1977, 1984)	• Dynamic capability theory: promoted by firm's latent abilities to renew, augment and adapt its core competence over time (Teece et al., 1997)
• Institutional theory: results from coercive, normative and mimetic isomorphism; maintaining congruence with shifting industry norms and shared logics (DiMaggio and Powell, 1983; Greenwood and Hinings, 1996)	• Behavioural theory of the firm: determined primarily by the availability and control of organizational slack and by the strategic intent to allocate slack to innovation (Cyert and March, 1963)
• Evolutionary theory: based on proliferation of routines and reinforcement of incremental improvements (Nelson and Winter, 1982)	• Learning theories: process of alignment of firm and environment based on unique skills for learning, unlearning or relearning (Argyris and Schön, 1978; Fiol and Lyles, 1985; Huber, 1991)
• Resource-based theory: converging trajectories of exploitation of unique core competencies (Learned et al., 1965; Penrose, 1959; Wernerfelt, 1984)	• Strategic choice theories: dynamic process subject to managerial action and environmental forces (Child, 1972, 1997; Hrebiniak and Joyce, 1985; Miles and Snow, 1978)

Source: Adapted from Lewin and Volberda, 1999

Instead of focusing on naïve selection or naïve adaptation processes of capability development, new research efforts should consider the joint outcomes of managerial adaptation and environmental selection. With a few exceptions (Baum and Singh, 1994; Bruderer and Singh, 1996; Lant and Mezias, 1990; Levinthal, 1997; Teece et al., 1997) researchers have tended not to address the inter-relationships between processes of firm level adaptation and population level selection pressures. Adaptation and selection are not wholly opposed forces but are fundamentally inter-related. Such a co-evolutionary approach assumes that capability development is not an outcome of managerial adaptation or environmental selection but rather the joint outcome of intention and environmental effects.

Co-evolutionary Studies on Dynamic Capabilities

Co-evolutionary studies on routines, capabilities and competencies are not new in strategic management. For example, Levitt and March (1988) and Nelson and Winter (1982) have proposed variations of mutual learning frameworks that retain and reinforce learning and incremental improvements of successful routines. Also, Levinthal and Myatt (1994) studied the macro-evolution of the mutual fund industry in terms of the co-evolution of industry market activities and distinctive capabilities of firms within the industry. These studies, which incorporate both firm and industry levels of analysis, subsume possible interactions between genealogical processes (replication of routines, capabilities, competencies) and ecological processes (dynamics of competition and selection).

Firm–industry analysis also points to potential for search behaviour in moving toward a co-evolutionary view of capabilities and competition (Huygens, 1999). In a study on evolution among Illinois banks, Barnett and Hansen (1996) report findings that support dynamic interactions between firm learning and adaptation on the one hand and higher levels of competition and selection on the other. This form of persistent co-evolution is dubbed an 'arms race' or 'the Red Queen effect' (Beinhocker, 1997; Kauffman, 1995; van Valen, 1973) after her comment to Alice, 'It takes all the running you can do to keep in the same place' (Carroll, 1946). The concept of hypercompetition (D'Aveni and Gunther, 1994), in which escalating competition results in short periods of advantage punctuated by frequent disruptions, represents a similar approach (Ilinitch et al., 1998). In these co-evolutionary models, the assumed symmetry between forces of adaptation and selection results in their cancelling each other out. That is to say, search behaviour on the firm level may lead to unique capabilities and competitive advantage, but as a result of increased competitive dynamics, these advantages are quickly eroded. The implication is that all species keep changing in a never ending race only to sustain their current level of fitness.

Of course, a much larger variety of co-evolutionary systems can be studied. Levinthal (1997) shows the relative impact of different levels of firm adaptation and population selection in a changing environment by simulating adaptation on smooth versus rugged fitness landscapes. In addition, on the basis of Heylighen and Campbell's (1995) competitive configurations, Baum (1999: 120) illustrates various alternatives to zero-sum, purely competitive co-evolutionary systems that are supercompetitive (increase in a firm's fitness results in a decrease in rival firms' fitness), partly competitive (some resources are shared and others not), synergistic (an increase in one firm's fitness results in an increase in rival firms' fitness) or independent (an increase in one firm's fitness does not affect rival firms' fitness).

In addition to various competitive co-evolutionary configurations, there are several studies that investigate co-operative co-evolutionary systems. For example, Hamel (1991) concludes that international alliances thought initially to be synergistic turn out to be supercompetitive (see also Chapter 11). Moreover, Koza and Lewin (1998) argue that strategic alliances are embedded in the firm's strategic portfolio and co-evolve with the firm's strategy, institutional, organizational and competitive environment and managerial intention for the alliance.

Other studies beyond aggregate studies on dynamic competitive and co-operative interactions between firms involve intra-organization evolution or microco-evolution. These studies consider co-evolution of intrafirm resources, dynamic capabilities and competencies in an intrafirm competitive context (Barnett et al., 1994; Burgelman, 1991, 1994, 1996; Galunic and Eisenhardt, 1996). For instance, Galunic and Eisenhardt's study (1996) shows that capability development in a particular multiunit firm, the M-firm, involves a mix of selection and adaptation processes. Moreover, Burgelman's (1994, 1996) intra-organizational process model shifts the locus of capability selection from the firm as a whole to classes of capabilities inside the firm and views managing intra-organizational ecological processes as a means by which the firm can achieve the learning benefits of both external and internal selection.

Future Research Directions on Methodology

Studies of simultaneous evolution, or co-evolution, of organizations and their environments are still rare. Although the co-evolution construct has been gaining adherents, co-evolutionary effects are far from being well accepted or understood. We shall, therefore, now consider some of the essential properties of co-evolution of dynamic capabilities and their implications for strategic management (Lewin and Volberda, 1999).

- Multilevel research of capabilities. Co-evolutionary effects take place at multiple levels within firms as well as between firms. While co-evolution of capabilities has been studied on a single level of analysis, McKelvey (1997: 360) argues that co-evolution takes place at multiple levels. He makes a distinction between co-evolution within the firm (micro co-evolution) and co-evolution between firms and their niche (macro co-evolution). The focus of macro co-evolutionary theory is on firms existing in a co-evolutionary competitive context, while micro co-evolution considers co-evolution of intrafirm resources, dynamic capabilities and competencies in an intrafirm competitive context. In the same vein, Thomas (Chapter 16) argues that in determining a firm's core competencies and how they affect firm performance, it may be useful in future strategy research to consider their impact at two or more levels of analysis (business unit, firm, strategic group, product market, process market, industry) simultaneously.

- Multidirectional causalities. Organizations and their parts do not merely evolve. They co-evolve with each other and with a changing organizational environment (Baum, 1999; Kauffman, 1993; McKelvey, 1997). In such complex systems of relationships, dependent–independent variable distinctions become less meaningful because changes in any one variable may be caused endogenously by changes in others.
- Nonlinear interactions. Scholars in strategy have removed nonlinear interactions for the sake of analytical tractability (Andersson, 1999a). A co-evolutionary approach, however, requires that sets of co-acting organizations and their environments be the object of study and that changes in all interacting organizations be allowed to result not only from the direct interactions between pairs of organizations, but also by indirect feedback through the rest of the system.
- Path and history dependence strategy research. Adaptation in a co-evolutionary process is path or history dependent (Calori et al., 1997; Kieser, 1989; McKelvey, 1997). Variation in adaptations among constituent firms in a population may reflect heterogeneity in the capabilities of firms at earlier points in time (Levinthal, 1997; Stinchcombe, 1965), rather than variation in niches in the environment (as suggested in population ecology) or a set of distinct external conditions (as generally suggested by contingency theories).

On the basis of these properties of co-evolution of dynamic capabilities, future research in the dynamic capabilities school should at least (Lewin et al., 1999) consider the following requirements.

- Capability co-evolution should be studied over a long period of time (Levinthal, 1997; McKelvey, 1997) by using longitudinal time series of micro-state adaptation events and measures of rate of change or pace of change; this suggests a change in focus from the absolute values of measures towards the change in values of measures or measures over time (Chapter 16).
- Capability development should be examined within a historical context of the firm and its environment (Calori et al., 1997; Kieser, 1989; Kieser, 1994; Stinchcombe, 1965).
- Multidirectional causalities should be considered between micro and macro co-evolution of capabilities (McKelvey, 1997), as well as between and across other system elements (Baum, 1999). In such systems of relationships among variables, the dependent–independent variable distinction becomes less meaningful. Changes in any one variable are caused endogenously by changes in the other.
- Mutual, simultaneous, lagged and nested effects should be incorporated. Such effects are not very likely to be linear and as a consequence of feedback flows, changes in one variable can produce counterintuitive changes in another variable.
- Path dependence should be considered. This enables and restricts capability leveraging and building at the firm level and at the population level, thereby driving both retention and variation at different rates.

Future Research Directions on the Development of Capabilities: What is in it for Management?[2]

Besides changes in how we study dynamic capabilities, as discussed above, we should also more precisely define dynamic capabilities in future (Chapters 13 and 16) and delineate the managerial roles in capability development. In other words, the dynamic capabilities through which competencies or resources are developed and leveraged should be considered more explicitly, rather than just be assumed to occur. More importantly, we must consider what management can do in these co-evolutionary processes of capabilities and competition.

Managerial Dimensions of Dynamic Capabilities

What is it exactly that makes a capability dynamic? We consider (based on Volberda, 1998: 108–11) these to be managerial dimensions of dynamic capabilities that differentiate them from ordinarily static routines:

- dynamic competition
- broad knowledge base/variety of managerial expertise
- absorptive capacity
- managerial experimentation and broad managerial mindsets
- development time and higher order learning.

Dynamic competition Specialized or static routines in terms of managerial directions, policies or procedures embody management's capacity to replicate previously performed tasks (Teece et al., 1997). These routines are perfectly illustrated by McDonald's operating manuals or KLM's directives, policies and procedures for aircraft maintenance. In contrast with dynamic capabilities, specialized routines are based on static control and static models of competition, which do not view the capacity to change as an essential feature of sustained success. For certain competitive changes, a standard or pre-programmed behaviour is prescribed. The primary virtue of specialized routines is that they eliminate the need for further communication and co-ordination among subunits and positions. Consequently, they provide a memory for handling routine situations. They are limited to those competitive changes that can be anticipated and to which an appropriate response can be identified.

Broad knowledge base/variety of managerial expertise Instead of limited expertise, dynamic capabilities require a broad and deep knowledge base (technological, market, product or distribution knowledge) and a variety of managerial expertise in order to devise appropriate responses. For instance, new products today are more likely than not to emerge through innovation at the interface of different specialities (Grant, 1996). The managerial ability to combine knowledge bases housed in different core technologies often distinguishes dynamic and innovative companies. For example, when 3M consumer research showed that customers complained about rusting steelwool pads, experts from 3M's adhesives, abrasives, coatings and nonwoven technologies divisions got together to create Never Rust plastic soap pads (Leonard-Barton, 1995: 67). Similarly, Corning views its knowledge about glass and ceramic processes as a strategic resource and continuously invests in its enhancement. By managing a broad knowledge base emerging from a variety of expertise, Corning is able to develop dynamic capabilities such as rapid product innovation and customization in order to exploit rapid, unpredictable product opportunities (Boynton and Victor, 1991). Finally, the credit card industry discovered how an outsider firm's broad knowledge base can result in a formidable new competitor when AT&T used its marketing and distribution knowledge to enter the credit card market. These examples illustrate that depth of the knowledge base is necessary for solving complex problems, but that breadth of the knowledge base is especially important for creating new dynamic capabilities.

Absorptive capacity   Related to a broad knowledge base, dynamic capabilities requires management to have a high absorptive capacity (Cohen and Levinthal, 1990) for recognizing the need to change. Successfully absorbing signals beyond the periphery of the firm is essential for developing capabilities. The ability of management to recognize the value of new, external information, then to assimilate and apply it to commercial ends is critical to the firm's dynamic capabilities. Absorptive capacity requires porous boundaries, scanning broadly for new soft information and identifying and using effectively those employees who serve as gatekeepers and boundary spanners (Leonard-Barton, 1995). Liebeskind et al. (1996) show that successful new biotechnology firms were able to develop dynamic capabilities in new product development because their management developed high levels of absorptive capacity through social networks and boundary spanning. This absorptive capacity helped the firms to source new knowledge from various universities and research institutes more quickly.

Managerial experimentation and broad managerial mindsets   Management must have an ability to identify and support new ideas, rather than exploiting existing routines to the maximum. Experimentation is limited when knowledge extension is based on routines, which work like well-worn grooves to channel managerial activities. By relying on these routines, management concentrates on its own specialized areas and avoids the need to construct its notion of the whole for new activities. As a consequence, routines exacerbate the separation of functional areas, impede learning processes and further restrict the development of new capabilities by imposing old knowledge. However, experimentation and broad mindsets can contribute to an increasing variety of dynamic capabilities. For instance, Sharp was able to develop dynamic capabilities in the electronic calculator industry while Texus Instruments was not, because of it's limited managerial mindsets, which were narrowly focused on the semiconductor market. Also, Honda's success in the American motorcycle market was based primarily on managerial latitude for experimentation and complementary managerial mindsets. While Sochiro Honda, the inventive founder of the company with a large ego and mercurial temperament, had a strong bias towards motor technology, his partner Takeo Fujisawa's primary focus was on market, distribution and financial knowledge.

Development time and higher-order learning   Dynamic capabilities such as flexible manufacturing or fast product development cannot be purchased off the shelf but require strategic vision, development time and sustained investment (Amit and Schoemaker, 1993). They take time to identify, nurture and leverage and tend not to be the kind of assets that management can turn on or off as they please. Firms simply lack the capacity to develop new capabilities quickly (Teece et al., 1997). That is, dynamic capabilities cannot be easily bought, but they must be built; skills acquisition and learning, therefore, become fundamental issues. While routines also require learning and take time to develop, they can often be built on an extrapolation of trends, imitation of others or past experience. These modes of single-loop learning are all based on repetitive reinforcement in which no cognitive change takes place in the organization. By contrast, dynamic capabilities requires higher-order learning such as double-loop learning, which hinges on the ability to challenge operating assumptions fundamentally.

To conclude, the development of dynamic capabilities requires

- managers' absorptive capacity to recognize quickly the need to change
- managers' knowledge base, expertise or ability to devise appropriate responses
- managerial experimentation and broad mindsets to increase the variety of dynamic capabilities
- higher-order managerial learning abilities to sustain an adequate repertoire of dynamic capabilities.

Managerial Roles in Capability Development[3]

Future research in the dynamic capabilities school should elaborate on these essential dimensions of dynamic capabilities and consider their implications for firm performance (van den Bosch et al., 1999). Based on the literature, however, a rough distinction can be made of three types of managerial roles: cross hierarchy, cross functional and cross value (Volberda, 1998: 111–16). Of course, we realize that developing dynamic capabilities is not exclusively the role of the manager. While in many situations managers do indeed dominate this process, in principle every member of the organization participates in it. That is, capabilities grow through the actions of employees at all organizational levels (Leonard-Barton, 1995: 28).

Vertical Management: Cross-Hierarchical Capabilities

Traditionally, identifying and building capabilities is viewed as a hierarchical process with the CEO and top management playing a central role (Chandler, 1962; Schumpeter, 1934). In particular, capability development is considered a top-down, deliberate managerial process, where the exploration of capabilities created by heuristics, skill development and fundamentally new insights takes place at the corporate management level, while the exploitation of these capabilities takes place at the business unit or lower levels. This perspective was recently supported by Prahalad and Hamel (1990) and Stalk et al. (1992), who argued that the development of adequate capabilities depends on the strategic intent

(Hamel and Prahalad, 1989) of the CEO or corporate management, based on superior industry foresight.

Examples of such a predominantly top-down capability development process include General Electric's corporate revitalization guided by its CEO Jack Welch and Philips' corporate change initiated by Jan Timmer and further accelerated by its new CEO Cor Boonstra. What is unique about these companies is the fact that their CEOs drove the entire process of capability development, starting by introducing new concepts, communicating them in an understandable manner through the use of metaphors and analogies and reiterating them repeatedly. Consequently, new capabilities such as speed, simplicity and market responsiveness were passed down the organization almost as an order or instruction to be followed. However, not every firm can simply copy this top-down approach, given the fact that strategy in large complex firms is often less centralized in top management, more multifaceted and generally less integrated.

In contrast, building on Bower's work (1970) on the management of the resource allocation process, a rich body of literature has suggested that perhaps the most effective process of capability development is through originating, developing and promoting strategic initiatives from the front-line managers (Burgelman, 1983; Kimberly, 1979; Quinn, 1985). This research finds that capabilities typically emerge from the autonomous strategic behaviour of individuals or small groups in lower levels of the organization. Front-line managers typically have the most current knowledge and expertise and are closer to the sources of information critical to new capabilities.

Within the reactive bottom-up, emergent perspective, the role of top management is described as 'retroactive legitimizer' (Burgelman, 1983) or judge and arbiter (Angle and van de Ven, 1989) and that of middle management as supporter and intermediary of lower-level initiatives. Exploration of new capabilities takes place at the lowest level by double-loop learning or generative learning (Senge, 1990); the interactions with the market and demanding clients spur front-line managers to call into question their norms, objectives and basic policies. At the upper managerial levels, the exploitation of already developed capabilities takes place by single-loop or adaptive learning, which helps the firm to exploit previous experiences, to detect causalities and to extrapolate to the future. It permits top corporate management to persist in its set policies and achieve its formulated objectives. An example of a more reactive bottom-up process of capability development can be found in 3M. In this highly innovative firm, the role of top management is limited to sponsor, coach or mentor; dynamic capabilities as innovation and speed of innovation clearly derive from initiatives at the bottom. Not surprisingly, the names of successive CEOs at 3M are relatively unknown, while the inventors and intrapreneurs of the lower levels of the company have received the most attention (for example, Scotch tape™ invented by Dick Drew or Post-It Notes™ by Art Fry).

By contrast, in the proactive bottom-up, emergent perspective, the role of top management is considered to be more than retroactive sense making of bottom-up initiatives; it is the creator of purpose and challenger of the status quo of the firm (Bartlett and Ghoshal, 1993). This creative tension (Senge, 1990) at the level of corporate management forces the firm to balance exploitation of capabilities with the cost of adaptability to new capability development. One could argue that in the proactive bottom-up, emergent perspective, top management is involved in single-loop and double-loop learning at the same time, sometimes called deutero learning (Argyris and Schön, 1978; Bateson, 1936). That is, top management's exploration of unknown futures and its exploitation of known pasts balance each other (Hedberg and Jönsson, 1978: 50). Asea Brown Boveri (ABB) can be considered as a firm in which capabilities are developed in a proactive, bottom-up fashion. New capabilities derive from front-line managers, but the direction is partly inspired by Percy Barnevick's very ambitious, future-oriented sense of mission.

Given these divergent views on vertical or cross-hierarchical capability development, it is impossible to give an integrated perspective on the managerial roles of different hierarchical levels. Vertical capability development can arise from lower as well as middle and upper levels. Essential for both top-down and bottom-up cross-hierarchy perspectives on capability development is that management must guarantee that, in the end, all levels are involved. If not, the firm will not be able to create corporate-wide dynamic capabilities but instead suffer from the tyranny of the business unit or the tyranny of top management and the resulting fragmentation of capabilities.

Horizontal Management: Cross-Functional Capabilities

In contrast to vertical capability development, horizontal capability development refers to more democratic and more participative forms of capability development in organizations, which may be explicitly designed, for example, teams, projects or task forces, but may also emerge out of a process of interaction. As an illustration of the difference between horizontal and vertical capability development, one could argue that the Taylorist principles of incentives and staff organization are cross-hierarchical capabilities for accomplishing standardized production at lower costs. On the other hand, we could classify Toyota's principles of decentralized authority and lateral communication across functions, buyers and suppliers as cross-functional capabilities to generate speed and flexibility.

In many contemporary firms, the role of management has shifted from vertical co-ordination through a hierarchical command and control structure to providing appropriate organizational support for horizontal exchange of knowledge. In all such firms, horizontal or self-co-ordination among experts is more efficient than vertical co-ordination by managers. However, self-co-ordination across functional and organizational boundaries cannot take place without managerial permission or active managerial support (Liebeskind et al., 1996). Nonetheless, horizontal or cross-functional capability development is in many cases disrupted by managerial meddling (Weick, 1979: 8). Management intervenes in the mistaken belief that single individuals develop capabilities, denying that capabilities may be developed implicitly in causal circuits and interpersonal influence processes. Failure to acknowledge these forms of self-control, coupled with interventions that actively disrupt these self-regulating activities, are the source of much mismanagement in organizations.

Ideological Management: Cross-Value Capabilities

In addition to vertical capability development by means of hierarchy and horizontal capability development by means of teams, we can distinguish an ideological type of capability development. A shared ideology may facilitate capability development among various parts or subcultures of the company by specifying broad, tacitly understood rules for appropriate action under unspecified contingencies (Camerer and Vepsalainen, 1988; De Leeuw and Volberda, 1996). These cross-value capabilities refer to the ability of the firm to produce a shared ideology that offers members an attractive identity as well as convincing interpretations of reality. The infusion of beliefs and values into an organization takes place over time and produces a distinct identity for its participants, colouring all aspects of organizational life and giving it a social integration that goes far beyond the vertical cross-hierarchical and horizontal cross-functional capabilities discussed above. These cross-value capabilities determine what kinds of knowledge are sought and nurtured and what kind of capability-building activities are tolerated and encouraged. They serve as capability-screening and control mechanisms. Japanese companies like Canon and Honda try to enhance cross-value capabilities by facilitating dialogue, camp sessions or brainstorming seminars held outside the workplace and even drinking sessions (Nonaka and Takeuchi, 1995).

Mintzberg connected cross-value capabilities to his concept of the missionary form and the ideological strategy (Mintzberg, 1979; Mintzberg and Waters, 1985). In addition, Ouchi's (1980) concept of clan control shows that shared norms and values facilitate exchange of tacit knowledge without resort to market pricing, contracts or managerial authority. In a similar vein, Bradach and Eccles (1989) defined trust as the alternative mode of knowledge exchange, where trust is engendered by shared norms. Furthermore, a recent study by Liebeskind et al. (1996) on new biotechnology firms illustrates that the sourcing of tacit external knowledge is possible only through shared social norms.

Ideological capability development rests in firms with a core identity, in which one can find a coherent set of beliefs, shared values and common language. Through it, every member identifies strongly with, and professes loyalty to, the goal of preserving, extending or perfecting the organization's mission and so can be trusted to make decisions in the organization's interests. Hewlett-Packard's corporate values, such as trust and respect for individuals, uncompromising integrity and teamwork (the 'HP Way') or 3M's eleventh commandment, 'thou shalt not kill ideas for new products', tolerance for failure and culture biased toward action help these firms to develop dynamic capabilities easily.

Of course, capability development can take place vertically, horizontally and ideologically, sequentially or even at the same time (see Figure 21.4). For instance, Leonard-Barton (1995) discussed T-shaped capabilities, which are cross-functional as well as cross-hierarchical and essential for successful innovations. These capabilities imply deep know-how and expertise within a functional area (the stem) completed with more superficial knowledge about the interaction with other functional areas (the crossbar). Nonaka (1994) describes middle-up-down management in Japanese firms such as Honda, Canon and Toyota in which all members of the organization work together horizontally and vertically. Teams

Vertical	Horizontal	Ideological
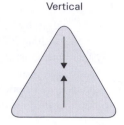	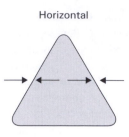	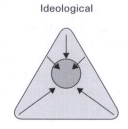

*Cross hierarchy: top-down/bottom-up

*Cross function: teaming

*Cross value: core culture

*Command and control structure/flat hierarchy

*Self-control

*Ideological control

*Extrinsic management: enforcing capability development by distinct leadership tasks at various levels varying from executive champion, product champion or intrapreneur

*Intrinsic management: supporting capability development by horizontal linking

*Intrinsic management: facilitating capability development by creating a vision, shared ideology or identity

FIGURE 21.4 *Various managerial roles in dynamic capability development (Volberda, 1998)*

play a central role in this kind of dual organization, with middle managers serving as team leaders who are at the intersection of the vertical and horizontal flows of information. Non-hierarchical, self-organizing team activities are indispensable for generating new capabilities through intensive, focused research. On the other hand, hierarchy is more efficient and effective for exploitation of capabilities (Romme, 1996).

We think that a co-evolutionary approach to dynamic capabilities development as sketched out here, together with a focus on productive managerial roles in this process may really develop the dynamic capabilities school into a serious alternative to the traditional IO approaches in strategy.

The Configurational School

Key Issues

There is a growing recognition of the need for a measure of synthesis and a more explicit understanding of the dynamics of strategic change (Greenwood and Hinings, 1988). The configurational school argues that an understanding of the process of strategic change requires a concerted return to classification (Child, 1997; Greenwood and Hinings, 1988; McKelvey, 1982) and that such a concern is the very basis of strategic management theory. Key issues in this school are analysing the contingencies in which strategy configurations are effective and defining the underlying dimensions that explain the variety in strategy configurations. In line with this, several authors have suggested archetypes (Miles and Snow, 1978), gestalts or configurations (Miller and Friesen, 1980; Mintzberg, 1979) in order to produce theoretical coherence. Some of them are based on theoretical typologies or more empirical taxonomies.

Others have begun the search for factors explaining the transitions of organizations and their transformation (Kimberly and Quinn, 1984; Miller and Friesen, 1980; Pettigrew, 1985). Key issues here are not so much describing cross-sectional variation of strategy configurations, but much more systemizing change from one configuration to another, resulting in transition modes, transformation modes, trajectories, periods and lifecycles.

There is, in short, an emerging focus on the incidence and nature of strategy configurations and the dynamics that control and propel movement from one configuration to another. Central to this emerging focus is the recognition of strategic change as involving a mutual penetration of static (contingency) theories, with their essentially 'mechanistic' assumption of configurations changing in response to altered contingencies and dynamic (evolutionary and revolutionary) theories, which emphasize the direction and scope of strategic change.

From a static perspective, the concept of configuration derives from the idea that organizations operate within a limited number of configurations of structure, strategy and environment (internal and external coherence). In Miller and Friesen's terminology (1984), configurations are composed of tightly interdependent and mutually supportive elements such that the importance of each element can be best understood by making reference to the whole configuration.

From a more dynamic perspective, configurations exhibit momentum and inertia. That is, most change occurs within an existing configuration rather than between such configurations. There is continuity in the direction or evolution in line with goals, structures, programmes and expectations. Organizations exhibit inertia precisely because they are caught within an archetype. Radical or quantum change occurs only when there are important problems to be faced.

Based on these static and dynamic perspectives of configurations, the following premises of the configurational school can be derived (Mintzberg, 1990b: 182).

- The strategic behaviours of organizations are best described in terms of configurations – distinct, integrated clusters of dimensions concerning state and time.
- In particular, strategy formation is an episodic process in which a particular configuration engages in a particular form of the process for a distinguishable period of time.
- Accordingly, each configuration must be found at its own time and in its own context.
- These periods of the clustered dimensions tend to sequence themselves over time in patterned ways that define common trajectories of transformation.

Mintzberg (Chapter 17) shows that the contribution of the configurational school in strategic management has been clear. The theoretically or empirically deduced configurations have helped us to understand the complex phenomena of strategy

TABLE 21.2   *Chandler's strategy–structure configuration of multinational corporations*

Strategy	Structure
Volume expansion	Centrally co-ordinated corporation
Geographical expansion	Functional corporation
Vertical integration	Complex functional corporation
Product diversification	Multidivisional corporation

formation (Chapter 18) and to teach students in the field. However, sometimes we need more fine-grained work that exposes all the complex inter-relationships among attributes (Chapter 20). Finally, for progress in this school of strategy synthesis we need configurations that are based on theory and empirical facts (Chapter 19) instead of armchair theorizing or data reduction methods.

Theoretical Background

Of course, the configurational school has a long tradition in strategy and organization theory. However, this school really came about through the work of Khandwalla (1977), who has given a systematic categorization of relevant dimensions, Miller and Friesen (1980), who have developed a typology of strategic archetypes and, of course, Mintzberg (1973a, 1978), who gave us strategy modes and organizational configurations.

In contrast to an integrative research approach, this school not only shows interest when certain configurations are plausible but also tries to explain dynamic trajectories of change. In doing so, its work is based on socially oriented organizational sciences that, with the aid of ideal types, try to explain the variety in strategy and structure configurations (Lammers, 1987; Perrow, 1986; Weber, 1946). At the same time, this school has a strongly historical streak, because some 'business recipes' are dominant in certain periods. In this respect, Chandler (1962) in his historical research into strategy–structure configurations in large multinational enterprises has distinguished four phases (see Table 21.2), which were later confirmed by Rumelt (1974) and many European researchers (Franco, 1974; Stopford and Wells, 1972).

Biology also contributes to this school in the form of dynamic equilibrium models, which indicate when certain lifeforms are adequate (morphostasis) and when structural transition (morphogenesis) is necessary. But also complex mathematical theories such as catastrophe theory and the chaos theory of cybernetics II (Maturana and Varela, 1980; Prigogine, 1976) give insight into when certain configurations are capable of self-reproduction and maintenance of their identity and when certain configurations are no longer viable. Miller (1982) has used the abovementioned insights for his 'quantum view of structural change in organizations'.

Tools for Problem Solving

Problem-solving techniques and typologies have been developed in great numbers and include Mintzberg's (1978, 1979) strategy modes and structural configurations and Greiner's growth model (1972). Although many of these

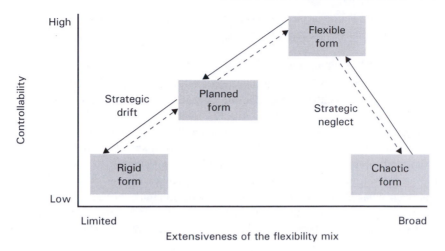

FIGURE 21.5 *A typology of alternative flexible forms for coping with hyper-competition; — natural trajectory of routinization; – – – reverse trajectory of revitalization (Volberda, 1998)*

categories are purely conceptual, the configurational school is distinct from the others due to its strongly empirical orientation and its systematic measurement of configurations. In this sense one can refer to Miles and Snow's (1978) empirical distinction of strategy types (defender, prospector, analyser, reactor), a typology which was later tested by other empirical researchers. One can also point to Miller and Friesen's (1980) archetypes of strategic transformation, based on a hundred historical case-studies.

In addition, Volberda (1996b, 1998) constructed a rich typology of alternative flexible forms (see Figure 21.5). On the basis of the two central building blocks of his framework – the extensiveness of the flexibility mix and the controllability of the organization – many organizational forms are possible for coping with changing levels of competition. There are four ideal types: rigid, planned, flexible and chaotic. Each type represents a particular way of addressing the flexibility paradox of change versus preservation and some are more effective than others. Using this typology, Volberda examined different trajectories of organizational development over time in several companies (Philips, KLM, Ericsson, ING), concentrating on those trajectories relating to revitalization. These trajectories gave insight both into methods for building flexible firms and into how these organizations can be transformed so that they can deal with the tensions of flexibility over time. On the basis of the typology, the flexibility audit and redesign (FAR) method has been developed for diagnosing organizational flexibility and guiding the transition process. This method uses the building blocks of the strategic framework and related data-gathering and data-analysis instruments to assess an organization's actual flexibility and, if necessary, to find ways to increase its flexibility. The FAR method thus pinpoints how an organization should create new flexible capabilities (managerial task) and reconfigure the organization (organization design task). The software tool FARSYS

(Volberda and Rutges, 1999) supports the data-gathering (FARSYS I) as well as the decision-making process of the consultant (FARSYS II).

Contributions of the Chapters

Mintzberg (Chapter 17) gives a thorough review of the configurational school and argues that its contribution to the strategy field has been clear. Configurations bring order to the messy world of strategy formation, particularly to its diverse literature and practice. Mintzberg argues that although configurational approaches in terms of ideal types have been rather common in social sciences, it was the configuration studies at McGill University in particular that really launched the configurational school in strategic management. Of course, the flipside of this has been what Donaldson (1996) calls 'McGillomania', the fact that each configuration is too crude when it comes to describing the diversity in the strategy landscape. Still, Mintzberg argues that we need configurations, although we must be aware of their limitations.

Building on six archetypical theoretical explanations of strategy development processes (planning, incremental, political, cultural, visionary, enforced choice), Bailey and Johnson (Chapter 18) try to understand the strategy development process as perceived by management. Instead of unidimensional perceptions of strategy development, they found combinations of primarily two or more perspectives depending on industry (for example, public versus professional service), organization (for example, history, power distribution) and individual (for example, function, tenure) attributes. Moreover, they found patterns of strategy development over time. Their results clearly show that unitary perspectives such as planning versus incremental are ineffective in conveying the complexity of the strategy development process. Rather, we should try to find viable configurations of strategy development that combine two or more perspectives. Bailey and Johnson only describe managerial perceptions of strategy development, however, and do not prescribe effective combinations of strategy development. They admit that contingent explanations of effective strategy configurations run the risk of exponential complexity.

In contrast, Lawless (Chapter 19) argues that configurations have taken on a role that is broader and more conceptually profound. They are indeed accepted as a means of simplifying the diverse, complex patterns of firms' conduct. However, configurations are very often assigned a key role, not only in describing, but also in predicting and evaluating firms' conduct. As Lawless puts it, configurations that have been variously labelled strategic groups, strategy archetypes, etc. have been used in empirical studies as having potentially the main effect on performance at the firm level.

Lawless argues that the reasoning behind the configurations construct itself is not well developed. Configurations are understood chiefly as similar behaviour in subpopulations of firms in markets. For the most part, their existence as an empirical phenomenon seems sufficient to include configurations in explanations of firms' performance, but Lawless proposes that we must have more convincing conceptual arguments for the existence of configurations themselves. As they have been commonly used in the strategy literature for some time, he says that concept development is important both for evaluating the literature to a large extent and for evaluating the paradigm under which future studies of patterns in firms' conduct is studied.

We should approach his argument carefully, since both purposes have the potential for wide-ranging impact on strategy research. What is the explanation that Lawless proposes for the existence of configurations and for patterns in their defining characteristics, membership, size, etc. over time? Simply put, it is the co-evolution of markets and the firms that occupy them. Within niches, or regions within markets, ecological forces elicit similar strategies among firms. The salient features of configurations, then, are central tendencies in strategies and capabilities. In mounting such strategies, firms tend to accumulate similar capabilities. History dependence in both strategies and capabilities then affects the cohesiveness and robustness of each configuration and intensity of rivalry among group members. Individual firms are constrained to a greater or lesser degree by their irreversible investments in capabilities, including routines that develop in support of strategy. It is not only strategy patterns, but also the ability to escape them, that is, to change configuration, which is affected by these commitments.

While it is not the perfect solution, Lawless offers a coherent explanation for the formation and persistence of configurations. The model offers a direction to a field of enquiry where intellectual development has been rather slow. At the least, there is value in responding to the need, in offering an explanation, and in stimulating debate about the theory behind configurations. Certainly, his model warrants validation through tests of deduced hypotheses.

New Developments

Pennings (Chapter 20) rightly remarks that the configurational school is not a coherent school in the way that its members hang together as a paradigmatic community. In fact, its progress largely depends on how strategy typologies and taxonomies can be used as tools for theory building and managerial practice. According to Pennings, typologies are usually of the armchair variety. Apart from the rich typologies of Burns and Stalker (1961), Miles and Snow (1978) and Mintzberg (1979), most typologies appear thin and arbitrary. Either they attend to too few components or they fail to make any serious attempt to show how and why these components inter-relate (Miller, 1996). Occasionally, we also encounter empirical taxonomies in which the researcher employs actual statistical data reduction mechanisms such as cluster analysis and multidimensional scaling (Miller and Friesen, 1980; McKelvey, 1982; Pugh et al., 1969). Compared to typologies, taxonomies tend to be more firmly based on facts or, at least, on quantitative data. However, many taxonomies have justly been criticized for their lack of theoretical significance, their arbitrary and narrow selection of variables and their unreliable or unstable results (Chapter 19; Miller, 1996). The strategic groups' literature, for example, has often produced conflicting findings (Barney and Hoskisson, 1990).

So how can we make progress in the configurational school? While the armchair theorist depends on cognitive simplification and psychological closure, the statistical algorithm relies on the smallest sums of squares. How can we develop strategy typologies and taxonomies that drive progress in strategic management? As a result of the *Strategic Management Journal* best paper award 1995, Miller (1996) reflects on strategy configurations and brings forward suggestions for further progress.

Conceptually Derived Typologies

Typologies at their best are memorable, neat and evocative. According to Miller (1996), successful typologies have to possess at least three important features:

1 the various strategy types are well informed by theory
2 they invoke contrasts that facilitate empirical progress, that is, they resolve persistent debates and conflicts
3 the elements or variables used to describe each type are shown to cohere in thematic and interesting ways, ways that have important conceptual, evolutionary or normative implications.

Regarding the first requirement, the review and classification of strategy types should have strong support from theories in strategic management. In other words, each type should have a long respectable history of academic work that has developed concepts and evidence. Second, perhaps more intriguingly, the types should point to important lessons for practising managers and for those who teach them. Finally, typologies should illuminate empirical work too.

Empirically Based Taxonomies

According to Miller (1996), the added value of any taxonomy relies on its ability to generate insight or to advance a predictive task. 'One must ask, for example, whether the clusters found suggest distinctions with theoretical or practical implications, or whether at a minimum they derive reliable and valid findings that can make knowledge more cumulative' (Miller, 1996: 507). Most taxonomies do not fulfill these requirements. Milller's (1996) remedial suggestions are therefore as follows.

- Look for orchestrating themes and networks of relationships. Since configurations are about organizational wholes, more should be done to discover their thematic and systematic aspects. Organizing themes, in a sense, can serve as the seeds of configuration. Qualitative studies can help researchers discover the themes that drive configurations, while multivariate analyses within configurations can dissolve relevant quantitative relationships.
- Study configurations as they emerge. Configurations are in essence dynamic and thus their attributes can be best revealed by studying organizations over time. Insights into the emergence of strategy configurations can be gained from evolutionary theories, complexity theory and co-evolutionary approaches.
- Connect configuration to theory. Too many taxonomies are disconnected from theory. In fact, many taxonomies in strategic management are too focused, in the sense that they only consider parts of strategies rather than wholes. For instance, competitive analysis only centres on generic strategies (content) for attaining competitive advantage (Porter, 1980, 1985) and ignores

the organizational attributes. Similarly, the resource-based theory of the firm only considers resources and skills for generating superior rents, but does not take into account the relationships of resources with organizational forms, learning mechanisms and market conditions. As a result, managers face major problems in developing and implementing a comprehensive strategy on the basis of these theories. In order to make progress, we have to understand how all these parts fit together.

- Develop taxonomies others can replicate. Replication can further improve the validity and reliability of strategy configurations. For instance, the many contextual replication studies of Miles and Snow's (1978) strategy types, Porter's generic strategies (1980), Woodward's (1965) classification of modes of production and Mintzberg's (1978) structural configurations have validated the taxonomies but also generated new insights as well as new configurations.

Configuration as a Source of Competitive Advantage
Besides these recommendations for developing better typologies or taxonomies, Miller also considers tight and coherent configuration of elements in a firm as a variable in itself. In other words, competitive advantage may reside in the orchestrating theme and integrative mechanisms that ensure complementarity between a firm's various components: its market domain, its skills, resources and routines, its technologies, its departments and its decision-making processes. This point is also made by Lawless and illustrated in terms of configurations of specialized capabilities and niches. Indeed, it goes back to the ideas of internal consistency among design variables of contingency theories and new economics of complementarities (Ichniowski et al., 1997; Milgrom and Roberts, 1995). These authors all emphasize the holistic, aggregated and systemic nature of configurations. They have pushed performance analysis beyond simple interactions between disaggregated variables to a more aggregated comparison of the performance of whole types. Whittington et al. (1999), for example, show on the basis of a large-scale survey of strategic and organizational change among medium and large firms throughout western Europe, that piecemeal changes were found to deliver little performance benefit, while those firms that exploited systemic change and complementarities (in boundaries, structure and processes) enjoyed high-performance premiums.

The Paradox of Configuration: not too little, not too much
The advantage of a high degree of configuration may, therefore, include synergy, clarity of direction and co-ordination, difficulty of imitation, distinctive competence, commitment, speed and economy. However, Miller (1990a) and Miller and Chen (1996) have rightly highlighted the dangers of strategy configurations that are too simple or monolithic, that is, too narrowly focused on a few key elements. Miller has also described this as the Icarus paradox (1990b), and in others theories it is referred to as a core rigidity (Leonard-Barton, 1992), competence trap (Levinthal and March, 1993), path dependence, sticky resources and structural and cognitive inertia (Hannan and Freeman, 1984; Teece et al., 1997).

New Viable Strategy Configurations of the Future

So what are the new effective strategy configurations that are not too loose, but also not too tight? Tightly coupled configurations result in inertia while, on the other hand, loosely coupled configurations cannot retain competitive advantage over time (Weick, 1982). Many popular and academic writers have recently speculated on the features or characteristics of new configurations (Lewin and Stephens, 1993; Volberda, 1996a, 1998). Management futurologists conceptualize the new landscape variously as a virtual corporation (Davidow and Malone, 1992), a hollow corporation, a dynamic network form (Miles and Snow, 1986), a cellular organization (Miles et al., 1997), a platform organization (Ciborra, 1996), and a shamrock organization (Handy, 1995). Most of these studies, however, represent retrospective accounts of single case examples of a successful adaptive configuration at a particular time using (Sun Microsystems' virtual organization (Davidow and Malone, 1992), Dell Computers' dynamic network (Miles and Snow, 1986), Acer's cellular form (Miles et al., 1997), Olivetti's platform organization (Ciborra, 1996) or F International's electronic shamrock (Handy, 1995)). The popular business press accounts of new forms serve as an important signpost, but the theory underlying these ideas remains to be developed more fully.

From a more theoretical perspective, the new configurations are assumed to develop new higher order capabilities to explore new opportunities effectively, as well as to exploit effectively those opportunities of flexibility and adaptivity (Volberda, 1998). These so-called hyperadaptive forms have been variously described as disposable organizations (March, 1995), poised organizations (Kauffman, 1995), at the edge of chaos (Brown and Eisenhardt, 1998; Kauffman, 1995), dissipative structures (Prigogine and Stengers, 1984), semi-structures (Brown and Eisenhardt, 1998), hypertext form (Nonaka and Takeuchi, 1995) or, more generally, flexible organizations that somehow internalize friction between change and preservation (Volberda, 1996b, 1998). At this 'edge of chaos', an organization is assumed to optimize the benefits of stability, while retaining the capacity to change, by combining and recombining both path dependence and path creation processes (Baum and Korn, 1999). Such an organization creates sufficient structure to maintain basic order but minimizes structural interdependencies. It evolves internal processes that unleash emergent processes such as improvization (Weick, 1998), self-organizing (Andersson, 1999b), emergent strategies (Brown and Eisenhardt, 1998; Ilinitch et al., 1998) and stage actors (for example, product champions). It involves a new underlying management logic founded on principles of self-organization, trust in bottom-up processes and effectiveness of eventual outcomes (Dijksterhuis et al., 1999; Lewin, 1999). Future research in the configurational school must analyse, explain and predict these new viable configurations.

Schools of Strategy Synthesis and Beyond

How can we evaluate the efforts in this book for synthesis, which have resulted in the emergence of three strategy schools? Our choice for synthesis was triggered by the potential to escape the dilemma of differentiation–integration. Synthesis is less far-reaching than integration. It does not attempt to develop a single paradigm consisting of universal concepts and laws covering the entire strategy field. The argument is that such a straitjacket is not required to achieve accumulation of knowledge. The main concern of the proponents of integration was the lack of accumulation of knowledge due to the fragmented state of the field. Instead of full-blown integration we believe that synthesis concerning particular domains of inquiry would be sufficient to address the problem of the accumulation of knowledge. The other dimensions of fragmentation, such as the perspectives of the underlying disciplines, the methodological approach and the purpose of the enquiry are not forced into a rigid single paradigm in order to reduce fragmentation. In fact, there are many arguments in this book that diversity concerning these dimensions is important for the development of the field. Spender (Chapter 2), for example, argues that descriptive approaches need to be confronted with normative practices in order to remain relevant. In most of the chapters on the boundary, dynamic capabilities and configurational schools it has been shown that different base disciplines have contributed to the advances of each particular area of research.

In our proposal for schools of strategy synthesis it is only the domain of inquiry that is regulated into three distinct schools. It is regulated along three clusters of problems in the strategy field. The three schools are not intended to be unique and mutually exclusive and new ones may emerge. In addition, there is overlap between the three schools. The main purpose of distinguishing these schools is to give some guidance. Research efforts can now more easily be evaluated in terms of their contribution to improve our understanding of a particular set of problems. Not developing new schools per se but accumulation of knowledge, has been our primary concern.

The main issue at this point is whether the establishment of synthesizing schools will improve knowledge accumulation and how this process might work. To start with the 'how' issue, the pragmatic research approach as discussed by Foss (Chapter 9), concerning the development of the boundary school, is illustrative of how that process works. It is an eclectic approach in which complementary parts of different theories are used to explain particular problems. The ability to solve that problem or to gain new insight into that problem is the criterion by which the contribution of the new combination of theories may be evaluated. As the schools of synthesis are based on a particular cluster of problems, this eclectic approach continuously tries to improve our understanding of those problems. As a result, knowledge accumulates within particular clusters of problems and our three emerging schools of synthesis are defined to encapsulate particular problem fields.

Of course, the proof of the pudding is in the eating. What is the evidence in this book that the three schools of synthesis facilitate and stimulate accumulation of knowledge? As has been discussed in the schools of strategy synthesis, each school has a long history in theory, builds on various base disciplines and further develops, extends and recombines strategic concepts (see Table 21.3). Moreover, each school gives directions for theory and concept development as

TABLE 21.3 *Synthetic schools in strategic management*

	The boundary school	The dynamic capabilities school	The configurational school
Questions	• Where should the boundary be drawn?	• With whom and how do firms compete?	• What are the contingencies? • Which strategy configurations are effective?
	• How can we manage across the divide?	• How do they sustain their competitive advantage over time?	• What are the underlying dimensions of strategy configurations?
Base disciplines/ theories	• Agency theory (economics/ psychology) • Transaction costs theory • Industrial organization • Control theories (sociology) • Decision-making theories (psychology)	• Resource-based theory of the firm (economics) • Entrepreneurship (economics) • Innovation theories (organization theory) • Learning theories (organizational behaviour)	• Social sciences • History • Equilibrium models (biology) • Catastrophe theories (mathematics)
Problem-solving tools	• The strategy sourcing process (Venkatesan, 1992) • Porter's value chain (Porter, 1980)	• The roots of competitiveness (Prahalad and Hamel, 1990) • The capability matrix (Schoemaker, 1992)	• Archetypes (Miller and Friesen, 1980) • Strategic types (Miles and Snow, 1978) • FAR method (Volberda, 1998)
New directions	• Strategizing • Joint value creation • Building trust • Learning across boundaries	• Co-evolution of capabilities and competition • Managerial dimensions of dynamic capabilities	• Conceptually derived typologies • Empirically based taxonomies • Configurations as source of competitive advantage

well as development of practical tools. Instead of substitution of concepts and theories, our major aim is much more further development and proliferation of concepts within a given problem domain. That is, transactions and boundaries are still central concepts in the boundary school, the dynamic capabilities school still focuses on resources and capabilities and clustering strategic phenomena into ex-ante or ex-post configurations is key in the configurational school.

As an example, in the boundary school the concept of transaction cost has grown and been expanded substantially in the 1970s and 1980s. Zajac and Olsen (1993) have combined the notion of transaction cost with the complementary concept of transaction value. This novel concept appeared to have generated substantial research efforts to elaborate, refine and extend the application of that concept in the 1990s. For example, in the section on new research directions in the boundary school we discussed how the notion of transaction value was refined by introducing the difference between private and common benefits in alliances. A similar trajectory of concept development emerged in the dynamic capabilities school, starting with an emphasis mainly on resources and assets, then moving on to skills and routines, to tacit knowledge, to core competencies and finally to dynamic capabilities.

Of course, one might argue that these schools of strategy synthesis act as a new straitjacket, which may limit openness to new theories and hamper absorption of outside developments. However, in our conceptualization of schools of strategy synthesis new theories are not ignored but invited to contribute. For instance, complexity theory, especially the concept of complex adaptive systems, has boosted new developments in the configurational school. The key criterion by which to judge whether a new concept may be embraced is its potential to improve the ability to explain certain problems. The overlap between the schools of synthesis can be seen as proof of this openness to other influences. For example, in the boundary school the competence concept has been introduced to illuminate the desire to share and learn across the boundaries of the firm. The competence concept has been able to enrich the transaction cost and transaction value theories as we have shown earlier in this discussion. Finally, building configurations based on types of capabilities and environmental conditions (Chapter 19) can also been seen as a hybrid of the dynamic capabilities and configurational school.

There are no fixed borders between the three proposed schools of synthesis. Besides some overlap between the schools, there is also some rivalry to provide a better understanding of relative new strategic phenomena. For instance, in all three schools efforts are made to improve our insight into networks. In the boundary school the issue is the ability to share and transfer knowledge across the boundaries of the firms participating in the network. In the dynamic capabilities school the issue is to absorb and develop new competences in a network environment. Lastly, the configurational school attempts to improve our understanding of networks by conceptualizing them as a new viable configuration.

Finally, besides the issues of rivalry and overlap between these schools of strategy synthesis we want to raise the issue of completeness. Our claim is not that these schools of synthesis cover the whole strategy field. There is probably room for new schools of strategy synthesis. However, we do think that our proposal of the three schools of strategy synthesis shows the most promising new directions in strategy: redrawing firm boundaries, developing new dynamic capabilities and discovering new viable strategy configurations. More importantly, from a practitioner perspective, the application of these schools of strategy synthesis may open up new sources of competitive advantage.

Notes

1 This section is, to a large extent, adapted from Lewin and Volberda (1999).
2 This section is, to a large extent, adapted from Volberda (1998: 108–19).
3 This section is, to a large extent, adapted from Volberda (1998: 111–16).

References

Abbott, A. (1988) *The system of professions: An essay on the division of expert labor.* Chicago, IL: University of Chicago Press.

Abernathy, W.J. and Clark, K.B. (1985) 'Innovation: mapping the winds of creative destruction', *Research Policy*, 14: 3–22.

Ackoff, R.L. (1993) 'Idealized design: creative corporate visioning', *OMEGA International Journal of Management Science*, 21 (4): 401–10.

Aguilar, F.J. (1967) *Scanning the Business Environment.* New York: Macmillan.

Alcar Group. (1989) *IBM's Acquisition of Rolm.* Case study developed by Alcar Group Inc., Chicago.

Alchian, A.A. and Demsetz, H. (1972) 'Production, information costs, and economic organizations', *American Economic Review*, 62 (5): 772–95.

Aldrich, H.E. (1979) *Organisations and Environments.* Englewood Cliffs, NJ: Prentice Hall.

Aldrich, H.E. and Mueller, S. (1982) 'The evolution of organisational form: technology coordination and control', in B.M. Staw and L.L. Cummings (eds), *Research in Organisational Behavior*, 4: 33–89.

Aldrich, H. and Pfeffer, J. (1976) 'Environments of organizations', *Annual Review of Sociology*, 2: 79–105.

Allison, G.T. (1971) *Essence of Decision – Explaining the Cuban Missile Crisis.* Boston, MA: Little, Brown and Company.

Amit, R.H. and Schoemaker, P.J.H. (1993) 'Strategic assets and organizational rents', *Strategic Management Journal*, 14 (1): 33–46.

Andersen, D. (1987) 'Vision management', *European Management Journal*, 5: 24–8.

Anderson, E. and Weitz, B. (1989) 'Determinants of continuity in conventional industrial channel dyads', *Marketing Science*, 8 (4): 310–23.

Anderson, J. and Narus, J. (1990) 'A model of distributor firm and manufacturing firm working partnerships', *Journal of Marketing*, 54: 42–58.

Andersson, P. (1999a) 'Complexity theory and organization science'. *Organization Science*, 10 (5): 216–32.

Andersson, P. (1999b) 'The role of the manager in a self-organizing enterprise', in J. Clippinger (ed.), *The Biology of Business: Decoding the Natural Laws of Enterprise.* San Fransisco, CA: Jossey-Bass.

Andreu, R. and Ciborra, C. (1994) 'Information systems for the learning organization', proceedings of the 'IT and Organizational Change' conference, Nijenrode University, Holland 28–9 April.

Andrews, K.R. (1965) 'The concept of corporate strategy', in E.P. Learned, C.R. Christensen and K.R. Andrews (eds), *Business Policy: Text and Cases*, Homewood, IL: Dow Jones-Irwin.

Andrews, K.R. (1971) *The Concept of Corporate Strategy*, Homewood, IL: Dow Jones-Irwin.

Angle, H.L. and van de Ven, A.H. (1989) 'Suggestions for managing the innovation journey', in A.H. van de Ven, H.L. Angle and M.S. Poole (eds), *Research on the Management of Innovation.* New York: Harper & Row, pp. 663–97.

Ansoff, H.I. (1965) *Corporate Strategy.* New York: McGraw Hill.

Ansoff, H.I. (1988) *The New Corporate Strategy.* New York: Wiley.

Ansoff, H.I. (1991) 'A critique of Henry Mintzberg's design school: reconsidering the basic premises of strategic management', *Strategic Management Journal*, 12 (6): 449–61.

Argyris, C. and Schön, D.A. (1974) *Theory in Practice: Increasing Professional Effectiveness.* San Francisco, CA: Josey-Bass.

Argyris, C. and Schön, D.A. (1978) *Organizational Learning: a Theory of Action Perspective*. Reading, MA: Addison-Wesley.

Arrow, K.J. (1974) *The Limits of Organization*. New York: Norton.

Ashmos, D.P., McDaniel, R.R. and Duchon, D. (1990) 'Differences in perception of strategic decision-making processes: the case of physicians and administrators', *Journal of Applied Behavioural Sciences*, 26 (2): 201–18.

Astley, W.G. and van de Ven, A.H. (1983) 'Central perspectives and debates in organisation theory', *Administrative Science Quarterly*, 28: 245–73.

Axelrod, R.M. (1984) *The Evolution of Cooperation*. New York: Basic Books.

Axelsson, B. and Easton, G. (eds) (1992) *Industrial Networks: A New View of Reality*. London: Routledge.

Badaracco, J.L. (1991) *The Knowledge Link*. Boston, MA: Harvard Business School Press.

Baden-Fuller, C. and Stopford, J.M. (1991) 'Globalisation Frustrated', *Strategic Management Journal*, 12: 493–507.

Baden-Fuller, C. and Stopford, J.M. (1994) *Rejuvenating the mature business*. Boston, MA: Harvard Business School Press.

Baden-Fuller, C. and Volberda, H.W. (1997) 'Strategic renewal in large complex organizations: a competence-based view', in A. Heene and R. Sanchez (eds), *Competence-Based Strategic Management*. Chichester: John Wiley, pp. 89–110.

Bahrami, H. and Evans, S. (1995) 'Flexible re-cycling and high technology entrepreneurship', *California Management Review*, 37 (3): 62–89.

Bailey, A. and Johnson, G. (1992) 'How strategies develop in organisations', in D. Faulkner and G. Johnson (eds), *The Challenge of Strategic Management*. London: Kogan Page, pp. 147–78.

Bailey, A. and Johnson, G. (1993) 'Managerial understanding of strategy development', paper presented at the Strategic Management Society conference, Chicago.

Bain, J.S. (1968) *Industrial Organization*, 2nd edn. New York: John Wiley.

Baldwin, C. and Clark, K.B. (1994) 'Modularity-in-design: an analysis based on the theory of real options', working paper, Boston, MA: Harvard Business School.

Barker III, V.L. and Mone, M.A. (1994) 'Retrenchement: cause of turnaround or consequence of decline?', *Strategic Management Journal*, 15: 395–405.

Barnard, C.I. (1938) *The Functions of the Executive*. Boston, MA: Harvard University Press.

Barnett, W.P., Greve, H.R. and Park, D.Y. (1994) 'An evolutionary model of organizational performance', *Strategic Management Journal*, 15: 11–28.

Barnett, W.P. and Hansen, M.T. (1996) 'The Red Queen in organizational evolution', *Strategic Management Journal*, 17 (special issue): 139–57.

Barney, J.B. (1986a) 'Strategic factor markets: expectations, luck, and business strategy', *Management Science*, 32 (10): 1231–41.

Barney, J.B. (1986b) 'Organizational culture: can it be a source of sustained competitive advantage?', *Academy of Management Review*, 11 (3): 656–65.

Barney, J.B. (1991) 'Firm resources and sustained competitive advantage', *Journal of Management*, 17 (1): 99–120.

Barney, J.B. and Hansen, M.H. (1994) 'Trustworthiness as a source of competitive advantage', *Strategic Management Journal*, 15: 175–90.

Barney, J.B. and Hoskisson, R. (1990) 'Strategic groups: untested assertions and research proposals', *Managerial and Decision Economics*, 11: 187–98.

Barr, P.S., Stimpert, J.L. and Huff, A.S. (1992) 'Cognitive change, strategic action, and organizational renewal', *Strategic Management Journal*, 13: 15–36.

Bartlett, C.A. (1993) 'Commentary: strategic flexibility, firm organization, and managerial work in dynamic markets', in P. Shrivastava, A.S. Huff and J. Dutton (eds), *Advances in Strategic Management*. Greenwich, CT: JAI Press, pp. 292–8.

Bartlett, C.A. and Ghoshal, S. (1989) *Managing Across Borders: the Transnational Solution*. London: Hutchinson Business Books.

Bartlett, C.A. and Ghoshal, S. (1993) 'Beyond the M-form: toward a managerial theory of the firm', *Strategic Management Journal*, 14 (special issue): 23–46.

Bartunek, J.M. (1984) 'Changing interpretative schemes and organizational restructuring: the examples of a religious order', *Administrative Science Quarterly*, 29: 355–72.

Bastien, D.T. (1987) 'Common patterns of behaviour and communication in corporate mergers and acquisitions', *Human Resource Management*, 26: 17–33.

Bastien, D.T. and van de Ven, A.H. (1986) 'Managerial and organisational dynamics of mergers and acquisitions', discussion paper 46, Strategic Management Research Centre, University of Minnesota, Minneapolis.

Bateson, G. (1936) *Naven*. Cambridge: Cambridge University Press.

Bateson, G. (1972) *Steps to an Ecology of Mind*. New York: Ballantine.

Baum, J.A.C. (1999) 'Whole-part coevolutionary competition in organizations', in J.A.C. Baum and B. McKelvey (eds), *Variations in Organization Science: in Honor of Donald T. Campbell*. London: Sage Publications Ltd, pp. 113–35.

Baum, J.A.C. and Korn, H.J. (1999) 'Dynamics of dyadic competitive interaction', *Strategic Management Journal*, 20 (3): 251–78.

Baum, J.A.C. and Singh, J.V. (1994) *Evolutionary Dynamics of Organizations*. New York: Oxford University Press.

Behrman, J.N. and Levin, R.I. (1984) 'Are business schools doing their job?', *Harvard Business Review*, 62 (1): 140–5.

Beinhocker, E. (1997) 'Strategy at the edge of chaos', *The McKinsey Quarterly*, (1): 25–39.

Bennis, W. and Nanus, B. (1985) *Leaders: the Strategies for Taking Charge*. New York: Harper & Row.

Berg, S.V., Duncan, J. and Friedman, P. (1981) *Joint Venture Strategies and Corporate Innovation*. Cambridge: Oelgeschlager, Gunn and Hain.

Berman, R.J. and Wade, M.R. (1981) 'The planned approach to acquisitions', in S.J. Lee and R.D. Coleman (eds), *Handbook of Mergers, Acquisitions and Buyouts*. Englewood Cliffs, NJ: Prentice Hall.

Bettenhausen, K.L. and Murnighan, J.K. (1985) 'The emergence of norms in competitive decision making groups', *Administrative Science Quarterly*, 36 (1): 350–72.

Bettis, R.A. (1991) 'Strategic management and the straightjacket: an editorial essay', *Organizational Science*, 2 (3): 315–19.

Bettis, R.A., Bradley, S.P. and Hamel, G. (1992) 'Outsourcing and industrial decline', *Academy of Management Executives*, 6: 7–22.

Beyer, J.M. (1981) 'Ideologies, values, and decision making in organisations', in P.C. Nystrom and W.H. Starbuck (eds), *Handbook of Organisational Design*, vol. 2. Oxford: Oxford University Press.

Biggadike, E.R. (1981) 'The contribution of marketing to strategic management', *Academy of Management Review*, 6: 621–32.

Bijker, W.E., Hughes, T.P. and Pinch, T.J. (1987) *The Social Construction of Technological Systems: New Directions in the Sociology and History of Technology*. Cambridge, MA: MIT Press.

Black, J.A. and Boal, K.B. (1994) 'Strategic resources: traits, configurations and paths to sustainable competitive advantage', *Strategic Management Journal*, 15 (special issue): 131–48.

Blau, P.M. (1964) *Exchange and Power in Social Life*. New York: John Wiley.

Blau, P.M. (1977) *Inequality and Heterogeneity*. New York: Free Press.

Bleeke, J. and Ernst, D. (1991) 'The way to win in cross-border alliances', *Harvard Business Review*, 69 (6): 127–35.

Bogaert, I., Martens, R. and van Cauwenbergh, A. (1994) 'Strategy as situational puzzle: the fit of components', in G. Hamel and A. Heene (eds), *Competence-Based Competition*. Chichester: John Wiley.

Boisot, M.H. (1998) *Knowledge Assets: Securing Competitive Advantage in the Information Economy*. Oxford: Oxford University Press.

Boland, L. (1982) *The Foundations of Economic Method*. London: Allen and Unwin.

Boltanski, L. and Thévenot, L. (1991) *De la Justification: les Economies de la Grandeur*. Paris: Seuil.

Bonora, E.A. and Revang, O. (1991) 'A strategic framework for analyzing professional service firms', paper presented at the Strategic Management Society international conference, Toronto, Canada, 23–6 October.

Boswell, J.S. (1983) *Business Policies in the Making: Three Steel Companies Compared.* London: Allen and Unwin.

Bougon, M., Weick, K.E. and Binkhorst, D. (1977) 'Cognition in organizations: an analysis of the Utrecht Jazz Orchestra', *Administrative Science Quarterly*, 22: 606–39.

Bourdieu, P. (1993) *Sociology in Question.* London: Sage Publications Ltd.

Bourgeois, L.J. (1984) 'Strategic management and determinism', *Academy of Management Review*, 9: 586–96.

Bourgeois, L.J. and Brodwin, D.R. (1984) 'Strategic implementation: five approaches to an exclusive phenomenon', *Strategic Management Journal*, 5: 241–64.

Bower, J.L. (1970) *Managing the Resource Allocation Process.* Boston, MA: Harvard Business School Press.

Bower, J.L. (1982) 'Business policy in the 1980s', *Academy of Management Review*, 7: 630–8.

Bowman, E.H. (1990) 'Strategy changes: possible worlds and actual minds', in J.W. Fredrickson (ed.), *Perspectives on Strategic Management.* New York: Harper & Row, pp. 9–38.

Bowman, C. and Daniels, K. (1995) 'The influence of functional experience on perceptions of strategic priorities', *British Journal of Management*, 6 (3): 157–68.

Bowman, E.H. and Hurry, D. (1993) 'Strategy through the options lens: an integrated view of resource investments and the incremental choice process', *Academy of Management Review*, 18 (4): 760–82.

Boyer, R. and Orléan, A. (1995) 'Stabilité de la Coopération dans les jeux évolutionnistes stochastiques', *Revue Economique*, 46 (3): 797–806.

Boynton, A.C. and Victor, B. (1991) 'Beyond flexibility: building and managing the dynamically stable organization', *California Management Review*, 34: 53–66.

Bracker, J. (1980) 'The historical development of the strategic management concept', *Academy of Management Review*, 5: 219–24.

Bradach, J.L. and Eccles, R.G. (1989) 'Price, authority, and trust: from ideal types to plural forms', *Annual Review of Sociology*, 15: 97–118.

Bradley, J.W. and Korn, D.H. (1981) 'The changing role of acquisitions', *Journal of Business Strategy*, 2: 30–2.

Brealy, R. and Myers, S. (1988) *Principles of Corporate Finance.* New York: McGraw Hill.

Brege, S. and Brandes, O. (1993) 'The successful double turnaround of ASEA and ABB – twenty lessons', *Journal of Strategic Change*, 2: 185–205.

Brenner, R. (1983) *History – the Human Gamble.* Chicago: University of Chicago Press.

Bromiley, P. and Cummings, L.L. (1995) 'Transaction costs in organizations with trust', in R. Bies, B. Sheppard and R. Lewicki (eds), *Research on Negotiation in Organizations*, vol. 5. Greenwich, CT, pp. 219–47.

Brown, R.B. (1993) 'The history of the paradigm', paper presented at the 11th EGOS Colloquium on the production and diffusion of managerial and organizational knowledge. Paris: ESCP.

Brown, J.S. and Duguid, P. (1991) 'Organizational learning and communities-of-practice: towards a unified view of working, learning, and innovation', *Organization Science*, 2: 40–57.

Brown, S.L. and Eisenhardt, K.M. (1998) *Competing on the Edge: Strategy as Structured Chaos.* Boston, MA: Harvard Business School Press.

Bruderer, E. and Singh, J.V. (1996) 'Organizational evolution, learning, and selection: a genetic algorithm-based model', *Academy of Management Journal*, 39 (5): 1322–49.

Bryson, J.M. (1993) *Strategic Planning for Public Service and Non Profit Organisations.* Oxford: Pergamon Press.

Brytting, T. (1991) *Organizing in the Small Growing Firm.* Stockholm: Stockholm School of Economics, Economic Research Institute.

Buckley, P.J. and Casson, M. (1988) 'A theory of cooperation in international business', in F. Contractor and P. Lorange (eds), *Cooperative Strategies in International Business*. Lexington, MA: Lexington Books, pp. 31–54.

Buono, A.F. and Bowditch, J.L. (1989) *The Human Side of Mergers and Acquisitions: Managing Collisions Between People and Organisations*. San Francisco, CA: Jossey-Bass.

Buono, A.F., Bowditch, J.L. and Lewis, J.W. (1988) 'The cultural dynamics of transformation: the case of a bank merger', in R. Kilmann and T. Covin (eds), *Corporate Transformation: Revitalising Organisations for a Competitive World*. San Fransisco, CA: Jossey-Bass, pp. 497–522.

Burgelman, R.A. (1983) 'A model of the interaction of strategic behavior, corporate context, and the concept of strategy', *Academy of Management Review*, 8 (1): 61–70.

Burgelman, R.A. (1991) 'Intraorganizational ecology of strategy making and organizational adaptation: theory and field research', *Organization Science*, 2: 239–62.

Burgelman, R.A. (1994) 'Fading memories: a process theory of strategic business exit in dynamic environments', *Administrative Science Quarterly*, 39 (1): 24–56.

Burgelman, R.A. (1996) 'A process model of strategic business exit: implications for an evolutionary perspective on strategy', *Strategic Management Journal*, 17: 193–214.

Burns, T. and Stalker, G.M. (1961) *The Management of Innovation*, 2nd edn. London: Tavistock.

Burrell, G. and Morgan, G. (1979) *Sociological Paradigms and Organisational Analysis*. London: Heinemann.

Calori, R., Lubatkin, M., Very, P. and Veiga, J.F. (1997) 'Modelling the origins of nationally bound administrative heritages: a historical institutional analysis of French and British firms', *Organization Science*, 8 (6): 681–96.

Camerer, C. (1985) 'Redirecting research in business policy and strategy', *Strategic Management Journal*, 6: 1–15.

Camerer, C. and Vepsalainen, A. (1988) 'The economic efficiency of corporate culture', *Strategic Management Journal*, 9: 115–26.

Cannella, A. and Paetzold, L. (1994) 'Pfeffer's barriers to the advance of organisational science: a rejoinder', *Academy of Management Review*, 19 (2): 331–41.

Carroll, L. (1946) *Through the Looking Glass and What Alice Found There*. New York: Grosset & Dunlap.

Cassell, J. (1991) *Expected Miracles: Surgeons at Work*. Philadelphia, PA: Temple University Press.

Cattell, R.B. (1966) 'The scree test for the number of factors', *Multivariate Behavioral Research*, 1: 245–76.

Caves, R. and Porter, M. (1977) 'From entry barriers to mobility barriers: conjectural decisions and contrived deterrence to new competition', *Quarterly Journal of Economics*, 91: 241–62.

Chaffee, E.E. (1985) 'Three models of strategy', *Academy of Management Review*, 10 (1): 89–98.

Chakravarthy, B.S. and Doz, Y. (1992) 'Strategy process research: focusing on corporate self-renewal', *Strategic Management Journal*, 13 (special issue): 5–14.

Chamberlin, E.H. (1933) *The Theory of Monopolistic Competition*. Boston, MA: Harvard University Press.

Chandler, A.D. (1962) *Strategy and Structure: Chapters in the History of the American Industrial Enterprise*. Cambridge, MA: The Massachusetts Institute of Technology Press.

Chandler, A.D. (1977) *The Visible Hand: The Managerial Revolution in American Business*. Cambridge, MA: Harvard University Press.

Chandler, A.D. (1990a) 'The enduring logic of industrial success', *Harvard Business Review*, 66: 130–40.

Chandler, A.D. (1990b) *Scale and Scope*. Boston, MA: Harvard Business School Press.

Chang, M.H. (1993) 'Flexible manufacturing, uncertain consumer tastes, and strategic entry deterrence', *Journal of Industrial Economics*, 41: 77–90.

Chatman, J.A. and Jehn, K.A. (1994) 'Assessing the relationship between industry characteristics and organizational culture: how different can you be?', *Academy of Management Journal*, 37 (3): 522–53.

Chatterjee, S. (1986) 'Types of synergy and economic value: the impact of acquisitions on merging and rival firms', *Strategic Management Journal*, 7: 119–40.

Chesbrough, H.W. and Teece, D.J. (1996) 'When is virtual virtuous?', *Harvard Business Review*, 74 (1): 65–73.

Cheung, S.S.N. (1983) 'The contractual nature of the firm', *Journal of Law and Economics*, 26: 1–22.

Child, J. (1972) 'Organization structure, environment and performance: the role of strategic choice', *Sociology*, 6 (1): 1–22.

Child, J. (1997) 'Strategic choice in the analysis of action, structure, organisations and environment: retrospect and prospect', *Organization Studies*, 18 (1): 43–76.

Christensen, C.R. and Hansen, A.J. (1987) *Teaching and the Case Method: Texts, cases and readings*. Boston, MA: Harvard Business School Press.

Ciborra, C.U. (1996) 'The platform organization: recombining strategies, structures, and surprises', *Organization Science*, 7 (2): 103–18.

Clark, K.B. (1985) 'The interaction of design hierarchies and market concepts in technological evolution', *Research Policy*, 14 (5): 235–51.

Clark, K.B. and Fujimoto, T. (1991) *Product Development Performance: Strategy, Organization, and Management in the World Auto Industry*. Boston, MA: Harvard University Press.

Clark, K.B. and Wheelwright, S.C. (1995) *The Product Development Challenge: Competing Through Speed, Quality and Creativity*. Boston, MA: Harvard University Press.

Coase, R.H. (1937) 'The nature of the firm', *Economica*, 4: 386–405.

Cohen, M.D., March, J.G. and Olsen, J.P. (1972) 'A garbage can model of organizational choice', *Administrative Science Quarterly*, 17: 1–25.

Cohen, W.M. and Levinthal, D.A. (1990) 'Absorptive capacity: a new perspective on learning and innovation', *Administrative Science Quarterly*, 35 (1): 128–52.

Cohen, M.D. and Sproull, L.S. (1996) *Organizational learning*. Thousand Oaks, CA: Sage Publications Ltd.

Cole, S. (1983) 'The hierarchy of the sciences', *American Journal of Sociology*, 89: 111–39.

Coleman, J. (1990) *Foundations of Social Theory*. Boston, MA: Harvard University Press.

Collis, D.J. (1994) 'How valuable are organizational capabilities?', *Strategic Management Journal*, 15: 143–52.

Collis, D.J. and Montgomery, C.A. (1995) 'Competing on resources: strategy in the 1990s', *Harvard Business Review*, 73 (4): 118–28.

Comrey, A.L. (1973) *A First Course in Factor Analysis*. New York: Academic Press.

Comrey, A.L. (1988) 'Factor analytic methods of scale development in personality and clinical psychology', *Journal of Consulting and Clinical Psychology*, 56: 754–61.

Conner, K.R. (1991) 'A historical comparison of resource-based theory and five schools of thought within industrial organization economics: do we have a new theory of the firm?', *Journal of Management*, 17: 121–54.

Conner, K.R. and Prahalad, C.K. (1996) 'A resource-based theory of the firm: knowledge versus opportunism', *Organization Science*, 7 (5): 477–501.

Connolly, T. (1984) 'Towards a reintegration of organisational behaviour', *Organisational Behaviour Teaching Review*, 9: 1–3.

Cyert, R.B. and March, J.G. (1963) *A Behavioural Theory of the Firm*. Engelwood Cliffs, NJ: Prentice Hall.

Daems, H. and Thomas, H. (1994) *Strategic Groups, Strategic Moves and Performance*. Oxford: Pergamon-Elsevier.

Daft, R.L. and Buenger, V. (1990) 'Hitchhiking a ride on a fast train to nowhere: the past and the future of strategic management research', in J.W. Fredrickson (ed.), *Perspectives on Strategic Management*. New York: Harper & Row, pp. 81–103.

Daft, R.L., Griffin, R.W. and Yates, V. (1987) 'Retrospective accounts of research factors', *Academy of Management Journal*, 30: 763–85.

Daft, R.L., Sormunen, J. and Parks, D. (1988) 'Chief executive scanning, environmental characteristics, and company performance: an empirical study', *Strategic Management Journal*, 9: 123–39.

Daft, R.L. and Weick, K.E. (1984) 'Toward a model of organizations as interpretation systems', *Academy of Management Review*, 9 (2): 284–95.

Das, T.K. (1991) 'Time: the hidden dimension in strategic planning', *Long Range Planning*, 24: 49–57.

Dasgupta, P. (1988) 'Trust as a commodity', in D. Gambetta (ed.), *Trust: Making and Breaking Cooperative Relations*. Oxford: Blackwell. pp. 49–72.

D'Aveni, R.A. and Gunther, R.E. (1994) *Hypercompetition: Managing the Dynamics of Strategic Maneuvering*. New York: Free Press.

Davidow, W.H. and Malone, M.S. (1992) *The Virtual Corporation*. New York: HarperCollins.

De Leeuw, A.C.J. and Volberda, H.W. (1996) 'On the concept of flexibility: a dual control perspective', *OMEGA*, 24 (2): 121–39.

Deal, T.E. and Kennedy, A.A. (1982) *Corporate Culture*. Reading, MA: Addison-Wesley.

Denzin, N.K. (1989) *The Research Act*. Englewood Cliffs, NJ: Prentice Hall.

Derkinderen, F.G.J. and Crum, R.L. (1988) 'The development and empirical validation of strategic decision models', *International Studies of Management and Organisation*, 18 (2): 29–55.

Deutsch, M. (1962) 'Cooperation and trust: some theoretical notes', in M.R. Jones (ed.), *Nebraska Symposium on Motivation*. Lincoln, NE: University of Nebraska Press. pp. 275–319.

Devine, I. (1984) 'Organisational adaptation to crisis conditions and effects on organisational members', paper presented at the 44th Academy of Management conference, August, Boston, MA.

Devlin, G. and Bleackley, M. (1988) 'Strategic alliances – guidelines for success', *Long Range Planning*, 21 (5): 18–23.

Dewey, J. (1929) *The Quest for Certainty*. New York: Minton, Balch.

Dierickx, I. and Cool, K. (1989) 'Asset stock accumulation and sustainability of competitive advantage', *Management Science*, 35: 1504–11.

Dijksterhuis, M., van den Bosch, F. and Volberda, H.W. (1999) 'Where do new organizational forms come from? Management logics as a source of co-evolution', *Organization Science*, 10 (5): 569–82.

DiMaggio, P.J. and Powell, W.W. (1983) 'The iron cage revisited: institutional isomorphism and collective rationality in organizational fields', *American Sociological Review*, 48: 147–60.

Dodd, P. (1976) 'Corporate takeovers and the Australian equity market', *Australian Journal of Management*, 1: 15–35.

Dodgson, M. (1993) 'Organizational learning: a review of some literatures', *Organization Studies*, 14 (3): 375–94.

Donaldson, G. and Lorsch, J.W. (1983) *Decision Making at the Top*. New York: Basic Books.

Donaldson, L. (1996) 'For Cartesianism: against organizational types and quantum jumps', in *For Positivist Organization Theory: Providing the Hard Core*. London: Sage Publications Ltd, pp. 108–29.

Doz, Y. (1992) 'The role of partnerships and alliances in the European industrial restructuring', in K. Cool, D. Nevan and L. Walters (eds), *European Industrial Restructuring in the 1990s*. London: Macmillan.

Doz, Y. and Prahalad, C.K. (1987) 'A process model of strategic redirection in large complex firms: the case of multinational corporations', in A. Pettigrew (ed.), *The Management of Strategic Change*. Oxford: Basil Blackwell.

Drazin, R. and van de Ven, A.H. (1985) 'Alternative forms of fit in contingency theory', *Administrative Science Quarterly*, 30: 514–39.

Dutton, J.E. (1988) 'Understanding strategic agenda building and its implications for managing change', in L.J. Boland and H. Thomas (eds), *Managing Change and Ambiguity*, Chichester: John Wiley, pp. 127–44.

Dutton, J.E. and Dukerich, J. (1991) 'Keeping and eye on the mirror: image and identity in organization adaptation', *Academy of Management Journal*, 34: 517–54.

Dutton, J.E., Stumpf, S. and Wagner, D. (1990) 'Diagnosing strategic issues and managerial investment of revenues', in P. Shrivastava and R. Lamb (eds), *Advances in Strategic Management*, Greenwich, CT: JAI Press, pp. 143–67.

Dyer, J.H. (1997) 'Effective interfirm collaboration: how firms minimize transaction costs and maximize transaction value', *Strategic Management Journal*, 18 (7): 535–56.

Eckbo, B.E. (1986) 'Mergers and the market for corporate control: the Canadian evidence', *Canadian Journal of Economics*, 19: 236–60.

Eckbo, B.E. and Langohr, H. (1985) 'Disclosure regulations and determinants of takeover premiums', unpublished paper, University of British Columbia and INSEAD, Vancouver and Fontainbleau.

Eisenhardt, K.M. (1989a) 'Building theories from case study research', *Academy of Management Review*, 14 (4): 532–50.

Eisenhardt, K.M. (1989b) 'Agency theory: an assessment and review', *Strategic Management Review*, 14: 57–74.

Eisenhardt, K.M. and Bourgeois III, L.J. (1988) 'Politics of strategic decision making in high-velocity environments: towards a midrange-theory', *Academy of Management Journal*, 31 (4) (special issue): 737–70.

Eisenhardt, K.M. and Zbaracki, M.J. (1992) 'Strategic decision making', *Strategic Management Journal*, 13 (special issue): 17–37.

Elgers, P.T. and Clarke, J.J. (1980) 'Merger types and stockholder returns: additional evidence', *Financial Management*, 9: 66–72.

Emery, F.E. and Trist, E.L. (1965) 'The causal texture of organizational environments', *Human Relations*, 18: 21–32.

Ernst, D. and Bleeke, J. (1993) *Collaborating to Compete*. New York: John Wiley.

Etzioni, A. (1968) *The Active Society*, New York: Free Press, pp. 282–309.

Fahey, L. and King, W.R. (1977) 'Environmental scanning for corporate planning', *Business Horizons*, 20 (4): 61–71.

Favereau, O. (1993) 'Objets de gestion et objets de la théorie economique', *Revue Française de Gestion*, 96: 6–12.

Feyeraband, P. (1975) *Against Method*. Thetford: Thetford Press.

Fiol, M.C. and Huff, A.S. (1992) 'Maps for managers. Where are we? Where are we go from here?', *Journal of Management Studies*, 29 (3): 267–85.

Fiol, C.M. and Lyles, M.A. (1985) 'Organizational learning', *Academy of Management Review*, 10 (4): 803–13.

Floyd, S.W. and Wooldridge, B. (1992) 'Middle management involvement in strategy and its association with strategic type: a research note', *Strategic Management Journal*, 13: 153–67.

Fombrun, C.J. (1986) 'Structural dynamics within and between organizations', *Administrative Science Quarterly*, 31: 403–21.

Fombrun, C.J. (1992) *Turning Points – Creating Strategic Change in Corporations*, New York: Mc-Graw Hill.

Foss, N.J. (1993) 'Theories of the firm: contractual and competence perspectives', *Journal of Evolutionary Economics*, 3: 127–44.

Foss, N.J. (1997a) *Resources, Firms, and Strategy: a Reader in the Resource-based Perspective*. Oxford: Oxford University Press.

Foss, N.J. (1997b) 'On the rationales of corporate headquarters', *Industrial and Corporate Change*, 6: 313–39.

Foss, N.J. (1999) 'Networks, capabilities, and competitive advantage', *Scandinavian Journal of Management*, 15: 1–15.

Foss, N.J. (2000) 'Evolutionary theories of the firm: reconstruction and relation to contractual theories', in Kurt Dopfer (ed.), *Evolutionary Principles of Economics*. Boston: Kluwer.

Foss, N.J. and Koch, C.A. (1996) 'Opportunism, organizational economics, and the network approach', *Scandinavian Journal of Management*, 12: 189–205.

Fowler, K.L. and Schmidt, D.R. (1989) 'Determinants of tender offer post-acquisition financial performance', *Strategic Management Journal*, 10: 339–50.

Franco, L. (1974) 'The move towards a multi-dimensional structure in European organizations', *Administrative Science Quarterly*, 19: 493–506.

Franks, J., Broyles, J. and Hecht, M. (1977) 'An industry study of the profitability of mergers in the United Kingdom', *Journal of Finance*, 32: 339–50.

Fredrickson, J.W. (1983) 'Strategic process research: questions and recommendations', *Academy of Management Review*, 8 (4): 565–75.

Fredrickson, J.W. (1992) *Perspectives on Strategy Formation*. London: Harper & Row.

Fredrickson, J.W. and Mitchell, T.R. (1984) 'Strategic decision processes: extension, observations, future directions', *Academy of Management Journal*, 27 (3): 445–66.

Friedlander, F. (1983) 'Patterns of individual and organizational learning', in S. Shrivastava (ed.), *The Executive Mind*. San Francisco, CA: Jossey-Bass.

Fudenberg, D. and Maskin, E. (1986) 'A folk theorem in repeated games with imperfect information', *Econometrica*, 54: 533–54.

Fukuyama, F. (1995) *Trust: Social Virtues and the Creation of Prosperity*. New York: Free Press.

Fuld, L.M. (1984) *Competitor Intelligence – How to get it – How to Use it*. New York: John Wiley.

Gagnon, J.M., Brehain, P., Broquet, C. and Guerra, F. (1982) 'Stock market behaviour of merging firms: the Belgian experience', *European Economic Review*, 17: 187–211.

Galunic, D.C. and Eisenhardt, K.M. (1996) 'The evolution of intracorporate domains: divisional charter losses in high-technology, multidivisional corporations', *Organization Science*, 7 (3): 255–82.

Galunic, D.C. and Rodan, S. (1998) 'Resource recombinations in the firm: knowledge structures and the potential for Schumpeterian innovation', *Strategic Management Journal*, 19 (12): 1193–1201.

Gambetta, D. (1988) 'Can we trust trust?', in D. Gambetta (ed.), *Trust: Making and Breaking Cooperative Relations*. Oxford: Blackwell.

Garud, R. and Kumaraswamy, A. (1993) 'Changing competitive dynamics in network industries: an exploration of Sun Microsystems' open systems strategy', *Strategic Management Journal*, 14 (5): 351–69.

Garvin, D.A. (1993) 'Building a learning organization', *Harvard Business Review*, 71 (4): 78–91.

Geringer, J.M. (1988) *Joint Venture Partner Selection: Strategies for Developed Countries*. Westport, CT: Quorum Books.

Geringer, J.M. (1991) 'Strategic determinants of partner selection criteria in international joint ventures', *Journal of International Business Studies*, 22 (1): 41–62.

Gersick, C.J.G. (1991) 'Revolutionary change theories: a multilevel exploration of the punctuated equilibrium paradigm', *Academy of Management Review*, 16: 10–36.

Gerwin, D. (1993) 'Manufacturing flexibility: a strategic perspective', *Management Science*, 39 (4): 395–410.

Ghemawat, P. (1991) *Commitment: The Dynamic of Strategy*. New York: Free Press.

Ghoshal, S. and Kim, S.K. (1986) 'Building effective intelligence systems for competitive advantage', *Sloan Management Review*, 27: 49–58.

Ghoshal, S. and Moran, P. (1996) 'Bad for practice: a critique of transaction cost theory', *Academy of Management Review*, 21: 13–47.

Ghoshal, S. and Westney, D.E. (1991) 'Organizing competitor analysis systems', *Strategic Management Journal*, 12: 17–31.

Giddens, A. (1990) *The Consequences of Modernity*, London: Polity Press.

Gilad, B. (1989) 'The role of organized competitive intelligence in corporate strategy', *Columbia Journal of World Business*, XXIV: 29–35.

Gilad, B. (1994) *Business Blindspots*. Chicago, IL: Probus Publishing Company.

Gilmore, F.F. (1970) *Formulation and Advocacy of Business Policy*. Ithaca, NY: Cornell University Press.

Gioia, D.A. (1986) 'Symbols, scripts and sensemaking. Creating meaning in the organizational experience', in H.P. Sims Jr and D.A. Gioia (eds), *The Thinking Organization. Dynamics of Organizational Social Cognition*. San Francisco, CA: Jossey-Bass, pp. 49–74.

Gioia, D.A. and Manz, C. (1985) 'Linking cognition and behavior: a script processing interpretation and vicarious learning', *Academy of Management Review*, 10: 527–39.

Gioia, D.A. and Poole, P.P. (1984) 'Scripts in organisational behaviour', *Academy of Management Review*, 9 (3): 449–59.

Gioia, D.A. and Sims Jr, H.P. (1986) 'Introduction: social cognition in organizations', in H.P. Sims Jr and D.A. Gioia (eds), *The Thinking Organization*. San Francisco, CA: Jossey-Bass.

Goffman, E. (1959) *The Presentation of Self in Everyday Life*. Garden City, NY: Doubleday.

Goldenberg, S. (1988) *International Joint Ventures in Action: How to Establish, Manage and Profit From International Strategic Alliances*. London: Hutchinson Business Books.

Grandori, A. (1987) *Perspectives on Organization Theory*. Cambridge, MA: Ballinger Publishing Company.

Granovetter, M. (1985) 'Economic action and social structure: the problem of embeddedness', *American Journal of Sociology*, 91: 481–510.

Grant, R.M. (1991) 'The resource-based theory of competitive advantage: implications for strategy formulation', *California Management Review*, 33 (3): 114–35.

Grant, R.M. (1995) *Contemporary Strategic Analysis: Concepts, Techniques, Applications*, 2nd edn. Cambridge, MA: Blackwell.

Grant, R.M. (1996) 'Prospering in dynamically-competitive environments: organizational capability as knowledge integration', *Organization Science*, 7 (4): 375–87.

Graves, D. (1981) 'Individual reactions to a merger of two small firms in the re-insurance industry: a total population survey', *Journal of Management Studies*, 18: 89–113.

Gray, B. and Yan, A. (1992) 'A negotiations model of joint venture formation, structure and performance', *Advances in International Comparative Management*, 7: 41–75.

Greenwood, R. and Hinings, C.R. (1988) 'Design archetypes, tracks and the dynamics of strategic change', *Organization Studies*, 9: 293–316.

Greenwood, R. and Hinings, C.R. (1993) 'Understanding strategic change: the contribution of archetypes', *Academy of Management Journal*, 36 (5): 1052–81.

Greenwood, R. and Hinings, C.R. (1996) 'Understanding radical organizational change: bringing together the old and new institutionalism', *Academy of Management Review*, 31 (4): 1022–54.

Greenwood, R., Walsh, K., Hinings, C.R. and Ranson, S. (1980) *Patterns of Management in Local Government*. Oxford: Martin Robertson.

Greiner, L.E. (1972) 'Evolution and revolution as organizations grow', *Harvard Business Review*, 50 (4): 37–46.

Grinyer, P.H., Mayes, D. and McKiernan, P. (1988) *Sharpbenders: The Secret of Unleashing Corporate Potential*, Oxford: Blackwell.

Grinyer, P. and McKiernan, P. (1992) 'Strategic planning in the ASEAN region', *Long Range Planning*, 25 (5): 80–91.

Grinyer, P.H. and Spender, J.-C. (1979a) 'Recipes, crises and adaptation in mature business', *International Studies of management and Organization*, 9: 113–23.

Grinyer, P.H. and Spender, J.-C. (1979b) *Turnabout: Managerial Recipes for Strategic Success: The Fall and Rise of the Newton Chambers Group*. London: Associated Business Press.

Grossman, S. and Hart, O. (1986) 'The costs and benefits of ownership: a theory of lateral and vertical integration', *Journal of Political Economy*, 94: 691–719.

Gulati, R. (1995) 'Does familiarity breed trust?', *Academy of Management Journal*, 38 (1): 85–112.

Håkansson, H. and Snehota, I. (1989) 'No business is an island: the network concept of strategy', *Scandinavian Journal of Management*, 5: 187–200.

Hald, A. and Konsynski, B.R. (1993) 'Seven technologies to watch in globalization', in S.P. Bradley, J.A. Hausman and R.L. Nolan (eds), *Globalization, Technology, and Competition: The Fusion of Computers and Telecommunications in the 1990s*. Boston, MA: Harvard Business School Press, pp. 335–58.

Hambrick, D.C. (1981) 'Strategic awareness within top management teams', *Strategic Management Journal*, 2 (3): 263–79.

Hambrick, D.C. (1982) 'Environmental scanning and organizational strategy', *Strategic Management Journal*, 3: 159–74.

Hambrick, D.C. (1990) 'The adolescence of strategic management, 1980–1985: critical perceptions and reality', in J.W. Fredrickson, *Perspectives on Strategic Management*. New York: Harper Business.

Hamel, G. (1990) 'Competitive collaboration: learning, power and dependence in international strategic alliances', unpublished thesis, University of Michigan, MI.

Hamel, G. (1991) 'Competition for competence and inter-partner learning within international strategic alliances', *Strategic Management Journal*, 12: 67–103.

Hamel, G. (1994) 'The concept of core competence', in G. Hamel and A. Heene (eds), *Competence-Based Competition*. Chichester: John Wiley, pp. 11–33.

Hamel, G., Doz, Y. and Prahalad, C.K. (1989) 'Collaborate with your competitors and win', *Harvard Business Review*, 67 (1): 133–9.

Hamel, G. and Heene, A. (eds) (1994) *Competence-Based Competition*. Chichester: John Wiley.

Hamel, G. and Prahalad, C.K. (1989) 'Strategic intent', *Harvard Business Review*, 67 (3): 63–76.

Hamel, G. and Prahalad, C.K. (1994) *Competing for the Future*. Boston, MA: Harvard Business School Press.

Handy, C. (1995) *The Age of Unreason*. London: Arrow Business Books.

Hannan, M.T. and Freeman, J.H. (1977) 'The population ecology of organizations', *American Journal of Sociology*, 82 (5): 929–64.

Hannan, M.T. and Freeman, J.H. (1984) 'Structural inertia and organisational change', *American Sociology Review*, 29: 149–64.

Hannan, M.T. and Freeman, J.H. (1989) *Organisational Ecology*. Boston, MA: Harvard University Press.

Hansen, G.S. and Wernerfelt, B. (1989) 'Determinants of firm performance: the relative importance of economic and organizational factors', *Strategic Management Journal*, 10: 399–411.

Harrigan, K.R. (1985a) 'An application of clustering to strategic group analysis', *Strategic Management Journal*, 6: 55–73.

Harrigan, K.R. (1985b) *Strategic Flexibility*, New York: Free Press.

Harrigan, K.R. (1986) *Managing for Joint Venture Success*. Lexington, MA: Lexington Books.

Harrigan, K.R. (1987) 'Joint ventures: a mechanism for creating strategic change' in A.M. Pettigrew (ed.), *The Management of Strategic Change*. London: Blackwell.

Harrigan, K.R. (1988) 'Joint ventures and competitive strategy', *Strategic Management Journal*, 9 (2): 141–58.

Harrigan, K.R. and Dalmia, D. (1991) 'Knowledge workers: the last bastion of competitive advantage', *Planning Review*, 19 (6): 4–9.

Hart, O.D. (1995) *Firms, Contracts, and Financial Structure*. Oxford: Clarendon Press.

Hart, S.L. (1992) 'An integrative framework for strategy-making processes', *Academy of Management Review*, 17 (2): 327–51.

Hart, S.L. and Banbury, C. (1994) 'How strategy-making processes can make a difference', *Strategic Management Journal*, 15 (4): 251–69.

Haspeslagh, P.C. (1986) 'Making acquisitions work', *Acquisitions Monthly*, 3 (1): 14–16.

Haspeslagh, P.C. and Farquhar, A. (1987) 'The acquisition integration process: a contingent framework', paper presented at the 7th international conference of the Strategic Management Society, Boston, MA, October 14–17.

Haspeslagh, P.C. and Jemison, D.B. (1987) 'Acquisitions: myth and reality. *Sloan Management Review*, 28: 53–8.

Haspeslagh, P.C. and Jemison, D.B. (1991) *Managing Acquisitions: Creating Value Through Corporate Renewal*. New York: Free Press.

Hay, M. and Williamson, P. (1991) *The Strategy Handbook*. Oxford: Blackwell.

Hayek, F.A. (1945) 'The use of knowledge in society', *American Economic Review*, 35: 519–30.

Hayek, F.A. (1978) 'Competition as a discovery procedure', in F.A. Hayek, *New Studies in Philosophy, Politics, Economics and the History of Ideas*. Chicago, IL: University of Chicago Press, pp. 179–90.

Hayes, R.H. (1979) 'The human side of acquisitions', *Management Review*, 68: 41–6.

Hayes, R.H. (1985) 'Strategic forward planning in reverse?', *Harvard Business Review*, 63 (6): 111–19.

Healy, A.F. and Bourne, Jr L.E. (1995) *Learning and Memory of Knowledge and Skills: Durability and Specificity*. Thousand Oaks, CA: Sage Publications Ltd.

Hébert, L. and Geringer, M. (1993) 'Division of control and performance outcome in international joint-ventures: a social exchange framework', paper presented at the 53rd Academy of Management conference, August, Atlanta, GA.

Hedberg, B.L.T. (1981) 'How Organizations Learn and Unlearn', in P.C. Nyström and W. Starbuck (eds), *Handbook of Organizational Design*, vol. 1. New York: Oxford University Press.

Hedberg, B. and Jönsson, S. (1977) 'Strategy formulation as a discontinuous process', *International Studies of Management and Organizations*, 7 (2): 89–109.

Hedberg, B. and Jönsson, S. (1978) 'Designing semi-confusing information systems for organizations in changing environments', *Accounting, Organizations and Society*, 3 (1): 47–64.

Hedberg, B.L.T., Nyström, P.C. and Starbuck, W. (1976) 'Camping on seesaws: prescriptions for a self-designing organization', *Administration Science Quarterly*, 2: 39–52.

Hedlund, G. (1994) 'A model of knowledge management and the N-form corporation', *Strategic Management Journal*, 15 (special issue): 73–90.

Hedlund, G. and Nonaka, I. (1993) 'Models of knowledge management in the West and Japan', in P. Lorange, B. Chakravarthy, J. Roos and A. van de Ven (eds), *Implementing Strategic Processes: Change, Learning and Co-operation*. Oxford: Blackwell, pp. 117–44.

Hedlund, G. and Rolander, D. (1990) 'Action in heterarchies – new approaches to managing the MNC', in C.A. Bartlett, Y. Doz and G. Hedlund (eds), *Managing the Global Firm*. London: Routledge, pp. 15–46.

Heene, A. and Sanchez, R. (1997) *Competence-Based Strategic Management*. Chichester: John Wiley.

Heide, J.B. and John, G. (1988) 'The role of dependence balancing in safeguarding transaction-specific assets in conventional channels', *Journal of Marketing*, 52: 20–35.

Heller, F., Drenth, P., Koopman, P. and Rus, V. (1988) *Decisions in Organisations: A Three Country Comparative Study*. London: Sage Publications Ltd.

Hellgren, B. and Melin, L. (1992) 'Business system industrial wisdom and corporate strategies', in R. Whitley (ed.), *European Business Systems: Firms and Markets in their National Contexts*, Sage Publications Ltd, pp. 180–97.

Hellgren, B. and Melin, L. (1993) 'The role of strategists' way-of-thinking in strategic change processes', in G. Johnson, J. Hendry and J. Newton (eds), *Strategic Thinking: Leadership and the Management of Change*, Chichester: John Wiley, pp. 251–71.

Hellgren, B., Melin, L. and Pettersson, A. (1993) 'Structure and change: the industrial field approach, industrial networks', in *Advances in International Marketing*. Greenwich, CT: JAI Press, pp. 87–106.

Henderson, R.M. and Clark, K.B. (1990) 'Architectural innovation: the reconfiguration of existing product technologies and the failure of established firms', *Administrative Science Quarterly*, 35: 9–30.

Hendry, J. (1995) 'Culture, community and networks: the hidden cost of outsourcing', *European Management Journal*, 13 (2): 193–200.

Hennart, J.F. (1988) 'A transaction costs theory of equity joint ventures', *Strategic Management Journal*, 9: 361–74.

Heylighen, F. and Campbell, D.T. (1995) 'Selection of organization at the social level: obstacles and facilitators of metasystem transitions', *World Futures: The Journal of General Evolution*, 6 (special issue): 181–212.

Hickson, D.J., Butler, R.J., Gray, D., Mallory, G.R. and Wilson, D.C. (1986) *Top Decisions – Strategic decision-making in organisations*. Oxford: Blackwell.

Hickson, D.J., Hinings, C.R., Lee, C.A., Schneck, R.E. and Pennings, J.M. (1971) 'A strategic contingencies theory of intraorganizational power', *Administrative Science Quarterly*, 16 (2): 216.

Hinings, C. and Greenwood, R. (1988) *The Dynamics of Strategic Change*. New York: Blackwell.

Hinings, C.R., Hickson, D.J., Pennings, J.M. and Schneck, R.E. (1974) 'Structural conditions of intraorganisational power', *Administrative Science Quarterly*, 19 (1): 22–44.

Hirsch, P.M., Friedman, R. and Mitchell, P.K. (1990) 'Collaboration or paradigm shift? Caveat emptor: the risk of romance with economic models for strategy and policy research', *Organization Science*, 1 (1): 87–97.

Hirshleifer, J. (1985) 'The expanding domain of economics', *American Economic Review*, 75 (6): 53–68.

Hogarth, R.M. and Makridakis, S. (1981) 'Forecasting and planning: an evaluation', *Management Science*, 27: 115–38.

Holland, J.H. (1975) *Adaptation in Natural and Artificial Systems*. Ann Arbor, MI: University of Michigan Press.

Hosking, D.M. and Morley, I.E. (1991) *A Social Psychology of Organizing*. New York: Harvester Wheatsheaf.

Hosmer, L.T. (1995) 'Trust: the connecting link between organizational theory and philosophical ethics', *Academy of Management Review*, 20 (2): 379–403.

Houghton, J.R. (1990) 'Corning cultivates joint-ventures that endure', *Planning Review*, 18 (5): 15–17.

Howell, R.A. (1970) 'Plan how to integrate your acquisitions', *Harvard Business Review*, 48 (6): 66–76.

Hrebiniak, L.G. and Joyce, W.F. (1985) 'Organizational adaptation: strategic choice and environmental determinism', *Administrative Science Quarterly*, 30 (3): 336–49.

Huber, G.P. (1991) 'Organizational learning: the contributing processes and the literatures', *Organization Science*, 2 (1): 88–115.

Huff, A.S. (1989) 'Book reviews: advances in strategic management, vols 1–5', *Administrative Science Quarterly*, 34 (4): 658–61.

Huff, J.O., Huff, A.S. and Thomas, H. (1992) 'Strategic renewal and the interaction of cumulative stress and inertia', *Strategic Management Journal*, 13: 55–75.

Huff, A.S. and Reger, R.K. (1987) 'A review of strategic process research', *Journal of Management*, 13 (2): 211–36.

Hurst, D.K. (1995) *Crisis and Renewal: Meeting the Challenge of Organizational Change*. Boston: Harvard Business School Press.

Huygens, M. (1999) Coevolution of capabilities and competition: a study of the music industry. PhD Series in General Management, Rotterdam School of Management (33). Rotterdam, The Netherlands.

Ichniowski, C., Shaw, K. and Prenushi, G. (1997) 'The effects of human resource management practices on productivity: a study of steel finishing lines', *American Economic Review*, 87 (3): 291–313.

Ilinitch, A.Y., Lewin, A.Y. and D'Aveni, R.A. (1998) *Managing in Times of Disorder: Hypercompetitive Organizational Responses*. Thousand Oaks, CA: Sage Publications.

Inzerilli, G. (1990) 'The Italian alternative: flexible organization and social management', *International Studies of Management and Organization*, 20 (4): 6–21.

Ireland, R.D., Hitt, M.A., Bettis, R.A. and DePorras, D.A. (1987) 'Strategy formulation processes: differences in perceptions of strength and weaknesses indicators and environmental uncertainty by managerial level', *Strategic Management Journal*, 8 (5): 469–85.

Itami, H. (1987) *Mobilizing Invisible Assets*. Boston, MA: Harvard University Press.

Ivancevich, J.M., Schweiger, D.M. and Power, F.R. (1987) 'Strategies for managing human resources during mergers and acquisitions', *Human Resource Planning*, 10: 19–35.

Jacquemin, A. (1988) 'Cooperative agreements in R&D and European antitrust policy', *European Economic Review*, 32 (2–3): 551–60.

Jain, S.C. (1984) 'Environmental scanning in U.S. corporations', *Long Range Planning*, 17 (2): 117–28.

Janis, I.L. (1972) *Victims of Groupthink*. Boston: Houghton-Mifflin.

Jaques, E. and Clement, S.D. (1991) *Executive Leadership: A Practical Guide to Managing Complexity*. Oxford: Blackwell.

Jarrell, G.A., Brickley, J.A. and Netter, J.M. (1988) 'The market for corporate control: the empirical evidence since 1980', *Journal of Economic Perspectives*, 2: 21–48.

Jarillo, J.C. (1988) 'On strategic networks', *Strategic Management Journal*, 9: 31–41.

Jarillo, J.C. (1993) *Strategic Networks*. London: Butterworth-Heinemann.

Jemison, D.B. (1981a) 'Organisational versus environmental sources of influence in strategic decision making', *Strategic Management Journal*, 2 (1): 77–89.

Jemison, D.B. (1981b) 'The importance of an integrative approach to strategic management research', *Academy of Management Review*, 1: 601–8.

Jemison, D.B. (1988) 'Process constraints on strategic capability transfer in acquisition integration', working paper, Graduate School of Business, TX.

Jemison, D.B. and Sitkin, S.B. (1986a) 'Corporate acquisitions: a process perspective', *Academy of Management Review*, 11 (1): 145–63.

Jemison, D.B. and Sitkin, S.B. (1986b) 'Acquisitions: the process can be a problem', *Harvard Business Review*, 64: 107–16.

Jensen, M.C. (1987) 'The free cash-flow theory of take-overs: a financial perspective on mergers and acquisitions and the economy', in L.E. Brown and E.S. Rosengren (eds), *The Merger Boom*. Boston: Federal Reserve Bank.

Jensen, M.C. and Meckling, W. (1976) 'Theory of the firm: managerial behaviour, agency costs, and ownership structure', in P.J. Buckley and J. Michie (eds) (1996) *Firms, Organizations, and Contracts*. Oxford: Oxford University Press.

Jensen, M.C. and Ruback, R.S. (1983) 'The market for corporate control: the scientific evidence', *Journal of Financial Economics*, 11: 5–50.

Jick, T. (1979) 'Process and impacts of a merger: individual and organisational perspectives', doctoral dissertation, Ithaca, NY: Cornell University.

Johanson, J. and Mattsson, L.-G. (1987) 'Interorganizational relations in industrial systems: a network approach compared with a transaction cost approach', *International Studies of Management and Organization*, 17: 34–48.

Johanson, J. and Mattsson, L.-G. (1993) 'Internationalization in industrial systems: a network approach', in P.J. Buckley and P. Ghauri (eds), *The Internationalization of the Firm: a Reader*. London: Academic Press.

Johnson, G. (1987) *Strategic Change and the Management Process*. Oxford: Blackwell.

Johnson, G. (1988) 'Re-thinking incrementalism', *Strategic Management Journal*, 9 (1): 75–91.

Johnson, G. (1990) 'Managing strategic change: the role of symbolic action', *British Journal of Management*, 1: 183–200.

Jones, K. and Shill, W.E. (1991) 'Allying for advantage', *McKinsey Quarterly*, 3: 73–101.

Joynt, P. (1990) 'Organizational research involving internal networks and external strategic alliances: a theoretical review of strategic alliances', working paper, Bergen Norway: Handelshoyskolen Norwegian School of Management.

Katz, D. and Kahn, R.L. (1978) *The Social Psychology of Organisations*. New York: John Wiley.

Kauffman, S.A. (1993) *The Origins of Order: Self-organization and Selection in Evolution*. New York: Oxford University Press.

Kauffman, S.A. (1995) 'Technology and evolution: escaping the Red Queen effect', *The McKinsey Quarterly*, 1995 (1): 118–29.

Kay, J.A. (1993) *The Foundations of Competitive Success*. Oxford: Oxford University Press.

Keegan, W.J. (1974) 'Multinational scanning: a study of the information sources utilized by headquarters executives in multinational companies', *Administrative Science Quarterly*, 19 (3): 411–21.

Khandwalla, P.N. (1970) 'The effect of the environment on the organizational structure of the firm'. Doctoral dissertation, Carnegie-Mellon University.

Khandwalla, P.N. (1977) *The Design of Organizations*. New York: Harcourt Brace Jovanovich.

Khanna, T., Gulati, R. and Nohria, N. (1998) 'The dynamics of learning alliances: competition, cooperation, and relative scope', *Strategic Management Journal*, 19 (3): 193–210.

Kieser, A. (1989) 'Organizational, institutional, and societal evolution: medieval craft guilds and the genesis of formal organizations', *Administrative Science Quarterly*, 34 (4): 540–64.

Kieser, A. (1994) 'Why organization theory needs historical analyses – and how this should be performed', *Organization Science*, 5 (4): 608–20.

Kim, D.H. (1993) 'The link between individual and organizational learning', *Sloan Management Review*, 35 (1): 37–50.

Kim, W.C. (1989) 'Developing a global diversification measure', *Management Science*, 35: 375–87.

Kim, W.C., Hwang, P. and Burgess, W.P. (1989) 'Global diversification strategy and corporate profit performance', *Strategic Management Journal*, 10: 45–57.

Kimberly, J.R. (1979) 'Issues in the creation of organizations: initiation, innovation, and institutionalization', *Academy of Management Journal*, 22: 437–57.

Kimberly, J.R. and Quinn, R.E. (1984) *Managing Organizational Transitions*. Homewood, IL: Irwin.

Kirzner, I. (1973) *Competition and Entrepreneurship*. Chicago, IL: University of Chicago Press.

Kitching, J. (1967) 'Why do mergers mis-carry?', *Harvard Business Review*, 45 (6): 84–101.

Kitching, J. (1974) 'Winning and losing with European acquisitions', *Harvard Business Review*, 52 (2): 124–36.

Klein, K.J., Damereau, F. and Hall, R.J. (1994) 'Levels issues in theory development: data collection and analysis', *Academy of Management Review*, 19 (2): 195–229.

Kleindorfer, P., Kunreuther, H. and Schoemaker, P.J.H. (1993) *Decision Sciences: An Integrative Perspective*. Cambridge: Cambridge University Press.

Koenig, C. and van Wijk, G. (1991) 'Interfirm cooperation: the role of trust', in J. Thépot and R.A. Thiétart, *Microeconomic Contributions to Strategic Management*. Amsterdam: North-Holland.

Kogut, B. (1988) 'Joint ventures: theoretical and empirical perspectives', *Strategic Management Journal*, 9: 319–22.

Kogut, B. (1989) 'The stability of joint-ventures: reciprocity and competitive rivalry', *Journal of Industrial Economics*, 38 (2): 183–98.

Kogut, B. and Bowman, E.H. (1994) 'Modularity and permeability as principles of design', working paper, Philadelphia, PA: Wharton School of Business.

Kogut, B. and Kulatilaka, N. (1994) 'Operating flexibility, global manufacturing, and the option value of a multinational network', *Management Science*, 40 (1): 123–39.

Kogut, B. and Zander, U. (1992) 'Knowledge of the firm, combinative capabilities, and the replication of technology', *Organization Science*, 3 (3): 383–97.

Kolb, D.A. (1984) *Experiential Learning: Experience as the Source of Learning and Development*. Englewood Cliffs, NJ: Prentice Hall.

Kotter, J.P. (1996) *Leading Change*. Boston, MA: Harvard Business School Press.

Koza, M.P. and Lewin, A.Y. (1998) 'The co-evolution of strategic alliances', *Organization Science*, 9 (3): 255–64.

Krajewski, W. (1977) *Correspondence Principle and Growth of Science*. Dordrecht: Reidel.

Kramer, R.M. and Tyler, T.R. (eds) (1996) *Trust in Organizations*. London: Sage Publications Ltd.

Kreps, D.M. (1990) 'Corporate culture and economic theory', in J.E. Alt and K.A. Shepsle (eds), *Perspectives on Positive Political Economy*. Cambridge: Cambridge University Press.

Kreps, D.M., Milgrom P., Roberts J. and Wilson, R. (1982) 'Rational cooperation in the finitely-repeated prisoner's dilemma', *Journal of Economic Theory*, 27: 245–52.

Kuhn, T.S. (1970) *The Structure of Scientific Revolutions*, 2nd edn. Chicago: University of Chicago Press.

Lacity, M.C., Willcocks, M.P. and Feeny, D.F. (1995) 'IT outsourcing: maximize flexibility and control', *Harvard Business Review*, 73 (3): 84–93.

Lahdenpää, M. (1991) 'The value of deliberate strategy making processes', in J. Näsi (ed.), *Arenas of Strategic Thinking*. Helsinki: Foundation for Economic Education, pp. 91–102.

Lakatos, I. (1970) 'Falsification and the methodology of research programmes', in L. Lakatos and A. Musgrave (eds), *Criticisms and the Growth of Knowledge*. Cambridge: Cambridge University Press, pp. 91–6.

Lamb, R.B. (ed.) (1984) *Competitive Strategic Management*. Englewood Cliffs, NJ: Prentice Hall.

Lammers, C.J. (1987) 'Transience and persistence of ideal types in organization theory', in N. DiTomaso and S. Bacharach, *Research in the Sociology of Organizations: A Research Annual*. Greenwich, CT, pp. 1–41.

Lane, C. and Bachmann, R. (1995) 'Cooperation in inter-firm relations in Britain and Germany: the role of social institutions', paper presented at the 12th European Group on Organization Studies (EGOS) Colloquium, July, Istanbul.

Lane, C. and Bachmann, R. (1996) 'The social constitution of trust', *Organization Studies*, 17 (3): 365–95.

Lange, O. (1936) 'On the economic theory of socialism', *Review of Economic Studies*, 4 (1): 53–71.

Langlois, R.N. and Foss, N.J. (1997) 'Capabilities and governance: the rebirth of production in the theory of economic organization', working paper, Danish Research Unit for Industrial Dynamics, Frederiksburg, Denmark.

Langlois, R.N. and Robertson, P.L. (1992) 'Networks and innovation in a modular system: lessons from the microcomputer and stereo components industries', *Research Policy*, 21 (4): 297–313.

Langlois, R.N. and Robertson, P.L. (1995) *Firms, Markets, and Economic Change: A Dynamic Theory of Business Institutions*. London: Routledge.

Lant, T.K. and Mezias, S. (1990) 'Managing discontinuous change: a simulation study of organizational learning and entrepreneurship', *Strategic Management Journal*, 11: 147–79.

Latour, B. (1996) *Aramis or the Love of Technology*. Boston, MA: Harvard University Press.

Lawler, E.E. III (1977) 'Adaptive experiments: an approach to organizational behavior research', *Academy of Management Review*, 2: 567–85.

Lawless, M. (1998) Performance Effects of Fit and Focus in Strategy Configurations, working paper, Fuqua School of Business, Duke University.

Lawless, M. and Anderson, P. (1996) 'Generational technological change: effects of innovation and local rivalry on performance', *Academy of Management Journal*, 39 (5): 1185–217.

Lawrence, P.R. and Lorsch, J.W. (1967) *Organization and Environment: Managing Differentianation and Integration*. Boston, MA: Harvard Business School Press.

Lazonick, William (1991) *The Myth of the Market Economy*. Cambridge: Cambridge University Press.

Learned, A., Christensen, E.P., Andrews, C.R. and Guth, W.R. (1965) *Business Policy: Text and Cases*. Homewood, IL: Irwin.

Lehtimäki, J. (1993) 'Towards a theory of the university as a knowledge-intensive organization', Publications of Turku School of Economics and Business Administration, series A-5. Turku, Finland.

Lei, D. (1993) 'Offensive and defensive uses of alliances', *Long Range Planning*, 26 (4): 32–41.

Lei, D. and Slocum, J.W. (1992) 'Global strategy competence-building and strategic alliances', *California Management Review*, 35 (1): 81–97.

Leibenstein, H. (1966) 'Allocative efficiency vs. X-efficiency', *American Economic Review*, 56: 392–415.

Leibenstein, H. (1976) *Beyond Economic Man*. Boston, MA: Harvard University Press.

Leighton, C.M. and Tod, G.R. (1969) 'After the acquisition: continuing challenge', *Harvard Business Review*, 47: 90–102.

Lenz, R.T. and Engledow, J.L. (1986) 'Environmental analysis units and strategic decision-making: a field study of selected "Leading-edge" corporations', *Strategic Management Journal*, 7: 69–89.

Leonard-Barton, D. (1988) 'Implementation as mutual adaptation of technology and organization', *Research Policy*, 17 (4): 251–67.

Leonard-Barton, D. (1992) 'Core capabilities and core rigidities: a paradox in managing new product development', *Strategic Management Journal*, 13: 111–25.

Leonard-Barton, D. (1995) *Wellsprings of Knowledge: Building and Sustaining the Sources of innovation*. Boston, MA: Harvard Business School Press.

Leontiades, M. (1982) 'The confusing words of business policy', *Academy of Management Review*, 7: 45–8.

Levinthal, D.A. (1997) 'Adaptation on rugged landscapes', *Management Science*, 43 (7): 934–50.

Levinthal, D.A. and March, J.G. (1993) 'The myopia of learning', *Strategic Management Journal*, 14: 95–112.

Levinthal, D. and Myatt, J. (1994) 'Co-evolution of capabilities and industry: the evolution of mutual fund processing', *Strategic Management Journal*, 15 (special issue): 45–62.

Levison, H. (1970) 'A psychologist diagnoses merger failures', *Harvard Business Review*, 48 (2): 139–47.

Levitt, B. and March, J.G. (1988) 'Organizational learning', *Annual Review of Sociology*, 14: 319–40.

Lewin, A.Y. (1999) 'Application of complexity theory to organization science', *Organization Science*, 10 (3): 215.

Lewin, A.Y., Long, C.P. and Carroll, T.N. (1999) 'The coevolution of new organizational forms', *Organization Science*, 10 (5): 535–50.

Lewin, A.Y. and Stephens, C.U. (1993) 'Designing postindustrial organizations: combining theory and practice', in G.P. Huber and W.H. Glick, *Organizational Change and Redesign*. New York: Oxford University Press, pp. 393–409.

Lewin, A.Y. and Volberda, H.W. (1999) 'Prolegomena on coevolution: A framework for Research on strategy and new organizational forms', *Organization Science*, 10 (5): 519–34.

Lewin, K. (1947) 'Frontiers in group dynamics', *Human Relations*, 1: 5–41.

Lewis, J.D. (1990) *Partnerships for Profit: Structuring and Managing Strategic Alliances*. New York: Macmillan.

Lewis, J.D. and Weigert, A. (1985) 'Trust as social reality', *Social Forces*, 63: 967–85.

Liebeskind, J.P., Oliver, A.L., Zucker, L. and Brewer, M. (1996) 'Social networks, learning and flexibility: sourcing scientific knowledge in new biotechnology firms', *Organization Science*, 7 (4): 428–43.

Likert, R. (1961) *New Patterns of Management*. New York: McGraw Hill.

Lindblom, C.E. (1959) 'The science of muddling through', *Public Administration Review*, 19 (2): 79–88.

Lindblom, C.E. (1987) 'Alternatives to validity: some thought suggested by Campbell's guidelines', *Creation, Diffusion, Utilization*, 8: 509–20.

Lippman, S.A. and Rumelt, R.P. (1982) 'Uncertain imitability: an analysis of interfirm differences in efficiency under competition', *Bell Journal of Economics*, 12: 413–38.

Lodahl, J.B. and Gordon, G. (1972) 'The structure of scientific fields and the functioning of university graduate departments', *American Sociological Review*, 37: 57–72.

Lorange, P. and Roos, J. (1992) *Strategic Alliances: Formation, Implementation and Evolution*. Oxford: Blackwell.

Lorange, P., Roos, J. and Bronn, P.S. (1992) 'Building successful strategic alliances', *Long Range Planning*, 25 (6): 10–18.

Lord, R.G. and Foti, R.J. (1986) 'Schema theories, information processing and organizational behaviour', in H.P. Sims Jr and D.A. Gioia (eds), *The Thinking Organization*. San Francisco, CA: Jossey-Bass.

Lorenzoni, G. and Lipparini, A. (1999) 'The leveraging of interfirm relationships as a distinctive organizational capability: a longitudinal study', *Strategic Management Journal*, 20 (4): 317–38.

Lubatkin, M. (1987) 'Merger strategies and stockholder value', *Strategic Management Journal*, 8: 39–53.

Luhmann, N. (1973) *Vertrauen.* Stuttgart: Ferdinand Enke Verlag.

Luhmann, N. (1988) 'Familiarity, confidence, trust: problems and alternatives', in D. Gambetta (ed.), *Trust: Making and Breaking Cooperating Relations*. Oxford: Blackwell, pp. 94–107.

Lyles, M.A. (1981) 'Formulating strategic problems: empirical analysis and model development', *Strategic Management Journal*, 2 (1): 61–75.

Lyles, M.A. and Schwenk, C.R. (1992) 'Top management, strategy and organizational knowledge structures', *Journal of Management Studies*, 29 (2): 155–74.

Lynch, G. (1989) *The Practical Guide to Joint-Ventures and Corporate Alliances*. London: John Wiley.

Lynch, R.P. (1990) 'Building alliances to penetrate European markets', *Journal of Business Strategy*, 11 (2): 4–8.

Lyons, M.P. (1991) 'Joint venture as strategic choice – a literature review', *Long Range Planning*, 24 (4): 130–44.

Macaulay, S. (1963) 'Non contractual relations in business: a preliminary study', *American Sociological Review*, 28: 55–67.

MacMillan, I.C. (1989) 'Delineating a forum for business policy scholars', *Strategic Management Journal*, 10: 391–5.

Mahoney, J.T. (1992) 'The choice of organizational form: vertical financial ownership versus other methods of vertical integration, *Strategic Management Journal*, 13: 31–41.

Mahoney, J.T. (1993) 'Strategic management and determinism: sustaining the conversation', *Journal of Management Studies*, 30 (1): 173–91.

Mahoney, J.T. (1995) 'The management of resources and the resource of management', *Journal of Business Research*, 33: 91–101.

Mahoney, J.T. and Pandian, J.R. (1992) 'The resource-based view within the conversation of strategic management', *Strategic Management Journal*, 13: 363–80.

Maister, D.H. (1993) *Managing the Professional Service Firm*. New York: Free Press.

Malone, T.J., Yates, J. and Benjamin, R. (1987) 'Electronic markets and electronic hierarchies', *Communications of the ACM*, 30 (6): 484–97.

Manne, H.G. (1965) 'Mergers and the market for corporate control', *Journal of Political Economy*, 73: 110–20.

March, J.G. (1978) 'Bounded rationality, ambiguity and the engineering of choice', *Bell Journal of Economics*, 9: 587–608.

March, J.G. (1981) 'Footnotes to organizational change', *Administrative Science Quarterly*, 26: 563–77.

March, J.G. (1991a) 'Exploration and exploitation in organizational learning', *Organization Science*, 2 (1): 71–87.

March, J.G. (1991b) 'Learning from experience in ecologies of organizations', research paper, Stanford University, Stanford, CA.

March, J.G. (1995) 'The future, disposable organizations, and the rigidities of imagination', *Organization*, 2 (3–4): 427–40.

March, J.G. and Olsen, J.P. (1989) *Rediscovering Institutions: The Organizational Basis of Politics*. New York: Free Press.

March, J.G. and Sevón, G. (1988) 'Behavioral perspectives on theories of the firm', in W.F. van Raaij and K.E. Wärneryd (eds), *Handbook of Economic Psychology*. Dordrecht, Netherlands: Kluwer Academic Publishers, pp. 369–402.

March, J.G. and Simon, H.A. (1958) *Organizations*. New York: John Wiley and Sons.

Marino, K.E. (1996) 'Developing consensus on firm competencies and capabilities', *Academy of Management Executives*, 10 (3): 40–51.

Markides, C. (1995) 'Diversification, restructuring and economic performance', *Strategic Management Journal*, 16: 101–18.

Marks, M.L. (1982) 'Merging human resources: a review of current research', *Mergers and Acquisitions*, 17: 38–44.

Marks, M.L. and Mirvis, P. (1985) 'Merger syndrome stress and uncertainty', *Mergers and Acquisitions*, 20 (2): 50–5.

Marsden, R. (1993) 'The politics of organisational analysis', *Organisation Studies*, 14: 93–124.

Martin, J. and Siehl, C. (1983) 'Organisational cultures and the counter culture: an uneasy symbiosis', *Organisational Dynamics*, 12 (2): 52–64.

Maturana, H. and Varela, F. (1980) *Autopoesis and Cognition: The Realization of the Living*. London: Reidl.

Mayer, R.C., Davis, J.H. and Schoorman, F.D. (1995) 'An integrative model of interorganizational trust', *Academy of Management Review*, 20 (3): 709–34.

McCann, J.E. and Selsky, J. (1984) 'Hyperturbulence and the emergence of type 5 environments', *Academy of Management Review*, 9 (3): 460–70.

McGee, J. and Thomas, H. (1986) 'Strategic groups: theory, research and taxonomy', *Strategic Management Journal*, 7: 141–60.

McKelvey, B. (1982) *Organizational Systematics*. Berkley, CA: University of California Press.

McKelvey, B. (1997) 'Quasi-natural organization science', *Organization Science*, 8 (4): 352–80.

Melin, L. (1985) 'Strategies in managing turnaround', *Long Range Planning*, 18 (1): 80–6.

Melin, L. (1987) 'Commentary on business strategy and strategy change in a hostile environment: failure and success among British cutlery producers', in A. Pettigrew (ed.), *The Management of Strategic Change*. Oxford: Basil Blackwell, pp. 154–65.

Melin, L. (1989) 'The field-force metaphor', *Advances in International Marketing*, 3: 161–79.

Melin, L. (1991) 'Omorientering och strategiska tänkesätt', in G. Arvidsson and R. Lind (eds), *Ledning av företag och förvaltningar – Förutsättningar, former, förnyelse*, Kristianstad: SNS Förlag, p. 193.

Meyer, A.D., Tsui, A.S. and Hinings, C.R. (1993) 'Configurational approaches to organisational analysis', *Academy of Management Journal*, 36 (6): 1175–95.

Meyer, H.E. (1987) *Real World Intelligence*. New York: Weidenfeld and Nicolson.

Meyer, J.W. and Rowan, B. (1977) 'Institutional organisations: formal structures as myth and ceremony', *American Journal of Sociology*, 83: 340–63.

Mezirow, J. (1990) *Fostering Critical Reflection in Adulthood. A Guide to Transformative and Emancipatory Learning*. San Francisco, CA: Jossey-Bass.

Michel, J. and Hambrick, D. (1992) 'Diversification posture and top management team characteristics', *Academy of Management Journal*, 35 (1): 9–37.

Miles, R.E. and Snow, C.C. (1978) *Organizational Strategy, Structure and Process*. New York: McGraw Hill.

Miles, R.E. and Snow, C.C. (1986) 'Organizations: new concepts for new forms', *California Management Review*, 28 (3): 62–73.

Miles, R.E. and Snow, C.C. (1994) *Fit, Failure and the Hall of Fame*. New York: Free Press.

Miles, R.E., Snow, C.C., Meyer, A.D. and Coleman Jr, H.J. (1978) 'Organizational strategy, structure and process', *American Management Review*, July: 546–62.

Miles, R.E., Snow, C.C., Mathews, J.A., Miles, G. and Coleman Jr, H.J. (1997) 'Organizing in the knowledge age: anticipating the cellular form', *Academy of Management Executives*, 11 (4): 7–20.

Milgrom, P. and Roberts, J.D. (1992) *Economics, Organization, and Management*. New York: Prentice Hall.

Milgrom, P. and Roberts, J.D. (1995) 'Complementarities and fit: strategy, structure and organizational change in manufacturing', *Journal of Accounting and Economy*, 19 (2–3): 179–208.

Miller, A. (1988) 'A taxonomy of technological settings, with related strategies and performance levels', *Strategic Management Journal*, 9: 239–54.

Miller, D. (1976) 'Strategy making in context: ten empirical archetypes', PhD thesis, McGill University, Montreal.

Miller, D. (1979) 'Strategy, structure and environment: context influences upon some bivariate associations', *Journal of Management Studies*, 16: 294–316.

Miller, D. (1982) 'Evolution and revolution: a quantum view of structural change in organizations', *Journal of Management Studies*, 19: 131–51.

Miller, D. (1987) 'The structural and environmental correlates of business strategy', *Strategic Management Journal*, 6 (1): 55–76.

Miller, D. (1990a) 'Organizational configurations: cohesion, change and prediction', *Human Relations*, 43: 771–89.

Miller, D. (1990b) *The Icarus Paradox: How Exceptional Companies Bring about their Own Downfall*. New York: Harper Collins.

Miller, D. (1993) 'The architecture of simplicity', *Academy of Management Review*, 18 (1): 116–38.

Miller, D. (1996) 'Configurations revisited', *Strategic Management Journal*, 17 (7): 505–12.

Miller, D. and Chen, M.-J. (1994) 'Sources and consequences of competitive inertia: a study of the U.S. airline industry', *Administrative Science Quarterly*, 39: 1–23.

Miller, D. and Chen, M.-J. (1996) 'The simplicity of competitive repertoires: an empirical analysis', *Strategic Management Journal*, 17 (6): 419–39.

Miller, D. and Friesen, P.H. (1980) 'Archetypes of organizational transition', *Administrative Science Quarterly*, 25 (2): 269–99.

Miller, D. and Friesen, P.H. (1982) 'Structural change and performance: quantum versus piecemeal incremental approaches', *Academy of Management Journal*, 25 (4): 867–92.

Miller, D. and Friesen, P.H. (1984) *Organizations: A Quantum View*. Englewood Cliffs, NJ: Prentice Hall.

Miller, D. and Mintzberg, H. (1983) 'The case for configuration', in G. Morgan (ed.), *Beyond Method: Strategies for Social Research*. Beverley Hills, CA: Sage Publications, pp. 57–73.

Mintzberg, H. (1973a) 'Strategy making in three modes', *California Management Review*, 16 (2): 44–53.

Mintzberg, H. (1973b) *The Nature of Managerial Work*. New York: Harper & Row.

Mintzberg, H. (1975) 'The manager's job: folklore and fact', *Harvard Business Review*, 53: 49–61.

Mintzberg, H. (1976) 'Planning on the left side and managing on the right', *Harvard Business Review*, 54: 49–58.

Mintzberg, H. (1978) 'Patterns in strategy formation', *Management Science*, 24 (9): 934–48.

Mintzberg, H. (1979) *The Structuring of Organizations*. Englewood Cliffs, NJ: Prentice Hall.

Mintzberg, H. (1983) *Structure in Fives. Designing Effective Organizations*. Englewood Cliffs, NJ: Prentice Hall.

Mintzberg, H. (1987a) 'Crafting strategy', *Harvard Business Review*, 65 (4): 65–75.

Mintzberg, H. (1987b) 'The strategy concept 1: five P's for strategy', *California Management Review*, 30 (1): 11–24.

Mintzberg, H. (1989) *Mintzberg on Management Inside our Strange World of Organizations*. New York: Free Press.

Mintzberg, H. (1990a) 'The design school: reconsidering the basic premises of strategic management', *Strategic Management Journal*, 11: 171–95.

Mintzberg, H. (1990b) 'Strategy formation: schools of thought', in J.W. Fredrickson (ed.), *Perspectives on Strategic Management*. New York: Harper & Row, pp. 105–235.

Mintzberg, H. (1991) 'Learning 1, planning 0: reply to Igor Ansoff', *Strategic Management Journal*, 12 (6): 463–6.

Mintzberg, H. (1994) *The Rise and Fall of Strategic Planning: Reconceiving Roles for Planning, Plans, and Planners*. New York: Free Press.

Mintzberg, H., Lampel, J. and Ahlstrand, B.W. (1998) *Strategy Safari: A Guided Tour Through the Wilds of Strategic Management*, New York: Free Press.

Mintzberg, H., Raisinghani, D. and Théoret, A. (1976) 'The structure of "unstructured" decision processes', *Administrative Science Quarterly*, 21 (2): 246–75.

Mintzberg, H. and McHugh, A. (1985) 'Strategy formation in an adhocracy', *Administrative Science Quarterly*, 30 (2): 160–97.

Mintzberg, H. and Waters, J.A. (1982) 'Tracking strategy in an entrepreneurial firm', *Academy of Management Journal*, 25 (3): 465–99.

Mintzberg, H. and Waters, J.A. (1985) 'Of strategies, deliberate and emergent', *Strategic Management Journal*, 6: 257–72.

Mohr, J. and Nevin, J.R. (1990) 'Communication strategies in marketing channels: a theoretical perspective', *Journal of Marketing*, 54: 36–51.

Mohr, J. and Spekman, R. (1994) 'Characteristics of partnership success: partnership attributes, communication, behaviour, and conflict resolution techniques', *Strategic Management Journal*, 15 (2): 135–52.

Moingeon, B. and Edmondson, A. (1996) *Organizational Learning and Competitive Advantage*. Thousand Oaks, CA: Sage Publications Inc.

Montgomery, C.A. (1994) 'Corporate diversification', *Journal of Economic Perspectives*, 8: 163–78.

Morgan, G. (1986) *Images of Organization*. Beverly Hills: Sage Publications Ltd.

Moss Kanter, R. (1983) *The Change Masters*. London: Allen & Unwin.

Nadler, D.A. and Tushman, M. (1989) 'Organizational frame bending: principles for managing reorientation', *Academy of Management Executive*, 1: 194–204.

Napier, N.K., Simmons, G. and Stratton, K. (1989) 'Communication during a merger: experience of two banks', *Human Resource Planning*, 12: 105–22.

Narayanan, V.K. and Fahey, L. (1982) 'The micro politics of strategy formulation', *Academy of Management Review*, 7 (1): 25–34.

Nelson, R.R. and Winter, S.G. (1982) *An Evolutionary Theory of Economic Change*. Boston, MA: The Belknap Press of Harvard University Press.

Nishiguchi, T. (1994) *Strategic Industrial Sourcing: The Japanese Industrial Advantage*. Oxford: Oxford University Press.

Nonaka, I. (1988) 'Creating organizational order out of chaos: self-renewal in Japanese firms', *California Management Review*, 30: 57–73.

Nonaka, I. (1990a) 'Managing globalization as a self-renewing process: experience of Japanese MNCs', in C.A. Bartlett, Y. Doz and G. Hedlund (eds), *Managing the Global Firm*. London: Routledge, pp. 69–94.

Nonaka, I. (1990b) 'Redundant, overlapping organization: a Japanese approach to innovation', *California Management Review*, 32 (3): 27–38.

Nonaka, I. (1991) 'The knowledge-creating company', *Harvard Business Review*, 69: 96–104.

Nonaka, I. (1994) 'A dynamic theory of organizational knowledge creation', *Organization Science*, 5 (1): 14–37.

Nonaka, I. and Takeuchi, H. (1995) *The Knowledge-creating Company: How Japanese Companies Create the Dynamics of Innovation*. New York: Oxford University Press.

Norman, D. (1989) *The Design of Everyday Things*. New York: Doubleday.

Normann, R. (1976) *Memory and Attention*. New York: John Wiley.

Normann, R. (1977) *Management for Growth*. Chichester: John Wiley.

Normann, R. (1984) *Service Management: Strategy and Leadership in Service Businesses*. Chichester: John Wiley.

Normann, R. (1985) 'Developing capabilities for organizational learning', in J.M. Pennings (ed.), *Organizational Strategy and Change*, San Francisco, CA: Jossey-Bass, pp. 217–47.

Normann, R. and Ramirez, R. (1993) 'From value chain to value constellation: designing interactive strategy', *Harvard Business Review*, 71: 65–77.

Nyström, P. and Starbuck, W.H. (1984) 'To avoid organizational crises, unlearn', *Organizational Dynamics*, 12 (4): 53–65.

Orton, D.J. and Weick, K.E. (1990) 'Loosely coupled systems: a reconceptualization', *Academy of Management Review*, 15 (2): 203–23.

Ouchi, W.G. (1980) 'Markets, bureaucracies and clans', *Administrative Science Quarterly*, 25: 129–41.

Parkhe, A. (1993) 'Many research, methodological predispositions and theory development in international joint ventures', *Academy of Management Review*, 18 (2): 227–68.

Pearce II, J.A. and Robbins, K.D. (1994) 'Retrenchement remains the foundation of business turnaround', *Strategic Management Journal*, 15: 407–17.

Pedler, M., Burgoyne, J. and Boydell, T. (1991) *The Learning Company: A Strategy for Sustainable Development*. London: McGraw Hill.

Pekar, P. and Allio, R. (1994) 'Making alliances work – guidelines for success', *Long Range Planning*, 27 (4): 54–65.

Penrose, E.T. (1959) *The Theory of the Growth of the Firm*. London: Oxford University Press.

Penrose, E.T. (1985) *The Theory of the Growth of the Firm: Twenty Five Years Later*. Uppsala, Sweden: Acta Universitatis Upsaliensis.

Pennings, J.M., Lee, K. and Van Witteloostuijn, A. (1998) 'Human capital, social capital and firm dissolution', *Academy of Management Journal*, 41 (4): 425–40.

Pepper, S. (1942) *World Hypotheses*. Berkeley, CA: University of California Press.

Perrow, C. (1967) 'A framework for the comparative analysis of organizations', *American Sociological Review*, 32 (2): 194–208.

Perrow, C. (1970) *Organizational Analysis: A Sociological View*. Belmont, CA: Wadsworth.

Perrow, C. (1986) *Complex Organizations – A Critical Essay*. New York: Random House.

Peteraf, M.A. (1993) 'The cornerstones of competitive advantage: a resource-based view', *Strategic Management Journal*, 14 (3): 179–91.

Peters, T.J. (1987) *Thriving on Chaos*, New York: Alfred A. Knopf.

Peters, T.J. and Waterman, Jr R.H. (1982) *In Search of Excellence*, New York: Warner Books.

Pettigrew, A.M. (1973) *The Politics of Organisational Decision Making*. London: Tavistock Publications.

Pettigrew, A.M. (1977) 'Strategy formulation as a political process', *International Studies of Management and Organisation*, 7 (2): 78–87.

Pettigrew, A.M. (1985) *The Awakening Giant: Continuity and Change in ICI*. Oxford: Blackwell.

Pettigrew, A.M. (1987) 'Context and action in transformation of the firm', *Journal of Management Studies*, 24 (6): 649–70.

Pettigrew, A.M. (1990) 'Longitudinal Field Research on Change: Theory and Practice', *Organization Science*, 1 (3): 267–92.

Pettigrew, A.M. (1992a) 'The character and significance of strategy process research', *Strategic Management Journal*, 13: 5–16.

Pettigrew, A.M. (1992b) 'On studying managerial elites', *Strategic Management Journal*, 13 (special issue): 163–82.

Pettigrew, A.M. and Hendry, C. (1992) 'Patterns of strategic change in the development of human resource management', *British Journal of Management*, 3 (3): 137–56.

Pettigrew, A.M. and Whipp, R. (1991) *Managing Change For Competitive Success*. Oxford: Blackwell.

Pfeffer, J. (1982) *Organizations and Organization Theory*. Boston, MA: Pitman.

Pfeffer, J. (1993) 'Barriers to the advance of organisational science: paradigm development as a dependent variable', *Academy of Management Review*, 18 (4): 599–620.

Pfeffer, J. and Salancik, G.R. (1978) *The External Control of Organisations: A Resource Dependence Perspective*. New York: Harper & Row.

Phillips, L.W. (1981) 'Assessing measurement error in key informant reports: a methodological note on organisational analysis in marketing', *Journal of Marketing Research*, 18: 395–415.

Polanyi, M. (1958) *Personal Knowledge*. London: Routledge & Kegan Paul.

Polanyi, M. (1962) *Personal Knowledge: Towards a Post Critical Philosophy*. Chicago, IL: University of Chicago Press.

Ponssard, J.P. (1994) 'Formalisation des connaissances, apprentissage organisationnel et rationalité interactive', in A. Orléan (ed.), *Analyse Economique des Conventions*. Paris: PUF, pp. 169–85.

Porac, J.F., Thomas, H. and Baden-Fuller, C. (1989) 'Competitive groups as cognitive communities: the case of Scottish knitwear manufacturers', *Journal of Management Studies*, 26: 397–416.

Porac, J.F., Thomas, H., Wilson, F., Paton, D. and Kanfer, A. (1995) 'Rivalry and the industry model of Scottish knitwear producers', *Administrative Science Quarterly*, 40: 203–27.

Porter, L.W. and McKibbin, L. (1988) *Management Education and Development*. New York: McGraw Hill.

Porter, M.E. (1980) *Competitive Strategy: Techniques for Analyzing Industries and Competitors*. New York: Free Press.

Porter, M.E. (1981) 'The contributions of industrial organization to strategic management', *Academy of Management Review*, 6: 609–20.

Porter, M.E. (1985) *Competitive Advantage*. New York: Free Press.

Porter, M.E. (1990) *The Competitive Advantage of Nations*. New York: Free Press.

Porter, M.E. (1991) 'Towards a dynamic theory of strategy', *Strategic Management Journal*, 12 (special issue): 95–117.

Porter, M.E. and Fuller, D. (1986) 'Coalitions and global strategy', in M.E. Porter (ed.), *Competition in Global Industries*. Boston, MA: Harvard Business School Press.

Powell, W.W. (1987) 'Hybrid organizational arrangements: new forms of transnational development', *California Management Review*, 29: 67–87.

Powell, W.W. (1996) 'Trust-based forms of governance', in R.M. Kramer and T.R. Tyler (eds), *Trust in Organizations*. London: Sage Publications Ltd, pp. 51–67.

Powell, W.W. and DiMaggio, P.J. (1991) *New Institutionalism in Organizational Analysis*. Chicago: University of Chicago Press.

Powell, W.W., Koput, K. and Smith-Doerr, L. (1996) 'Interorganizational collaboration and the locus of innovation: networks of learning in biotechnology', *Administrative Science Quarterly*, 41: 116–45.

Prahalad, C.K. and Bettis, R.A. (1986) 'The dominant logic: a new linkage between diversity and performance', *Strategic Management Journal*, 7 (6): 485–501.

Prahalad, C.K. and Hamel, G. (1990) 'The core competence of the corporation', *Harvard Business Review*, 68: 79–93.

Prahalad, C.K. and Hamel, G. (1993) 'Strategy as stretch and leverage', *Harvard Business Review*, 71 (2): 75–85.

Prescott, J.E. and Smith, D.C. (1989) 'A framework for the design and implementation of competitive intelligence systems', in C.C. Snow (ed.), *Strategy, Organization Design and Human Resource Management*. Greenwich, CT: JAI Press, pp. 161–201.

Prigogine, I. (1976) 'Order through fluctuation: self-organization and social system', in E. Jantsch and Waddington, C.H., *Evolution and Consciousness: Human Systems in Transition*. Reading, MA: Addison-Wesley, pp. 93–133.

Prigogine, I. and Stengers, E. (1984) *Order Out of Chaos: Man's New Dialogue with Nature*. New York: Bantam Books.

Pritchett, P. (1985) *After the Merger: Managing the Shockwaves*. Homewood, IL: Irwin.

Pritchett, P. (1987) *Making Mergers Work: A Guide to Managing Mergers and Acquisitions*. Homewood, IL: Irwin.

Pugh, D.S., Hickson, D.J. and Hinings, C.R. (1969) 'An empirical taxonomy of structures of work organizations', *Administrative Science Quarterly*, 14 (1): 115–26.

Pugh, D.S., Hickson, D.J., Hinings, C.R. and Turner, C. (1968) 'Dimensions of organizational structure', *Administrative Science Quarterly*, 13 (1): 65–105.

Quinn, J.B. (1980a) *Strategies for Change – Logical Incrementalism*. Homewood, IL: Irwin.

Quinn, J.B. (1980b) 'Managing strategic change', *Sloan Management Review*, 21 (4): 3–20.

Quinn, J.B. (1985) 'Managing innovation: controlled chaos', *Harvard Business Review*, 63 (3): 73–84.

Quinn, J.B. (1992) *Intelligent Enterprise: A Knowledge and Service Based Paradigm for Industry*. New York: Free Press.

Quinn, J.B. and Hilmer, F.G. (1994) 'Strategic outsourcing', *Sloan Management Review*, 72: 43–55.

Rajagopalan, N., Rasheed, A.M.A. and Datta, D.K. (1993) 'Strategic decision processes: an integrative framework and future directions', in P. Lorange, B. Chakravarthy, J. Roos, and A.H. van de Ven (eds), *Implementing Strategic Processes: Change, Learning and Co-operation*. Oxford: Blackwell, pp. 274–312.

Ramanujam, V. and Varadarajan, P. (1989) 'Research on corporate diversification: a synthesis', *Strategic Management Journal*, 10 (6): 523–51.

Raphael, R. (1976) *Backcountry Lives in America Today on the Borderlands Between the Old Ways and the New*. New York: Knopf.

Redlich, F. (1957) 'Academic education for business: its development and the contribution of Ignaz Jastrow (1856–1937)', *Business History Review*, 31: 35–91.

Reed, M.I. (1985) *Redirections in Organisational Analysis*. London: Tavistock.

Reger, R. and Huff, A.S. (1993) 'Strategic groups: a cognitive perspective', *Strategic Management Journal*, 14: 103–24.

Reve, T. (1990) 'The firm as a nexus of internal and external contracts', in M. Aoki, B. Gustaffson and O.E. Williamson (eds), *The Firm as a Nexus of Treaties*. London: Sage Publications Ltd.

Richardson, G.B. (1972) 'The organisation of industry', *Economic Journal*, 82: 883–96.

Ring, P.S. and van de Ven, A.H. (1989) 'Formal and informal dimensions of transactions', in A.H. van de Ven, H.L. Angle and M.S. Poole (eds), *Research on the Management of Innovation: The Minnesota Studies*. New York: Praeger.

Ring, P.S. and van de Ven, A.H. (1993) *Developmental Processes of Cooperative Interorganizational Relationships*. Strategic Management Research Center, University of Minnesota, Minneapolis.

Ring, P.S. and van de Ven, A.H. (1994) 'Developmental processes of cooperative interorganizational relationships', *Academy of Management Review*, 19 (1): 90–118.

Ritzer, G. (1975) 'Sociology: a multiple paradigm science', *American Sociologist*, 10: 156–67.

Robbins, D.K. and Pearce, J.A. (1992) 'Turnaround: retrenchement and recovery', *Strategic Management Journal*, 13: 287–309.

Romanelli, E. and Tushman, M.L. (1994) 'Organizational transformation as punctuated equilibrium: an empirical test', *Academy of Management Journal*, 37 (5): 1141–66.

Romme, A.G.L. (1996) 'A note on the hierarchy-team debate', *Strategic Management Journal*, 17 (5): 411–17.

Roos, J. and von Krogh, G. (1992) 'Figuring out your competence configuration', *European Management Journal*, 10 (4): 422–27.

Rosenberg, N. (1972) *Technology and American Economic Growth*. New York: Harper Torch Books.

Ross, J. (1994) 'Cable and Wireless: managing strategic alliances', keynote speech (unpublished) given at Strategic Planning conference on Strategic Alliances, 1994.

Rouleau, L. and Séquin, F. (1995) 'Strategy and organization theories: common forms of discourse', *Journal of Management Studies*, 32: 101–16.

Rubin, P. (1990) *Managing Business Transactions*. New York: Free Press.

Rugmann, A.M. (1979) *International Diversification and the Multinational Enterprise*. Lexington, MA: Heath.

Rumelt, R.P. (1974) *Strategy, Structure, and Economic Performance, Division of Research*. Boston, MA: Harvard Business School Press.

Rumelt, R.P. (1979) 'Evaluation of strategy: theory and models', in D.E. Schendel and C.W. Hofer (eds), *Strategic Management: A New View of Business Policy and Planning*. Boston, MA: Little Brown, pp. 197–211.

Rumelt, R.P. (1984) 'Towards a strategic theory of the firm', in R. Lamb (ed.), *Competitive Strategic Management*. Englewood Cliffs, NJ: Prentice Hall, pp. 556–70.

Rumelt, R.P. (1987) 'Theory, strategy, and entrepreneurship', in D.J. Teece (ed.), *The competitive challenge*. Cambridge, MA: Ballinger, pp. 137–58.

Rumelt, R.P. (1991) 'How much does industry matter?', *Strategic Management Journal*, 12 (3): 167–86.

Rumelt, R.P. (1994) 'Foreword', in G. Hamel and A. Heene (eds), *Competence-Based Competition*, New York: John Wiley, pp. xv–xix.

Rumelt, R.P., Schendel, D.E. and Teece, D.J. (1991) 'Strategic management and economics', *Strategic Management Journal*, 12 (special issue): 5–29.

Rumelt, R.P., Schendel, D.E. and Teece, D.J. (1994) *Fundamental Issues in Strategy*. Boston, MA: Harvard Business School Press.

Sabel, C. (1993) 'Studied trust', *Human Relations*, 46 (9): 1133–70.

Salais, R. (1994) 'Incertitude et interactions de travail: des produits aux conventions', in A. Orléan (ed.) *Analyse Economique des Coventions*. Paris: PUF, pp. 371–403.

Sales, A. and Mirvis, P.H. (1985) 'When cultures collide: issues in acquisitions', in J.R. Kimberly and R.E. Quinn (eds), *New Futures: The Challenge of Managing Corporate Transitions*. Homewood, IL: Irwin.

Salter, M.S. and Weinhold, W.S. (1979) *Diversification Through Acquisition*. New York: Free Press.

Sammon, W.L., Kurland, M.A. and Spitalnic, R. (eds) (1984) *Business Competitor Intelligence Methods for Collecting, Organizing and Using Information*. New York: John Wiley.

Sanchez, R. (1991) 'Strategic flexibility, real options, and product-based strategy', PhD dissertation, Massachusetts Institute of Technology, Cambridge, MA.

Sanchez, R. (1993) 'Strategic flexibility, firm organization, and managerial work in dynamic markets: a strategic options perspective', *Advances in Strategic Management*, 9: 251–91.

Sanchez, R. (1995a) 'Strategic flexibility in product competition', *Strategic Management Journal*, 16 (special issue): 135–59.

Sanchez, R. (1995b) 'Integrating technology strategy and marketing strategy', in H. Thomas, D. O'Neal and E. Zajac (eds), *Strategic Integration*. Chichester: John Wiley, pp. 337–63.

Sanchez, R. (1996a) 'Strategic product creation: managing new interactions of technology, markets, and organizations', *European Management Journal*, 14 (2): 121–38.

Sanchez, R. (1996b) 'Quick-connect technologies for product creation: implications for competence-based competition', in R. Sanchez, A. Heene and H. Thomas (eds), *Dynamics of Competence Based Competition*. Oxford: Elsevier Pergamon, pp. 299–322.

Sanchez, R. (1996c) 'Managing articulated knowledge in competence-based competition', in R. Sanchez and A. Heene (eds), *Strategic Learning and Knowledge Management*. Chichester: John Wiley, pp. 163–87.

Sanchez, R. (1997) 'Strategic management at the point of inflection: systems, complexity, and competence theory', *Long Range Planning*, 30 (6): 939–46.

Sanchez, R. and Heene, A. (1997a) 'A competence perspective on strategic learning and knowledge management', in R. Sanchez and A. Heene (eds), *Strategic Learning and Knowledge Management*, Chichester: John Wiley.

Sanchez, R. and Heene, A. (eds) (1997b) *Strategic Learning and Knowledge Management*. Chichester: John Wiley.

Sanchez, R., Heene, A. and Thomas, H. (1996) 'Towards the theory and practice of competence-based competition', in R. Sanchez, A. Heene and H. Thomas (eds), *Dynamics of Competence-Based Competition: Theory and Practice in the New Strategic Management*, Oxford: Elsevier Pergamon.

Sanchez, R. and Mahoney, J.T. (1996) 'Modularity, flexibility, and knowledge management in product and organization design', *Strategic Management Journal*, 17 (special issue): 63–76.

Sanchez, R. and Sudharshan, D. (1993) 'Real-time market research: Learning-by-doing in the development of new products', *Marketing Intelligence and Planning*, 11 (7): 29–38.

Sanchez, R. and Thomas, H. (1996) 'Strategic goals', in R. Sanchez, A. Heene and H. Thomas (eds), *Dynamics of Competence-Based Competition*. Oxford: Elsevier, pp. 63–84.

Sanderson, S.W. and Uzumeri, V. (1990) 'Strategies for new product development and renewal: design-based incrementalism', working paper, Center for Science and Technology Policy, Rensselaer Polytechnic Institute, Troy, New York.

Schank, R.C. and Abelson, R.P. (1977) *Scripts, Plans, Goals and Understanding*. Hillsdale, NJ: Erlbaum.

Schein, E.H. (1985) *Organizational Culture and Leadership*. San Francisco, CA: Jossey-Bass.

Schelling, T.C. (1960) *The Strategy of Conflict*. Cambridge MA: Harvard University Press.

Schendel, D. (1991) 'Editor's comments on the winter special issue', *Strategic Management Journal*, 12: 1–3.

Schendel, D. (1994) 'Introduction to the summer 1994 special issue – Strategy: the search for new paradigms', *The Strategic Management Journal*, 15 (special issue): 1–4.

Schendel, D. and Hofer, C. (eds) (1979) *Strategic Management: A New View of Business Policy and Planning*. Boston, MA: Little, Brown.

Scherer, F.M. (1980) *Industrial Market Structure and Economic Performance*. Boston, MA: Honghton Mifflin.

Schoemaker, P.J.H. (1982) 'The expected utility model: its variants, purposes, evidence and limitations', *Journal of Economic Literature*, 20: 529–63.

Schoemaker, P.J.H. (1990) 'Strategy, complexity and economic rent', *Management Science*, 36 (10): 1178–92.

Schoemaker, P.J.H. (1991) 'The quest for optimality: a positive heuristic of science?', *The Behavioral and Brain Sciences*, 14 (2): 205–15.

Schoemaker, P.J.H. (1992) 'How to link strategic vision to core capabilities', *Sloan Management Review*, 34 (1): 67–81.

Schoemaker, P.J.H. (1993) 'Strategic decisions in organisations: rational and behavioural views', *Journal of Management Studies*, 30 (1): 107–29.

Schön, D.A. (1983) *The Reflective Practioner: How Professionals Think in Action.* London: Temple Smith.

Schön, D.A. (1984) 'The crisis of professional knowledge and the pursuit of an epistemology of practice', 75th anniversary colloquium on teaching by the case method, Harvard Business School, Boston, MA.

Schumpeter, J.A. (1934) *The Theory of Economic Development.* Boston, MA: Harvard Business School Press.

Schweiger, D. and Walsh, J. (1990) 'Mergers and acquisitions: an interdisciplinary view', in K.M. Roland and G.R. Ferris (eds), *Research in Personnel and Human Resource Management.* Greenwich, CT: Jail Press.

Schwenk, C.R. (1984) 'Cognitive simplification processes in strategic decision-making', *Strategic Management Journal*, 5: 111–28.

Schwenk, C.R. (1988a) *The Essence of Strategic Decision Making.* Lexington, MA: D.C. Heath and Co.

Schwenk, C.R. (1988b) 'The cognitive perspective on strategic decision making', *Journal of Management Studies*, 25 (1): 41–55.

Schwenk, C.R. (1989) 'Linking cognitive, organizational and political factors in explaining strategic change', *Journal of Management Studies*, 26 (2): 177–87.

Scott, R.W. (1987) *Organizations: rational, natural and open systems.* London: Prentice Hall.

Scott, R.W. (1992) *Organizations: Rational, Natural, and Open Systems*, 3rd edn. Englewood Cliffs, NJ: Prentice Hall.

Searby, F.W. (1969) 'Control post merger change', *Harvard Business Review*, 47 (5): 4–12.

Selznick, P. (1957) *Leadership in Administration: A Sociological Interpretation.* New York: Row Peterson.

Senge, P.M. (1990) *The Fifth Discipline: The Art and Practice of the Learning Organization.* New York: Currency Doubleday.

Shanley, M. (1987) 'Post acquisition management approaches: an exploratory study', doctoral dissertation, Wharton School, University of Pennsylvania, PA.

Shapiro, C. (1989) 'The theory of business strategy', *The RAND Journal of Economics*, 20: 125–37.

Shapiro, S. (1987) 'The social control of impersonal trust', *American Journal of Sociology*, 93 (3): 623–58.

Shelton, L.M. (1988) 'Strategic business fits and corporate acquisition: empirical evidence', *Strategic Management Journal*, 9: 279–88.

Shirley, R.C. (1977) 'The human side of merger planning', *Long Range Planning*, 10: 35–9.

Shrivastava, P. (1983) 'A typology of organizational learning systems', *Journal of Management Studies*, 20 (1): 7–29.

Shrivastava, P. (1986) 'Is strategic management ideological?', *Journal of Management*, 12: 363–77.

Shrivastava, P. (1987) 'Rigor and practical usefulness of research in strategic management', *Strategic Management Journal*, 8: 77–92.

Shrivastava, P. and Grant, J.H. (1985) 'Empirically derived models of strategic decision making processes', *Strategic Management Journal*, 6 (2): 97–113.

Simon, H.A. (1955) 'A behavioral model of rational choice', *Quarterly Journal of Economics*, 69: 99–118.

Simon, H.A. (1962) 'The architecture of complexity', *Proceedings of the American Philosophical Society*, 106 (6): 467–82.

Simon, H.A. (1976) *Administrative Behavior.* New York: Free Press.

Simon, H.A. (1981) *The Sciences of the Artificial.* Cambridge, MA: Massachusetts Institute of Technology Press.

Simon, H.A. (1982) *Models of Bounded Rationality: Behavioral Economics and Business Organization.* Cambridge, MA: Massachusetts Institute of Technology Press.

Sinetar, M. (1981) 'Mergers, morale and productivity', *Personnel Journal*, 60 (11): 863–7.

Singer, A.E. (1994) 'Strategy as moral philosophy', *Strategic Management Journal*, 15: 191–213.

Singh, H. and Montgomery, C.A. (1987) 'Corporate acquisition strategies and economic performance', *Strategic Management Journal*, 8: 377–86.

Smircich, L. (1983) 'Concepts of culture and organizational analysis', *Administrative Science Quarterly*, 28: 339–58.

Smircich, L. and Stubbart, C. (1985) 'Strategic management in an enacted world', *Academy of Management Review*, 10 (4): 724–36.

Smith, C.E. (1994) 'The Merlin factor: leadership and strategic intent', *Business Strategy Review*, 5 (1): 67–84.

Souder, W.S. and Chakrabarti, A.K. (1984) 'Acquisitions: do they really work out?', *Interfaces*, 14: 41–7.

Spender, J.-C. (1989) *Industry Recipes: The Nature and Sources of Managerial Judgement*. Oxford: Blackwell Publishers.

Spender, J.-C. (1996) 'Organizational knowledge, learning and memory: three concepts in search of a theory', *Journal of Organizational Change Management*, 9: 63–79.

Stalk, G., Evans, P. and Schulman, L. (1992) 'Competing on capabilities: the new rules of corporate strategy', *Harvard Business Review*, 70 (2): 57–69.

Stalk, G. Jr and Hout, T.M. (1990) 'Competing against time', *Research Technology Management*, 33 (2): 19–25.

Starbuck, W.H. (1992) 'Learning by knowledge-intensive firms', *Journal of Management Studies*, 29 (6): 713–40.

Steiner, G.A. (1969) *Top Management Planning*. New York: Macmillan.

Stiles, J. (1994) 'Strategic alliances: making them work', *Long Range Planning*, 27 (4): 133–7.

Stinchcombe, A. (1965) 'Social structure and organizations' in J. March (ed.), *Handbook of Organizations*. Chicago, IL: Rand McNally, pp. 142–93.

Stopford, J.M. and Wells Jr, L.T. (1972) *Managing the Multinational Enterprise: Organization of the Firm and Ownership of the Subsidiaries*. London: Longman.

Summer, C., et al. (1990) 'Doctoral education in the field of business policy and strategy', *Journal of Management*, 16 (2): 361–98.

Sutton, R.I. (1983) 'Managing organisational death', *Human Resource Management*, 22: 391–412.

Sveiby, K.E. and Lloyd, T. (1987) *Managing Knowhow*. London: Bloomsbury.

Takec, P.F. and Singh, C.P. (1992) 'Strategic alliances in banking', Management Decisions, 30 (1): 32–43.

Tampoe, M. (1994) 'Exploiting the core competences of your organization', *Long Range Planning*, 27 (4): 66–77.

Tang, M.J. and Thomas, H. (1994) 'Developing theories of strategy using dominance criteria', *Journal of Management Studies*, 31: 209–24.

Taylor, B. and Macmillan, K. (1973) *Business Policy: Teaching and Research*. Bradford: Bradford University Press.

Taylor, M. (1987) *The Possibility of Cooperation*. Cambridge: Cambridge University Press.

Teece, D.J. (1982) 'Towards an economic theory of the multiproduct firm', *Journal of Economic Behavior and Organization*, 3: 39–63.

Teece, D.J. (1986) 'Firm boundaries, technological innovation and strategic management', in L.G. Thomas (ed.), *The Economics of Strategic Planning*. Lexington, MA: Lexington Books.

Teece, D.J. (1987) 'Profiting from technological innovation: implications for integration, collaboration, licensing and public policy', in D.J. Teece (ed.), *The Competitive Challenge*. Cambridge, MA: Ballinger Publishing Company, pp. 185–219.

Teece, D.J. (1990) 'Contributions and impediments of economic analysis to the study of strategic management', in J.W. Fredrickson (ed.), *Perspectives on Strategic Management*. New York: Harper & Row, pp. 39–80.

Teece, D.J., Pisano, G. and Shuen, A. (1990) 'Dynamic capabilities and strategic management', working paper, University of California, Berkeley, CA.

Teece, D.J., Pisano, G. and Shuen, A. (1994) 'Dynamic capabilities and strategic management', working paper no. 94–9. University of California, Berkeley, CA.

Teece, D.J., Pisano, G. and Shuen, A. (1997) 'Dynamic capabilities and strategic management', *Strategic Management Journal*, 18 (7): 509–33.

Thomas, H., Gorman, P. and Sanchez, R. (1996) 'Industry dynamics in competence-based competition', in R. Sanchez, A. Heene and H. Thomas (eds), *Dynamics of Competence-Based Competition*. Oxford: Elsevier.

Thomas, K.W. and Tymon, W.G. Jr (1982) 'Necessary properties of relevant research: lessons from recent criticism of the organizational science', *Academy of Management Review*, 7 (3): 345–52.

Thompson, J.D. (1967) *Organizations in Action*, New York: McGraw Hill.

Thorelli, H.B. (1986) 'Networks: between markets and hierarchies', *Strategic Management Journal*, 7: 37–51.

Tirole, J. (1988) *The Theory of Industrial Organization*. Cambridge, MA: Massachusetts Institute of Technology Press.

Trice, H.M. and Beyer, J.M. (1986) 'The concept of charisma', *Research in Organisational Behavior*, 8: 118–64.

Trompenaars, F. (1993) *Riding the Waves of Culture, Understanding Cultural Diversity in Business*. London: Nicholas Brealy Publishing.

Tsoukas, H. (1994) 'Types of knowledge in management studies', *Journal of Management Studies*, 31: 761–80.

Turner, D. and Crawford, M. (1994) 'Managing current and future competitive performance: the role of competence', in G. Hamel and A. Heene (eds), *Competence-Based Competition*. Chichester: John Wiley.

Tushman, M.L. and Romanelli, E. (1990) 'Organizational evolution: a metamorphosis model of convergence and reorientation', in B.M. Staw and L.L. Cummings (eds), *The Evolution and Adaptation of Organizations*. JAI Press, pp. 139–90.

Tyson, K.W.M. (1986) *Business Intelligence – Putting It All Together*. Lombard, IL: Leading Edge Publications.

van den Bosch, F.A.J. (1997) 'Porter's contribution to more general and dynamic strategy frameworks', in F.A.J. van den Bosch and A.P. de Man (eds), *Perspectives on Strategy, Contributions of Michael E. Porter*. Boston, MA: Kluwer Academic Publishers, pp. 91–100.

van den Bosch, F.A.J. and de Man, A.P. (eds) (1997) *Perspectives on Strategy, Contributions of Michael E. Porter*, Boston, MA: Kluwer Academic Publishers.

van den Bosch, F.A.J., Volberda, H.W. and de Boer, M. (1999) 'Co-evolution of firm absorptive capacity and knowledge environment: organizational forms and combinative capabilities', *Organization Science*, 10 (5): 551–68.

van de Ven, A.H. (1986) 'Central problems in the management of innovation', *Management Science*, 32 (5): 590–607.

van de Ven, A. (1992) 'Suggestions for studying strategy process: a research note', *Strategic Management Journal*, 13 (special issue): 169–88.

van Valen, L. (1973) 'A new evolutionary law', *Evolutionary Theory*, 1: 1–30.

van Wijk, G. (1985) 'The role of shared understanding and trust in loan decisions', unpublished doctoral dissertation, Columbia University, New York.

Venkatesan, R. (1992) 'Strategic sourcing: to make or not to make', *Sloan Management Review*, 70 (6): 98–107.

Venkatraman, N. and Grant, J.H. (1986) 'Construct measurement in organisational strategy research: a critique and proposal', *Academy of Management Review*, 11 (1): 71–87.

Venkatraman, N. and Prescott, J.E. (1990) 'Environment–strategy coalignment: an empirical test of its performance implications', *Strategic Management Journal*, 11: 1–23.

Vickers, J. (1985) 'Pre-emptive patenting, joint ventures and the persistence of oligopoly', *International Journal of Industrial Organization*, 3: 261–73.

Vinton, D.E. (1992) 'A new look at time, speed, and the manager', *The Executive* VI: 7–16.

Volberda, H.W. (1992) *Organizational Flexibility: Change and Preservation*. Groningen: Wolters-Noordhoff.

Volberda, H.W. (1993) 'In search of a disciplined methodology: a synthetic research approach', 11th EGOS colloquium, Paris.

Volberda, H.W. (1996a) 'Flexible configuration strategies within Philips Semiconductors: a strategic process of entrepreneurial revitalization', in R. Sanchez, A. Heene and H. Thomas (eds), *Dynamics of Competence-Based Competition: Theory and Practice in the New Strategic Management*. Oxford: Elsevier Pergamon.

Volberda, H.W. (1996b) 'Toward the flexible form: how to remain vital in hypercompetitive environments', *Organization Science*, 7 (4): 359–74.

Volberda, H.W. (1998) *Building the Flexible Firm: How to Remain Competitive*. Oxford: Oxford University Press.

Volberda, H.W. and Baden-Fuller, C. (1998) 'Strategic renewal and competence building: four dynamic mechanisms', in G. Hamel, C.K. Prahalad, H. Thomas and D. O'Neal (eds), *Strategic Flexibility: Managing in a Turbulent Environment*. Chichester: John Wiley, pp. 371–89.

Volberda, H.W. and Rutges, A. (1999) 'FARSYS: a knowledge-based system for managing strategic change', *Decision Support Systems*, 26 (2): 99–123.

von Krogh, G. and Roos, J. (1996) *Managing Knowledge: Perspectives on Cooperation and Competition*. London: Sage Publications Ltd.

von Krogh, G. and Vicari, S. (1993) 'An autopoiesis approach to experimental strategic learning', in P. Lorange, B. Chakravarty, J. Roos and A. van de Ven (eds), *Implementing Strategic Processes: Change, Learning and Co-operation*. Oxford: Blackwell.

von Neumann, J. and Morgenstern, O. (1944) *The Theory of the Games and Economic Behaviour*. New York: John Wiley.

Walsh, J.P. (1988) 'Top management turnover feelings following mergers and acquisitions', *Strategic Management Journal*, 9: 173–83.

Walsh, J.P. and Ungson, G.R. (1991) 'Organizational memory', *Academy of Management Review*, 16 (1): 57–91.

Walter, G.A. (1985) 'Culture collisions in mergers and acquisitions', in P.J. Frost, L.F. Moore, M.R. Louis and C.C. Lundberg (eds), *Organisational Culture*. Beverly Hills: Sage Publications Inc, pp. 301–14.

Weber, M. (1946) 'From Max Weber: essays in sociology', in H.H. Gerth and C. Wright (eds), *From Max Weber: Essays in Sociology*. New York: Mills.

Webster, J. and Starbuck, W.H. (1988) 'Theory building in industrial and organisational psychology', in C.L. Cooper and I. Robertson (eds), *International Review of Industrial and Organisational Psychology*. London: John Wiley, pp. 54–67.

Weick, K.E. (1979) *The Social Psychology of Organizing*. London: Addison-Wesley.

Weick, K.E. (1982) 'Management of organizational change among loosely coupled elements', in P.S. Goodman (ed.), *Change in Organizations: New Perspectives in Theory, Research, and Practice*. San Francisco, CA: Jossey-Bass, pp. 375–408.

Weick, K.E. (1989) 'Theory construction as disciplined imagination', *Academy of Management Review*, 14 (4): 516–31.

Weick, K.E. (1995) *Sensemaking in Organizations*. Thousand Oaks, CA: Sage Publications Ltd.

Weick, K.E. (1998) 'Improvisation as a mindset for organizational analysis', *Organization Science*, 9 (5): 543–55.

Wernerfelt, B. (1984) 'A resource-based view of the firm', *Strategic Management Journal*, 5: 171–80.

Wernerfelt, B. (1995) 'The resource-based view of the firm: ten years after', *Strategic Management Journal*, 16: 171–4.

Westley, F. and Mintzberg, H. (1989) 'Visionary leadership and strategic management', *Strategic Management Journal*, 10 (special issue): 17–32.

Weston, J.F. and Copeland, T.E. (1986) *Managerial Finance*. Fortworth, FL: Dryden Press.

Wheatcroft, S. and Lipman, G. (1990) *European Liberalisation and World Air Transport Special Report. No. 2015*. London: Economist Intelligence Unit.

Wheelwright, S.C. and Sasser Jr, E. (1989) 'The new product development map', *Harvard Business Review*, 67 (3): 112–22.

Whitley, R. (1984) 'The fragmented state of management studies: reasons and consequences', *Journal of Management Studies*, 21 (3): 331–48.

Whittington, R. (1993) *What is Strategy – and does it matter?* London: Routledge.

Whittington, R., Pettigrew, A., Peck, S., Fenton, E. and Conyon, M. (1999) 'Change and complementarities in the new competitive landscape: a European panel study, 1992–1996', *Organization Science*, 10 (5): 583–600.

Wiersema, M.F. and Bantel, K.A. (1992) 'Top management demography and corporate strategic change', *Academy of Management Journal*, 35 (1): 91–121.

Williamson, O.E. (1975) *Markets and Hierarchies: Analysis and Antitrust Implications*. New York: Free Press.

Williamson, O.E. (1976) 'Franchise bidding for natural monopolies – in general and with respect to CATV', *Bell Journal of Economics*, 7: 73–104.

Williamson, O.E. (1985) *The Economic Institutions of Capitalism*. New York: Free Press.

Williamson, O.E. (1986) *Economic Organization: Firms, Markets and Policy Control*. New York: New York University Press.

Williamson, O.E. (1991) 'Economic institutions: spontaneous and intentional governance', *Journal of Law, Economics and Organization,* 7 (special issue): 159–87.

Williamson, O.E. (1993a) 'Transaction cost economics and organization theory', *Industrial and Corporate Change*, 2 (2): 107–56.

Williamson, O.E. (1993b) 'Calculativeness, trust and economic organization', *Journal of Law and Economics*, XXXVI: 453–86.

Williamson, O.E. (1994) 'Strategizing, economizing, and economic organization', in R.P. Rumelt, D.E. Schendel and D.J. Teece (eds), *Fundamental Issues in Strategy*. Boston, MA: Harvard Business School Press.

Williamson, O.E. (1996) *The Mechanisms of Governance*. New York: Free Press.

Winter, S.G. (1987) 'Knowledge and competence as strategic assets', in D.J. Teece (ed.), *The Competitive Challenge*. Cambridge, MA: Ballinger Publishing Company, pp. 159–84.

Woodward, J. (1965) *Industrial Organisation: Theory and Practice*. London: Oxford University Press.

Woolsey, J.P. (1994) '777', *Air Transport World*, 31 (4): 22–31.

Wrapp, H.E. (1967) 'Good managers don't make policy decisions', *Harvard Business Review*, 45: 91–9.

Yao, D.A. (1988) 'Beyond the reach of the invisible hand: impediments to economic activity, market failures, and profitability', *Strategic Management Journal*, 9: 59–70.

Yoffie, D.B. (1996) 'Competing in the age of digital convergence', *California Management Review*, 48 (4): 31–53.

Zaheer, A. and Venkatraman, N. (1995) 'Relational governance as an interorganizational strategy: an empirical test of the rate of trust in economic exchange', *Strategic Management Journal*, 16: 373–92.

Zajac, E.J. and Olsen, C.P. (1993) 'From transaction cost to transaction value analysis: implications for the study of interorganizational strategies', *Journal of Management Studies*, 30 (1): 131–45.

Zammuto, R. and Connolly, T. (1984) 'Coping with disciplinary fragmentation', *Organisational Behaviour Teaching Review*, 9: 30–7.

Ziman, J. (1968) *Public Knowledge*. Cambridge: Cambridge University Press.

Zucker, L.G. (1986) 'Production of trust: institutional sources of economic structure', in B.M. Staw and L.L. Cummings (eds), *Research in Organizational Behavior*, vol. 8. Greenwich, CT: JAI Press, pp. 53–112.

Zuckerman, H. and Merton, R.K. (1971) 'Patterns of evaluation in science: institutionalisation, structure and function of the referee system', *Minerva*, 9: 66–101.

Index